EVERYMAN'S LIBRARY

EVERYMAN,
I WILL GO WITH THEE,
AND BE THY GUIDE,
IN THY MOST NEED
TO GO BY THY SIDE

MAXINE HONG KINGSTON

THE
WOMAN
WARRIOR

CHINA MEN

WITH AN INTRODUCTION
BY MARY GORDON

EVERYMAN'S LIBRARY

Alfred A. Knopf NewYork Toronto

MAXINE HONG
KINGSTON
———

THIS IS A BORZOI BOOK
PUBLISHED BY ALFRED A. KNOPF

First included in Everyman's Library, 2005

The Woman Warrior
Copyright © 1975, 1976 by Maxine Hong Kingston
First published by Alfred A. Knopf, Inc., in 1976
'No Name Woman' originally appeared, in slightly different form,
in the January 1975 issue of *Viva*.

China Men
Copyright © 1977, 1978, 1979, 1980 by Maxine Hong Kingston
First published by Alfred A. Knopf, Inc., in 1980
Portions of this book have been published in different forms in
Bamboo Ridge, Hawaii Review, The New Yorker, and *Seattle Weekly*.

Introduction Copyright © 2005 by Mary Gordon
Chronology Copyright © 2005 by Everyman's Library
Fourth printing

Grateful acknowledgment is made to the University of California
Press for permission to reprint from *The State of the Language*, edited
by Leonard Michaels and Christopher Ricks, 1980.

www.randomhouse.com/everymans

ISBN 978-1-4000-4384-2

Book design by Barbara de Wilde and Carol Devine Carson

Printed and bound in Germany by GGP Media GmbH, Pössneck

CONTENTS

INTRODUCTION

These are impossible books. They should not exist. Their source is a world that refers to girls as maggots, as a curse, as something to be sold into slavery, one that warns against speaking to the outside world to the point that it renders its gifted daughters mute or mad. How can this world have produced a storyteller of such incandescent vision, such mastery of language, that she has created a masterpiece, work that lives, painfully and brilliantly, forever, in the minds of its readers? Impossible. And yet we have them, these two astonishing memoirs: *The Woman Warrior* and *China Men*.

They were part of a certain moment in history. *The Woman Warrior* was published in 1976 and *China Men* in 1980. It was a time when those Americans who had been classified as minorities were searching for new ways of understanding identity. People were beginning to question the sacred notion of assimilation and to wonder if it required too high a price, too much of the past and the self repressed or erased in favor of what would be, in any case, a fruitless quest for acceptance and approval by the majority. It was also a moment when feminism insisted upon questioning the ways women came to know themselves: the stories of women – even the stories of girls – were newly important. And it must be remembered that these books were written before the wave of memoirs hit the cultural landscape – Nabokov's *Speak, Memory* was an anomaly in its artful presentation of an imagined, re-created past.

And so, of course, *The Woman Warrior* and *China Men* were of their time, and yet they struck readers with a shocking and exhilarating force. We had not seen anything like them before, with their poetic prose, with their interweavings of tales exotic and familiar, with their mix of white-hot rage and cool-eyed analysis. Maxine Hong Kingston had created what seemed almost a new form: she took us on a journey we had never before embarked upon.

It was, and is, a journey of knowing. Knowing the self and the world, the self in the world, the self through the world.

ix

These books take up the complex business of trying to find the meaning of the word 'I'. Kingston tells us that as a child, 'I' was difficult for her to understand.

I could not understand 'I.' The Chinese 'I' has seven strokes, intricacies. How could the American 'I,' assuredly wearing a hat like the Chinese, have only three strokes, the middle so straight? Was it out of politeness that this writer left off strokes the way a Chinese has to write her own name small and crooked? No, it was not politeness; 'I' is a capital and 'you' is a lower-case. I stared at that middle line and waited so long for its black center to resolve into tight strokes and dots that I forgot to pronounce it.

And yet the Chinese word for the female 'I' means 'slave.' So the child speaker, in attempting to understand the 'I' is rendered mute. But the adult writer has found her voice, and in finding it has found herself. She has found it in myth and song and rant and curse and incantation. She is a warrior of words:

The swordsman and I are not so dissimilar. May my people understand the resemblance soon so that I can return to them. What we have in common are the words at our backs. The idioms for *revenge* are 'report a crime' and 'report to five families.' The reporting is the vengeance – not the beheading, not the gutting, but the words.

Whose voice is this? In what terms, using what categories, does it define itself? And by what word would it be named: female, daughter, Chinese, American, storyteller, writer, keeper of memory, betrayer, citizen – all these would seem to apply. For these books tell us that the self cannot know itself properly in a vacuum, that the self is composed in the company of the living and the dead. 'Memoirs of a Girlhood Among Ghosts' is the subtitle of *The Woman Warrior* – and the word 'ghosts' has two meanings. There is the meaning that is more familiar to us: the disembodied spirits of the dead. But in the Chinese community that nurtured Maxine Hong Kingston 'ghost' is simply a synonym for white person, one of those in power, those who make the rules, at once god-like and despised: they are ridiculous, ignorant no-nothings without manners and tradition or even good sense, but they hold in their hands the key, for the Chinese who are at their mercy, to life and death. So the Chinese American must negotiate her way through the land of white ghosts, but there is another sense in which she makes her way, among other ghosts: she is accompanied by them, through their stories, both factual and mythical: they tell her who she is, and perhaps more importantly, who she might be.

In the realm of fact, what might be called the realm of psychological realism, the territory limned by both Freud and the great nineteenth-century novelists, Maxine Hong Kingston is a frightened child who grows up in a harsh world almost entirely without affection, praise, or encouragement. She is afraid of being sent back to China to be sold as a slave. She is afraid of being sold off to a retarded man because he has money and she fears that her parents see her as damaged and therefore the fit mate for this damaged creature whom they allow to sit in their laundry and provide their children with toys. Insult seems to be her daily bread: the insults of her parents and the casual insults of the white world that misunderstands and undervalues her and yet provides her with the ambiguous freedom offered by modern America. Kingston understands very well the geography of this world.

I had to leave home in order to see the world logically, logic the new way of seeing. I learned to think that mysteries are for explanation. I enjoy the simplicity. Concrete pours out of my mouth to cover the forests with freeways and sidewalks. Give me plastics, periodical tables, t.v. dinners with vegetables no more complex than peas mixed with diced carrots. Shine floodlights into dark corners: no ghosts.

But this world, this American world, this logical world, is not the only world, nor is it necessarily the most important one. Alongside it there is the world of story, of talk-story, a concept passed on from Kingston's mother. And from this world of words, the shy girl creates a triumphant image for herself: the warrior she may be in the process of becoming.

It is clear to Kingston that the Chinese Americans she knows have other identities than the ones legible to American ghosts. To them, her mother is a source of cheap labor: she works as a near-slave both in her husband's laundry and picking tomatoes in the California fields. But Kingston knows the truth about her mother. Her mother is Brave Orchid, who was trained as a doctor in China, carried in a palinquin, feared, honored and revered by the people in her village who saw her as their savior, the bringer of life, since she refused to treat patients who seemed near death.

The name of the mother: *Brave Orchid*. A name whose meaning seems elusive to ghost ears. How can an orchid be brave? An orchid is vivid and sensual, but fragile. It is a sign of rare and opulent beauty. Against what could it contend, what could be the terms of its vanquishing, and what its victories? What might its weapons be? For this brave orchid, this mother of the writer, the main weapons against the dangerous world are the weapons of energy and voice. Brave Orchid is fearless, she is tireless.

MaMa worked in the fields and the canneries. She showed us how to use her new tools, the pitters and curved knives. We tried on her cap pinned with union buttons and her rubber gloves that smelled like rubber tomatoes. She emptied her buckets, thermoses, shopping bags, lunch pail, apron, and scarf; she brought home every kind of vegetable and fruit grown in San Joaquin County. She said she was tired after work but kept moving, busy, banged doors, drawers, pots and cleaver, turned faucets off and on with *ka-chunks* in the pipes. Her cleaver banged on the chopping block for an hour straight as she minced pork and steak into patties. Her energy slammed BaBa back into his chair. She took care of everything; he did not have a reason to get up. He stared at his toes and fingers. 'You've lost your sense of emergency,' she said; she kept up her sense of emergency every moment.

What can it mean to have a mother who keeps up her sense of emergency every moment? Invaluable when an emergency does occur and necessary for survival against brutal odds, it provides no possibility of rest. The Hong household, presided over by Brave Orchid, does not seem like a place where rest is possible. There is no silence; work is always being done, scolding is always happening. When Maxine wants to tell her mother the 'list of over two hundred things . . . so that she would know the true things about me and to stop the pain in my throat,' Brave Orchid is too tired to listen; she doesn't want her own hard-won silence polluted by her daughter's ravings: she tells the anguished, guilty child to 'Leave me alone.' But Kingston is never without her mother, who in cutting her frenum has freed her tongue, and somehow activated her daughter's endlessly active, endlessly lively imagination, peopled with creatures as inventive and unstill as acrobats. And the daughter becomes the acrobat/warrior who with her nimbleness can escape the juggernaut of the mother, as some, including her sister, Moon Orchid, cannot.

One of the most moving sections of *The Woman Warrior* is the one entitled 'At the Western Palace.' It concerns the arrival of Brave Orchid's sister, Moon Orchid, who comes as an old woman from China to California. Brave Orchid insists that Moon Orchid track down her husband who left her half a century before. Moon Orchid's daughter by this husband has revealed that her father has a new wife and a new family. Brave Orchid says that her sister, still elegant at eighty, must move into her husband's house and take her place as First Wife. The sisters plan to confront the husband, a successful doctor, in his office. His new wife is serving as his nurse. Brave Orchid devises a scheme for entrapping him into their car. He refuses to acknowledge his old wife.

Shattered by the pressure of these events and unable to find her place in America, Moon Orchid loses her mind and ends her days in a mental hospital, where she is happy in a world of 'sisters.' The destruction brought about by Brave Orchid's relentless certainty is not discussed. And yet the child of this mother sees it and notes it, as she sees and notes the destructiveness in herself. Resolutely unsentimental, Kingston is aware that the cruelty that may be a necessary concomitant of survival results in cruelty passed on to others. One of the most harrowing recountings in *China Men* is the drawn-out description of the abashed girl-child Maxine torturing a classmate more abashed than she, trying to force the girl to talk and literally making herself sick in the process. Her guilt drives her to a sickbed, where, in her convalescence, she reads and makes up stories. But she longs to confess to her mother, to recite the list of her sins, her crimes. 'If only I could let my mother know the list, she –and the world – would become more like me, and I would never be alone again.' But Brave Orchid has neither the time nor the inclination to listen to such a list, and no notion of the power of listening to absolve and to transform.

And what of the father, who was 'slammed back into his chair' by his wife's torrential force? What of this father who is roused out of his catatonia only by rage against his children? What does the writer/warrior learn about men from him?

'Father, I have seen you lighthearted ... But usually you did not play. You were angry. You scared us. Every day we listened to you swear, 'Dog vomit. Your mother's cunt. Your mother's smelly cunt.' You slammed the iron on the shirt while muttering, 'Stink pig. Mother's cunt.' Obscenities ... What I want from you is for you to tell me that those curses are only common Chinese sayings. That you did not mean to make me sicken at being female. 'Those were only sayings,' I want you to say to me. 'I didn't mean you or your mother. I didn't mean your sisters or grandmothers or women in general.'

For Kingston, the world of the father is not only the world of the literal father, any more than the world of the mother is only that of the literal mother. The world of the fathers is the world of the China Men, who are not to be confused with the Chinamen, a derogatory name invented by American Ghosts. If the world of the mothers is marked most importantly by the danger of enslavement and punishment, the world of the fathers is one of physical danger, where what is required is not only cunning, but brute strength. To support their families – to earn the money that would spare their families starvation– Kingston's forebears built America's railroads and cleared its forests. And of course, they cleaned America's clothes. Kingston's father's dreams of glory ended in his owning his own laundry, and she evokes it in terms whose power comes from their spare dryness.

When the thermometer in our laundry reached one hundred and eleven degrees on summer afternoons, either my mother or my father would say that it was time to tell another ghost story so that we could get some good chills up our backs. My parents, my brothers, sisters, great-uncle, and 'Third Aunt,' who wasn't really our aunt but a fellow villager, someone else's third aunt, kept the presses crashing and hissing and shouted out the stories. Those were our successful days, when so much laundry came in, my mother did not have to pick tomatoes. For breaks we changed from pressing to sorting.

This passage is emblematic of Maxine Hong Kingston's vision and her method. Both insist on an endlessly shifting reality, in which the hissing of the presses mixes with the shouted tales of ghosts, tales which work as hard as the laundry workers: they preserve the past and they cool the skin. For Kingston, nothing is static, everything is what it appears to be and what is behind it, silent and invisible. So behind the enraged sullen father is a 'silent magician' who as a young man danced down Fifth Avenue pretending he was Fred Astaire. The mutterer of curses about the bodies of women is the enchanting companion who takes his daughter along to be part of his life as a gambler. The sweating toiler in the laundry has a closet full of beautiful suits: 'Power suits. Money suits. Two hundred-dollars-apiece New York suits. Businessmen-in-the-movies suits.' As the mother in her tomato-smelling rubber gloves, shouting that her children are worthless, is the scientist in a silk gown and the tender granter of freedom who allows her child the world, stroking her hair and whispering, 'Of course, you must go, little Dog.'

The structure of these books reflects an awareness of the essential shaping power of myth, and yet it speaks from the limits of post-Enlightenment understanding. Only the power of myths and the ghosts who tell them allows this daughter of a despised and starving and endangered people the power of language. Language is her sword; she is the swordsman of words. And yet what, she asks herself, have her words changed? She lives in late twentieth-century America, and there she is ineffectual; when she tries to take a stand against her bigoted employers, she only croaks out her objections, and then is fired. Her kin in China continue to starve. She does not even feel able to sort out the reality of China under Mao from the horror stories that her parents believe.

So what can she do? What good is she, this girl with her straight A's and her loosened tongue, and the ferocity of her language? She can witness. She can transform the sorrow and humiliation of a people into the gold of radiant words. She can preserve what is in danger of being lost. Like Ts'ai Yen, the poetess born in 175 AD, she can sing from her tent, apart from the others. 'Her words seemed to be Chinese, but the barbarians understood their sadness and anger.'

From sadness and anger to the barbarians' understanding. This is the victory achieved by the Warrior of Words, whose sword (her loosened tongue, her sharpened pen) slashes our spirits and incises our hearts.

Mary Gordon

Further Reading
Conversations with Maxine Hong Kingston, edited by Paul Skenazy and Tera Martin, University of Mississippi Press, 1998.

CHRONOLOGY

———

DATE	AUTHOR'S LIFE	LITERARY CONTEXT
		1937 Hurston: *Their Eyes Were Watching God.*
		1939 Steinbeck: *The Grapes of Wrath.*
1940	Maxine Ting Ting Hong is born on 27 October in Stockton, California, the eldest of six children of first-generation Chinese immigrants. Her father Tom is a scholar, manager of a gambling house, and a laundry worker. Her mother, Ling Yang or Brave Orchid, a doctor in China, works in the laundry and as a farm laborer. Tom names his daughter Maxine after a blond woman lucky at the gambling tables.	1940 Greene: *The Power and the Glory.* Hemingway: *For Whom the Bell Tolls.* Stead: *The Man Who Loved Children.*
		1941 Fitzgerald: *The Last Tycoon.* O'Neill: *Long Day's Journey into Night.* Hurston: *Dust Tracks on a Road.* Woolf: *Between the Acts.*
		1942 Hisaye Yamamoto and her family are evacuated to the detention camp in Poston, Arizona. Yamamoto publishes *Death Rides the Rails to Poston*, a serialized mystery story, in the camp newspaper.
		1945 Orwell: *Animal Farm.*

HISTORICAL EVENTS

1937 Sino-Japanese War (to 1945).

1939 Outbreak of World War II.

1940 US refuses France's appeal for help: fall of France. Battle of Britain. Italy joins the war in alliance with Germany. Penicillin developed as an antibiotic.

1941 Canadian Government starts moving citizens of Japanese descent into internment camps, where conditions are so bad that food is sent to them from Japan through the Red Cross. US and Britain freeze Japanese assets to claims in Indo-China. Japanese bomb Pearl Harbor. US and Britain declare war on Japan. Hong Kong, Malaya, Singapore and Burma fall to the Japanese.

1942 Franklin D. Roosevelt signs Executive Order 9066, leading to the internment of some 12,000 Japanese Americans living on the West Coast. Many Japanese Canadians have possessions and property confiscated under the War Measures Act.

1943 Chinese Exclusion Act of 1882 finally repealed though quota for entry to the US remains at a mere 105 per annum. By the end of the 1940s all restrictions on Asians acquiring US citizenship are abolished.
1945 Germany surrenders. Britain, US and China demand the unconditional surrender of Japan. Massive air raids on Tokyo; atomic bombs dropped on Hiroshima and Nagasaki. United Nations founded. Wives and children of Chinese Americans able to enter the US under terms of the War Brides Act. Death of Roosevelt: Truman US President.

DATE	AUTHOR'S LIFE	LITERARY CONTEXT
		1947 Williams: *A Streetcar Named Desire.* Levi: *If This Is a Man.* 1948 Norman Mailer: *The Naked and the Dead.* Graham Greene: *The Heart of the Matter.* 1949 Yamamoto: *Seventeen Syllables.* Amy Tan's mother is forced to leave three children behind in China as she escapes on the last boat from Shanghai before the Communist takeover. De Beauvoir: *The Second Sex.* 1950 Hemingway: *Across the River and into the Trees.* Pound: *Seventy Cantos.*
		1951 Yamamoto: *Yoneko's Earthquake.* Salinger: *The Catcher in the Rye.* 1952 Amy Tan is born in Oakland, California to Chinese parents. Beckett: *Waiting for Godot.* Lessing: *Martha Quest.*
1954	Attends Edison High School in Stockton (to 1958).	1954 Yamamoto: *Appointment in Japan.* Bellow: *The Adventures of Augie March.*
1955	Publishes her first essay, 'I am an American,' in *American Girl* magazine.	1955 *The Diary of Anne Frank* is published. Nabokov: *Lolita.* Flannery O'Connor: *A Good Man Is Hard to Find.* Miller: *A View From the Bridge.*
1958	Wins a journalism scholarship to the University of California, Berkeley. Writes for student newspaper, *The Daily Californian.*	1958 Pasternak: *Doctor Zhivago.* Capote: *Breakfast at Tiffany's.* Achebe: *Things Fall Apart.*

CHRONOLOGY

1946 Civil War in China (to 1949). Beginning of Cold War.

1947 Marshall Plan: US aid for postwar European recovery. Puppet Communist states set up in Eastern Europe. Independence of India and Pakistan.

1948 Chiang Kai-shek resumes presidency of China and is granted dictatorial powers. Communists announce birth of the North China People's Republic. State of Israel founded. South African government adopts *apartheid* as official policy.

1949 Chiang Kai-shek resigns presidency of China. Communist People's Republic of China proclaimed. NATO founded.

1950 McCarthy leads Communist witch hunts in the US. Peking offers Tibet regional autonomy in exchange for joining the Communist system. Tibet appeals to UN against Chinese aggression; China refuses UN appeal for a ceasefire. Korean War (to 1953).

1951 North Korean and Chinese Communists break through UN lines, taking Seoul. China rejects UN peace proposal for the Far East. China extends rule over Tibet.

1952 US tests hydrogen bomb. Chinese Communists accuse US forces of deploying germ warfare in Korea. McCarran-Walter Act abolishes race as an immigration criterion and sets quotas by nation.

1954 Vietnam War begins when the French colonists are defeated by the communists at Dieu Bien Phu.

1955 Montgomery Bus Boycoctt (to 1956) heralds a decade of non-violent protests, student sit-ins and marches in support of the civil rights movement.

1956 Khrushchev denounces Stalin. Hundred Flowers in China: population allowed to voice their opinion of the Communist regime (forcibly ended 1957). California repeals alien landownership laws.

1958 The Beatnik movement begins amongst young poets in California. US Supreme court forces Little Rock High School, Arkansas to admit African-American pupils. Great Leap Forward in China: unsuccessful attempt to accelerate industrialization and improve agricultural production.

DATE	AUTHOR'S LIFE	LITERARY CONTEXT
		1961 Yamamoto: *Nip in the Bud.* Updike: *Rabbit Run.* Heller: *Catch-22.* Naipaul: *A House for Mr Biswas.*
1962	Graduates. Marries Earll Kingston.	1962 Lessing: *The Golden Notebook.* Solzhenitsyn: *One Day in the Life of Ivan Denisovich.*
1963	Joseph Lawrence Chung Mei Kingston is born.	1963 Plath: *The Bell Jar.* McCarthy: *The Group.* Friedan: *The Feminine Mystique.* 1964 Yamamoto: *A Slight Case of Mistaken Identity.*
1965	Teaches at a Californian High School. Takes part in protests against the Vietnam War and becomes involved in the Free Speech Movement.	1965 Mailer: *An American Dream.* Drabble: *The Millstone.* 1966 Plath: *Ariel.* Rhys: *Wide Sargasso Sea.* Nabokov: *Speak, Memory.*
1967	Moves to Hawaii with her husband and son.	1967 Márquez: *One Hundred Years of Solitude.* Sexton: *Live or Die.* 1969 Oates: *Them.* Sontag: *Styles of Radical Will.* Rich: *Leaflets.* Angelou: *I Know Why the Caged Bird Sings.* 1970 Greer: *The Female Eunuch.* Atwood: *The Edible Woman.* 1973 Rich: *Diving into the Wreck.* Sarton: *Journal of a Solitude.* 1974 Kagawa: *A Choice of Dreams.* Bellow: *Humboldt's Gift.* Jong: *Fear of Flying.* Lorde: *New York Head Shop and Museum.*

CHRONOLOGY

1961 US cuts off diplomatic relations with Cuba. Bay of Pigs invasion. President John F. Kennedy takes up office. Construction of the Berlin Wall. Yuri Gagarin becomes the first man in space.

1962 Cuban Missile Crisis.

1963 Over 250,000 people march on Washington in support of the Civil Rights Bill. Assassination of John F. Kennedy in Dallas, Texas. Beatles' first LP is released.

1964 Congress passes Civil Rights Act. US enters Vietnam War. Khrushchev deposed and replaced by Brezhnev. Mandela imprisoned in South Africa (to 1990).

1965 Congress passes Voting Rights Act. Immigration Act abolishes country preferences; Asian immigration increases. Malcolm X assassinated.

1966 Cultural Revolution in China. Betty Friedan founds National Organization for Women in the US.

1967 Six-Day War between Israel and Arab states. Biafran War (to 1970). First successful heart transplant (Christian Barnard).

1968 Assassination of Martin Luther King. Soviet-led invasion of Czechoslovakia. Student unrest throughout Europe and US.

1969 Neil Armstrong becomes the first man to set foot on the moon. First Concorde flight.

1972 Strategic Arms Limitation Treaty is signed by the US and USSR. President Nixon visits China.

1973 US withdraws from Vietnam War. General Pinochet stages coup in Chile.

1974 Resignation of Nixon following the Watergate scandal.

DATE	AUTHOR'S LIFE	LITERARY CONTEXT
		1975 Alther: *Kinflicks*.
1976	*The Woman Warrior: Memoirs of a Girlhood Among Ghosts* is published, winning the National Book Critics Circle Award for non-fiction.	1976 Yamamoto: *I Still Carry It Around*. Lorde: *Coal*.
1977	*Duck Boy* is published in the *New York Times Magazine*. Appointed Visiting Professor of English, University of Hawaii, Honolulu (to 1981).	1977 Morrison: *Song of Solomon*. Cheever: *Falconer*.
		1978 Kagawa: *Jericho Road*. French: *The Women's Room*.
1979	*Woman Warrior* is rated as one of the top ten non-fiction works of the decade by *Time* magazine.	1979 Carter: *The Bloody Chamber*.
1980	*China Men* is published, winning the National Book Award for non-fiction. The author receives a National Endowment for the Arts Writing Fellowship and is named a 'Living Treasure of Hawaii' by a Buddhist church in Honolulu. Increasing involvement in the anti-draft movement.	1980 Joy Kagawa publishes *Obasan*, winning the first Nobel prize for a book in Canada.
1981	*China Men* is a runner-up for the Pulitzer Prize. Kingston is awarded a Guggenheim Fellowship.	1981 Moore: *The Complete Poems*. Updike: *Rabbit is Rich*. Rushdie: *Midnight's Children*. 1982 Walker: *The Color Purple*. Allende: *The House of the Spirits*. 1983 Walker: *In Search of Our Mothers' Gardens*. Atwood: *The Handmaid's Tale*. Weldon: *The Life and Loves of a She-Devil*.
1984	The author travels to China for the first time along with a group of other writers including Allen Ginsberg and Toni Morrison. Moves from Hawaii to Los Angeles.	1984 Yamamoto: *An Abandoned Pot of Rice*. Carter: *Nights at the Circus*.

CHRONOLOGY

1975 End of the Vietnam War. Immigrants arrive from Communist regimes in Vietnam, Cambodia, and Laos.
1976 Death of Chairman Mao; Gang of Four compete for power in China. Jimmy Carter elected US President. Soweto massacre.

1977 Deng Xiaoping gains power in China.

1978 Camp David Agreement between Carter, Begin and Sadat. Boat people leaving Vietnam. First test-tube baby born.
1979 SALT 2 signed. Soviet forces invade Afghanistan. Shah of Iran deposed in Islamic revolution. Pol Pot deposed in Cambodia. Diplomatic relations between the US and China resumed. Margaret Thatcher first woman Prime Minister in UK.

1981 President Sadat is assassinated in Egypt. Ronald Reagan is elected President in the US.

1983 US troops invade Grenada.

DATE	AUTHOR'S LIFE	LITERARY CONTEXT
		1986 DeLillo: *The End Zone.*
		Simpson: *Anywhere but Here.*
		1987 Yamamoto: *A Day in Little Tokyo.*
		Morrison: *Beloved.*
		Ondaatje: *In the Skin of a Lion.*
		1988 Wolfe: *The Bonfire of the Vanities.*
		Carver: *Where I'm Calling From.*
		Gellhorn: *A View from the Ground.*
		Rushdie: *The Satanic Verses.*
		Carey: *Oscar and Lucinda.*
1989	Publishes *Tripmaster Monkey: His Fake Book* (PEN USA West Award) and 'Students of Tiananmen: Braving a Way of Peace.'	1989 Tan: *The Joy Luck Club.* Ozick: *The Shawl.*
1990	Invited back to the University of California, Berkeley, as a Chancellor's Distinguished Professor of English.	1990 Oates: *Because It Is Bitter, and Because It Is My Heart.* Byatt: *Possession.* Kureishi: *The Buddha of Suburbia.*
1991	The author's father dies in September. In October the Oakland Hills firestorm burns Kingston's home to the ground. All her manuscripts are destroyed, including the unfinished *Fourth Book of Peace.*	1991 Tan: *The Kitchen God's Wife.* Yamamoto: *Broccoli and Spinach.* Jung Chang: *Wild Swans: Three Daughters of China.*
1992	Wins Lila Wallace Reader's Digest writing award; dedicates prize money to fund writing workshops for war veterans.	1992 Yamamoto: *Florentine Garden.* Kagawa: *Itsuka.* Oates: *Black Water.* Ondaatje: *The English Patient.*
1993	Chairs a series of workshops for veterans.	1993 Okri: *Songs of Enchantment.*
1994	*The Woman Warrior* is adapted for stage and receives its first performance at Berkeley.	1994 Angelou: *The Complete Collected Poems.* Jong: *Fear of Fifty.* Atwood: *The Robber Bride.*
1995	Chairs a reading of Vietnamese and US poets and novelists at a conference investigating the legacy of the Vietnam War.	1995 Kagawa: *The Rain Ascends.* Guterson: *Snow Falling on Cedars.* Viramontes: *Under the Feet of Jesus.*

HISTORICAL EVENTS

1986 Gorbachev–Reagan summit. Nuclear explosion at Chernobyl.

1988 George Bush is elected President of the US. Gorbechev announces significant troop reductions. Terrorist bomb destroys Pan Am flight over Lockerbie, Scotland.

1989 Fall of the Berlin Wall. Tiennamen Square massacre in China. De Klerk is elected President of South Africa. Collapse of Communism in Eastern Europe. President Bush signs law to pay each survivor of Japanese internment camps $20,000.

1990 Nelson Mandela is released from prison after 27 years. Immigration Act raises the total quota and reorganizes system of preferences. Nearly 5 million immigrants arrive in the US from Asian countries.

1991 Gulf War. Gorbachev deposed by coup: demise of USSR. War begins in former Yugoslavia. End of Apartheid in South Africa.

1992 Riots in Los Angeles. Bill Clinton is elected US President.

1993 Palestinian leader Arafat and Israeli Prime Minister Rabin sign peace agreement in the US.
1994 Massacres in Rwanda. Mandela leads the ANC party to victory in South African elections. Russia initiates military action against Chechen Republic.

DATE	AUTHOR'S LIFE	LITERARY CONTEXT
		1996 Atwood: *Alias Grace.* Updike: *In the Beauty of the Lilies.*
1997	Speaks at a peace conference in San Francisco, alongside Alice Walker and the Dalai Lama of Tibet. Awarded the National Humanities Medal by President Clinton.	1997 Roth: *American Pastoral.* Ozick: *The Puttermesser Papers.* Roy: *The God of Small Things.*
1998	*Hawai'i One Summer* is published. Awarded the John Dos Passos Prize for Literature.	1998 Tan: *The Hundred Secret Senses.* Morrison: *Paradise.* DeLillo: *Underworld.* Roth: *I Married a Communist.*
1999	*Hawai'i One Summer* receives the Ka Palapola Po'okala Award from the Hawai'i Publishers Association.	1999 Sontag: *In America.*
2000	Alumna of the Year, University of California, Berkeley.	2000 Atwood: *The Blind Assassin.* Roth: *The Human Stain.* 2001 Tan: *The Bonesetter's Daughter.* Kagawa: *Song of Lilith.* Lessing: *The Sweetest Dream.* Sontag: *Where the Stress Falls.* Franzen: *The Corrections.*
2002	Gives the Massey Lectures at Harvard University, published by Harvard University Press as *To be the Poet.*	
2003	Retires from teaching at Berkeley. Publishes *The Fifth Book of Peace.* Along with Alice Walker, Kingston is arrested for civil disobedience in front of the White House at a rally to protest against the bombing of Iraq.	2003 Atwood: *Oryx and Crake.* Lessing: *The Grandmothers.*
2004	Accepts honorary doctorate from the University of the Pacific.	

CHRONOLOGY

1996 President Clinton is re-elected in the US.

1997 Britain hands Hong Kong over to China.

1998 Clinton–Lewinski scandal breaks. Clinton orders air strikes against Iraq.

1999 Serbs attack ethnic Albanians in Kosovo; US leads NATO in the bombing of Belgrade.

2000 Milosevic's regime in the former Yugoslavia collapses. George W. Bush becomes President.

2001 Al-Qaeda terrorist attacks of 9/11. US and allied military attacks against the Taliban in Afghanistan.

2003 Iraq weapons crisis. American and British troops invade Iraq.

2004 George W. Bush re-elected.

THE WOMAN WARRIOR

Memoirs of a Girlhood among Ghosts

CONTENTS

3

To Mother and Father

NO NAME WOMAN

"You must not tell anyone," my mother said, "what I am about to tell you. In China your father had a sister who killed herself. She jumped into the family well. We say that your father has all brothers because it is as if she had never been born.

"In 1924 just a few days after our village celebrated seventeen hurry-up weddings – to make sure that every young man who went 'out on the road' would responsibly come home – your father and his brothers and your grandfather and his brothers and your aunt's new husband sailed for America, the Gold Mountain. It was your grandfather's last trip. Those lucky enough to get contracts waved good-bye from the decks. They fed and guarded the stowaways and helped them off in Cuba, New York, Bali, Hawaii. 'We'll meet in California next year,' they said. All of them sent money home.

"I remember looking at your aunt one day when she and I were dressing; I had not noticed before that she had such a protruding melon of a stomach. But I did not think, 'She's pregnant,' until she began to look like other pregnant women, her shirt pulling and the white tops of her black pants showing. She could not have been pregnant, you see, because her husband had been gone for years. No one said anything. We did not discuss it. In early summer she was ready to have the child, long after the time when it could have been possible.

"The village had also been counting. On the night the baby was to be born the villagers raided our house. Some were crying. Like a great saw, teeth strung with lights, files of people walked zigzag across our land, tearing the rice. Their lanterns doubled in the disturbed black water, which drained away through the broken bunds. As the villagers closed in, we could see that some of them, probably men and women we knew well, wore white masks. The people with long hair hung it over their faces. Women with short hair made it stand up on end. Some had tied white bands around their foreheads, arms, and legs.

"At first they threw mud and rocks at the house. Then they threw eggs and began slaughtering our stock. We could hear the animals scream their deaths – the roosters, the pigs, a last great roar from the ox. Familiar wild heads flared in our night windows; the villagers encircled us. Some of the faces stopped to peer at us, their eyes rushing like searchlights. The hands flattened against the panes, framed heads, and left red prints.

"The villagers broke in the front and the back doors at the same time, even though we had not locked the doors against them. Their knives dripped with the blood of our animals. They smeared blood on the doors and walls. One woman swung a chicken, whose throat she had slit, splattering blood in red arcs about her. We stood together in the middle of our house, in the family hall with the pictures and tables of the ancestors around us, and looked straight ahead.

"At that time the house had only two wings. When the men came back, we would build two more to enclose our courtyard and a third one to begin a second courtyard. The villagers pushed through both wings, even your grandparents' rooms, to find your aunt's, which was also mine until the men returned. From this room a new wing for one of the younger families would grow. They ripped up her clothes and shoes and broke her combs, grinding them underfoot. They tore her work from the loom. They scattered the cooking fire and rolled the new weaving in it. We could hear them in the kitchen breaking our bowls and banging the pots. They overturned the great waist-high earthenware jugs; duck eggs, pickled fruits, vegetables burst out and mixed in acrid torrents. The old woman from the next field swept a broom through the air and loosed the spirits-of-the-broom over our heads. 'Pig.' 'Ghost.' 'Pig,' they sobbed and scolded while they ruined our house.

"When they left, they took sugar and oranges to bless themselves. They cut pieces from the dead animals. Some of them took bowls that were not broken and clothes that were not torn. Afterward we swept up the rice and sewed it back up into sacks. But the smells from the spilled preserves lasted. Your aunt gave birth in the pigsty that night. The next morning when I went for the water, I found her and the baby plugging up the family well.

"Don't let your father know that I told you. He denies her. Now that you have started to menstruate, what happened to her could happen to you. Don't humiliate us. You wouldn't like to be forgotten as if you had never been born. The villagers are watchful."

Whenever she had to warn us about life, my mother told stories that ran like this one, a story to grow up on. She tested our strength to establish realities. Those in the emigrant generations who could not reassert brute survival died young and far from home. Those of us in the first American generations have had to figure out how the invisible world the emigrants built around our childhoods fits in solid America.

The emigrants confused the gods by diverting their curses, misleading them with crooked streets and false names. They must try to confuse their offspring as well, who, I suppose, threaten them in similar ways – always trying to get things straight, always trying to name the unspeakable. The Chinese I know hide their names; sojourners take new names when their lives change and guard their real names with silence.

Chinese-Americans, when you try to understand what things in you are Chinese, how do you separate what is peculiar to childhood, to poverty, insanities, one family, your mother who marked your growing with stories, from what is Chinese? What is Chinese tradition and what is the movies?

If I want to learn what clothes my aunt wore, whether flashy or ordinary, I would have to begin, "Remember Father's drowned-in-the-well sister?" I cannot ask that. My mother has told me once and for all the useful parts. She will add nothing unless powered by Necessity, a riverbank that guides her life. She plants vegetable gardens rather than lawns; she carries the odd-shaped tomatoes home from the fields and eats food left for the gods.

Whenever we did frivolous things, we used up energy; we flew high kites. We children came up off the ground over the melting cones our parents brought home from work and the American movie on New Year's Day – *Oh, You Beautiful Doll* with Betty Grable one year, and *She Wore a Yellow Ribbon* with John Wayne another year. After the one carnival ride each, we paid in guilt; our tired father counted his change on the dark walk home.

Adultery is extravagance. Could people who hatch their own chicks and eat the embryos and the heads for delicacies and boil the feet in vinegar for party food, leaving only the gravel, eating even the gizzard lining – could such people engender a prodigal aunt? To be a woman, to have a daughter in starvation time was a waste enough. My aunt could not have been the lone romantic who gave up everything for sex. Women in the old China did not choose. Some man had commanded her to lie with him and be his secret evil. I wonder whether he masked himself when he joined the raid on her family.

Perhaps she had encountered him in the fields or on the mountain where the daughters-in-law collected fuel. Or perhaps he first noticed her in the marketplace. He was not a stranger because the village housed no strangers. She had to have dealings with him other than sex. Perhaps he worked an adjoining field, or he sold her the cloth for the dress she sewed and wore. His demand must have surprised, then terrified her. She obeyed him; she always did as she was told.

When the family found a young man in the next village to be her husband, she had stood tractably beside the best rooster, his proxy, and promised before they met that she would be his forever. She was lucky that he was her age and she would be the first wife, an advantage secure now. The night she first saw him, he had sex with her. Then he left for America. She had almost forgotten what he looked like. When she tried to envision him, she only saw the black and white face in the group photograph the men had had taken before leaving.

The other man was not, after all, much different from her husband. They both gave orders: she followed. "If you tell your family, I'll beat you. I'll kill you. Be here again next week." No one talked sex, ever. And she might have separated the rapes from the rest of living if only she did not have to buy her oil from him or gather wood in the same forest. I want her fear to have lasted just as long as rape lasted so that the fear could have been contained. No drawn-out fear. But women at sex hazarded birth and hence lifetimes. The fear did not stop but permeated everywhere. She told the man, "I think I'm pregnant." He organized the raid against her.

On nights when my mother and father talked about their life back home, sometimes they mentioned an "outcast table" whose business they still seemed to be settling, their voices tight. In a commensal tradition, where food is precious, the powerful older people made wrongdoers eat alone. Instead of letting them start separate new lives like the Japanese, who could become samurais and geishas, the Chinese family, faces averted but eyes glowering sideways, hung on to the offenders and fed them leftovers. My aunt must have lived in the same house as my parents and eaten at an outcast table. My mother spoke about the raid as if she had seen it, when she and my aunt, a daughter-in-law to a different household, should not have been living together at all. Daughters-in-law lived with their husbands' parents, not their own; a synonym for marriage in Chinese is "taking a daughter-in-law." Her husband's parents could have sold her, mortgaged her, stoned her. But they had sent her back to her own mother and father, a mysterious act hinting at disgraces not told me. Perhaps they had thrown her out to deflect the avengers.

She was the only daughter; her four brothers went with her father, husband, and uncles "out on the road" and for some years became western men. When the goods were divided among the family, three of the brothers took land, and the youngest, my father, chose an education. After my grandparents gave their daughter away to her husband's family, they had dispensed all the adventure and all the property. They expected her alone to keep the traditional ways, which her brothers, now among the barbarians, could fumble without detection. The heavy, deep-rooted women were to maintain the past against the flood, safe for returning. But the rare urge west had fixed upon our family, and so my aunt crossed boundaries not delineated in space.

The work of preservation demands that the feelings playing about in one's guts not be turned into action. Just watch their passing like cherry blossoms. But perhaps my aunt, my forerunner, caught in a slow life, let dreams grow and fade and after some months or years went toward what persisted. Fear at the enormities of the forbidden kept her desires delicate, wire and bone. She looked at a man because she liked the way the hair was tucked behind his ears, or she liked the question-mark line of a long torso curving at the shoulder and straight at the hip. For warm eyes or a soft voice or a slow walk – that's all – a few hairs, a line, a brightness, a sound, a pace, she gave up family. She offered us up for a charm that vanished with tiredness, a pigtail that didn't toss when the wind died. Why, the wrong lighting could erase the dearest thing about him.

It could very well have been, however, that my aunt did not take subtle enjoyment of her friend, but, a wild woman, kept rollicking company. Imagining her free with sex doesn't fit, though. I don't know any women like that, or men either. Unless I see her life branching into mine, she gives me no ancestral help.

To sustain her being in love, she often worked at herself in the mirror, guessing at the colors and shapes that would interest him, changing them frequently in order to hit on the right combination. She wanted him to look back.

On a farm near the sea, a woman who tended her appearance reaped a reputation for eccentricity. All the married women blunt-cut their hair in flaps about their ears or pulled it back in tight buns. No nonsense. Neither style blew easily into heart-catching tangles. And at their weddings they displayed themselves in their long hair for the last time. "It brushed the backs of my knees," my mother tells me. "It was braided, and even so, it brushed the backs of my knees."

At the mirror my aunt combed individuality into her bob. A bun could have been contrived to escape into black streamers blowing in the wind or in quiet wisps about her face, but only the older women in our picture album wear buns. She brushed her hair back from her forehead, tucking the flaps behind her ears. She looped a piece of thread, knotted into a circle between her index fingers and thumbs, and ran the double strand across her forehead. When she closed her fingers as if she were making a pair of shadow geese bite, the string twisted together catching the little hairs. Then she pulled the thread away from her skin, ripping the hairs out neatly, her eyes watering from the needles of pain. Opening her fingers, she cleaned the thread, then rolled it along her hairline and the tops of her eyebrows. My mother did the same to me and my sisters and herself. I used to believe that the expression "caught by the short hairs" meant a captive held with a depilatory string. It especially hurt at the temples, but my mother said we were lucky we didn't have to have our feet bound when we were seven. Sisters used to sit on their beds and cry together, she said, as their mothers or their slaves removed the bandages for a few minutes each night and let the blood gush back into their veins. I hope that the man my aunt loved appreciated a smooth brow, that he wasn't just a tits-and-ass man.

Once my aunt found a freckle on her chin, at a spot that the almanac said predestined her for unhappiness. She dug it out with a hot needle and washed the wound with peroxide.

More attention to her looks than these pullings of hairs and pickings at spots would have caused gossip among the villagers. They owned work clothes and good clothes, and they wore good clothes for feasting the new seasons. But since a woman combing her hair hexes beginnings, my aunt rarely found an occasion to look her best. Women looked like great sea snails – the corded wood, babies, and laundry they carried were the whorls on their backs. The Chinese did not admire a bent back; goddesses and warriors stood straight. Still there must have been a marvelous freeing of beauty when a worker laid down her burden and stretched and arched.

Such commonplace loveliness, however, was not enough for my aunt. She dreamed of a lover for the fifteen days of New Year's, the time for families to exchange visits, money, and food. She plied her secret comb. And sure enough she cursed the year, the family, the village, and herself.

Even as her hair lured her imminent lover, many other men looked at her. Uncles, cousins, nephews, brothers would have looked, too, had they been home between journeys. Perhaps they had already been restraining their curiosity, and they left, fearful that their glances, like a field of nesting birds, might be startled and caught. Poverty hurt, and that was their first reason for leaving. But another, final reason for leaving the crowded house was the never-said.

She may have been unusually beloved, the precious only daughter, spoiled and mirror gazing because of the affection the family lavished on her. When her husband left, they welcomed the chance to take her back from the in-laws; she could live like the little daughter for just a while longer. There are stories that my grandfather was different from other people, "crazy ever since the little Jap bayoneted him in the head." He used to put his naked penis on the dinner table, laughing. And one day he brought home a baby girl, wrapped up inside his brown western-style greatcoat. He had traded one of his sons, probably my father, the youngest, for her. My grandmother made him trade back. When he finally got a daughter of his own, he doted on her. They must have all loved her, except perhaps my father, the only brother who never went back to China, having once been traded for a girl.

Brothers and sisters, newly men and women, had to efface their sexual color and present plain miens. Disturbing hair and eyes, a smile like no other, threatened the ideal of five generations living under one roof. To focus blurs, people shouted face to face and yelled from room to room. The immigrants I know have loud voices, unmodulated to American tones even after years away from the village where they called their friendships out across the fields. I have not been able to stop my mother's screams in public libraries or over telephones. Walking erect (knees straight, toes pointed forward, not pigeon-toed, which is Chinese-feminine) and speaking in an inaudible voice, I have tried to turn myself American-feminine. Chinese communication was loud, public. Only sick people had to whisper. But at the dinner table, where the family members came nearest one another, no one could talk, not the outcasts nor any eaters. Every word that falls from the mouth is a coin lost. Silently they gave and accepted food with both hands. A preoccupied child who took his bowl with one hand got a sideways glare. A complete moment of total attention is due everyone alike. Children and lovers have no singularity here, but my aunt used a secret voice, a separate attentiveness.

She kept the man's name to herself throughout her labor and dying; she did not accuse him that he be punished with her. To save her inseminator's name she gave silent birth.

He may have been somebody in her own household, but intercourse with a man outside the family would have been no less abhorrent. All the village were kinsmen, and the titles shouted in loud country voices never let kinship be forgotten. Any man within visiting distance would have been neutralized as a lover – "brother," "younger brother," "older brother" – one hundred and fifteen relationship titles. Parents researched birth charts probably not so much to assure good fortune as to circumvent incest in a population that has but one hundred surnames. Everybody has eight million relatives. How useless then sexual mannerisms, how dangerous.

As if it came from an atavism deeper than fear, I used to add "brother" silently to boys' names. It hexed the boys, who would or would not ask me to dance, and made them less scary and as familiar and deserving of benevolence as girls.

But, of course, I hexed myself also – no dates. I should have stood up, both arms waving, and shouted out across libraries, "Hey, you! Love me back." I had no idea, though, how to make attraction selective, how to control its direction and magnitude. If I made myself American-pretty so that the five or six Chinese boys in the class fell in love with me, everyone else – the Caucasian, Negro, and Japanese boys – would too. Sisterliness, dignified and honorable, made much more sense.

Attraction eludes control so stubbornly that whole societies designed to organize relationships among people cannot keep order, not even when they bind people to one another from childhood and raise them together. Among the very poor and the wealthy, brothers married their adopted sisters, like doves. Our family allowed some romance, paying adult brides' prices and providing dowries so that their sons and daughters could marry strangers. Marriage promises to turn strangers into friendly relatives – a nation of siblings.

In the village structure, spirits shimmered among the live creatures, balanced and held in equilibrium by time and land. But one human being flaring up into violence could open up a black hole, a maelstrom that pulled in the sky. The frightened villagers, who depended on one another to maintain the real, went to my aunt to show her a personal, physical representation of the break she had made in the "roundness." Misallying couples snapped off the future, which was to be embodied in true offspring. The villagers punished her for acting as if she could have a private life, secret and apart from them.

If my aunt had betrayed the family at a time of large grain yields and peace, when many boys were born, and wings were being built on many houses, perhaps she might have escaped such severe punishment. But the men – hungry, greedy, tired of planting in dry soil – had been forced to leave the village in order to send food-money home. There were ghost plagues, bandit plagues, wars with the Japanese, floods. My Chinese brother and sister had died of an unknown sickness. Adultery, perhaps only a mistake during good times, became a crime when the village needed food.

The round moon cakes and round doorways, the round tables of graduated sizes that fit one roundness inside another, round windows and rice bowls – these talismans had lost their power to warn this family of the law: a family must be whole, faithfully keeping the descent line by having sons to feed the old and the dead, who in turn look after the family. The villagers came to show my aunt and her lover-in-hiding a broken house. The villagers were speeding up the circling of events because she was too shortsighted to see that her infidelity had already harmed the village, that waves of consequences would return unpredictably, sometimes in disguise, as now, to hurt her. This roundness had to be made coin-sized so that she would see its circumference: punish her at the birth of her baby. Awaken her to the inexorable. People who refused fatalism because they could invent small resources insisted on culpability. Deny accidents and wrest fault from the stars.

After the villagers left, their lanterns now scattering in various directions toward home, the family broke their silence and cursed her. "Aiaa, we're going to die. Death is coming. Death is coming. Look what you've done. You've killed us. Ghost! Dead ghost! Ghost! You've never been born." She ran out into the fields, far enough from the house so that she could no longer hear their voices, and pressed herself against the earth, her own land no more. When she felt the birth coming, she thought that she had been hurt. Her body seized together. "They've hurt me too much," she thought. "This is gall, and it will kill me." With forehead and knees against the earth, her body convulsed and then relaxed. She turned on her back, lay on the ground. The black well of sky and stars went out and out and out forever; her body and her complexity seemed to disappear. She was one of the stars, a bright dot in blackness, without home, without a companion, in eternal cold and silence. An agoraphobia rose in her, speeding higher and higher, bigger and bigger; she would not be able to contain it; there would be no end to fear.

Flayed, unprotected against space, she felt pain return, focusing her body. This pain chilled her – a cold, steady kind of surface pain. Inside, spasmodically, the other pain, the pain of the child, heated her. For hours she lay on the ground, alternately body and space. Sometimes a vision of normal comfort obliterated reality: she saw the family in the evening gambling at the dinner table, the young people massaging their elders' backs. She saw them congratulating one another, high joy on the mornings the rice shoots came up. When these pictures burst, the stars drew yet further apart. Black space opened.

She got to her feet to fight better and remembered that old-fashioned women gave birth in their pigsties to fool the jealous, pain-dealing gods, who do not snatch piglets. Before the next spasms could stop her, she ran to the pigsty, each step a rushing out into emptiness. She climbed over the fence and knelt in the dirt. It was good to have a fence enclosing her, a tribal person alone.

Laboring, this woman who had carried her child as a foreign growth that sickened her every day, expelled it at last. She reached down to touch the hot, wet, moving mass, surely smaller than anything human, and could feel that it was human after all – fingers, toes, nails, nose. She pulled it up on to her belly, and it lay curled there, butt in the air, feet precisely tucked one under the other. She opened her loose shirt and buttoned the child inside. After resting, it squirmed and thrashed and she pushed it up to her breast. It turned its head this way and that until it found her nipple. There, it made little snuffling noises. She clenched her teeth at its preciousness, lovely as a young calf, a piglet, a little dog.

She may have gone to the pigsty as a last act of responsibility: she would protect this child as she had protected its father. It would look after her soul, leaving supplies on her grave. But how would this tiny child without family find her grave when there would be no marker for her anywhere, neither in the earth nor the family hall? No one would give her a family hall name. She had taken the child with her into the wastes. At its birth the two of them had felt the same raw pain of separation, a wound that only the family pressing tight could close. A child with no descent line would not soften her life but only trail after her, ghost-like, begging her to give it purpose. At dawn the villagers on their way to the fields would stand around the fence and look.

Full of milk, the little ghost slept. When it awoke, she hardened her breasts against the milk that crying loosens. Toward morning she picked up the baby and walked to the well.

Carrying the baby to the well shows loving. Otherwise abandon it. Turn its face into the mud. Mothers who love their children take them along. It was probably a girl; there is some hope of forgiveness for boys.

"Don't tell anyone you had an aunt. Your father does not want to hear her name. She has never been born." I have believed that sex was unspeakable and words so strong and fathers so frail that "aunt" would do my father mysterious harm. I have thought that my family, having settled among immigrants who had also been their neighbors in the ancestral land, needed to clean their name, and a wrong word would incite the kinspeople even here. But there is more to this silence: they want me to participate in her punishment. And I have.

In the twenty years since I heard this story I have not asked for details nor said my aunt's name; I do not know it. People who can comfort the dead can also chase after them to hurt them further – a reverse ancestor worship. The real punishment was not the raid swiftly inflicted by the villagers, but the family's deliberately forgetting her. Her betrayal so maddened them, they saw to it that she would suffer forever, even after death. Always hungry, always needing, she would have to beg food from other ghosts, snatch and steal it from those whose living descendants give them gifts. She would have to fight the ghosts massed at crossroads for the buns a few thoughtful citizens leave to decoy her away from village and home so that the ancestral spirits could feast unharassed. At peace, they could act like gods, not ghosts, their descent lines providing them with paper suits and dresses, spirit money, paper houses, paper automobiles, chicken, meat, and rice into eternity — essences delivered up in smoke and flames, steam and incense rising from each rice bowl. In an attempt to make the Chinese care for people outside the family, Chairman Mao encourages us now to give our paper replicas to the spirits of outstanding soldiers and workers, no matter whose ancestors they may be. My aunt remains forever hungry. Goods are not distributed evenly among the dead.

My aunt haunts me — her ghost drawn to me because now, after fifty years of neglect, I alone devote pages of paper to her, though not origamied into houses and clothes. I do not think she always means me well. I am telling on her, and she was a spite suicide, drowning herself in the drinking water. The Chinese are always very frightened of the drowned one, whose weeping ghost, wet hair hanging and skin bloated, waits silently by the water to pull down a substitute.

WHITE TIGERS

When we Chinese girls listened to the adults talk-story, we learned that we failed if we grew up to be but wives or slaves. We could be heroines, swordswomen. Even if she had to rage across all China, a swordswoman got even with anybody who hurt her family. Perhaps women were once so dangerous that they had to have their feet bound. It was a woman who invented white crane boxing only two hundred years ago. She was already an expert pole fighter, daughter of a teacher trained at the Shao-lin temple, where there lived an order of fighting monks. She was combing her hair one morning when a white crane alighted outside her window. She teased it with her pole, which it pushed aside with a soft brush of its wing. Amazed, she dashed outside and tried to knock the crane off its perch. It snapped her pole in two. Recognizing the presence of great power, she asked the spirit of the white crane if it would teach her to fight. It answered with a cry that white crane boxers imitate today. Later the bird returned as an old man, and he guided her boxing for many years. Thus she gave the world a new martial art.

This was one of the tamer, more modern stories, mere introduction. My mother told others that followed swordswomen through woods and palaces for years. Night after night my mother would talk-story until we fell asleep. I couldn't tell where the stories left off and the dreams began, her voice the voice of the heroines in my sleep. And on Sundays, from noon to midnight, we went to the movies at the Confucius Church. We saw swordswomen jump over houses from a standstill; they didn't even need a running start.

At last I saw that I too had been in the presence of great power, my mother talking-story. After I grew up, I heard the chant of Fa Mu Lan, the girl who took her father's place in battle. Instantly I remembered that as a child I had followed my mother about the house, the two of us singing about how Fa Mu Lan fought gloriously and returned alive from war to settle in the village. I had forgotten this chant that was once mine, given me by my mother, who may not have known its power to remind. She said I would grow up a wife and a slave, but she taught me the song of the warrior woman, Fa Mu Lan. I would have to grow up a warrior woman.

The call would come from a bird that flew over our roof. In the brush drawings it looks like the ideograph for "human," two black wings. The bird would cross the sun and lift into the mountains (which look like the ideograph "mountain"), there parting the mist briefly that swirled opaque again. I would be a little girl of seven the day I followed the bird away into the mountains. The brambles would tear off my shoes and the rocks cut my feet and fingers, but I would keep climbing, eyes upward to follow the bird. We would go around and around the tallest mountain, climbing ever upward. I would drink from the river, which I would meet again and again. We would go so high the plants would change, and the river that flows past the village would become a waterfall. At the height where the bird used to disappear, the clouds would gray the world like an ink wash.

Even when I got used to that gray, I would only see peaks as if shaded in pencil, rocks like charcoal rubbings, everything so murky. There would be just two black strokes – the bird. Inside the clouds – inside the dragon's breath – I would not know how many hours or days passed. Suddenly, without noise, I would break clear into a yellow, warm world. New trees would lean toward me at mountain angles, but when I looked for the village, it would have vanished under the clouds.

The bird, now gold so close to the sun, would come to rest on the thatch of a hut, which, until the bird's two feet touched it, was camouflaged as part of the mountainside.

The door opened, and an old man and an old woman came out carrying bowls of rice and soup and a leafy branch of peaches.

"Have you eaten rice today, little girl?" they greeted me.

"Yes, I have," I said out of politeness. "Thank you."

("No, I haven't," I would have said in real life, mad at the Chinese for lying so much. "I'm starved. Do you have any cookies? I like chocolate chip cookies.")

"We were about to sit down to another meal," the old woman said. "Why don't you eat with us?"

They just happened to be bringing three rice bowls and three pairs of silver chopsticks out to the plank table under the pines. They gave me an egg, as if it were my birthday, and tea, though they were older than I, but I poured for them. The teapot and the rice pot seemed bottomless, but perhaps not; the old couple ate very little except for peaches.

When the mountains and the pines turned into blue oxen, blue dogs, and blue people standing, the old couple asked me to spend the night in the hut. I thought about the long way down in the ghostly dark and decided yes. The inside of the hut seemed as large as the outdoors. Pine needles covered the floor in thick patterns; someone had carefully arranged the yellow, green, and brown pine needles according to age. When I stepped carelessly and mussed a line, my feet kicked up new blends of earth colors, but the old man and old woman walked so lightly that their feet never stirred the designs by a needle.

A rock grew in the middle of the house, and that was their table. The benches were fallen trees. Ferns and shade flowers grew out of one wall, the mountainside itself. The old couple tucked me into a bed just my width. "Breathe evenly, or you'll lose your balance and fall out," said the woman, covering me with a silk bag stuffed with feathers and herbs. "Opera singers, who begin their training at age five, sleep in beds like this." Then the two of them went outside, and through the window I could see them pull on a rope looped over a branch. The rope was tied to the roof, and the roof opened up like a basket lid. I would sleep with the moon and the stars. I did not see whether the old people slept, so quickly did I drop off, but they would be there waking me with food in the morning.

"Little girl, you have now spent almost a day and a night with us," the old woman said. In the morning light I could see her earlobes pierced with gold. "Do you think you can bear to stay with us for fifteen years? We can train you to become a warrior."

"What about my mother and father?" I asked.

The old man untied the drinking gourd slung across his back. He lifted the lid by its stem and looked for something in the water. "Ah, there," he said.

At first I saw only water so clear it magnified the fibers in the walls of the gourd. On the surface, I saw only my own round reflection. The old man encircled the neck of the gourd with his thumb and index finger and gave it a shake. As the water shook, then settled, the colors and lights shimmered into a picture, not reflecting anything I could see around me. There at the bottom of the gourd were my mother and father scanning the sky, which was where I was. "It has happened already, then," I could hear my mother say. "I didn't expect it so soon." "You knew from her birth that she would be taken," my father answered. "We'll have to harvest potatoes without her help this year," my mother said, and they turned away toward the fields, straw baskets in their arms. The water shook and became just water again. "Mama. Papa," I called, but they were in the valley and could not hear me.

"What do you want to do?" the old man asked. "You can go back right now if you like. You can go pull sweet potatoes, or you can stay with us and learn how to fight barbarians and bandits."

"You can avenge your village," said the old woman. "You can recapture the harvests the thieves have taken. You can be remembered by the Han people for your dutifulness."

"I'll stay with you," I said.

So the hut became my home, and I found out that the old woman did not arrange the pine needles by hand. She opened the roof; an autumn wind would come up, and the needles fell in braids – brown strands, green strands, yellow strands. The old woman waved her arms in conducting motions; she blew softly with her mouth. I thought, nature certainly works differently on mountains than in valleys.

"The first thing you have to learn," the old woman told me, "is how to be quiet." They left me by streams to watch for animals. "If you're noisy, you'll make the deer go without water."

When I could kneel all day without my legs cramping and my breathing became even, the squirrels would bury their hoardings at the hem of my shirt and then bend their tails in a celebration dance. At night, the mice and toads looked at me, their eyes quick stars and slow stars. Not once would I see a three-legged toad, though; you need strings of cash to bait them.

The two old people led me in exercises that began at dawn and ended at sunset so that I could watch our shadows grow and shrink and grow again, rooted to the earth. I learned to move my fingers, hands, feet, head, and entire body in circles. I walked putting heel down first, toes pointing outward thirty to forty degrees, making the ideo-graph "eight," making the ideograph "human." Knees bent, I would swing into the slow, measured "square step," the powerful walk into battle. After five years my body became so strong that I could control even the dilations of the pupils inside my irises. I could copy owls and bats, the words for "bat" and "blessing" homonyms. After six years the deer let me run beside them. I could jump twenty feet into the air from a standstill, leaping like a monkey over the hut. Every creature has a hiding skill and a fighting skill a warrior can use. When birds alighted on my palm, I could yield my muscles under their feet and give them no base from which to fly away.

But I could not fly like the bird that led me here, except in large, free dreams.

During the seventh year (I would be fourteen), the two old people led me blindfolded to the mountains of the white tigers. They held me by either elbow and shouted into my ears, "Run. Run. Run." I ran and, not stepping off a cliff at the edge of my toes and not hitting my forehead against a wall, ran faster. A wind buoyed me up over the roots, the rocks, the little hills. We reached the tiger place in no time – a mountain peak three feet three from the sky. We had to bend over.

The old people waved once, slid down the mountain, and disappeared around a tree. The old woman, good with the bow and arrow, took them with her; the old man took the water gourd. I would have to survive bare-handed. Snow lay on the ground, and snow fell in loose gusts – another way the dragon breathes. I walked in the direction from which we had come, and when I reached the timberline, I collected wood broken from the cherry tree, the peony, and the wal-nut, which is the tree of life. Fire, the old people had taught me, is stored in trees that grow red flowers or red berries in the spring or whose leaves turn red in the fall. I took the wood from the protected spots beneath the trees and wrapped it in my scarf to keep dry. I dug where squirrels might have come, stealing one or two nuts at each place. These I also wrapped in my scarf. It is possible, the old people said, for a human being to live for fifty days on water. I would save the roots and nuts for hard climbs, the places where nothing grew, the emergency should I not find the hut. This time there would be no bird to follow.

The first night I burned half of the wood and slept curled against the mountain. I heard the white tigers prowling on the other side of the fire, but I could not distinguish them from the snow patches. The morning rose perfectly. I hurried along, again collecting wood and edibles. I ate nothing and only drank the snow my fires made run.

The first two days were gifts, the fasting so easy to do, I so smug in my strength that on the third day, the hardest, I caught myself sitting on the ground, opening the scarf and staring at the nuts and dry roots. Instead of walking steadily on or even eating, I faded into dreams about the meat meals my mother used to cook, my monk's food forgotten. That night I burned up most of the wood I had collected, unable to sleep for facing my death — if not death here, then death someday. The moon animals that did not hibernate came out to hunt, but I had given up the habits of a carnivore since living with the old people. I would not trap the mice that danced so close or the owls that plunged just outside the fire.

On the fourth and fifth days, my eyesight sharp with hunger, I saw deer and used their trails when our ways coincided. Where the deer nibbled, I gathered the fungus, the fungus of immortality.

At noon on the tenth day I packed snow, white as rice, into the worn center of a rock pointed out to me by a finger of ice, and around the rock I built a fire. In the warming water I put roots, nuts, and the fungus of immortality. For variety I ate a quarter of the nuts and roots raw. Oh, green joyous rush inside my mouth, my head, my stomach, my toes, my soul – the best meal of my life.

One day I found that I was striding long distances without hindrance, my bundle light. Food had become so scarce that I was no longer stopping to collect it. I had walked into dead land. Here even the snow stopped. I did not go back to the richer areas, where I could not stay anyway, but, resolving to fast until I got halfway to the next woods, I started across the dry rocks. Heavily weighed down by the wood on my back, branches poking maddeningly, I had burned almost all of the fuel not to waste strength lugging it.

Somewhere in the dead land I lost count of the days. It seemed as if I had been walking forever; life had never been different from this. An old man and an old woman were help I had only wished for. I was fourteen years old and lost from my village. I was walking in circles. Hadn't I been already found by the old people? Or was that yet to come? I wanted my mother and father. The old man and old woman were only a part of this lostness and this hunger.

One nightfall I ate the last of my food but had enough sticks for a good fire. I stared into the flames, which reminded me about helping my mother with the cooking and made me cry. It was very strange looking through water into fire and seeing my mother again. I nodded, orange and warm.

A white rabbit hopped beside me, and for a moment I thought it was a blob of snow that had fallen out of the sky. The rabbit and I studied each other. Rabbits taste like chickens. My mother and father had taught me how to hit rabbits over the head with wine jugs, then skin them cleanly for fur vests. "It's a cold night to be an animal," I said. "So you want some fire too, do you? Let me put on another branch, then." I would not hit it with the branch. I had learned from rabbits to kick backward. Perhaps this one was sick because normally the animals did not like fire. The rabbit seemed alert enough, however, looking at me so acutely, bounding up to the fire. But it did not stop when it got to the edge. It turned its face once toward me, then jumped into the fire. The fire went down for a moment, as if crouching in surprise, then the flames shot up taller than before. When the fire became calm again, I saw the rabbit had turned into meat, browned just right. I ate it, knowing the rabbit had sacrificed itself for me. It had made me a gift of meat.

When you have been walking through trees hour after hour — and I finally reached trees after the dead land — branches cross out everything, no relief whichever way your head turns until your eyes start to invent new sights. Hunger also changes the world — when eating can't be a habit, then neither can seeing. I saw two people made of gold dancing the earth's dances. They turned so perfectly that together they were the axis of the earth's turning. They were light; they were molten, changing gold — Chinese lion dancers, African lion dancers in midstep. I heard high Javanese bells deepen in midring to Indian bells, Hindu Indian, American Indian. Before my eyes, gold bells shredded into gold tassles that fanned into two royal capes that softened into lions' fur. Manes grew tall into feathers that shone — became light rays. Then the dancers danced the future — a machine-future — in clothes I had never seen before. I am watching the centuries pass in moments because suddenly I understand time, which is spinning and fixed like the North Star. And I understand how working and hoeing are dancing; how peasant clothes are golden, as king's clothes are golden; how one of the dancers is always a man and the other a woman.

The man and the woman grow bigger and bigger, so bright. All light. They are tall angels in two rows. They have high white wings on their backs. Perhaps there are infinite angels; perhaps I see two angels in their consecutive moments. I cannot bear their brightness and cover my eyes, which hurt from opening so wide without a blink. When

I put my hands down to look again, I recognize the old brown man and the old gray woman walking toward me out of the pine forest.

It would seem that this small crack in the mystery was opened, not so much by the old people's magic, as by hunger. Afterward, whenever I did not eat for long, as during famine or battle, I could stare at ordinary people and see their light and gold. I could see their dance. When I get hungry enough, then killing and falling are dancing too.

The old people fed me hot vegetable soup. Then they asked me to talk-story about what happened in the mountains of the white tigers. I told them that the white tigers had stalked me through the snow but that I had fought them off with burning branches, and my great-grandparents had come to lead me safely through the forests. I had met a rabbit who taught me about self-immolation and how to speed up transmigration: one does not have to become worms first but can change directly into a human being – as in our own humaneness we had just changed bowls of vegetable soup into people too. That made them laugh. "You tell good stories," they said. "Now go to sleep, and tomorrow we will begin your dragon lessons."

"One more thing," I wanted to say. "I saw you and how old you really are." But I was already asleep; it came out only a murmur. I would want to tell them about that last moment of my journey; but it was only one moment out of the weeks that I had been gone, and its telling would keep till morning. Besides, the two people must already know. In the next years, when I suddenly came upon them or when I caught them out of the corners of my eyes, he appeared as a handsome young man, tall with long black hair, and she, as a beautiful young woman who ran bare-legged through the trees. In the spring she dressed like a bride; she wore juniper leaves in her hair and a black embroidered jacket. I learned to shoot accurately because my teachers held the targets. Often when sighting along an arrow, there to the side I would glimpse the young man or young woman, but when I looked directly, he or she would be old again. By this time I had guessed from their manner that the old woman was to the old man a sister or a friend rather than a wife.

After I returned from my survival test, the two old people trained me in dragon ways, which took another eight years. Copying the tigers, their stalking kill and their anger, had been a wild, bloodthirsty joy. Tigers are easy to find, but I needed adult wisdom to know dragons. "You have to infer the whole dragon from the parts you can see and touch," the old people would say. Unlike tigers, dragons are so immense, I would never see one in its entirety. But I could explore the mountains, which are the top of its head. "These mountains are also *like* the tops of *other* dragons' heads," the old people would tell me. When climbing the slopes, I could understand that I was a bug riding on a dragon's forehead as it roams through space, its speed so different from my speed that I feel the dragon solid and immobile. In quarries I could see its strata, the dragon's veins and muscles; the minerals, its teeth and bones. I could touch the stones the old woman wore – its bone marrow. I had worked the soil, which is its flesh, and harvested the plants and climbed the trees, which are its hairs. I could listen to its voice in the thunder and feel its breathing in the winds, see its breathing in the clouds. Its tongue is the lightning. And the red that the lightning gives to the world is strong and lucky – in blood, poppies, roses, rubies, the red feathers of birds, the red carp, the cherry tree, the peony, the line alongside the turtle's eyes and the mallard's. In the spring when the dragon awakes, I watched its turnings in the rivers.

The closest I came to seeing a dragon whole was when the old people cut away a small strip of bark on a pine that was over three thousand years old. The resin underneath flows in the swirling shapes of dragons. "If you should decide during your old age that you would like to live another five hundred years, come here and drink ten pounds of this sap," they told me. "But don't do it now. You're too young to decide to live forever." The old people sent me out into thunderstorms to pick the red-cloud herb, which grows only then, a product of dragon's fire and dragon's rain. I brought the leaves to the old man and old woman, and they ate them for immortality.

I learned to make my mind large, as the universe is large, so that there is room for paradoxes. Pearls are bone marrow; pearls come from oysters. The dragon lives in the sky, ocean, marshes, and mountains; and the mountains are also its cranium. Its voice thunders and jingles like copper pans. It breathes fire and water; and sometimes the dragon is one, sometimes many.

I worked every day. When it rained, I exercised in the downpour, grateful not to be pulling sweet potatoes. I moved like the trees in the wind. I was grateful not to be squishing in chicken mud, which I did not have nightmares about so frequently now.

On New Year's mornings, the old man let me look in his water gourd to see my family. They were eating the biggest meal of the year, and I missed them very much. I had felt loved, love pouring from their fingers when the adults tucked red money in our pockets. My two old people did not give me money, but, each year for fifteen years, a bead. After I unwrapped the red paper and rolled the bead about between thumb and fingers, they took it back for safekeeping. We ate monk's food as usual.

By looking into the water gourd I was able to follow the men I would have to execute. Not knowing that I watched, fat men ate meat; fat men drank wine made from the rice; fat men sat on naked little girls. I watched powerful men count their money, and starving men count theirs. When bandits brought their share of raids home, I waited until they took off their masks so I would know the villagers who stole from their neighbors. I studied the generals' faces, their rank-stalks quivering at the backs of their heads. I learned rebels' faces, too, their foreheads tied with wild oaths.

The old man pointed out strengths and weaknesses whenever heroes met in classical battles, but warfare makes a scramble of the beautiful, slow old fights. I saw one young fighter salute his opponent – and five peasants hit him from behind with scythes and hammers. His opponent did not warn him.

"Cheaters!" I yelled. "How am I going to win against cheaters?"

"Don't worry," the old man said. "You'll never be trapped like that poor amateur. You can see behind you like a bat. Hold the peasants back with one hand and kill the warrior with the other."

Menstrual days did not interrupt my training; I was as strong as on any other day. "You're now an adult," explained the old woman on the first one, which happened halfway through my stay on the mountain. "You can have children." I had thought I had cut myself when jumping over my swords, one made of steel and the other carved out of a single block of jade. "However," she added, "we are asking you to put off children for a few more years."

"Then can I use the control you taught me and stop this bleeding?"

"No. You don't stop shitting and pissing," she said. "It's the same with the blood. Let it run." ("Let it walk" in Chinese.)

To console me for being without family on this day, they let me look inside the gourd. My whole family was visiting friends on the other side of the river. Everybody had on good clothes and was exchanging cakes. It was a wedding. My mother was talking to the hosts: "Thank you for taking our daughter. Wherever she is, she must be happy now. She will certainly come back if she is alive, and if she is a spirit, you have given her a descent line. We are so grateful."

Yes, I would be happy. How full I would be with all their love for me. I would have for a new husband my own play-mate, dear since childhood, who loved me so much he was to become a spirit bridegroom for my sake. We will be so happy when I come back to the valley, healthy and strong and not a ghost.

The water gave me a close-up of my husband's wonderful face — and I was watching when it went white at the sudden approach of armored men on horseback, thudding and jan-gling. My people grabbed iron skillets, boiling soup, knives, hammers, scissors, whatever weapons came to hand, but my father said, "There are too many of them," and they put down the weapons and waited quietly at the door, open as if for guests. An army of horsemen stopped at our house; the foot soldiers in the distance were coming closer. A horse-man with silver scales afire in the sun shouted from the scroll in his hands, his words opening a red gap in his black beard. "Your baron has pledged fifty men from this district, one from each family," he said, and then named the family names.

"No!" I screamed into the gourd.

"I'll go," my new husband and my youngest brother said to their fathers.

"No," my father said, "I myself will go," but the women held him back until the foot soldiers passed by, my husband and my brother leaving with them.

As if disturbed by the marching feet, the water churned; and when it stilled again ("Wait!" I yelled. "Wait!"), there were strangers. The baron and his family — all of his family — were knocking their heads on the floor in front of their ancestors and thanking the gods out loud for protecting them from conscription. I watched the baron's piggish face chew open-mouthed on the sacrificial pig. I plunged my hand into the gourd, making a grab for his thick throat, and he broke into pieces, splashing water all over my face and clothes. I turned the gourd upside-down to empty it, but no little people came tumbling out.

"Why can't I go down there now and help them?" I cried. "I'll run away with the two boys and we'll hide in the caves."

"No," the old man said. "You're not ready. You're only fourteen years old. You'd get hurt for nothing."

"Wait until you are twenty-two," the old woman said. "You'll be big then and more skillful. No army will be able to stop you from doing whatever you want. If you go now, you will be killed, and you'll have wasted seven and a half years of our time. You will deprive your people of a champion."

"I'm good enough now to save the boys."

"We didn't work this hard to save just two boys, but whole families."

Of course.

"Do you really think I'll be able to do that – defeat an army?"

"Even when you fight against soldiers trained as you are, most of them will be men, heavy footed and rough. You will have the advantage. Don't be impatient."

"From time to time you may use the water gourd to watch your husband and your brother," the old man said.

But I had ended the panic about them already. I could feel a wooden door inside of me close. I had learned on the farm that I could stop loving animals raised for slaughter. And I could start loving them immediately when someone said, "This one is a pet," freeing me and opening the door. We had lost males before, cousins and uncles who were conscripted into armies or bonded as apprentices, who are almost as lowly as slave girls.

I bled and thought about the people to be killed; I bled and thought about the people to be born.

During all my years on the mountain, I talked to no one except the two old people, but they seemed to be many people. The whole world lived inside the gourd, the earth a green and blue pearl like the one the dragon plays with.

When I could point at the sky and make a sword appear, a silver bolt in the sunlight, and control its slashing with my mind, the old people said I was ready to leave. The old man opened the gourd for the last time. I saw the baron's messenger leave our house, and my father was saying, "This time I must go and fight." I would hurry down the mountain and take his place. The old people gave me the fifteen beads, which I was to use if I got into terrible danger. They gave me men's clothes and armor. We bowed to one another. The bird flew above me down the mountain, and for some miles, whenever I turned to look for them, there would be the two old people waving. I saw them through the mist; I saw them on the clouds; I saw them big on the mountain-top when distance had shrunk the pines. They had probably left images of themselves for me to wave at and gone about their other business.

When I reached my village, my father and mother had grown as old as the two whose shapes I could at last no longer see. I helped my parents carry their tools, and they walked ahead so straight, each carrying a basket or a hoe not to overburden me, their tears falling privately. My family surrounded me with so much love that I almost forgot the ones not there. I praised the new infants.

"Some of the people are saying the Eight Sages took you away to teach you magic," said a little girl cousin. "They say they changed you into a bird, and you flew to them."

"Some say you went to the city and became a prostitute," another cousin giggled.

"You might tell them that I met some teachers who were willing to teach me science," I said.

"I have been drafted," my father said.

"No, Father," I said. "I will take your place."

My parents killed a chicken and steamed it whole, as if they were welcoming home a son, but I had gotten out of the habit of meat. After eating rice and vegetables, I slept for a long time, preparation for the work ahead.

In the morning my parents woke me and asked that I come with them to the family hall. "Stay in your night-clothes," my mother said. "Don't change yet." She was holding a basin, a towel, and a kettle of hot water. My father had a bottle of wine, an ink block and pens, and knives of various sizes. "Come with us," he said. They had stopped the tears with which they had greeted me. Forebodingly I caught a smell – metallic, the iron smell of blood, as when a woman gives birth, as at the sacrifice of a large animal, as when I menstruated and dreamed red dreams.

My mother put a pillow on the floor before the ancestors. "Kneel here," she said. "Now take off your shirt." I kneeled with my back to my parents so none of us felt embarrassed. My mother washed my back as if I had left for only a day and were her baby yet. "We are going to carve revenge on your back," my father said. "We'll write out oaths and names."

"Wherever you go, whatever happens to you, people will know our sacrifice," my mother said. "And you'll never forget either." She meant that even if I got killed, the people could use my dead body for a weapon, but we do not like to talk out loud about dying.

My father first brushed the words in ink, and they fluttered down my back row after row. Then he began cutting; to make fine lines and points he used thin blades, for the stems, large blades.

My mother caught the blood and wiped the cuts with a cold towel soaked in wine. It hurt terribly – the cuts sharp; the air burning; the alcohol cold, then hot – pain so various. I gripped my knees. I released them. Neither tension nor relaxation helped. I wanted to cry. If not for the fifteen years of training, I would have writhed on the floor; I would have had to be held down. The list of grievances went on and on. If an enemy should flay me, the light would shine through my skin like lace.

At the end of the last word, I fell forward. Together my parents sang what they had written, then let me rest. My mother fanned my back. "We'll have you with us until your back heals," she said.

When I could sit up again, my mother brought two mirrors, and I saw my back covered entirely with words in red and black files, like an army, like my army. My parents nursed me just as if I had fallen in battle after many victories. Soon I was strong again.

A white horse stepped into the courtyard where I was polishing my armor. Though the gates were locked tight, through the moon door it came — a kingly white horse. It wore a saddle and bridle with red, gold, and black tassles dancing. The saddle was just my size with tigers and dragons tooled in swirls. The white horse pawed the ground for me to go. On the hooves of its near forefoot and hindfoot was the ideograph "to fly."

My parents and I had waited for such a sign. We took the fine saddlebags off the horse and filled them with salves and herbs, blue grass for washing my hair, extra sweaters, dried peaches. They gave me a choice of ivory or silver chopsticks. I took the silver ones because they were lighter. It was like getting wedding presents. The cousins and the villagers came bearing bright orange jams, silk dresses, silver embroidery scissors. They brought blue and white porcelain bowls filled with water and carp — the bowls painted with carp, fins like orange fire. I accepted all the gifts — the tables, the earthenware jugs — though I could not possibly carry them with me, and culled for travel only a small copper cooking bowl. I could cook in it and eat out of it and would not have to search for bowl-shaped rocks or tortoiseshells.

I put on my men's clothes and armor and tied my hair in a man's fashion. "How beautiful you look," the people said. "How beautiful she looks."

A young man stepped out of the crowd. He looked familiar to me, as if he were the old man's son, or the old man himself when you looked at him from the corners of your eyes.

"I want to go with you," he said.

"You will be the first soldier in my army," I told him.

I leapt onto my horse's back and marveled at the power and height it gave to me. Just then, galloping out of nowhere straight at me came a rider on a black horse. The villagers scattered except for my one soldier, who stood calmly in the road. I drew my sword. "Wait!" shouted the rider, raising weaponless hands. "Wait. I have traveled here to join you."

Then the villagers relinquished their real gifts to me – their sons. Families who had hidden their boys during the last conscription volunteered them now. I took the ones their families could spare and the ones with hero-fire in their eyes, not the young fathers and not those who would break hearts with their leaving.

We were better equipped than many founders of dynasties had been when they walked north to dethrone an emperor; they had been peasants like us. Millions of us had laid our hoes down on the dry ground and faced north. We sat in the fields, from which the dragon had withdrawn its moisture, and sharpened those hoes. Then, though it be ten thousand miles away, we walked to the palace. We would report to the emperor. The emperor, who sat facing south, must have been very frightened – peasants everywhere walking day and night toward the capital, toward Peiping. But the last emperors of dynasties must not have been facing in the right direction, for they would have seen us and not let us get this hungry. We would not have had to shout our grievances.

The peasants would crown as emperor a farmer who knew the earth or a beggar who understood hunger.

"Thank you, Mother. Thank you, Father," I said before leaving. They had carved their names and address on me, and I would come back.

Often I walked beside my horse to travel abreast of my army. When we had to impress other armies — marauders, columns of refugees filing past one another, boy gangs following their martial arts teachers — I mounted and rode in front. The soldiers who owned horses and weapons would pose fiercely on my left and right. The small bands joined us, but sometimes armies of equal or larger strength would fight us. Then screaming a mighty scream and swinging two swords over my head, I charged the leaders; I released my bloodthirsty army and my straining war-horse. I guided the horse with my knees, freeing both hands for sword-work, spinning green and silver circles all around me.

I inspired my army, and I fed them. At night I sang to them glorious songs that came out of the sky and into my head. When I opened my mouth, the songs poured out and were loud enough for the whole encampment to hear; my army stretched out for a mile. We sewed red flags and tied the red scraps around arms, legs, horses' tails. We wore our red clothes so that when we visited a village, we would look as happy as for New Year's Day. Then people would want to join the ranks. My army did not rape, only taking food where there was an abundance. We brought order wherever we went.

When I won over a goodly number of fighters, I built up my army enough to attack fiefdoms and to pursue the enemies I had seen in the water gourd.

My first opponent turned out to be a giant, so much bigger than the toy general I used to peep at. During the charge, I singled out the leader, who grew as he ran toward me. Our eyes locked until his height made me strain my neck looking up, my throat so vulnerable to the stroke of a knife that my eyes dropped to the secret death points on the huge body. First I cut off his leg with one sword swipe, as Chen Luan-feng had chopped the leg off the thunder god. When the giant stumped toward me, I cut off his head. Instantly he reverted to his true self, a snake, and slithered away hissing. The fighting around me stopped as the combatants' eyes and mouths opened wide in amazement. The giant's spells now broken, his soldiers, seeing that they had been led by a snake, pledged their loyalty to me.

In the stillness after battle I looked up at the mountain-tops; perhaps the old man and woman were watching me and would enjoy my knowing it. They'd laugh to see a creature winking at them from the bottom of the water gourd. But on a green ledge above the battlefield I saw the giant's wives crying. They had climbed out of their palanquins to watch their husband fight me, and now they were holding each other weeping. They were two sisters, two tiny fairies against the sky, widows from now on. Their long undersleeves, which they had pulled out to wipe their tears, flew white mourning in the mountain wind. After a time, they got back into their sedan chairs, and their servants carried them away.

I led my army northward, rarely having to sidetrack; the emperor himself sent the enemies I was hunting chasing after me. Sometimes they attacked us on two or three sides; sometimes they ambushed me when I rode ahead. We would always win, Kuan Kung, the god of war and literature riding before me. I would be told of in fairy tales myself. I over-heard some soldiers – and now there were many who had not met me – say that whenever we had been in danger of losing, I made a throwing gesture and the opposing army would fall, hurled across the battlefield. Hailstones as big as heads would shoot out of the sky and the lightning would stab like swords, but never at those on my side. "On *his* side," they said. I never told them the truth. Chinese executed women who disguised themselves as soldiers or students, no matter how bravely they fought or how high they scored on the examinations.

One spring morning I was at work in my tent repairing equipment, patching my clothes, and studying maps when a voice said, "General, may I visit you in your tent, please?" As if it were my own home, I did not allow strangers in my tent. And since I had no family with me, no one ever visited inside. Riverbanks, hillsides, the cool sloped rooms under the pine trees – China provides her soldiers with meeting places enough. I opened the tent flap. And there in the sunlight stood my own husband with arms full of wildflowers for me. "You are beautiful," he said, and meant it truly. "I have looked for you everywhere. I've been looking for you since the day that bird flew away with you." We were so pleased with each other, the childhood friend found at last, the childhood friend mysteriously grown up. "I followed you, but you skimmed over the rocks until I lost you."

"I've looked for you too," I said, the tent now snug around us like a secret house when we were kids. "Whenever I heard about a good fighter, I went to see if it were you," I said. "I saw you marry me. I'm so glad you married me."

He wept when he took off my shirt and saw the scar-words on my back. He loosened my hair and covered the words with it. I turned around and touched his face, loving the familiar first.

So for a time I had a partner – my husband and I, soldiers together just as when we were little soldiers playing in the village. We rode side by side into battle. When I became pregnant, during the last four months, I wore my armor altered so that I looked like a powerful, big man. As a fat man, I walked with the foot soldiers so as not to jounce the gestation. Now when I was naked, I was a strange human being indeed – words carved on my back and the baby large in front.

I hid from battle only once, when I gave birth to our baby. In dark and silver dreams I had seen him falling from the sky, each night closer to the earth, his soul a star. Just before labor began, the last star rays sank into my belly. My husband would talk to me and not go, though I said for him to return to the battlefield. He caught the baby, a boy, and put it on my breast. "What are we going to do with this?" he asked, holding up the piece of umbilical cord that had been closest to the baby.

"Let's tie it to a flagpole until it dries," I said. We had both seen the boxes in which our parents kept the dried cords of all their children. "This one was yours, and this yours," my mother would say to us brothers and sisters, and fill us with awe that she could remember.

We made a sling for the baby inside my big armor, and rode back into the thickest part of the fighting. The umbilical cord flew with the red flag and made us laugh. At night inside our own tent, I let the baby ride on my back. The sling was made of red satin and purple silk; the four paisley straps that tied across my breasts and around my waist ended in housewife's pockets lined with a coin, a seed, a nut, and a juniper leaf. At the back of the sling I had sewn a tiny quilted triangle, red at its center against two shades of green; it marked the baby's nape for luck. I walked bowed, and the baby warmed himself against me, his breathing in rhythm with mine, his heart beating like my heart.

When the baby was a month old, we gave him a name and shaved his head. For the full-month ceremony my husband had found two eggs, which we dyed red by boiling them with a flag. I peeled one and rolled it all over the baby's head, his eyes, his lips, off his bump of a nose, his cheeks, his dear bald head and fontanel. I had brought dried grapefruit peel in my saddlebag, and we also boiled that. We washed our heads and hands in the grapefruit water, dabbing it on the baby's forehead and hands. Then I gave my husband the baby and told him to take it to his family, and I gave him all the money we had taken on raids to take to my family. "Go now," I said, "before he is old enough to recognize me." While the blur is still in his eyes and the little fists shut tight like buds, I'll send my baby away from me. I altered my clothes and became again the slim young man. Only now I would get so lonely with the tent so empty that I slept outside.

My white horse overturned buckets and danced on them; it lifted full wine cups with its teeth. The strong soldiers lifted the horse in a wooden tub, while it danced to the stone drums and flute music. I played with the soldiers, throwing arrows into a bronze jar. But I found none of these antics as amusing as when I first set out on the road.

It was during this lonely time, when any high cry made the milk spill from my breasts, that I got careless. Wildflowers distracted me so that I followed them, picking one, then another, until I was alone in the woods. Out from behind trees, springing off branches came the enemy, their leader looming like a genie out of the water gourd. I threw fists and feet at them, but they were so many, they pinned me to the earth while their leader drew his sword. My fear shot forth – a quick, jabbing sword that slashed fiercely, silver flashes, quick cuts wherever my attention drove it. The leader stared at the palpable sword swishing unclutched at his men, then laughed aloud. As if signaled by his laughter, two more swords appeared in midair. They clanged against mine, and I felt metal vibrate inside my brain. I willed my sword to hit back and to go after the head that controlled the other swords. But the man fought well, hurting my brain. The swords opened and closed, scissoring madly, metal zinging along metal. Unable to leave my skysword to work itself, I would be watching the swords move like puppets when the genie yanked my hair back and held a dagger against my throat. "Aha!" he said. "What have we here?" He lifted the bead pouch out of my shirt and cut the string. I grabbed his arm, but one of his swords dived toward me, and I rolled out of the way. A horse galloped up, and he leapt on it, escaping into the forest, the beads in his fist. His swords fought behind him until I heard him shout, "I am here!" and they flew to his side. So I had done battle with the prince who had mixed the blood of his two sons with the metal he had used for casting his swords.

I ran back to my soldiers and gathered the fastest horsemen for pursuit. Our horses ran like the little white water horses in the surf. Across a plain we could see the enemy, a dustdevil rushing toward the horizon. Wanting to see, I focused my eyes as the eagles had taught me, and there the genie would be – shaking one bead out of the pouch and casting it at us. Nothing happened. No thunder, no earthquake that split open the ground, no hailstones big as heads.

"Stop!" I ordered my riders. "Our horses are exhausted, and I don't want to chase any farther south." The rest of the victories would be won on my own, slow and without shortcuts.

I stood on top of the last hill before Peiping and saw the roads below me flow like living rivers. Between roads the woods and plains moved too; the land was peopled – the Han people, the People of One Hundred Surnames, marching with one heart, our tatters flying. The depth and width of Joy were exactly known to me: the Chinese population. After much hardship a few of our millions had arrived together at the capital. We faced our emperor personally. We beheaded him, cleaned out the palace, and inaugurated the peasant who would begin the new order. In his rags he sat on the throne facing south, and we, a great red crowd, bowed to him three times. He commended some of us who were his first generals.

I told the people who had come with me that they were free to go home now, but since the Long Wall was so close,

I would go see it. They could come along if they liked. So, loath to disband after such high adventures, we reached the northern boundary of the world, chasing Mongols en route.

I touched the Long Wall with my own fingers, running the edge of my hand between the stones, tracing the grooves the builders' hands had made. We lay our foreheads and our cheeks against the Long Wall and cried like the women who had come here looking for their men so long building the wall. In my travels north, I had not found my brother.

Carrying the news about the new emperor, I went home, where one more battle awaited me. The baron who had drafted my brother would still be bearing sway over our village. Having dropped my soldiers off at crossroads and bridges, I attacked the baron's stronghold alone. I jumped over the double walls and landed with swords drawn and knees bent, ready to spring. When no one accosted me, I sheathed the swords and walked about like a guest until I found the baron. He was counting his money, his fat ringed fingers playing over the abacus.

"Who are you? What do you want?" he said, encircling his profits with his arms. He sat square and fat like a god.

"I want your life in payment for your crimes against the villagers."

"I haven't done anything to you. All this is mine. I earned it. I didn't steal it from you. I've never seen you before in my life. Who are you?"

"I am a female avenger."

Then – heaven help him – he tried to be charming, to appeal to me man to man. "Oh, come now. Everyone takes the girls when he can. The families are glad to be rid of them. 'Girls are maggots in the rice.' 'It is more profitable to raise geese than daughters.'" He quoted to me the sayings I hated.

"Regret what you've done before I kill you," I said.

"I haven't done anything other men – even you – wouldn't have done in my place."

"You took away my brother."

"I free my apprentices."

"He was not an apprentice."

"China needs soldiers in wartime."

"You took away my childhood."

"I don't know what you're talking about. We've never met before. I've done nothing to you."

"You've done this," I said, and ripped off my shirt to show him my back. "You are responsible for this." When I saw his startled eyes at my breasts, I slashed him across the face and on the second stroke cut off his head.

I pulled my shirt back on and opened the house to the villagers. The baron's family and servants hid in closets and under beds. The villagers dragged them out into the court-yard, where they tried them next to the beheading machine. "Did you take my harvest so that my children had to eat grass?" a weeping farmer asked.

"I saw him steal seed grain," another testified.

"My family was hiding under the thatch on the roof when the bandits robbed our house, and we saw this one take off his mask." They spared those who proved they could be reformed. They beheaded the others. Their necks were collared in the beheading machine, which slowly clamped shut. There was one last-minute reprieve of a bodyguard when a witness shouted testimony just as the vise was pinching blood. The guard had but recently joined the household in exchange for a child hostage. A slow killing gives a criminal time to regret his crimes and think of the right words to prove he can change.

I searched the house, hunting out people for trial. I came upon a locked room. When I broke down the door, I found women, cowering, whimpering women. I heard shrill insect noises and scurrying. They blinked weakly at me like pheasants that have been raised in the dark for soft meat. The servants who walked the ladies had abandoned them, and they could not escape on their little bound feet. Some crawled away from me, using their elbows to pull themselves along. These women would not be good for anything. I called the villagers to come identify any daughters they wanted to take home, but no one claimed any. I gave each woman a bagful of rice, which they sat on. They rolled the bags to the road. They wandered away like ghosts. Later, it would be said, they turned into the band of swordswomen who were a mercenary army. They did not wear men's clothes like me, but rode as women in black and red dresses. They bought up girl babies so that many poor families welcomed their visitations. When slave girls and daughters-in-law ran away, people would say they joined these witch amazons. They killed men and boys. I myself never encountered such women and could not vouch for their reality.

After the trials we tore down the ancestral tablets. "We'll use this great hall for village meetings," I announced. "Here we'll put on operas; we'll sing together and talk-story." We washed the courtyard; we exorcised the house with smoke and red paper. "This is a new year," I told the people, "the year one."

I went home to my parents-in-law and husband and son. My son stared, very impressed by the general he had seen in the parade, but his father said, "It's your mother. Go to your mother." My son was delighted that the shiny general was his mother too. She gave him her helmet to wear and her swords to hold.

Wearing my black embroidered wedding coat, I knelt at my parents-in-law's feet, as I would have done as a bride. "Now my public duties are finished," I said. "I will stay with you, doing farmwork and housework, and giving you more sons."

"Go visit your mother and father first," my mother-in-law said, a generous woman. "They want to welcome you."

My mother and father and the entire clan would be living happily on the money I had sent them. My parents had bought their coffins. They would sacrifice a pig to the gods that I had returned. From the words on my back, and how they were fulfilled, the villagers would make a legend about my perfect filiality.

My American life has been such a disappointment.

"I got straight A's, Mama."

"Let me tell you a true story about a girl who saved her village."

I could not figure out what was my village. And it was important that I do something big and fine, or else my parents would sell me when we made our way back to China. In China there were solutions for what to do with little girls who ate up food and threw tantrums. You can't eat straight A's.

When one of my parents or the emigrant villagers said, "'Feeding girls is feeding cowbirds,'" I would thrash on the floor and scream so hard I couldn't talk. I couldn't stop.

"What's the matter with her?"

"I don't know. Bad, I guess. You know how girls are. 'There's no profit in raising girls. Better to raise geese than girls.'"

"I would hit her if she were mine. But then there's no use wasting all that discipline on a girl. 'When you raise girls, you're raising children for strangers.'"

"Stop that crying!" my mother would yell. "I'm going to hit you if you don't stop. Bad girl! Stop!" I'm going to remember never to hit or to scold my children for crying, I thought, because then they will only cry more.

"I'm not a bad girl," I would scream. "I'm not a bad girl. I'm not a bad girl." I might as well have said, "I'm not a girl."

"When you were little, all you had to say was 'I'm not a bad girl,' and you could make yourself cry," my mother says, talking-story about my childhood.

I minded that the emigrant villagers shook their heads at my sister and me. "One girl – and another girl," they said, and made our parents ashamed to take us out together. The good part about my brothers being born was that people stopped saying, "All girls," but I learned new grievances. "Did you roll an egg on *my* face like that when *I* was born?" "Did you have a full-month party for *me*?" "Did you turn on all the lights?" "Did you send *my* picture to Grandmother?" "Why not? Because I'm a girl? Is that why not?" "Why didn't you teach me English?" "You like having me beaten up at school, don't you?"

"She is very mean, isn't she?" the emigrant villagers would say.

"Come, children. Hurry. Hurry. Who wants to go out with Great-Uncle?" On Saturday mornings my great-uncle, the ex-river pirate, did the shopping. "Get your coats, whoever's coming."

"I'm coming. I'm coming. Wait for me."

When he heard girls' voices, he turned on us and roared, "No girls!" and left my sisters and me hanging our coats back up, not looking at one another. The boys came back with candy and new toys. When they walked through China-town, the people must have said, "A boy – and another boy – and another boy!" At my great-uncle's funeral I secretly tested out feeling glad that he was dead – the six-foot bearish masculinity of him.

I went away to college – Berkeley in the sixties – and I studied, and I marched to change the world, but I did not turn into a boy. I would have liked to bring myself back as a boy for my parents to welcome with chickens and pigs. That was for my brother, who returned alive from Vietnam.

If I went to Vietnam, I would not come back; females desert families. It was said, "There is an outward tendency in females," which meant that I was getting straight A's for the good of my future husband's family, not my own. I did not plan ever to have a husband. I would show my mother and father and the nosey emigrant villagers that girls have no outward tendency. I stopped getting straight A's.

And all the time I was having to turn myself American-feminine, or no dates.

There is a Chinese word for the female I – which is "slave." Break the women with their own tongues!

I refused to cook. When I had to wash dishes, I would crack one or two. "Bad girl," my mother yelled, and sometimes that made me gloat rather than cry. Isn't a bad girl almost a boy?

"What do you want to be when you grow up, little girl?"

"A lumberjack in Oregon."

Even now, unless I'm happy, I burn the food when I cook. I do not feed people. I let the dirty dishes rot. I eat at other people's tables but won't invite them to mine, where the dishes are rotting.

If I could not-eat, perhaps I could make myself a warrior like the swordswoman who drives me. I will – I must – rise and plow the fields as soon as the baby comes out.

Once I get outside the house, what bird might call me; on what horse could I ride away? Marriage and childbirth strengthen the swordswoman, who is not a maid like Joan of Arc. Do the women's work; then do more work, which will become ours too. No husband of mine will say, "I could have been a drummer, but I had to think about the wife and kids. You know how it is." Nobody supports me at the expense of his own adventure. Then I get bitter: no one supports me; I am not loved enough to be supported. That I am not a burden has to compensate for the sad envy when I look at women loved enough to be supported. Even now China wraps double binds around my feet.

When urban renewal tore down my parents' laundry and paved over our slum for a parking lot, I only made up gun and knife fantasies and did nothing useful.

From the fairy tales, I've learned exactly who the enemy are. I easily recognize them — business-suited in their modern American executive guise, each boss two feet taller than I am and impossible to meet eye to eye.

I once worked at an art supply house that sold paints to artists. "Order more of that nigger yellow, willya?" the boss told me. "Bright, isn't it? Nigger yellow."

"I don't like that word," I had to say in my bad, small-person's voice that makes no impact. The boss never deigned to answer.

I also worked at a land developers' association. The building industry was planning a banquet for contractors, real estate dealers, and real estate editors. "Did you know the restaurant you chose for the banquet is being picketed by CORE and the NAACP?" I squeaked.

"Of course I know." The boss laughed. "That's why I chose it."

"I refuse to type these invitations," I whispered, voice unreliable.

He leaned back in his leather chair, his bossy stomach opulent. He picked up his calendar and slowly circled a date. "You will be paid up to here," he said. "We'll mail you the check."

If I took the sword, which my hate must surely have forged out of the air, and gutted him, I would put color and wrinkles into his shirt.

It's not just the stupid racists that I have to do something about, but the tyrants who for whatever reason can deny my family food and work. My job is my own only land.

To avenge my family, I'd have to storm across China to take back our farm from the Communists; I'd have to rage across the United States to take back the laundry in New York and the one in California. Nobody in history has conquered and united both North America and Asia. A descendant of eighty pole fighters, I ought to be able to set out confidently, march straight down our street, get going right now. There's work to do, ground to cover. Surely, the eighty pole fighters, though unseen, would follow me and lead me and protect me, as is the wont of ancestors.

Or it may well be that they're resting happily in China, their spirits dispersed among the real Chinese, and not nudging me at all with their poles. I mustn't feel bad that I haven't done as well as the swordswoman did; after all, no bird called me, no wise old people tutored me. I have no magic beads, no water gourd sight, no rabbit that will jump in the fire when I'm hungry. I dislike armies.

I've looked for the bird. I've seen clouds make pointed angel wings that stream past the sunset, but they shred into clouds. Once at a beach after a long hike I saw a seagull, tiny as an insect. But when I jumped up to tell what miracle I saw, before I could get the words out I understood that the bird was insect-size because it was far away. My brain had momentarily lost its depth perception. I was that eager to find an unusual bird.

The news from China has been confusing. It also had something to do with birds. I was nine years old when the letters made my parents, who are rocks, cry. My father screamed in his sleep. My mother wept and crumpled up the letters. She set fire to them page by page in the ashtray, but new letters came almost every day. The only letters they opened without fear were the ones with red borders, the holiday letters that mustn't carry bad news. The other letters said that my uncles were made to kneel on broken glass during their trials and had confessed to being landowners. They were all executed, and the aunt whose thumbs were twisted off drowned herself. Other aunts, mothers-in-law, and cousins disappeared; some suddenly began writing to us again from communes or from Hong Kong. They kept asking for money. The ones in communes got four ounces of fat and one cup of oil a week, they said, and had to work from 4 A.M. to 9 P.M. They had to learn to do dances waving red kerchiefs; they had to sing nonsense syllables. The Communists gave axes to the old ladies and said, "Go and kill yourself. You're useless." If we overseas Chinese would just send money to the Communist bank, our relatives said, they might get a percentage of it for themselves. The aunts in Hong Kong said to send money quickly; their children were begging on the sidewalks, and mean people put dirt in their bowls.

When I dream that I am wire without flesh, there is a letter on blue airmail paper that floats above the night ocean between here and China. It must arrive safely or else my grandmother and I will lose each other.

My parents felt bad whether or not they sent money. Sometimes they got angry at their brothers and sisters for asking. And they would not simply ask but have to talk-story too. The revolutionaries had taken Fourth Aunt and Uncle's store, house, and lands. They attacked the house and killed the grandfather and oldest daughter. The grandmother escaped with the loose cash and did not return to help. Fourth Aunt picked up her sons, one under each arm, and hid in the pig house, where they slept that night in cotton clothes. The next day she found her husband, who had also miraculously escaped. The two of them collected twigs and yams to sell while their children begged. Each morning they tied the faggots on each other's back. Nobody bought from them. They ate the yams and some of the children's rice. Finally Fourth Aunt saw what was wrong. "We have to shout 'Fuel for sale' and 'Yams for sale,'" she said. "We can't just walk unobtrusively up and down the street." "You're right," said my uncle, but he was shy and walked in back of her. "Shout," my aunt ordered, but he could not. "They think we're carrying these sticks home for our own fire," she said. "Shout." They walked about miserably, silently, until sundown, neither of them able to advertise themselves. Fourth Aunt, an orphan since the age of ten, mean as my mother, threw her bundle down at his feet and scolded Fourth Uncle, "Starving to death, his wife and children starving to death, and he's too damned shy to raise his voice." She left him standing by himself and afraid to return empty-handed to her. He sat under a tree to think, when he spotted a pair of nesting doves. Dumping his bag of yams, he climbed up and caught the birds. That was where the Communists trapped him, in the tree. They criticized him for selfishly taking food for his own family and killed him, leaving his body in the tree as an example. They took the birds to a commune kitchen to be shared.

It is confusing that my family was not the poor to be championed. They were executed like the barons in the stories, when they were not barons. It is confusing that birds tricked us.

What fighting and killing I have seen have not been glorious but slum grubby. I fought the most during junior high school and always cried. Fights are confusing as to who has won. The corpses I've seen had been rolled and dumped, sad little dirty bodies covered with a police khaki blanket. My mother locked her children in the house so we couldn't look at dead slum people. But at news of a body, I would find a way to get out; I had to learn about dying if I wanted to become a swordswoman. Once there was an Asian man stabbed next door, words on cloth pinned to his corpse. When the police came around asking questions, my father said, "No read Japanese. Japanese words. Me Chinese."

I've also looked for old people who could be my gurus. A medium with red hair told me that a girl who died in a far country follows me wherever I go. This spirit can help me if I acknowledge her, she said. Between the head line and heart line in my right palm, she said, I have the mystic cross. I could become a medium myself. I don't want to be a medium. I don't want to be a crank taking "offerings" in a wicker plate from the frightened audience, who, one after another, asked the spirits how to raise rent money, how to cure their coughs and skin diseases, how to find a job. And martial arts are for unsure little boys kicking away under fluorescent lights.

I live now where there are Chinese and Japanese, but no emigrants from my own village looking at me as if I had failed them. Living among one's own emigrant villagers can give a good Chinese far from China glory and a place. "That old busboy is really a swordsman," we whisper when he goes by, "He's a swordsman who's killed fifty. He has a tong ax in his closet." But I am useless, one more girl who couldn't be sold. When I visit the family now, I wrap my American successes around me like a private shawl; I *am* worthy of eating the food. From afar I can believe my family loves me fundamentally. They only say, "When fishing for treasures in the flood, be careful not to pull in girls," because that is what one says about daughters. But I watched such words come out of my own mother's and father's mouths; I looked at their ink drawing of poor people snagging their neighbors' flotage with long flood hooks and pushing the girl babies on down the river. And I had to get out of hating range. I read in an anthropology book that Chinese say, "Girls are necessary too"; I have never heard the Chinese I know make this concession. Perhaps it was a saying in another village. I refuse to shy my way anymore through our Chinatown, which tasks me with the old sayings and the stories.

The swordswoman and I are not so dissimilar. May my people understand the resemblance soon so that I can return to them. What we have in common are the words at our backs. The idioms for *revenge* are "report a crime" and "report to five families." The reporting is the vengeance – not the beheading, not the gutting, but the words. And I have so many words – "chink" words and "gook" words too – that they do not fit on my skin.

SHAMAN

Once in a long while, four times so far for me, my mother brings out the metal tube that holds her medical diploma. On the tube are gold circles crossed with seven red lines each – "joy" ideographs in abstract. There are also little flowers that look like gears for a gold machine. According to the scraps of labels with Chinese and American addresses, stamps, and postmarks, the family airmailed the can from Hong Kong in 1950. It got crushed in the middle, and whoever tried to peel the labels off stopped because the red and gold paint came off too, leaving silver scratches that rust. Somebody tried to pry the end off before discovering that the tube pulls apart. When I open it, the smell of China flies out, a thousand-year-old bat flying heavy-headed out of the Chinese caverns where bats are as white as dust, a smell that comes from long ago, far back in the brain. Crates from Canton, Hong Kong, Singapore, and Taiwan have that smell too, only stronger because they are more recently come from the Chinese.

Inside the can are three scrolls, one inside another. The largest says that in the twenty-third year of the National Republic, the To Keung School of Midwifery, where she has had two years of instruction and Hospital Practice, awards its Diploma to my mother, who has shown through oral and written examination her Proficiency in Midwifery, Pediatrics, Gynecology, "Medecine," "Surgary," Therapeutics, Ophthalmology, Bacteriology, Dermatology, Nursing, and Bandage. This document has eight stamps on it: one, the school's English and Chinese names embossed together in a circle; one, as the Chinese enumerate, a stork and a big baby in lavender ink; one, the school's Chinese seal; one, an orangish paper stamp pasted in the border design; one, the red seal of Dr. Wu Pak-liang, M.D., Lyon, Berlin, president and "Ex-assistant étranger à la clinique chirugicale et d'accouchement de l'université de Lyon"; one, the red seal of Dean Woo Yin-kam, M.D.; one, my mother's seal, her chop mark larger than the president's and the dean's; and one, the number 1279 on the back. Dean Woo's signature is followed by "(Hackett)." I read in a history book that Hackett Medical College for Women at Canton was founded in the nineteenth century by European women doctors.

The school seal has been pressed over a photograph of my mother at the age of thirty-seven. The diploma gives her age as twenty-seven. She looks younger than I do, her eyebrows are thicker, her lips fuller. Her naturally curly hair is parted on the left, one wavy wisp tendriling off to the right. She wears a scholar's white gown, and she is not thinking about her appearance. She stares straight ahead as if she could see me and past me to her grandchildren and grandchildren's grandchildren. She has spacy eyes, as all people recently from Asia have. Her eyes do not focus on the camera. My mother is not smiling; Chinese do not smile for photographs. Their faces command relatives in foreign lands – "Send money" – and posterity forever – "Put food in front of this picture." My mother does not understand Chinese-American snapshots. "What are you laughing at?" she asks.

The second scroll is a long narrow photograph of the graduating class with the school officials seated in front. I picked out my mother immediately. Her face is exactly her own, though forty years younger. She is so familiar, I can only tell whether or not she is pretty or happy or smart by comparing her to the other women. For this formal group picture she straightened her hair with oil to make a chin-length bob like the others'. On the other women, strangers,

I can recognize a curled lip, a sidelong glance, pinched shoulders. My mother is not soft; the girl with the small nose and dimpled underlip is soft. My mother is not humorous, not like the girl at the end who lifts her mocking chin to pose like Girl Graduate. My mother does not have smiling eyes; the old woman teacher (Dean Woo?) in front crinkles happily, and the one faculty member in the western suit smiles westernly. Most of the graduates are girls whose faces have not yet formed; my mother's face will not change anymore, except to age. She is intelligent, alert, pretty. I can't tell if she's happy.

The graduates seem to have been looking elsewhere when they pinned the rose, zinnia, or chrysanthemum on their precise black dresses. One thin girl wears hers in the middle of her chest. A few have a flower over a left or a right nipple. My mother put hers, a chrysanthemum, below her left breast. Chinese dresses at that time were dartless, cut as if women did not have breasts; these young doctors, unaccustomed to decorations, may have seen their chests as black expanses with no reference points for flowers. Perhaps they couldn't shorten that far gaze that lasts only a few years after a Chinese emigrates. In this picture too my mother's eyes are big with what they held – reaches of oceans beyond China, land beyond oceans. Most emigrants learn the barbarians' directness – how to gather themselves and stare rudely into talking faces as if trying to catch lies. In America my mother has eyes as strong as boulders, never once skittering off a face, but she has not learned to place decorations and phonograph needles, nor has she stopped seeing land on the other side of the oceans. Now her eyes include the relatives in China, as they once included my father smiling and smiling in his many western outfits, a different one for each photograph that he sent from America.

He and his friends took pictures of one another in bathing suits at Coney Island beach, the salt wind from the

Atlantic blowing their hair. He's the one in the middle with his arms about the necks of his buddies. They pose in the cockpit of a biplane, on a motorcycle, and on a lawn beside the "Keep Off the Grass" sign. They are always laughing. My father, white shirt sleeves rolled up, smiles in front of a wall of clean laundry. In the spring he wears a new straw hat, cocked at a Fred Astaire angle. He steps out, dancing down the stairs, one foot forward, one back, a hand in his pocket. He wrote to her about the American custom of stomping on straw hats come fall. "If you want to save your hat for next year," he said, "you have to put it away early, or else when you're riding the subway or walking along Fifth Avenue, any stranger can snatch it off your head and put his foot through it. That's the way they celebrate the change of seasons here." In the winter he wears a gray felt hat with his gray overcoat. He is sitting on a rock in Central Park. In one snapshot he is not smiling; someone took it when he was studying, blurred in the glare of the desk lamp.

There are no snapshots of my mother. In two small portraits, however, there is a black thumbprint on her forehead, as if someone had inked in bangs, as if someone had marked her.

"Mother, did bangs come into fashion after you had the picture taken?" One time she said yes. Another time when I asked, "Why do you have fingerprints on your forehead?" she said, "Your First Uncle did that." I disliked the unsureness in her voice.

The last scroll has columns of Chinese words. The only English is "Department of Health, Canton," imprinted on my mother's face, the same photograph as on the diploma. I keep looking to see whether she was afraid. Year after year my father did not come home or send for her. Their two children had been dead for ten years. If he did not return soon, there would be no more children. ("They were three and two years old, a boy and a girl. They could talk already.") My father did send money regularly, though, and she had nobody to spend it on but herself. She bought good clothes and shoes. Then she decided to use the money for becoming a doctor. She did not leave for Canton immediately after the children died. In China there was time to complete feelings. As my father had done, my mother left the village by ship. There was a sea bird painted on the ship to protect it against shipwreck and winds. She was in luck. The following ship was boarded by river pirates, who kidnapped every passenger, even old ladies. "Sixty dollars for an old lady" was what the bandits used to say. "I sailed alone," she says, "to the capital of the entire province." She took a brown leather suitcase and a seabag stuffed with two quilts.

At the dormitory the school official assigned her to a room with five other women, who were unpacking when she came in. They greeted her and she greeted them. But no one wanted to start friendships until the unpacking was done, each item placed precisely to section off the room. My mother spotted the name she had written on her application pinned to a headboard, and the annoyance she felt at not arriving early enough for first choice disappeared. The locks on her suitcase opened with two satisfying clicks; she enjoyed again how neatly her belongings fitted together, clean against the green lining. She refolded the clothes before putting them in the one drawer that was hers. Then she took out her pens and inkbox, an atlas of the world, a tea set and tea cannister, sewing box, her ruler with the real gold markings, writing paper, envelopes with the thick red stripe to signify no bad news, her bowl and silver chopsticks. These things she arranged one by one on her shelf. She spread the two quilts on top of the bed and put her slippers side by side underneath. She owned more – furniture, wedding jewelry, cloth, photographs – but she had left such troublesome valuables behind in the family's care. She never did get all of it back.

The women who had arrived early did not offer to help unpack, not wanting to interfere with the pleasure and the privacy of it. Not many women got to live out the daydream of women – to have a room, even a section of a room, that only gets messed up when she messes it up herself. The book would stay open at the very page she had pressed flat with her hand, and no one would complain about the field not being plowed or the leak in the roof. She would clean her own bowl and a small, limited area; she would have one drawer to sort, one bed to make.

To shut the door at the end of the workday, which does not spill over into evening. To throw away books after reading them so they don't have to be dusted. To go through boxes on New Year's Eve and throw out half of what is inside. Sometimes for extravagance to pick a bunch of flowers for the one table. Other women besides me must have this day-dream about a carefree life. I've seen Communist pictures showing a contented woman sitting on her bunk sewing. Above her head is her one box on a shelf. The words stenciled on the box mean "Fragile," but literally say, "Use a little heart." The woman looks very pleased. The Revolution put an end to prostitution by giving women what they wanted: a job and a room of their own.

Free from families, my mother would live for two years without servitude. She would not have to run errands for my father's tyrant mother with the bound feet or thread needles for the old ladies, but neither would there be slaves and nieces to wait on her. Now she would get hot water only if she bribed the concierge. When I went away to school my mother said, "Give the concierge oranges."

Two of my mother's roommates, who had organized their corners to their satisfaction, made tea and set a small table with their leftover travel food. "Have you eaten, Lady Scholar?" they invited my mother. "Lady Scholar, come drink tea," they said to each of the others. "Bring your own cup." This largess moved my mother – tea, an act of humility. She brought out meats and figs she had preserved on the farm. Everyone complimented her on their tastiness. The women told which villages they came from and the names they would go by. My mother did not let it be known that she had already had two children and that some of these girls were young enough to be her daughters.

Then everyone went to the auditorium for two hours of speeches by the faculty. They told the students that they would begin with a text as old as the Han empire, when the prescription for immortality had not yet been lost. Chang Chung-ching, father of medicine, had told how the two great winds, *yang* and *yin*, blew through the human body. The diligent students would do well to begin tonight memorizing his book on colds and fevers. After they had mastered the ancient cures that worked, they would be taught the most up-to-date western discoveries. By the time the students graduated – those of them who persevered – their range of knowledge would be wider than that of any other doctor in history. Women have now been practicing medicine for about fifty years, said one of the teachers, a woman, who complimented them for adding to their growing number and also for coming to a school that taught modern medicine. "You will bring science to the villages." At the end of the program, the faculty turned their backs to the students, and everyone bowed the three bows toward the picture of Doctor Sun Yat-sen, who was a western surgeon before he became a revolutionary. Then they went to the dining hall to eat. My mother began memorizing her books immediately after supper.

There were two places where a student could study: the dining hall with its tables cleared for work, everyone chanting during the common memorization sessions; or the table in her own room. Most students went to the dining hall for the company there. My mother usually stayed in her room or, when a roommate wanted the privacy of it also, went to a secret hiding place she had hunted out during the first week of school. Once in a while she dropped by the dining hall, chanted for a short while with the most advanced group, not missing a syllable, yawned early, and said good-night. She quickly built a reputation for being brilliant, a natural scholar who could glance at a book and know it.

"The other students fought over who could sit next to me at exams," says my mother. "One glimpse at my paper when they got stuck, and they could keep going."

"Did you ever try to stop them from copying your paper?"

"Of course not. They only needed to pick up a word or two, and they could remember the rest. That's not copying. You get a lot more clues in actual diagnosis. Patients talk endlessly about their ailments. I'd feel their pulses knocking away under my very fingertips – so much clearer than the paperdolls in the textbooks. I'd chant the symptoms, and those few words would start a whole chapter of cures tumbling out. Most people don't have the kind of brains that can do that." She pointed at the photograph of the thirty-seven graduates. "One hundred and twelve students began the course at the same time I did."

She suspected she did not have the right kind of brains either, my father the one who can recite whole poems. To make up the lack, she did secret studying. She also gave herself twenty years' headstart over the young girls, although she admitted to only ten, which already forced her to push. Older people were expected to be smarter; they are closer to the gods. She did not want to overhear students or teachers say, "She must be exceedingly stupid, doing no better than anyone else when she is a generation older. She's so dumb, she has to study day and night."

"I studied far in advance," says my mother. "I studied when the breathing coming from the beds and coming through the wood walls was deep and even. The night before exams, when the other students stayed up, I went to bed early. They would say, 'Aren't you going to study?' and I'd say, 'No, I'm going to do some mending,' or, 'I want to write letters tonight.' I let them take turns sitting next to me at the tests." The sweat of hard work is not to be displayed. It is much more graceful to appear favored by the gods.

Maybe my mother's secret place was the room in the dormitory which was haunted. Even though they had to crowd the other rooms, none of the young women would sleep in it. Accustomed to nestling with a bedful of siblings and grannies, they fitted their privacy tighter rather than claim the haunted room as human territory. No one had lived in it for at least five years, not since a series of hauntings had made its inhabitants come down with ghost fear that shattered their brains for studying. The haunted ones would give high, startled cries, pointing at the air, which sure enough was becoming hazy. They would suddenly turn and go back the way they had come. When they rounded a corner, they flattened themselves fast against the building to catch what followed unawares moving steadily forward. One girl tore up the photographs she had taken of friends in that room. The stranger with arms hanging at its sides who stood beside the wall in the background of the photograph was a ghost. The girl would insist there had been nobody there when she took the picture. "That was a Photo Ghost," said my mother when the students talked-story. "She needn't have been afraid. Most ghosts are only nightmares. Somebody should have held her and wiggled her ears to wake her up."

My mother relished these scare orgies. She was good at naming – Wall Ghost, Frog Spirit (frogs are "heavenly chickens"), Eating Partner. She could find descriptions of phenomena in ancient writings – the Green Phoenix stories, "The Seven Strange Tales of the Golden Bottle," "What Confucius Did Not Talk About." She could validate ghost sightings.

"But ghosts can't be just nightmares," a storyteller protested. "They come right out into the room. Once our whole family saw wine cups spinning and incense sticks waving through the air. We got the magic monk to watch all night. He also saw the incense tips tracing orange figures in the dark – ideographs, he said. He followed the glow patterns with his inkbrush on red paper. And there it was, a message from our great-grandfather. We needed to put bigger helpings and a Ford in front of his plaque. And when we did, the haunting stopped immediately."

"I like to think the ancestors are busier than that," my mother said, "or more at rest. Yes, they're probably more at rest. Perhaps it was an animal spirit that was bothering your house, and your grandfather had something to do with chasing it off." After what she thought was a suitably tactful pause, she said, "How do we know that ghosts are the continuance of dead people? Couldn't ghosts be an entirely different species of creature? Perhaps human beings just die, and that's the end. I don't think I'd mind that too much. Which would you rather be? A ghost who is constantly wanting to be fed? Or nothing?"

If the other storytellers had been reassuring one another with science, then my mother would have flown stories as factual as bats into the listening night. A practical woman, she could not invent stories and told only true ones. But tonight the younger women were huddling together under the quilts, the ghost room with its door open steps away.

"Did you hear that?" someone would whisper. And sure enough, whenever their voices stilled simultaneously, a thump or a creak would unmistakably sound somewhere inside the building. The girls would jump closer together giggling.

"That was the wind," my mother would say. "That was somebody who fell asleep reading in bed; she dropped her book." She neither jumped nor giggled.

"If you're so sure," said an impertinent girl, perhaps the one with the disdainful chin, "why don't you go out there and take a look?"

"Of course," said my mother. "I was just thinking about doing that," and she took a lamp and left her friends, impressed, in a dimmer room. She advanced steadily, waking the angular shadows up and down the corridor. She walked to both ends of the hallway, then explored another wing for good measure. At the ghost room, door open like a mouth, she stopped and, stepping inside, swung light into its corners. She saw cloth bags in knobby mounds; they looked like gnomes but were not gnomes. Suitcases and boxes threw shadow stairs up the walls and across the floor. Nothing unusual loomed at her or scurried away. No temperature change, no smell.

She turned her back on the room and slowly walked through one more wing. She did not want to get back too soon. Her friends, although one owes nothing to friends, must be satisfied that she searched thoroughly. After a suffi-ciently brave time, she returned to the storytellers. "I saw nothing," she said. "There's nothing to be afraid of in the whole dormitory, including the ghost room. I checked there too. I went inside just now."

"The haunting begins at midnight," said the girl with the adamantine chin. "It's not quite eleven."

My mother may have been afraid, but she would be a dragoness ("my totem, your totem"). She could make herself not weak. During danger she fanned out her dragon claws and riffled her red sequin scales and unfolded her coiling green stripes. Danger was a good time for showing off. Like the dragons living in temple eaves, my mother looked down on plain people who were lonely and afraid.

"I'm so sleepy," my mother said. "I don't want to wait up until midnight. I'll go sleep in the ghost room. Then if any-thing happens, I won't miss it. I hope I'll be able to recognize the ghost when I see it. Sometimes ghosts put on such mundane disguises, they aren't particularly interesting."

"Aiaa. Aiaa," the storytellers exclaimed. My mother laughed with satisfaction at their cries.

"I'll call out if something bad happens to me," she said. "If you come running all together, you will probably be able to scare any ghost away."

Some of them promised to come; some offered their talismans – a branch from a peach tree, a Christian cross, a red paper with good words written on it. But my mother refused them all. "If I take charms, then the ghost will hide from me. I won't learn what kind of ghost it is, or whether or not a ghost lives in there at all. I'll only bring a knife to defend myself and a novel in case I get bored and can't sleep. You keep the charms; should I call for help, bring them with you." She went to her own room and got weapon and book, though not a novel but a textbook.

Two of her roommates walked her to the ghost room. "Aren't you afraid?" they asked.

"What is there to be afraid of?" she asked. "What could a ghost do to me?" But my mother did pause at the door. "Listen," she said, "if I am very afraid when you find me, don't forget to tweak my ears. Call my name and tell me how to get home." She told them her personal name.

She walked directly to the back of the room, where the boxes formed a windowseat. She sat with the lamp beside her and stared at her yellow and black reflection in the night glass. "I am very pretty," she thought. She cupped her hands to the window to see out. A thin moon pricked through the clouds, and the long grass waved. "That is the same moon that they see in New Society Village," she thought, "the same stars." ("That is the same moon that they see in China, the same stars though shifted a little.")

When she set the lamp next to the bed, the room seemed darker, the uncurtained window letting in the bare night.

She wrapped herself well in her quilt, which her mother had made before dying young. In the middle of one border my grandmother had sewn a tiny satin triangle, a red heart to protect my mother at the neck, as if she were her baby yet.

My mother read aloud; perhaps the others could hear how calmly. The ghost might hear her too; she did not know whether her voice would evoke it or disperse it. Soon the ideographs lifted their feet, stretched out their wings, and flew like blackbirds; the dots were their eyes. Her own eyes drooped. She closed her book and turned off the lamp.

A new darkness pulled away the room, inked out flesh and outlined bones. My mother was wide awake again. She became sharply herself – bone, wire, antenna – but she was not afraid. She had been pared down like this before, when she had traveled up the mountains into rare snow – alone in white not unlike being alone in black. She had also sailed a boat safely between land and land.

She did not know whether she had fallen asleep or not when she heard a rushing coming out from under the bed. Cringes of fear seized her soles as something alive, rumbling, climbed the foot of the bed. It rolled over her and landed bodily on her chest. There it sat. It breathed airlessly, pressing her, sapping her. "Oh, no. A Sitting Ghost," she thought. She pushed against the creature to lever herself out from underneath it, but it absorbed this energy and got heavier. Her fingers and palms became damp, shrinking at the ghost's thick short hair like an animal's coat, which slides against warm solidity as human flesh slides against muscles and bones. She grabbed clutches of fur and pulled. She pinched the skin the hair grew out of and gouged into it with her fingernails. She forced her hands to hunt out eyes, furtive somewhere in the hair, but could not find any. She lifted her head to bite but fell back exhausted. The mass thickened.

She could see the knife, which was catching the moonlight, near the lamp. Her arm had become an immensity, though, too burdensome to lift. If she could only move it to the edge of the bed, perhaps it would fall off and reach the knife. As if feeding on her very thoughts, the ghost spread itself over her arm.

A high ringing sound somewhere had grown loud enough so that she heard it, and she understood that it had started humming at the edge of her brain before the ghost appeared. She breathed shallowly, panting as in childbirth, and could not shout out. The room sang, its air electric with the ringing; surely someone would hear and come help.

Earlier in the night, on the other side of the ringing, she could hear women's voices talking. But soon their conversations had ceased. The school slept. She could feel that the souls had gone traveling; there was a lightness not in the dormitory during the day. Without looking at the babies on her back or in their cribs, she had always been able to tell – after the rocking and singing and bedtime stories and keeping still not to startle them – the moment when they fell asleep. A tensing goes out of their bodies, out of the house. Beyond the horror in the ghost room, she felt this release throughout the dormitory. No one would come to see how she was doing.

"You will not win, Boulder," she spoke to the ghost. "You do not belong here. And I will see to it that you leave. When morning comes, only one of us will control this room, Ghost, and that one will be me. I will be marching its length and width; I will be dancing, not sliding and creeping like you. I will go right out that door, but I'll come back. Do you know what gift I will bring you? I'll get fire, Ghost. You made a mistake haunting a medical school. We have cabinets full of alcohol, laboratories full. We have a communal kitchen with human-sized jars of oil and cooking fat, enough to burn for a month without our skipping a single fried meal. I will pour alcohol into my washbucket, and I'll set fire to it. Ghost, I will burn you out. I will swing the bucket across the ceiling. Then from the kitchen my friends will come with the lard; when we fire it, the smoke will fill every crack and corner. Where will you hide, Ghost? I will make this room so clean, no ghost will ever visit here again.

"I do not give in," she said. "There is no pain you can inflict that I cannot endure. You're wrong if you think I'm afraid of you. You're no mystery to me. I've heard of you Sitting Ghosts before. Yes, people have lived to tell about you. You kill babies, you cowards. You have no power over a strong woman. You are no more dangerous than a nesting cat. My dog sits on my feet more heavily than you can. You think this is suffering? I can make my ears ring louder by taking aspirin. Are these all the tricks you have, Ghost? Sitting and ringing? That is nothing. A Broom Ghost can do better. You cannot even assume an interesting shape. Merely a boulder. A hairy butt boulder. You must not be a ghost at all. Of course. There are no such things as ghosts.

"Let me instruct you, Boulder. When Yen, the teacher, was grading the provincial exams one year, a thing with hair as ugly as yours plopped itself on his desk. (That one had glaring eyes, though, so it wasn't blind and stupid like you.) Yen picked up his ferule and hit it like a student. He chased it around the room. (It wasn't lame and lazy.) And it vanished. Later Yen taught us, 'After life, the rational soul ascends the dragon; the sentient soul descends the dragon. So in the world there can be no ghosts. This thing must have been a Fox Spirit.' That must be just what you are — a Fox Spirit. You are so hairy, you must be a fox that doesn't even know how to transform itself. You're not clever for a Fox Spirit, I must say. No tricks. No blood. Where are your hanged man's rotting noose and icy breath? No throwing shoes into the rafters? No metamorphosis into a beautiful sad lady? No disguises in my dead relatives' shapes? No drowned woman with seaweed hair? No riddles or penalty games? You are a puny little boulder indeed. Yes, when I get my oil, I will fry you for breakfast."

She then ignored the ghost on her chest and chanted her lessons for the next day's classes. The moon moved from one window to the other, and as dawn came, the thing scurried off, climbing quickly down the foot of the bed.

She fell asleep until time for school. She had said she was going to sleep in that room, and so she did.

She awoke when the students came tumbling into the room. "What happened?" they asked, getting under the quilt to keep warm. "Did anything happen?"

"Take my earlobes, please," said my mother, "and pull them back and forth. In case I lost any of my self, I want you to call me back. I was afraid, and fear may have driven me out of my body and mind. Then I will tell you the story." Two friends clasped her hands while a third held her head and took each earlobe between thumb and forefinger, wiggling them and chanting, "Come home, come home, Brave Orchid, who has fought the ghosts and won. Return to To Keung School, Kwangtung City, Kwangtung Province. Your classmates are here waiting for you, scholarly Brave Orchid. Come home. Come home. Come back and help us with our lessons. School is starting soon. Come for breakfast. Return, daughter of New Society Village, Kwangtung Province. Your brother and sisters call you. Your friends call you. We need you. Return to us. Return to us at the To Keung School. There's work to do. Come back, Doctor Brave Orchid, be unafraid. Be unafraid. You are safe now in the To Keung School. All is safe. Return."

Abundant comfort in long restoring waves warmed my mother. Her soul returned fully to her and nestled happily inside her skin, for this moment not traveling in the past where her children were nor to America to be with my father. She was back among many people. She rested after battle. She let friends watch out for her.

"There," said the roommate, giving her ear a last hearty tug, "you are cured. Now tell us what happened."

"I had finished reading my novel," said my mother, "and still nothing happened. I was listening to the dogs bark far away. Suddenly a full-grown Sitting Ghost loomed up to the ceiling and pounced on top of me. Mounds of hair hid its claws and teeth. No true head, no eyes, no face, so low in its level of incarnation it did not have the shape of a recognizable animal. It knocked me down and began to strangle me. It was bigger than a wolf, bigger than an ape, and growing. I would have stabbed it. I would have cut it up, and we would be mopping blood this morning, but – a Sitting Ghost mutation – it had an extra arm that wrested my hand away from the knife.

"At about 3 A.M. I died for a while. I was wandering, and the world I touched turned into sand. I could hear wind, but the sand did not fly. For ten years I lost my way. I almost forgot about you; there was so much work leading to other work and another life – like picking up coins in a dream. But I returned. I walked from the Gobi Desert to this room in the To Keung School. That took another two years, outwitting Wall Ghosts en route. (The way to do that is to go straight ahead; do not play their side-to-side games. In confusion they will instantly revert to their real state – weak and sad humanity. No matter what, don't commit suicide, or you will have to trade places with the Wall Ghost. If you are not put off by the foot-long lolling tongues and the popped-out eyes of the hanged ones or the open veins or the drowned skin and seaweed hair – and you shouldn't be because you're doctors – you can chant these poor souls on to light.)

"No white bats and no black bats flew ahead to guide me to my natural death. Either I would die without my whole life or I would not die. I did not die. I am brave and good. Also I have bodily strength and control. Good people do not lose to ghosts.

"Altogether I was gone for twelve years, but in this room only an hour had passed. The moon barely moved. By silver light I saw the black thing pulling shadows into itself, setting up magnetic whorls. Soon it would suck in the room and begin on the rest of the dormitory. It would eat us up. It threw boulders at me. And there was a sound like mountain wind, a sound so high it could drive you crazy. Didn't you hear it?"

Yes, they had. Wasn't it like the electric wires that one sometimes heard in the city? Yes, it was the sound of energy amassing.

"You were lucky you slept because the sound tears the heart. I could hear babies crying in it. I could hear tortured people screaming, and the cries of their relatives who had to watch."

"Yes, yes, I recognize that. That must have been the singing I heard in my dream."

"It may be sounding even now, though too strangely for our daytime ears. You cannot hit the ghost if you sweep under the bed. The ghost fattens at night, its dark sacs empty by daylight. It's a good thing I stopped it feeding on me; blood and meat would have given it strength to feed on you. I made my will an eggshell encasing the monster's fur so that the hollow hairs could not draw. I never let up willing its size smaller, its hairs to retract, until by dawn the Sitting Ghost temporarily disappeared.

"The danger is not over. The ghost is listening to us right now, and tonight it will walk again but stronger. We may not be able to control it if you do not help me finish it off before sundown. This Sitting Ghost has many wide black mouths. It is dangerous. It is real. Most ghosts make such brief and gauzy appearances that eyewitnesses doubt their own sightings. This one can conjure up enough substance to sit solidly throughout a night. It is a serious ghost, not at all playful. It does not twirl incense sticks or throw shoes and dishes.

It does not play peekaboo or wear fright masks. It does not bother with tricks. It wants lives. I am sure it is surfeited with babies and is now coming after adults. It grows. It is mysterious, not merely a copy of ourselves as, after all, the hanged men and seaweed women are. It could be hiding right now in a piece of wood or inside one of your dolls. Perhaps in daylight we accept that bag to be just a bag" – she pointed with the flat of her palm as if it balanced a top – "when in reality it is a Bag Ghost." The students moved away from the bag in which they collected their quilting scraps and pulled up their feet that were dangling over the edge of the bed.

"You have to help me rid the world of this disease, as invisible and deadly as bacteria. After classes, come back here with your buckets, alcohol, and oil. If you can find dog's blood too, our work will go fast. Act unafraid. Ghost chasers have to be brave. If the ghost comes after you, though I would not expect an attack during the day, spit at it. Scorn it. The hero in a ghost story laughs a nimble laugh, his life so full it splatters red and gold on all the creatures around him."

These young women, who would have to back up their science with magical spells should their patients be disappointed and not get well, now hurried to get to classes on time. The story about the ghost's appearance and the coming ghost chase grew, and students snatched alcohol and matches from the laboratories.

My mother directed the arrangement of the buckets and burners into orderly rows and divided the fuel. "Let's fire the oil all at once," she said. "Now."

"Whup. Whup." My mother told the sound of new fire so that I remember it. "Whup. Whup."

The alcohol burned a floating blue. The tarry oil, which someone had bought from her village witch, fumed in black clouds. My mother swung a big bucket overhead. The smoke curled in black boas around the women in their scholars' black gowns. They walked the ghost room, this circle of little black women, lifting smoke and fire up to the ceiling corners, down to the floor corners, moving clouds across the walls and floors, under the bed, around one another.

"I told you, Ghost," my mother chanted, "that we would come after you." "We told you, Ghost, that we would come after you," sang the women. "Daylight has come yellow and red," sang my mother, "and we are winning. Run, Ghost, run from this school. Only good medical people belong here. Go back, dark creature, to your native country. Go home. Go home." "Go home," sang the women.

When the smoke cleared, I think my mother said that under the foot of the bed the students found a piece of wood dripping with blood. They burned it in one of the pots, and the stench was like a corpse exhumed for its bones too soon. They laughed at the smell.

The students at the To Keung School of Midwifery were new women, scientists who changed the rituals. When she got scared as a child, one of my mother's three mothers had held her and chanted their descent line, reeling the frighted spirit back from the farthest deserts. A relative would know personal names and secrets about husbands, babies, renegades and decide which ones were lucky in a chant, but these out-side women had to build a path from scraps. No blood bonded friend to friend (though there were things owed beggars and monks), and they had to figure out how to help my mother's spirit locate the To Keung School as "home." The calling out of her real descent line would have led her to the wrong place, the village. These strangers had to make her come back to them. They called out their own names, women's pretty names, haphazard names, horizontal names of one generation. They pieced together new directions, and my mother's spirit followed them instead of the old footprints. Maybe that is why she lost her home village and did not reach her husband for fifteen years.

When my mother led us out of nightmares and horror movies, I felt loved. I felt safe hearing my name sung with hers and my father's, my brothers' and sisters', her anger at children who hurt themselves surprisingly gone. An old-fashioned woman would have called in the streets for her sick child. She'd hold its little empty coat unbuttoned, "Come put on your coat, you naughty child." When the coat puffed up, she'd quickly button up the spirit inside and hurry it home to the child's body in bed. But my mother, a modern woman, said our spells in private. "The old ladies in China had many silly superstitions," she said. "I know you'll come back without my making a fool of myself in the streets."

Not when we were afraid, but when we were wide awake and lucid, my mother funneled China into our ears: Kwangtung Province, New Society Village, the river Kwoo, which runs past the village. "Go the way we came so that you will be able to find our house. Don't forget. Just give your father's name, and any villager can point out our house." I am to return to China where I have never been.

After two years of study – the graduates of three-week and six-week courses were more admired by the peasants for learning at such wondrous speeds – my mother returned to her home village a doctor. She was welcomed with garlands and cymbals the way people welcome the "barefoot doctors" today. But the Communists wear a blue plainness dotted with one red Mao button. My mother wore a silk robe and western shoes with big heels, and she rode home carried in a sedan chair. She had gone away ordinary and come back miraculous, like the ancient magicians who came down from the mountains.

"When I stepped out of my sedan chair, the villagers said, 'Ahhh,' at my good shoes and my long gown. I always dressed well when I made calls. Some villages brought out their lion and danced ahead of me. You have no idea how much I have fallen coming to America." Until my father sent for her to live in the Bronx, my mother delivered babies in beds and pigsties. She stayed awake keeping watch nightly in an epidemic and chanted during air raids. She yanked bones straight that had been crooked for years while relatives held the cripples down, and she did all this never dressed less elegantly than when she stepped out of the sedan chair.

Nor did she change her name: Brave Orchid. Professional women have the right to use their maiden names if they like. Even when she emigrated, my mother kept Brave Orchid, adding no American name nor holding one in reserve for American emergencies.

Walking behind the palanquin so that the crowd took her for one of themselves following the new doctor came a quiet girl. She carried a white puppy and a rice sack knotted at the mouth. Her pigtails and the puppy's tail ended in red yarn. She may have been either a daughter or a slave.

When my mother had gone to Canton market to shop, her wallet had unfolded like wings. She had received her diploma, and it was time to celebrate. She had hunted out the seed shops to taste their lichees, various as wines, and bought a sack that was taller than a child to bedazzle the nieces and nephews. A merchant had given her one nut fresh on its sprig of narrow leaves. My mother popped the thin wood shell in her curled palm. The white fruit, an eye without an iris, ran juices like spring rivers inside my mother's mouth. She spit out the brown seed, iris after all.

She had bought a turtle for my grandfather because it would lengthen his life. She had dug to the bottom of fabric piles and explored the shadows underneath awnings. She gave beggars rice and letter-writers coins so that they would talk-story. ("Sometimes what I gave was all they had, and stories.") She let a fortuneteller read the whorls on her fin- gerprints; he predicted that she would leave China and have six more children. "Six," he said, "is the number of everything. You are such a lucky woman. Six is the universe's number. The four compass points plus the zenith and the nadir are six. There are six low phoenix notes and six high, six worldly environments, six senses, six virtues, six obligations, six classes of ideograph, six domestic animals, six arts, and six paths of metempsychosis. More than two thousand years ago, six states combined to overthrow Ch'in. And, of course, there are the hexagrams that are the *I Ching*, and there is the Big Six, which is China." As interesting as his list of sixes was, my mother hurried on her way; she had come to market to buy herself a slave.

Between the booths and stores, whoever could squeeze a space – a magician who could turn dirt into gold, twenty-five acrobats on one unicycle, a man who could swim – displayed his or her newest feat for money. From the country the villagers brought strange purple textiles, dolls with big feet, geese with brown tufts on their heads, chickens with white feathers and black skin, gambling games and puppet shows, intricate ways to fold pastry and ancestors' money, a new boxing stance.

Herders roped off alleys to pen their goats, which stared out of the dimness with rectangular pupils. Whisking a handful of grass, my mother coaxed them into the light and watched the tiny yellow windows close and open again as the goats skipped backward into the shade. Two farmers, each leading this year's cow, passed each other, shouting prices. Usually my mother would have given herself up to the pleasure of being in a crowd, delighting in the money game the people would play with the rival herders, who were now describing each other's cows – "skinny shoulder blades," "lame legs," "patchy hair," "ogre face." But today she hurried even when looking over the monkey cages stacked higher than her head. She paused only a while in front of the ducks, which honked madly, the down flying as some passer-by bumped into their cages. My mother liked to look at the ducks and plan how she would dig a pond for them near the sweet potato field and arrange straw for their eggs. She decided that the drake with the green head would be the best buy, the noblest, although she would not buy him unless she had money left over; she was already raising a nobler duck on the farm.

Among the sellers with their ropes, cages, and water tanks were the sellers of little girls. Sometimes just one man would be standing by the side of the road selling one girl. There were fathers and mothers selling their daughters, whom they pushed forward and then pulled back again. My mother turned her face to look at pottery or embroidery rather than at these miserable families who did not have the sense to leave the favored brothers and sisters home. All the children bore still faces. My mother would not buy from parents, crying and clutching. They would try to keep you talking to find out what kind of mistress you were to your slaves. If they could just hear from the buyer's own mouth about a chair in the kitchen, they could tell each other in the years to come that their daughter was even now resting in the kitchen chair. It was merciful to give these parents a few details about the garden, a sweet feeble grandmother, food.

My mother would buy her slave from a professional whose little girls stood neatly in a row and bowed together when a customer looked them over. "How do you do, Sir?" they would sing. "How do you do, Madam?" "Let a little slave do your shopping for you," the older girls chorused. "We've been taught to bargain. We've been taught to sew. We can cook, and we can knit." Some of the dealers merely had the children bow quietly. Others had them sing a happy song about flowers.

Unless a group of little girls chanted some especially clever riddle, my mother, who distrusts people with public concerns, braggarts, went over to the quiet older girls with the dignified bows. "Any merchant who advertises 'Honest Scales' must have been thinking about weighting them," she says. Many sellers displayed the sign "Children and Old Men Not Cheated."

There were girls barely able to toddle carrying infant slaves tied in slings to their backs. In the undisciplined groups the babies crawled into gutters and the older girls each acted as if she were alone, a daughter among slaves. The one- to two-year-old babies cost nothing.

"Greet the lady," the dealer commanded, just as the nice little girls' mothers had when visitors came.

"How do you do, Lady," said the girls.

My mother did not need to bow back, and she did not. She overlooked the infants and toddlers and talked to the oldest girls.

"Open your mouth," she said, and examined teeth. She pulled down eyelids to check for anemia. She picked up the girls' wrists to sound their pulses, which tell everything.

She stopped at a girl whose strong heart sounded like thunder within the earth, sending its power into her finger-tips. "I would not have sold a daughter such as that one," she told us. My mother could find no flaw in the beat; it matched her own, the real rhythm. There were people jumpy with silly rhythms; broken rhythms; sly, secretive rhythms. They did not follow the sounds of earth-sea-sky and the Chinese language.

My mother brought out the green notebook my father had given her when he left. It had a map of each hemisphere on the inside covers and a clasp that shut it like a pocket-book. "Watch carefully," she said. With an American pencil, she wrote a word, a felicitous word such as "longevity" or "double joy," which is symmetrical.

"Look carefully," she said into the girl's face. "If you can write this word from memory, I will take you with me. Concentrate now." She wrote in a plain style and folded the page a moment afterward. The girl took the pencil and wrote surely; she did not leave out a single stroke.

"What would you do," my mother asked, "if you lost a gold watch in a field?"

"I know a chant on the finger bones," said the girl. "But even if I landed on the bone that says to look no more, I would go to the middle of the field and search in a spiral going outward until I reached the field's edge. Then I would believe the chant and look no more." She drew in my mother's notebook the field and her spiraling path.

"How do you cast on yarn?"

The girl pantomimed her method with her large hands.

"How much water do you put in the rice pot for a family of five? How do you finish off weaving so that it doesn't unravel?"

Now it was time to act as if she were very dissatisfied with the slave's answers so that the dealer would not charge her extra for a skillful worker.

"You tie the loose ends into tassels," said the girl.

My mother frowned. "But suppose I like a finished border?"

The girl hesitated. "I could, uh, press the fibers under and sew them down. Or how about cutting the fibers off?"

My mother offered the dealer half the price he named. "My mother-in-law asked me to find a weaver for her, and obviously she and I will have to waste many months training this girl."

"But she can knit and cook," said the dealer, "and she can find lost watches." He asked for a price higher than her suggestion but lower than his first.

"I knit and cook and find things," said my mother. "How else do you suppose I think of such ingenious questions? Do you think I would buy a slave who could outwork me in front of my mother-in-law?" My mother walked off to look at a group of hungry slaves across the street. When she returned, the dealer sold her the girl with the finding chant at my mother's price.

"I am a doctor," she told her new slave, when they were out of the dealer's hearing, "and I shall train you to be my nurse."

"Doctor," said the slave, "do you understand that I do know how to finish off my weaving?"

"Yes, we fooled him very well," said my mother.

The unsold slaves must have watched them with envy. I watch them with envy. My mother's enthusiasm for me is duller than for the slave girl; nor did I replace the older brother and sister who died while they were still cuddly. Throughout childhood my younger sister said, "When I grow up, I want to be a slave," and my parents laughed, encouraging her. At department stores I angered my mother when I could not bargain without shame, poor people's shame. She stood in back of me and prodded and pinched, forcing me to translate her bargaining, word for word.

On that same day she bought at the dog dealer's a white puppy to train as her bodyguard when she made night calls. She tied pretty red yarn around its tail to neutralize the bad luck. There was no use docking the tail. No matter at what point she cut, the tip would have been white, the mourning color.

The puppy waved its red yarn at the nurse girl, and she picked it up. She followed my mother back to the village, where she always got enough to eat because my mother became a good doctor. She could cure the most spectacular diseases. When a sick person was about to die, my mother could read the fact of it a year ahead of time on the daughters-in-law's faces. A black veil seemed to hover over their skin. And though they laughed, this blackness rose and fell with their breath. My mother would take one look at the daughter-in-law who answered the door at the sick house and she'd say, "Find another doctor." She would not touch death; therefore, untainted, she brought only health from house to house. "She must be a Jesus convert," the people from the far villages said. "All her patients get well." The bigger the talk, the farther the distances she traveled. She had customers everywhere.

Sometimes she went to her patients by foot. Her nurse-slave carried an umbrella when my mother predicted rain and a parasol when she predicted sun. "My white dog would be standing at the door waiting for me whenever I came home," she said. When she felt like it, my mother would leave the nurse-slave to watch the office and would take the white dog with her.

"What happened to your dog when you came to America, Mother?"

"I don't know."

"What happened to the slave?"

"I found her a husband."

"How much money did you pay to buy her?"

"One hundred and eighty dollars."

"How much money did you pay the doctor and the hospital when I was born?"

"Two hundred dollars."

"Oh."

"That's two hundred dollars American money."

"Was the one hundred and eighty dollars American money?"

"No."

"How much was it American money?"

"Fifty dollars. That's because she was sixteen years old. Eight-year-olds were about twenty dollars. Five-year-olds were ten dollars and up. Two-year-olds were about five dollars. Babies were free. During the war, though, when you were born, many people gave older girls away for free. And here I was in the United States paying two hundred dollars for you."

When my mother went doctoring in the villages, the ghosts, the were-people, the apes dropped out of trees. They rose out of bridge water. My mother saw them come out of cervixes. Medical science does not seal the earth, whose nether creatures seep out, hair by hair, disguised like the smoke that dispels them. She had apparently won against the one ghost, but ghost forms are various and many. Some can occupy the same space at the same moment. They permeate the grain in wood, metal, and stone. Animalcules somersault about our faces when we breathe. We have to build horns on our roofs so that the nagging once-people can slide up them and perhaps ascend to the stars, the source of pardon and love.

On a fine spring day the villagers at a place my mother had never visited before would wave peach branches and fans, which are emblems of Chung-li Ch'uan, the chief of the Eight Sages and keeper of the elixir of life. The pink petals would fall on my mother's black hair and gown. The villagers would set off firecrackers as on New Year's Day. If it had really been New Year's, she would have had to shut herself up in her own house. Nobody wanted a doctor's visit in the first days of the year.

But at night my mother walked quickly. She and bandits were the only human beings out, no palanquins available for midwives. For a time the roads were endangered by a fantastic creature, half man and half ape, that a traveler to the West had captured and brought back to China in a cage. With his new money, the man had built the fourth wing to his house, and in the courtyard he grew a stand of bamboo. The ape-man could reach out and touch the thin leaves that shaded its cage.

This creature had gnawed through the bars. Or it had tricked its owner into letting it play in the courtyard, and then leapt over the roof of the new wing. Now it was at large in the forests, living off squirrels, mice, and an occasional duck or piglet. My mother saw in the dark a denser dark, and she knew she was being followed. She carried a club, and the white dog was beside her. The ape-man was known to have attacked people. She had treated their bites and claw wounds. With hardly a rustle of leaves, the ape-man leapt live out of the trees and blocked her way. The white dog yelped. As big as a human being, the ape-thing jumped up and down on one foot. Its two hands were holding the other foot, hurt in the jump. It had long orange hair and beard. Its owner had clothed it in a brown burlap rice sack with holes for neck and arms. It blinked at my mother with human eyes, moving its head from shoulder to shoulder as if figuring things out. "Go home," she shouted, waving her club. It copied her waving with one raised arm and made complex motions with its other hand. But when she rushed at it, it turned and ran limping into the forest. "Don't you scare me again," she yelled after its retreating buttocks, tailless and hairless under the shirt. It was definitely not a gorilla; she has since seen some of those at the Bronx Zoo, and this ape-man was nothing like them. If her father had not brought Third Wife, who was not Chinese, back from his travels, my mother might have thought this orange creature with the great nose was a barbarian from the West. But my grandfather's Third Wife was black with hair so soft that it would not hang, instead blowing up into a great brown puffball. (At first she talked constantly, but who could understand her? After a while she never talked anymore. She had one son.) The owner of the ape-man finally recaptured it by luring it back into its cage with cooked pork and wine. Occasionally my mother went to the rich man's house to look at the ape-man. It seemed to recognize her and smiled when she gave it candy. Perhaps it had not been an ape-man at all, but one of the Tigermen, a savage northern race.

My mother was midwife to whatever spewed forth, not being able to choose as with the old and sick. She was not squeamish, though, and deftly caught spewings that were sometimes babies, sometimes monsters. When she helped the country women who insisted on birthing in the pigpen, she could not tell by starlight and moonlight what manner of creature had made its arrival on the earth until she carried it inside the house. "Pretty pigbaby, pretty piglet," she and the mother would croon, fooling the ghosts on the lookout for a new birth. "Ugly pig, dirty pig," fooling the gods jealous of human joy. They counted fingers and toes by touch, felt for penis or no penis, but not until later would they know for sure whether the gods let them get away with something good.

One boy appeared perfect, so round in the cool opal dawn. But when my mother examined him indoors, he opened up blue eyes at her. Perhaps he had looked without protection at the sky, and it had filled him. His mother said that a ghost had entered him, but my mother said the baby looked pretty.

Not all defects could be explained so congenially. One child born without an anus was left in the outhouse so that the family would not have to hear it cry. They kept going back to see whether it was dead yet, but it lived for a long time. Whenever they went to look at it, it was sobbing, heaving as if it were trying to defecate. For days the family either walked to the fields or used the night soil buckets.

As a child, I pictured a naked child sitting on a modern toilet desperately trying to perform until it died of congestion. I had to flick on the bathroom lights fast so that no small shadow would take a baby shape, sometimes seated on the edge of the bathtub, its hopes for a bowel movement so exaggerated. When I woke at night I sometimes heard an infant's grunting and weeping coming from the bathroom. I did not go to its rescue but waited for it to stop.

I hope this holeless baby proves that my mother did not prepare a box of clean ashes beside the birth bed in case of a girl. "The midwife or a relative would take the back of a girl baby's head in her hand and turn her face into the ashes," said my mother. "It was very easy." She never said she herself killed babies, but perhaps the holeless baby was a boy.

Even here on Gold Mountain grateful couples bring gifts to my mother, who had cooked them a soup that not only ended their infertility but gave them a boy.

My mother has given me pictures to dream – nightmare babies that recur, shrinking again and again to fit in my palm. I curl my fingers to make a cradle for the baby, my other hand an awning. I would protect the dream baby, not let it suffer, not let it out of my sight. But in a blink of inattention, I would mislay the baby. I would have to stop moving, afraid of stepping on it. Or before my very eyes, it slips between my fingers because my fingers cannot grow webs fast enough. Or bathing it, I carefully turn the righ-thand faucet, but it spouts hot water, scalding the baby until its skin tautens and its face becomes nothing but a red hole of a scream. The hole turns into a pinprick as the baby recedes from me.

To make my waking life American-normal, I turn on the lights before anything untoward makes an appearance. I push the deformed into my dreams, which are in Chinese, the language of impossible stories. Before we can leave our parents, they stuff our heads like the suitcases which they jam-pack with homemade underwear.

When the thermometer in our laundry reached one hundred and eleven degrees on summer afternoons, either my mother or my father would say that it was time to tell another ghost story so that we could get some good chills up our backs. My parents, my brothers, sisters, great-uncle, and "Third Aunt," who wasn't really our aunt but a fellow villager, someone else's third aunt, kept the presses crashing and hissing and shouted out the stories. Those were our successful days, when so much laundry came in, my mother did not have to pick tomatoes. For breaks we changed from pressing to sorting.

"One twilight," my mother began, and already the chills traveled my back and crossed my shoulders; the hair rose at the nape and the back of the legs, "I was walking home after doctoring a sick family. To get home I had to cross a foot-bridge. In China the bridges are nothing like the ones in Brooklyn and San Francisco. This one was made from rope, laced and knotted as if by magpies. Actually it had been built by men who had returned after harvesting sea swallow nests in Malaya. They had had to swing over the faces of the Malayan cliffs in baskets they had woven themselves. Though this bridge pitched and swayed in the updraft, no one had ever fallen into the river, which looked like a bright scratch at the bottom of the canyon, as if the Queen of Heaven had swept her great silver hairpin across the earth as well as the sky."

One twilight, just as my mother stepped on the bridge, two smoky columns spiraled up taller than she. Their swaying tops hovered over her head like white cobras, one at either handrail. From stillness came a wind rushing between the smoke spindles. A high sound entered her temple bones. Through the twin whirlwinds she could see the sun and the river, the river twisting in circles, the trees upside down. The bridge moved like a ship, sickening. The earth dipped. She collapsed to the wooden slats, a ladder up the sky, her fingers so weak she could not grip the rungs. The wind dragged her hair behind her, then whipped it forward across her face. Suddenly the smoke spindles disappeared. The world righted itself, and she crossed to the other side. She looked back, but there was nothing there. She used the bridge often, but she did not encounter those ghosts again.

"They were Sit Dom Kuei," said Great-Uncle. "Sit Dom Kuei."

"Yes, of course," said my mother. "Sit Dom Kuei."

I keep looking in dictionaries under those syllables. "Kuei" means "ghost," but I don't find any other words that make sense. I only hear my great-uncle's river-pirate voice, the voice of a big man who had killed someone in New York or Cuba, make the sounds – "Sit Dom Kuei." How do they translate?

When the Communists issued their papers on techniques for combating ghosts, I looked for "Sit Dom Kuei." I have not found them described anywhere, although now I see that my mother won in ghost battle because she can eat anything – quick, pluck out the carp's eyes, one for Mother and one for Father. All heroes are bold toward food. In the research against ghost fear published by the Chinese Academy of Science is the story of a magistrate's servant, Kao Chung, a capable eater who in 1683 ate five cooked chickens and drank ten bottles of wine that belonged to the sea monster with branching teeth. The monster had arranged its food around a fire on the beach and started to feed when Kao Chung attacked. The swan-feather sword he wrested from this monster can be seen in the Wentung County Armory in Shantung today.

Another big eater was Chou Yi-han of Changchow, who fried a ghost. It was a meaty stick when he cut it up and cooked it. But before that it had been a woman out at night.

Chen Luan-feng, during the Yuan Ho era of the T'ang dynasty (A.D. 806–820), ate yellow croaker and pork together, which the thunder god had forbidden. But Chen wanted to incur thunderbolts during drought. The first time he ate, the thunder god jumped out of the sky, its legs like old trees. Chen chopped off the left one. The thunder god fell to the earth, and the villagers could see that it was a blue pig or bear with horns and fleshy wings. Chen leapt on it, prepared to chop its neck and bite its throat, but the villagers stopped him. After that, Chen lived apart as a rainmaker, neither relatives nor the monks willing to bring lightning upon themselves. He lived in a cave, and for years whenever there was drought the villagers asked him to eat yellow croaker and pork together, and he did.

The most fantastic eater of them all was Wei Pang, a scholar-hunter of the Ta Li era of the T'ang dynasty (A.D. 766–779). He shot and cooked rabbits and birds, but he could also eat scorpions, snakes, cockroaches, worms, slugs, beetles, and crickets. Once he spent the night in a house that had been abandoned because its inhabitants feared contamination from the dead man next door. A shining, twinkling sphere came flying through the darkness at Wei. He felled it with three true arrows – the first making the thing crackle and flame; the second dimming it; and the third putting out its lights, sputter. When his servant came running in with a lamp, Wei saw his arrows sticking in a ball of flesh entirely covered with eyes, some rolled back to show the dulling whites. He and the servant pulled out the arrows and cut up the ball into little pieces. The servant cooked the morsels in sesame oil, and the wonderful aroma made Wei laugh. They ate half, saving half to show the household, which would return now.

Big eaters win. When other passers-by stepped around the bundle wrapped in white silk, the anonymous scholar of Hanchow took it home. Inside were three silver ingots and a froglike evil, which sat on the ingots. The scholar laughed at it and chased it off. That night two frogs the size of year-old babies appeared in his room. He clubbed them to death, cooked them, and ate them with white wine. The next night a dozen frogs, together the size of a pair of year-old babies, jumped from the ceiling. He ate all twelve for dinner. The third night thirty small frogs were sitting on his mat and staring at him with their frog eyes. He ate them too. Every night for a month smaller but more numerous frogs came so that he always had the same amount to eat. Soon his floor was like the healthy banks of a pond in spring when the tadpoles, having just turned, sprang in the wet grass. "Get a hedgehog to help eat," cried his family. "I'm as good as a hedgehog," the scholar said, laughing. And at the end of the month the frogs stopped coming, leaving the scholar with the white silk and silver ingots.

My mother has cooked for us: raccoons, skunks, hawks, city pigeons, wild ducks, wild geese, black-skinned bantams, snakes, garden snails, turtles that crawled about the pantry floor and sometimes escaped under refrigerator or stove, catfish that swam in the bathtub. "The emperors used to eat the peaked hump of purple dromedaries," she would say. "They used chopsticks made from rhinoceros horn, and they ate ducks' tongues and monkeys' lips." She boiled the weeds we pulled up in the yard. There was a tender plant with flowers like white stars hiding under the leaves, which were like the flower petals but green. I've not been able to find it since growing up. It had no taste. When I was as tall as the washing machine, I stepped out on the back porch one night, and some heavy, ruffling, windy, clawed thing dived at me. Even after getting chanted back to sensibility, I shook when I recalled that perched everywhere there were owls with great hunched shoulders and yellow scowls. They were a surprise for my mother from my father. We children used to hide under the beds with our fingers in our ears to shut out the bird screams and the thud, thud of the turtles swimming in the boiling water, their shells hitting the sides of the pot. Once the third aunt who worked at the laundry ran out and bought us bags of candy to hold over our noses; my mother was dismembering skunk on the chopping block. I could smell the rubbery odor through the candy.

In a glass jar on a shelf my mother kept a big brown hand with pointed claws stewing in alcohol and herbs. She must have brought it from China because I do not remember a time when I did not have the hand to look at. She said it was a bear's claw, and for many years I thought bears were hairless. My mother used the tobacco, leeks, and grasses swimming about the hand to rub our sprains and bruises.

Just as I would climb up to the shelf to take one look after another at the hand, I would hear my mother's monkey story. I'd take my fingers out of my ears and let her monkey words enter my brain. I did not always listen voluntarily, though. She would begin telling the story, perhaps repeating it to a homesick villager, and I'd overhear before I had a chance to protect myself. Then the monkey words would unsettle me; a curtain flapped loose inside my brain. I have wanted to say, "Stop it. Stop it," but not once did I say, "Stop it."

"Do you know what people in China eat when they have the money?" my mother began. "They buy into a monkey feast. The eaters sit around a thick wood table with a hole in the middle. Boys bring in the monkey at the end of a pole. Its neck is in a collar at the end of the pole, and it is screaming. Its hands are tied behind it. They clamp the monkey into the table; the whole table fits like another collar around its neck. Using a surgeon's saw, the cooks cut a clean line in a circle at the top of its head. To loosen the bone, they tap with a tiny hammer and wedge here and there with a silver pick. Then an old woman reaches out her hand to the monkey's face and up to its scalp, where she tufts some hairs and lifts off the lid of the skull. The eaters spoon out the brains."

Did she say, "You should have seen the faces the monkey made"? Did she say, "The people laughed at the monkey screaming"? It was alive? The curtain flaps closed like merciful black wings.

"Eat! Eat!" my mother would shout at our heads bent over bowls, the blood pudding awobble in the middle of the table.

She had one rule to keep us safe from toadstools and such: "If it tastes good, it's bad for you," she said. "If it tastes bad, it's good for you."

We'd have to face four- and five-day-old leftovers until we ate it all. The squid eye would keep appearing at breakfast and dinner until eaten. Sometimes brown masses sat on every dish. I have seen revulsion on the faces of visitors who've caught us at meals.

"Have you eaten yet?" the Chinese greet one another.

"Yes, I have," they answer whether they have or not. "And you?"

I would live on plastic.

My mother could contend against the hairy beasts whether flesh or ghost because she could eat them, and she could not-eat them on the days when good people fast. My mother was not crazy for seeing ghosts nor was she one of those the women teased for "longing" after men. She was a capable exorcist; she did not "long" ("mong" in Cantonese). The village crazy lady was somebody else, an inappropriate woman whom the people stoned.

It was just after this stoning that my mother left China. My father had made the money for the fare at last, but he sent for her instead of returning, one more postponement of home, this time because of the Japanese. By 1939 the Japanese had taken much of the land along the Kwoo River, and my mother was living in the mountains with other refugees. (I used to watch my mother and father play refugees, sleeping sitting up, huddled together with their heads on each other's shoulder, their arms about each other, holding up the blanket like a little tent. "Aiaa," they'd sigh. "Aiaa." "Mother, what's a refugee? Father, what's a refugee?") The Japanese, though "little," were not ghosts, the only foreigners considered not ghosts by the Chinese. They may have been descended from the Chinese explorers that the First Emperor of Ch'in (221–210 B.C.) had deployed to find longevity medicine. They were to look for an island beyond the Eastern Ocean, beyond the impassable wind and mist. On this island lived phoenixes, unicorns, black apes, and white stags. Magic orchids, strange trees, and plants of jasper grew on Penglai, a fairy mountain, which may have been Mount Fuji. The emperor would saw off the explorers' heads if they returned without the herbs of immortality. Another ancestor of the Japanese is said to be an ape that raped a Chinese princess, who then fled to the eastern islands to have the first Japanese child. Whichever the case, they were not a totally alien species, connected as they were even to royalty. Chinese without sons stole the boy babies of Japanese settlers who left them bundled up at the ends of the potato rows.

Now the villagers were watching for Japanese airplanes that strafed the mountainsides every day. "If you see a single plane, you needn't be afraid," my mother taught us. "But watch for planes in threes. When they spread apart, you know they're going to drop bombs. Sometimes airplanes covered the sky, and we could not see and we could not hear." She warned us because it was the same war still going on years after she crossed the ocean and had us. I huddled under my blankets when Pan Am and United Air Lines planes flew overhead, the engines sounding like insects at first and getting louder and louder.

In the mountains my mother set up a hospital in a cave, and she carried the wounded there. Some villagers had never seen an airplane before. Mothers stopped up their babies' mouths so their crying would not attract the planes. The bombing drove people insane. They rolled on the ground, pushed themselves against it, as if the earth could open a door for them. The ones who could not stop shaking after the danger passed would sleep in the cave. My mother explained airplanes to them as she wiggled their ears.

One afternoon peace and summer rested on the mountains. Babies napped in the tall grass, their blankets covering the wildflowers with embroidered flowers. It was so quiet; the bees hummed and the river water played the pebbles, the rocks, and the hollows. Cows under the trees whisked their tails; goats and ducks followed the children here and there; and the chickens scratched in the dirt. The villagers stood about in the sunshine. They smiled at one another. Here they all were together, idle above their fields, nobody hoeing, godlike; nobody weeding, New Year's in summer. My mother and the women her age talked about how similar this day was to the orderly days long ago when they walked up the mountain to collect firewood, only now they could dally without the mothers-in-law scolding.

The village crazy lady put on her headdress with the small mirrors, some of them waving quickly on red stalks. In her crazy lady clothes of reds and greens, she greeted the animals and the moving branches as she carried her porcelain cup to the river. Although her bindings had come loose, her tiny feet made her body sway pleasantly, her shoes like little bridges. She knelt singing at the river and filled her cup. Carrying the brimming water in two careful hands, she undulated toward a clearing where the light of the afternoon seemed to be concentrated. The villagers turned to look at her. She dipped her fingertips into the water and flung droplets into grass and air. Then she set the cup down and pulled out the long white undersleeves of her old-fashioned dress. She began to move in fanning circles, now flying the sleeves in the air, now trailing them on the grass, dancing in the middle of the light. The little mirrors in her headdress shot rainbows into the green, glinted off the water cup, caught water drops. My mother felt as if she were peering into Li T'ieh-kuai's magic gourd to check the fate of an impish mortal.

One villager whispered away the spell, "She's signaling the planes." The whisper carried. "She's signaling the planes," the people repeated. "Stop her. Stop her."

"No, she's only crazy," said my mother. "She's a harmless crazy lady."

"She's a spy. A spy for the Japanese."

Villagers picked up rocks and moved down the hill.

"Just take away the mirrors," my mother called. "Just take her headdress."

But the tentative first stones were already falling around the crazy lady. She dodged them; she tried to catch them, laughing, at last, people to play with.

The rocks hit harder as the villagers came within stoning range. "Here. Here. I'll get her mirrors," said my mother, who had come running down the mountain into the clearing. "Give me your headdress," she ordered, but the woman only shook her head coquettishly.

"See? She's a spy. Get out of the way, Doctor. You saw the way she flashed the signals. She comes to the river every day before the planes come."

"She's only getting drinking water," said my mother. "Crazy people drink water too."

Someone took the crazy lady's cup and threw it at her. It broke at her feet. "Are you a spy? Are you?" they asked her.

A cunning look narrowed her eyes. "Yes," she said, "I have great powers. I can make the sky rain fire. Me. I did that. Leave me alone or I will do it again." She edged toward the river as if she were about to run, but she wouldn't have been able to get away on her tiny feet.

A large stone rammed her head, and she fell in a flutter of sleeves, the ornaments jumping about her broken head. The villagers closed in. Somebody held a fragment of glass under her nostrils. When it clouded, they pounded her temples with the rocks in their fists until she was dead. Some villagers remained at the body beating her head and face, smashing the little mirrors into silver splinters.

My mother, who had turned her back and walked up

the mountain (she never treated those about to die), looked down at the mass of flesh and rocks, the sleeves, the blood flecks. The planes came again that very afternoon. The villagers buried the crazy lady along with the rest of the dead.

My mother left China in the winter of 1939, almost six months after the stoning, and arrived in New York Harbor in January, 1940. She carried the same suitcase she had taken to Canton, this time filled with seeds and bulbs. On Ellis Island the officials asked her, "What year did your husband cut off his pigtail?" and it terrified her when she could not remember. But later she told us perhaps this lapse was for the best: what if they were trying to trap him politically? The men had cut their pigtails to defy the Manchus and to help Sun Yat-sen, fellow Cantonese.

I was born in the middle of World War II. From earliest awareness, my mother's stories always timely, I watched for three airplanes parting. Much as I dream recurringly about shrinking babies, I dream that the sky is covered from horizon to horizon with rows of airplanes, dirigibles, rocket ships, flying bombs, their formations as even as stitches. When the sky seems clear in my dreams and I would fly, if I look too closely, there so silent, far away, and faint in the daylight that people who do not know about them do not see them, are shiny silver machines, some not yet invented, being moved, fleets always being moved from one continent to another, one planet to another. I must figure out a way to fly between them.

But America has been full of machines and ghosts – Taxi Ghosts, Bus Ghosts, Police Ghosts, Fire Ghosts, Meter Reader Ghosts, Tree Trimming Ghosts, Five-and-Dime Ghosts. Once upon a time the world was so thick with ghosts, I could hardly breathe; I could hardly walk, limping my way around the White Ghosts and their cars. There were

Black Ghosts too, but they were open eyed and full of laughter, more distinct than White Ghosts.

What frightened me most was the Newsboy Ghost, who came out from between the cars parked in the evening light. Carrying a newspaper pouch instead of a baby brother, he walked right out in the middle of the street without his parents. He shouted ghost words to the empty streets. His voice reached children inside the houses, reached inside the children's chests. They would come running out of their yards with their dimes. They would follow him just a corner too far. And when they went to the nearest house to ask directions home, the Gypsy Ghosts would lure them inside with gold rings and then boil them alive and bottle them. The ointment thus made was good for rubbing on children's bruises.

We used to pretend we were Newsboy Ghosts. We collected old Chinese newspapers (the Newsboy Ghost not giving us his ghost newspapers) and trekked about the house and yard. We waved them over our heads, chanting a chant: "Newspapers for sale. Buy a newspaper." But those who could hear the insides of words heard that we were selling a miracle salve made from boiled children. The newspapers covered up green medicine bottles. We made up our own English, which I wrote down and now looks like "eeeeeeeeee." When we heard the real newsboy calling, we hid, dragging our newspapers under the stairs or into the cellar, where the Well Ghost lived in the black water under a lid. We crouched on our newspapers, the San Francisco *Gold Mountain News*, and plugged up our ears with our knuckles until he went away.

For our very food we had to traffic with the Grocery Ghosts, the supermarket aisles full of ghost customers. The Milk Ghost drove his white truck from house to house every other day. We hid watching until his truck turned the corner, bottles rattling in their frames. Then we unlocked the front door and the screen door and reached for the milk. We were regularly visited by the Mail Ghost, Meter Reader Ghost, Garbage Ghost. Staying off the streets did no good. They came nosing at windows – Social Worker Ghosts; Public Health Nurse Ghosts; Factory Ghosts recruiting workers during the war (they promised free child care, which our mother turned down); two Jesus Ghosts who had formerly worked in China. We hid directly under the windows, pressed against the baseboard until the ghost, calling us in the ghost language so that we'd almost answer to stop its voice, gave up. They did not try to break in, except for a few Burglar Ghosts. The Hobo Ghosts and Wino Ghosts took peaches off our trees and drank from the hose when nobody answered their knocks.

It seemed as if ghosts could not hear or see very well. Momentarily lulled by the useful chores they did for whatever ghostly purpose, we did not bother to lower the windows one morning when the Garbage Ghost came. We talked loudly about him through the fly screen, pointed at his hairy arms, and laughed at how he pulled up his dirty pants before swinging his hoard onto his shoulders. "Come see the Garbage Ghost get its food," we children called. "The Garbage Ghost," we told each other, nodding our heads. The ghost looked directly at us. Steadying the load on his back with one hand, the Garbage Ghost walked up to the window. He had cavernous nostrils with yellow and brown hair. Slowly he opened his red mouth, "The . . . Gar . . . bage . . . Ghost," he said, copying human language. "Gar . . . bage . . . Ghost?" We ran, screaming to our mother, who efficiently shut the window. "Now we know," she told us, "the White Ghosts can hear Chinese. They have learned it. You mustn't talk in front of them again. Someday, very soon, we're going home, where there are Han people everywhere. We'll buy furniture then, real tables and chairs. You children will smell flowers for the first time."

"Mother! Mother! It's happening again. I taste something in my mouth, but I'm not eating anything."

"Me too, Mother. Me too. There's nothing there. Just my spit. My spit tastes like sugar."

"Your grandmother in China is sending you candy again," said my mother. Human beings do not need Mail Ghosts to send messages.

I must have tinkered too much wondering how my invisible grandmother, illiterate and dependent on letter writers, could give us candy free. When I got older and more scientific, I received no more gifts from her. She died, and I did not get "home" to ask her how she did it. Whenever my parents said "home," they suspended America. They suspended enjoyment, but I did not want to go to China. In China my parents would sell my sisters and me. My father would marry two or three more wives, who would spatter cooking oil on our bare toes and lie that we were crying for naughtiness. They would give food to their own children and rocks to us. I did not want to go where the ghosts took shapes nothing like our own.

As a child I feared the size of the world. The farther away the sound of howling dogs, the farther away the sound of the trains, the tighter I curled myself under the quilt. The trains sounded deeper and deeper into the night. They had not reached the end of the world before I stopped hearing them, the last long moan diminishing toward China. How large the world must be to make my grandmother only a taste by the time she reaches me.

When I last visited my parents, I had trouble falling asleep, too big for the hills and valleys scooped in the mattress by child-bodies. I heard my mother come in. I stopped moving. What did she want? Eyes shut, I pictured my mother, her white hair frizzy in the dark-and-light doorway, my hair white now too, Mother. I could hear her move furniture about. Then she dragged a third quilt, the thick, homemade Chinese kind, across me. After that I lost track of her location. I spied from beneath my eyelids and had to hold back a jump. She had pulled up a chair and was sitting by the bed next to my head. I could see her strong hands in her lap, not working fourteen pairs of needles. She is very proud of her hands, which can make anything and stay pink and soft while my father's became like carved wood. Her palm lines do not branch into head, heart, and life lines like other people's but crease with just one atavistic fold. That night she was a sad bear; a great sheep in a wool shawl. She recently took to wearing shawls and granny glasses, American fashions. What did she want, sitting there so large next to my head? I could feel her stare – her eyes two lights warm on my graying hair, then on the creases at the sides of my mouth, my thin neck, my thin cheeks, my thin arms. I felt her sight warm each of my bony elbows, and I flopped about in my fake sleep to hide them from her criticism. She sent light at full brightness beaming through my eyelids, her eyes at my eyes, and I had to open them.

"What's the matter, Mama? Why are you sitting there?"

She reached over and switched on a lamp she had placed on the floor beside her. "I swallowed that LSD pill you left on the kitchen counter," she announced.

"That wasn't LSD, Mama. It was just a cold pill. I have a cold."

"You're always catching colds when you come home. You must be eating too much *yin*. Let me get you another quilt."

"No, no more quilts. You shouldn't take pills that aren't prescribed for you. 'Don't eat pills you find on the curb,' you always told us."

"You children never tell me what you're really up to. How else am I going to find out what you're really up to?" As if her head hurt, she closed her eyes behind the gold wire rims.

"Aiaa," she sighed, "how can I bear to have you leave me again?"

How can I bear to leave her again? She would close up this room, open temporarily for me, and wander about cleaning and cleaning the shrunken house, so tidy since our leaving. Each chair has its place now. And the sinks in the bedrooms work, their alcoves no longer stuffed with laundry right up to the ceiling. My mother has put the clothes and shoes into boxes, stored against hard times. The sinks had been built of gray marble for the old Chinese men who boarded here before we came. I used to picture modest little old men washing in the mornings and dressing before they shuffled out of these bedrooms. I would have to leave and go again into the world out there which has no marble ledges for my clothes, no quilts made from our own ducks and turkeys, no ghosts of neat little old men.

The lamp gave off the sort of light that comes from a television, which made the high ceiling disappear and then suddenly drop back into place. I could feel that clamping down and see how my mother had pulled the blinds down so low that the bare rollers were showing. No passer-by would detect a daughter in this house. My mother would sometimes be a large animal, barely real in the dark; then she would become a mother again. I could see the wrinkles around her big eyes, and I could see her cheeks sunken without her top teeth.

"I'll be back again soon," I said. "You know that I come back. I think of you when I'm not here."

"Yes, I know you. I know you now. I've always known you. You're the one with the charming words. You have never come back. 'I'll be back on Turkeyday,' you said. Huh."

I shut my teeth together, vocal cords cut, they hurt so. I would not speak words to give her pain. All her children gnash their teeth.

"The last time I saw you, you were still young," she said.

"Now you're old."

"It's only been a year since I visited you."

"That's the year you turned old. Look at you, hair gone gray, and you haven't even fattened up yet. I know how the Chinese talk about us. 'They're so poor,' they say, 'they can't afford to fatten up any of their daughters.' 'Years in America,' they say, 'and they don't eat.' Oh, the shame of it – a whole family of skinny children. And your father – he's so skinny, he's disappearing."

"Don't worry about him, Mama. Doctors are saying that skinny people live longer. Papa's going to live a long time."

"So! I knew I didn't have too many years left. Do you know how I got all this fat? Eating your leftovers. Aiaa, I'm getting so old. Soon you will have no more mother."

"Mama, you've been saying that all my life."

"This time it's true. I'm almost eighty."

"I thought you were only seventy-six."

"My papers are wrong. I'm eighty."

"But I thought your papers are wrong, and you're seventy-two, seventy-three in Chinese years."

"My papers are wrong, and I'm eighty, eighty-one in Chinese years. Seventy. Eighty. What do numbers matter? I'm dropping dead any day now. The aunt down the street was resting on her porch steps, dinner all cooked, waiting for her husband and son to come home and eat it. She closed her eyes for a moment and died. Isn't that a wonderful way to go?"

"But our family lives to be ninety-nine."

"That's your father's family. My mother and father died very young. My youngest sister was an orphan at ten. Our parents were not even fifty."

"Then you should feel grateful you've lived so many extra years."

"I was so sure you were going to be an orphan too. In fact, I'm amazed you've lived to have white hair. Why don't you dye it?"

"Hair color doesn't measure age, Mother. White is just another pigment, like black and brown."

"You're always listening to Teacher Ghosts, those Scientist Ghosts, Doctor Ghosts."

"I have to make a living."

"I never do call you Oldest Daughter. Have you noticed that? I always tell people, 'This is my Biggest Daughter.' "

"Is it true then that Oldest Daughter and Oldest Son died in China? Didn't you tell me when I was ten that she'd have been twenty; when I was twenty, she'd be thirty? Is that why you've denied me my title?"

"No, you must have been dreaming. You must have been making up stories. You are all the children there are."

(Who was that story about — the one where the parents are throwing money at the children, but the children don't pick it up because they're crying too hard? They're writhing on the floor covered with coins. Their parents are going out the door for America, hurling handfuls of change behind them.)

She leaned forward, eyes brimming with what she was about to say: "I work so hard," she said. She was doing her stare — at what? My feet began rubbing together as if to tear each other's skin off. She started talking again, "The tomato vines prickle my hands; I can feel their little stubble hairs right through my gloves. My feet squish-squish in the rotten tomatoes, squish–squish in the tomato mud the feet ahead of me have sucked. And do you know the best way to stop the itch from the tomato hairs? You break open a fresh tomato and wash yourself with it. You cool your face in tomato juice. Oh, but it's the potatoes that will ruin my hands. I'll get rheumatism washing potatoes, squatting over potatoes."

She had taken off the Ace bandages around her legs for the night. The varicose veins stood out.

"Mama, why don't you stop working? You don't have to work anymore. Do you? Do you really have to work like that? Scabbing in the tomato fields?" Her black hair seems filleted with the band of white at its roots. She dyed her hair so that the farmers would hire her. She would walk to Skid Row and stand in line with the hobos, the winos, the junkies, and the Mexicans until the farm buses came and the farmers picked out the workers they wanted. "You have the house," I said. "For food you have Social Security. And urban renewal must have given you something. It was good in a way when they tore down the laundry. Really, Mama, it was. Otherwise Papa would never have retired. You ought to retire too."

"Do you think your father wanted to stop work? Look at his eyes; the brown is going out of his eyes. He has stopped talking. When I go to work, he eats leftovers. He doesn't cook new food," she said, confessing, me maddened at confessions. "Those Urban Renewal Ghosts gave us moving money. It took us seventeen years to get our customers. How could we start all over on moving money, as if we two old people had another seventeen years in us? Aa" – she flipped something aside with her hand – "White Ghosts can't tell Chinese age."

I closed my eyes and breathed evenly, but she could tell I wasn't asleep.

"This is terrible ghost country, where a human being works her life away," she said. "Even the ghosts work, no time for acrobatics. I have not stopped working since the day the ship landed. I was on my feet the moment the babies were out. In China I never even had to hang up my own clothes. I shouldn't have left, but your father couldn't have supported you without me. I'm the one with the big muscles."

"If you hadn't left, there wouldn't have been a me for you two to support. Mama, I'm really sleepy. Do you mind letting me sleep?" I do not believe in old age. I do not believe in getting tired.

"I didn't need muscles in China. I was small in China."

She was. The silk dresses she gave me are tiny. You would not think the same person wore them. This mother can carry a hundred pounds of Texas rice up- and downstairs. She could work at the laundry from 6:30 a.m. until midnight, shifting a baby from an ironing table to a shelf between packages, to the display window, where the ghosts tapped on the glass. "I put you babies in the clean places at the laundry, as far away from the germs that fumed out of the ghosts' clothes as I could. Aa, their socks and handkerchiefs choked me. I cough now because of those seventeen years of breathing dust. Tubercular handkerchiefs. Lepers' socks." I thought she had wanted to show off my baby sister in the display window.

In the midnight unsteadiness we were back at the laundry, and my mother was sitting on an orange crate sorting dirty clothes into mountains − a sheet mountain, a white shirt mountain, a dark shirt mountain, a work-pants mountain, a long underwear mountain, a short underwear mountain, a little hill of socks pinned together in pairs, a little hill of handkerchiefs pinned to tags. Surrounding her were candles she burned in daylight, clean yellow diamonds, footlights that ringed her, mysterious masked mother, nose and mouth veiled with a cowboy handkerchief. Before undoing the bundles, my mother would light a tall new candle, which was a luxury, and the pie pans full of old wax and wicks that sometimes sputtered blue, a noise I thought was the germs getting seared.

"No tickee, no washee, mama-san?" a ghost would say, so embarrassing.

"Noisy Red-Mouth Ghost," she'd write on its package, naming it, marking its clothes with its name.

Back in the bedroom I said, "The candles must have helped. It was a good idea of yours to use candles."

"They didn't do much good. All I have to do is think about dust sifting out of clothes or peat dirt blowing across a field or chick mash falling from a scoop, and I start coughing." She coughed deeply. "See what I mean? I have worked too much. Human beings don't work like this in China. Time goes slower there. Here we have to hurry, feed the hungry children before we're too old to work. I feel like a mother cat hunting for its kittens. She has to find them fast because in a few hours she will forget how to count or that she had any kittens at all. I can't sleep in this country because it doesn't shut down for the night. Factories, canneries, restaurants – always somebody somewhere working through the night. It never gets done all at once here. Time was different in China. One year lasted as long as my total time here; one evening so long, you could visit your women friends, drink tea, and play cards at each house, and it would still be twilight. It even got boring, nothing to do but fan ourselves. Here midnight comes and the floor's not swept, the ironing's not ready, the money's not made. I would still be young if we lived in China."

"Time is the same from place to place," I said unfeelingly. "There is only the eternal present, and biology. The reason you feel time pushing is that you had six children after you were forty-five and you worried about raising us. You shouldn't worry anymore, though, Mama. You should feel good you had so many babies around you in middle age. Not many mothers have that. Wasn't it like prolonging youth? Now wasn't it? You mustn't worry now. All of us have grown up. And you can stop working."

"I can't stop working. When I stop working, I hurt. My head, my back, my legs hurt. I get dizzy. I can't stop."

"I'm like that too, Mama. I work all the time. Don't worry about me starving. I won't starve. I know how to work. I work all the time. I know how to kill food, how to skin and pluck it. I know how to keep warm by sweeping and mopping. I know how to work when things get bad."

"It's a good thing I taught you children to look after

yourselves. We're not going back to China for sure now."

"You've been saying that since nineteen forty-nine."

"Now it's final. We got a letter from the villagers yesterday. They asked if it was all right with us that they took over the land. The last uncles have been killed so your father is the only person left to say it is all right, you see. He has written saying they can have it. So. We have no more China to go home to."

It must be all over then. My mother and father have stoked each other's indignation for almost forty years telling stories about land quarrels among the uncles, the in-laws, the grandparents. Episodes from their various points of view came weekly in the mail, until the uncles were executed kneeling on broken glass by people who had still other plans for the land. How simply it ended – my father writing his permission. Permission asked, permission given twenty-five years after the Revolution.

"We belong to the planet now, Mama. Does it make sense to you that if we're no longer attached to one piece of land, we belong to the planet? Wherever we happen to be standing, why, that spot belongs to us as much as any other spot." Can we spend the fare money on furniture and cars? Will American flowers smell good now?

"I don't want to go back anyway," she said. "I've gotten used to eating. And the Communists are much too mischievous. You should see the ones I meet in the fields. They bring sacks under their clothes to steal grapes and tomatoes from the growers. They come with trucks on Sundays. And they're killing each other in San Francisco." One of the old men caught his visitor, another old fellow, stealing his bantam; the owner spotted its black feet sticking out of his guest's sweater. We woke up one morning to find a hole in the ground where our loquat tree had stood. Later we saw a new loquat tree most similar to ours in a Chinese neighbor's yard. We knew a family who had a sign in their vegetable patch: "Since this is not a Communist garden but cabbages grown by private enterprise, please do not steal from my garden." It was dated and signed in good handwriting.

"The new immigrants aren't Communists, Mother. They're fugitives from the real Communists."

"They're Chinese, and Chinese are mischievous. No, I'm too old to keep up with them. They'd be too clever for me. I've lost my cunning, having grown accustomed to food, you see. There's only one thing that I really want anymore. I want you here, not wandering like a ghost from Romany. I want every one of you living here together. When you're all home, all six of you with your children and husbands and wives, there are twenty or thirty people in this house. Then I'm happy. And your father is happy. Whichever room I walk into overflows with my relatives, grandsons, sons-in-law. I can't turn around without touching somebody. That's the way a house should be." Her eyes are big, inconsolable. A spider headache spreads out in fine branches over my skull. She is etching spider legs into the icy bone. She pries open my head and my fists and crams into them responsibility for time, responsibility for intervening oceans.

The gods pay her and my father back for leaving their parents. My grandmother wrote letters pleading for them to come home, and they ignored her. Now they know how she felt.

"When I'm away from here," I had to tell her, "I don't get sick. I don't go to the hospital every holiday. I don't get pneumonia, no dark spots on my x-rays. My chest doesn't hurt when I breathe. I can breathe. And I don't get headaches at 3:00. I don't have to take medicines or go to doctors. Elsewhere I don't have to lock my doors and keep checking the locks. I don't stand at the windows and watch for movements and see them in the dark."

"What do you mean you don't lock your doors?"

"I do. I do. But not the way I do here. I don't hear ghost

sounds. I don't stay awake listening to walking in the kitchen. I don't hear the doors and windows unhinging."

"It was probably just a Wino Ghost or a Hobo Ghost looking for a place to sleep."

"I don't want to hear Wino Ghosts and Hobo Ghosts. I've found some places in this country that are ghost-free. And I think I belong there, where I don't catch colds or use my hospitalization insurance. Here I'm sick so often, I can barely work. I can't help it, Mama."

She yawned. "It's better, then, for you to stay away. The weather in California must not agree with you. You can come for visits." She got up and turned off the light. "Of course, you must go, Little Dog."

A weight lifted from me. The quilts must be filling with air. The world is somehow lighter. She has not called me that endearment for years – a name to fool the gods. I am really a Dragon, as she is a Dragon, both of us born in dragon years. I am practically a first daughter of a first daughter.

"Good night, Little Dog."

"Good night, Mother."

She sends me on my way, working always and now old, dreaming the dreams about shrinking babies and the sky covered with airplanes and a Chinatown bigger than the ones here.

AT THE WESTERN PALACE

When she was about sixty-eight years old, Brave Orchid took a day off to wait at San Francisco International Airport for the plane that was bringing her sister to the United States. She had not seen Moon Orchid for thirty years. She had begun this waiting at home, getting up a half-hour before Moon Orchid's plane took off in Hong Kong. Brave Orchid would add her will power to the forces that keep an airplane up. Her head hurt with the concentration. The plane had to be light, so no matter how tired she felt, she dared not rest her spirit on a wing but continuously and gently pushed up on the plane's belly. She had already been waiting at the airport for nine hours. She was wakeful.

Next to Brave Orchid sat Moon Orchid's only daughter, who was helping her aunt wait. Brave Orchid had made two of her own children come too because they could drive, but they had been lured away by the magazine racks and the gift shops and coffee shops. Her American children could not sit for very long. They did not understand sitting; they had wandering feet. She hoped they would get back from the pay t.v.'s or the pay toilets or wherever they were spending their money before the plane arrived. If they did not come back soon, she would go look for them. If her son thought he could hide in the men's room, he was wrong.

"Are you all right, Aunt?" asked her niece.

"No, this chair hurts me. Help me pull some chairs together so I can put my feet up."

She unbundled a blanket and spread it out to make a bed for herself. On the floor she had two shopping bags full of canned peaches, real peaches, beans wrapped in taro leaves, cookies, Thermos bottles, enough food for everybody, though only her niece would eat with her. Her bad boy and bad girl were probably sneaking hamburgers, wasting their money. She would scold them.

Many soldiers and sailors sat about, oddly calm, like little boys in cowboy uniforms. (She thought "cowboy" was what you would call a Boy Scout.) They should have been crying hysterically on their way to Vietnam. "If I see one that looks Chinese," she thought, "I'll go over and give him some advice." She sat up suddenly; she had forgotten about her own son, who was even now in Vietnam. Carefully she split her attention, beaming half of it to the ocean, into the water to keep him afloat. He was on a ship. He was in Vietnamese waters. She was sure of it. He and the other children were lying to her. They had said he was in Japan, and then they said he was in the Philippines. But when she sent him her help, she could feel that he was on a ship in Da Nang. Also she had seen the children hide the envelopes that his letters came in.

"Do you think my son is in Vietnam?" she asked her niece, who was dutifully eating.

"No. Didn't your children say he was in the Philippines?"

"Have you ever seen any of his letters with Philippine stamps on them?"

"Oh, yes. Your children showed me one."

"I wouldn't put it past them to send the letters to some Filipino they know. He puts Manila postmarks on them to fool me."

"Yes, I can imagine them doing that. But don't worry. Your son can take care of himself. All your children can take care of themselves."

"Not him. He's not like other people. Not normal at all. He sticks erasers in his ears, and the erasers are still attached to the pencil stubs. The captain will say, 'Abandon ship,' or, 'Watch out for bombs,' and he won't hear.

He doesn't listen to orders. I told him to flee to Canada, but he wouldn't go."

She closed her eyes. After a short while, plane and ship under control, she looked again at the children in uniforms. Some of the blond ones looked like baby chicks, their crew cuts like the downy yellow on baby chicks. You had to feel sorry for them even though they were Army and Navy Ghosts.

Suddenly her son and daughter came running. "Come, Mother. The plane's landed early. She's here already." They hurried, folding up their mother's encampment. She was glad her children were not useless. They must have known what this trip to San Francisco was about then. "It's a good thing I made you come early," she said.

Brave Orchid pushed to the front of the crowd. She had to be in front. The passengers were separated from the people waiting for them by glass doors and walls. Immigration Ghosts were stamping papers. The travelers crowded along some conveyor belts to have their luggage searched. Brave Orchid did not see her sister anywhere. She stood watching for four hours. Her children left and came back. "Why don't you sit down?" they asked.

"The chairs are too far away," she said.

"Why don't you sit on the floor then?"

No, she would stand, as her sister was probably standing in a line she could not see from here. Her American children had no feelings and no memory.

To while away time, she and her niece talked about the Chinese passengers. These new immigrants had it easy. On Ellis Island the people were thin after forty days at sea and had no fancy luggage.

"That one looks like her," Brave Orchid would say.

"No, that's not her."

Ellis Island had been made out of wood and iron. Here everything was new plastic, a ghost trick to lure immigrants into feeling safe and spilling their secrets. Then the Alien Office could send them right back. Otherwise, why did they lock her out, not letting her help her sister answer questions and spell her name? At Ellis Island when the ghost asked Brave Orchid what year her husband had cut off his pigtail, a Chinese who was crouching on the floor motioned her not to talk. "I don't know," she had said. If it weren't for that Chinese man, she might not be here today, or her husband either. She hoped some Chinese, a janitor or a clerk, would look out for Moon Orchid. Luggage conveyors fooled immigrants into thinking the Gold Mountain was going to be easy.

Brave Orchid felt her heart jump – Moon Orchid. "There she is," she shouted. But her niece saw it was not her mother at all. And it shocked her to discover the woman her aunt was pointing out. This was a young woman, younger than herself, no older than Moon Orchid the day the sisters parted. "Moon Orchid will have changed a little, of course," Brave Orchid was saying. "She will have learned to wear western clothes." The woman wore a navy blue suit with a bunch of dark cherries at the shoulder.

"No, Aunt," said the niece. "That's not my mother."

"Perhaps not. It's been so many years. Yes, it is your mother. It must be. Let her come closer, and we can tell. Do you think she's too far away for me to tell, or is it my eyes getting bad?"

"It's too many years gone by," said the niece.

Brave Orchid turned suddenly – another Moon Orchid, this one a neat little woman with a bun. She was laughing at something the person ahead of her in line said. Moon Orchid was just like that, laughing at nothing. "I would be able to tell the difference if one of them would only come closer," Brave Orchid said with tears, which she did not wipe. Two children met the woman with the cherries, and she shook their hands. The other woman was met by a young man. They looked at each other gladly, then walked away side by side.

Up close neither one of those women looked like Moon Orchid at all. "Don't worry, Aunt," said the niece. "I'll know her."

"I'll know her too. I knew her before you did."

The niece said nothing, although she had seen her mother only five years ago. Her aunt liked having the last word.

Finally Brave Orchid's children quit wandering and drooped on a railing. Who knew what they were thinking? At last the niece called out, "I see her! I see her! Mother! Mother!" Whenever the doors parted, she shouted, probably embarrassing the American cousins, but she didn't care. She called out, "Mama! Mama!" until the crack in the sliding doors became too small to let in her voice. "Mama!" What a strange word in an adult voice. Many people turned to see what adult was calling, "Mama!" like a child. Brave Orchid saw an old, old woman jerk her head up, her little eyes blinking confusedly, a woman whose nerves leapt toward the sound anytime she heard "Mama!" Then she relaxed to her own business again. She was a tiny, tiny lady, very thin, with little fluttering hands, and her hair was in a gray knot. She was dressed in a gray wool suit; she wore pearls around her neck and in her earlobes. Moon Orchid *would* travel with her jewels showing. Brave Orchid momentarily saw, like a larger, younger outline around this old woman, the sister she had been waiting for. The familiar dim halo faded, leaving the woman so old, so gray. So old. Brave Orchid pressed against the glass. *That* old lady? Yes, that old lady facing the ghost who stamped her papers without questioning her was her sister. Then, without noticing her family, Moon Orchid walked smiling over to the Suitcase Inspector Ghost, who took her boxes apart, pulling out puffs of tissue. From where she was, Brave Orchid could not see what her sister had chosen to carry across the ocean. She wished her sister would look her way. Brave Orchid thought that if *she* were entering a new country, she would be at the windows. Instead Moon Orchid hovered over the unwrapping, surprised at each reappearance as if she were opening presents after a birthday party.

"Mama!" Moon Orchid's daughter kept calling. Brave Orchid said to her children, "Why don't you call your aunt too? Maybe she'll hear us if all of you call out together." But her children slunk away. Maybe that shame-face they so often wore was American politeness.

"Mama!" Moon Orchid's daughter called again, and this time her mother looked right at her. She left her bundles in a heap and came running. "Hey!" the Customs Ghost yelled at her. She went back to clear up her mess, talking inaudibly to her daughter all the while. Her daughter pointed toward Brave Orchid. And at last Moon Orchid looked at her – two old women with faces like mirrors.

Their hands reached out as if to touch the other's face, then returned to their own, the fingers checking the grooves in the forehead and along the sides of the mouth. Moon Orchid, who never understood the gravity of things, started smiling and laughing, pointing at Brave Orchid. Finally Moon Orchid gathered up her stuff, strings hanging and papers loose, and met her sister at the door, where they shook hands, oblivious to blocking the way.

"You're an old woman," said Brave Orchid.

"Aiaa. *You're* an old woman."

"But you are really old. Surely, you can't say that about me. I'm not old the way you're old."

"But *you* really are old. You're one year older than I am."

"Your hair is white and your face all wrinkled."

"You're so skinny."

"You're so fat."

"Fat women are more beautiful than skinny women."

The children pulled them out of the doorway. One of Brave Orchid's children brought the car from the parking lot, and the other heaved the luggage into the trunk. They put the two old ladies and the niece in the back seat. All the way home − across the Bay Bridge, over the Diablo hills, across the San Joaquin River to the valley, the valley moon so white at dusk − all the way home, the two sisters exclaimed every time they turned to look at each other, "Aiaa! How old!"

Brave Orchid forgot that she got sick in cars, that all vehicles but palanquins made her dizzy. "You're so old," she kept saying. "How did you get so old?"

Brave Orchid had tears in her eyes. But Moon Orchid said, "You look older than I. You *are* older than I," and again she'd laugh. "You're wearing an old mask to tease me." It surprised Brave Orchid that after thirty years she could still get annoyed at her sister's silliness.

Brave Orchid's husband was waiting under the tangerine tree. Moon Orchid recognized him as the brother-in-law in photographs, not as the young man who left on a ship. Her sister had married the ideal in masculine beauty, the thin scholar with the hollow cheeks and the long fingers. And here he was, an old man, opening the gate he had built with his own hands, his hair blowing silver in twilight. "Hello," he said like an Englishman in Hong Kong. "Hello," she said like an English telephone operator. He went to help his children unload the car, gripping the suitcase handles in his bony fingers, his bony wrists locked.

Brave Orchid's husband and children brought everything into the dining room, provisions for a lifetime move heaped all over the floor and furniture. Brave Orchid wanted to have a luck ceremony and then to put things away where they belonged, but Moon Orchid said, "I've got presents for everybody. Let me get them." She opened her boxes again.

Her suitcase lids gaped like mouths; Brave Orchid had better hurry with the luck.

"First I've got shoes for all of you from Lovely Orchid," Moon Orchid said, handing them out to her nieces and nephews, who grimaced at one another. Lovely Orchid, the youngest aunt, owned either a shoe store or a shoe factory in Hong Kong. That was why every Christmas she sent a dozen pairs, glittering with yellow and pink plastic beads, sequins, and turquoise blue flowers. "She must give us the leftovers," Brave Orchid's children were saying in English. As Brave Orchid ran back and forth turning on all the lights, every lamp and bulb, she glared sideways at her children. They would be sorry when they had to walk barefoot through snow and rocks because they didn't take what shoes they could, even if the wrong size. She would put the slippers next to the bathtub on the linoleum floors in winter and trick her lazy children into wearing them.

"May I have some scissors? Oh, where are my scissors?" said Moon Orchid. She slit the heel of a black embroidered slipper and pulled out the cotton – which was entangled with jewels. "You'll have to let me pierce your ears," she told her nieces, rubbing their earlobes. "Then you can wear these." There were earrings with skewers like gold krisses. There was a jade heart and an opal. Brave Orchid interrupted her dashing about to rub the stones against her skin.

Moon Orchid laughed softly in delight. "And look here. Look here," she said. She was holding up a paper warrior-saint, and he was all intricacies and light. A Communist had cut a wisp of black paper into a hero with sleeves like butterflies' wings and with tassels and flags, which fluttered when you breathed on him. "Did someone really cut this out by hand?" the children kept asking. "Really?" The eyebrows and mustache, the fierce wrinkles between the eyes, the face, all were the merest black webs. His open hand had been cut out finger by finger. Through the spaces you could see light and the room and each other. "Oh, there's more. There's more," said Moon Orchid happily. She picked up another paper cutout and blew on it. It was the scholar who always carries a fan; her breath shook its blue feathers. His brush and quill and scrolls tied with ribbon jutted out of lace vases. "And more" – an orange warrior-poet with sword and scroll; a purple knight with doily armor, holes for scales; a wonderful archer on a red horse with a mane like fire; a modern Communist worker with a proud gold hammer; a girl Communist soldier with pink pigtails and pink rifle. "And this is Fa Mu Lan," she said. "She was a woman warrior, and really existed." Fa Mu Lan was green and beautiful, and her robes whirled out as she drew her sword.

"Paper dolls," said Brave Orchid to her children. "I'd have thought you were too old to be playing with dolls." How greedy to play with presents in front of the giver. How impolite ("untraditional" in Chinese) her children were. With a slam of her cleaver, she cracked rock candy into jagged pieces. "Take some," she urged. "Take more." She brought the yellow crystals on a red paper plate to her family, one by one. It was very important that the beginning be sweet. Her children acted as if this eating were a bother. "Oh, all right," they said, and took the smallest slivers. Who would think that children could dislike candy? It was abnormal, not in the nature of children, not human. "Take a big piece," she scolded. She'd make them eat it like medicine if necessary. They were so stupid, surely they weren't adults yet. They'd put the bad mouth on their aunt's first American day; you had to sweeten their noisy barbarous mouths. She opened the front door and mumbled something. She opened the back door and mumbled something.

"What do you say when you open the door like that?" her children used to ask when they were younger.

"Nothing. Nothing," she would answer.

"Is it spirits, Mother? Do you talk to spirits? Are you asking them in or asking them out?"

"It's nothing," she said. She never explained anything that was really important. They no longer asked.

When she came back from talking to the invisibilities, Brave Orchid saw that her sister was strewing the room. The paper people clung flat against the lampshades, the chairs, the tablecloths. Moon Orchid left fans unfolded and dragons with accordion bodies dangling from doorknobs. She was unrolling white silk. "Men are good at stitching roosters," she was pointing out bird embroidery. It was amazing how a person could grow old without learning to put things away.

"Let's put these things away," Brave Orchid said.

"Oh, Sister," said Moon Orchid. "Look what I have for you," and she held up a pale green silk dress lined in wool. "In winter you can look like summer and be warm like summer." She unbuttoned the frogs to show the lining, thick and plaid like a blanket.

"Now where would I wear such a fancy dress?" said Brave Orchid. "Give it to one of the children."

"I have bracelets and earrings for them."

"They're too young for jewelry. They'll lose it."

"They seem very big for children."

"The girls broke six jade bracelets playing baseball. And they can't endure pain. They scream when I squeeze their hands into the jade. Then that very day, they'll break it. We'll put the jewelry in the bank, and we'll buy glass and black wood frames for the silk scrolls." She bundled up the sticks that opened into flowers. "What were you doing carrying these scraps across the ocean?"

Brave Orchid took what was useful and solid into the back bedroom, where Moon Orchid would stay until they decided what she would do permanently. Moon Orchid picked up pieces of string, but bright colors and movements distracted her. "Oh, look at this," she'd say. "Just look at this.

You have carp." She was turning the light off and on in the goldfish tank, which sat in the rolltop desk that Brave Orchid's husband had taken from the gambling house when it shut down during World War II. Moon Orchid looked up at the grandparents' photographs that hung on the wall above the desk. Then she turned around and looked at the opposite wall; there, equally large, were pictures of Brave Orchid and her husband. They had put up their own pictures because later the children would not have the sense to do it.

"Oh, look," said Moon Orchid. "Your pictures are up too. Why is that?"

"No reason. Nothing," said Brave Orchid. "In America you can put up anybody's picture you like."

On the shelf of the rolltop desk, like a mantel under the grandparents' photos, there were bowls of plastic tangerines and oranges, crepe-paper flowers, plastic vases, porcelain vases filled with sand and incense sticks. A clock sat on a white runner crocheted with red phoenixes and red words about how lucky and bright life is. Moon Orchid lifted the ruffles to look inside the pigeon holes. There were also pen trays and little drawers, enough so that the children could each have one or two for their very own. The fish tank took up half the desk space, and there was still room for writing. The rolltop was gone; the children had broken it slat by slat when they hid inside the desk, pulling the top over themselves. The knee hole had boxes of toys that the married children's children played with now. Brave Orchid's husband had padlocked one large bottom cabinet and one drawer.

"Why do you keep it locked?" Moon Orchid asked. "What's in here?"

"Nothing," he said. "Nothing."

"If you want to poke around," said Brave Orchid, "why don't you find out what's in the kitchen drawers so you can help me cook?"

They cooked enough food to cover the dining room and kitchen tables. "Eat!" Brave Orchid ordered. "Eat!" She would not allow anybody to talk while eating. In some families the children worked out a sign language, but here the children spoke English, which their parents didn't seem to hear.

After they ate and cleaned up, Brave Orchid said, "Now! We have to get down to business."

"What do you mean?" said her sister. She and her daughter held one another's hands.

"Oh, no. I don't want to listen to this," said Brave Orchid's husband, and left to read in bed.

The three women sat in the enormous kitchen with the butcher's block and two refrigerators. Brave Orchid had an inside stove in the kitchen and a stove outside on the back porch. All day long the outside stove cooked peelings and gristle into chicken feed. It horrified the children when they caught her throwing scraps of chicken into the chicken feed. Both stoves had been turned off for the night now, and the air was cooling.

"Wait until morning, Aunt," said Moon Orchid's daughter. "Let her get some sleep."

"Yes, I do need rest after traveling all the way from China," she said. "I'm here. You've done it and brought me here." Moon Orchid meant that they should be satisfied with what they had already accomplished. Indeed, she stretched happily and appeared quite satisfied to be sitting in that kitchen at that moment. "I want to go to sleep early because of jet lag," she said, but Brave Orchid, who had never been on an airplane, did not let her.

"What are we going to do about your husband?" Brave Orchid asked quickly. That ought to wake her up.

"I don't know. Do we have to do something?"

"He does not know you're here."

Moon Orchid did not say anything. For thirty years she had been receiving money from him from America. But she had never told him that she wanted to come to the United States. She waited for him to suggest it, but he never did. Nor did she tell him that her sister had been working for years to transport her here. First Brave Orchid had found a Chinese-American husband for her daughter. Then the daughter had come and had been able to sign the papers to bring Moon Orchid over.

"We have to tell him you've arrived," said Brave Orchid.

Moon Orchid's eyes got big like a child's. "I shouldn't be here," she said.

"Nonsense. I want you here, and your daughter wants you here."

"But that's all."

"Your husband is going to have to see you. We'll make him recognize you. Ha. Won't it be fun to see his face? You'll go to his house. And when his second wife answers the door, you say, 'I want to speak to my husband,' and you name his personal name. 'Tell him I'll be sitting in the family room.' Walk past her as if she were a servant. She'll scold him when he comes home from work, and it'll serve him right. You yell at him too."

"I'm scared," said Moon Orchid. "I want to go back to Hong Kong."

"You can't. It's too late. You've sold your apartment. See here. We know his address. He's living in Los Angeles with his second wife, and they have three children. Claim your rights. Those are *your* children. He's got two sons. *You* have two sons. You take them away from her. You become their mother."

"Do you really think I can be a mother of sons? Don't you think they'll be loyal to her, since she gave birth to them?"

"The children will go to their true mother – you," said Brave Orchid. "That's the way it is with mothers and children."

"Do you think he'll get angry at me because I came without telling him?"

"He deserves your getting angry with him. For abandoning you and for abandoning your daughter."

"He didn't abandon me. He's given me so much money. I've had all the food and clothes and servants I've ever wanted. And he's supported our daughter too, even though she's only a girl. He sent her to college. I can't bother him. I mustn't bother him."

"How can you let him get away with this? Bother him. He deserves to be bothered. How dare he marry somebody else when he has you? How can you sit there so calmly? He would've let you stay in China forever. *I* had to send for your daughter, and *I* had to send for you. Urge her," she turned to her niece. "Urge her to go look for him."

"I think you should go look for my father," she said. "I'd like to meet him. I'd like to see what my father looks like."

"What does it matter what he's like?" said her mother. "You're a grown woman with a husband and children of your own. You don't need a father – or a mother either. You're only curious."

"In this country," said Brave Orchid, "many people make their daughters their heirs. If you don't go see him, he'll give everything to the second wife's children."

"But he gives us everything anyway. What more do I have to ask for? If I see him face to face, what is there to say?"

"I can think of hundreds of things," said Brave Orchid. "Oh, how I'd love to be in your place. I could tell him so many things. What scenes I could make. You're so wishy-washy."

"Yes, I am."

"You have to ask him why he didn't come home. Why he turned into a barbarian. Make him feel bad about leaving his mother and father. Scare him. Walk right into his house with your suitcases and boxes. Move right into the bedroom.

Throw her stuff out of the drawers and put yours in. Say, 'I am the first wife, and she is our servant.'"

"Oh, no, I can't do that. I can't do that at all. That's terrible."

"Of course you can. I'll teach you. 'I am the first wife, and she is our servant.' And you teach the little boys to call you Mother."

"I don't think I'd be very good with little boys. Little American boys. Our brother is the only boy I've known. Aren't they very rough and unfeeling?"

"Yes, but they're yours. Another thing I'd do if I were you, I'd get a job and help him out. Show him I could make his life easier; how I didn't need his money."

"He has a great deal of money, doesn't he?"

"Yes, he can do some job the barbarians value greatly."

"Could I find a job like that? I've never had a job."

"You could be a maid in a hotel," Brave Orchid advised. "A lot of immigrants start that way nowadays. And the maids get to bring home all the leftover soap and the clothes people leave behind."

"I would clean up after people, then?"

Brave Orchid looked at this delicate sister. She was such a little old lady. She had long fingers and thin, soft hands. And she had a high-class city accent from living in Hong Kong. Not a trace of village accent remained; she had been away from the village for that long. But Brave Orchid would not relent; her dainty sister would just have to toughen up. "Immigrants also work in the canneries, where it's so noisy it doesn't matter if they speak Chinese or what. The easiest way to find a job, though, is to work in Chinatown. You get twenty-five cents an hour and all your meals if you're working in a restaurant."

If she were in her sister's place, Brave Orchid would have been on the phone immediately, demanding one of those Chinatown jobs. She would make the boss agree that she start work as soon as he opened his doors the next morning. Immigrants nowadays were bandits, beating up store owners and stealing from them rather than working. It must've been the Communists who taught them those habits.

Moon Orchid rubbed her forehead. The kitchen light shined warmly on the gold and jade rings that gave her hands a completeness. One of the rings was a wedding ring. Brave Orchid, who had been married for almost fifty years, did not wear any rings. They got in the way of all the work. She did not want the gold to wash away in the dishwater and the laundry water and the field water. She looked at her younger sister whose very wrinkles were fine. "Forget about a job," she said, which was very lenient of her. "You won't have to work. You just go to your husband's house and demand your rights as First Wife. When you see him, you can say, 'Do you remember me?'"

"What if he doesn't?"

"Then start telling him details about your life together in China. Act like a fortuneteller. He'll be so impressed."

"Do you think he'll be glad to see me?"

"He better be glad to see you."

As midnight came, twenty-two hours after she left Hong Kong, Moon Orchid began to tell her sister that she really was going to face her husband. "He won't like me," she said.

"Maybe you should dye your hair black, so he won't think you're old. Or I have a wig you can borrow. On the other hand, he should see how you've suffered. Yes, let him see how he's made your hair turn white."

These many hours, her daughter held Moon Orchid's hand. The two of them had been separated for five years. Brave Orchid had mailed the daughter's young photograph to a rich and angry man with citizenship papers. He was a tyrant. Mother and daughter were sorry for one another. "Let's not talk about this anymore," said Moon Orchid. "We can plan tomorrow. I want to hear about my grandchildren.

Tell me about them. I have three grandchildren, don't I?" she asked her daughter.

Brave Orchid thought that her niece was like her mother, the lovely, useless type. She had spent so much time trying to toughen up these two. "The children are very smart, Mother," her niece was saying. "The teachers say they are brilliant. They can speak Chinese and English. They'll be able to talk to you."

"My children can talk to you too," said Brave Orchid. "Come. Talk to your aunt," she ordered.

Her sons and daughters mumbled and disappeared – into the bathroom, the basement, the various hiding places they had dug throughout the house. One of them locked herself in the pantry-storeroom, where she had cleared off a shelf for a desk among the food. Brave Orchid's children were antisocial and secretive. Ever since they were babies, they had burrowed little nests for themselves in closets and underneath stairs; they made tents under tables and behind doors. "My children are also very bright," she said. "Let me show you before you go to sleep." She took her sister to the living room where she had a glass case, a large upside-down fish tank, and inside were her children's athletic trophies and scholarship trophies. There was even a beauty contest trophy. She had decorated them with runners about luck.

"Oh my, isn't that wonderful?" said the aunt. "You must be so proud of them. Your children must be so smart." The children who were in the living room groaned and left. Brave Orchid did not understand why they were ashamed of the things they could do. It was hard to believe that they could do the things the trophies said they did. Maybe they had stolen them from the real winners. Maybe they had bought cups and medallions and pretended they'd won them. She'd have to accuse them and see how they reacted. Perhaps they fooled the Ghost Teachers and Ghost Coaches, who couldn't tell smart Chinese from dumb Chinese. Her children certainly didn't seem like much.

She made some of the children sleep on the floor and put Moon Orchid and her daughter in their room. "Will my mother be living at your house or my house?" her niece asked Brave Orchid.

"She's going to live with her own husband." Brave Orchid was firm. She would not forget about this subject in the morning.

The next day, immediately after breakfast, Brave Orchid talked about driving to Los Angeles. They would not take the coast route along mountainsides that dropped into the sea – the way her children, who liked carnival rides, would want to go. She would make them take the inland route, flat and direct.

"The first thing you've got to ask your husband," she said, "is why he never came back to China when he got rich."

"All right," said Moon Orchid. She was poking about the house, holding cans up to her ear, trailing after the children.

"He probably has a car," Brave Orchid persisted. "He can drive you places. Should he tell you to go away, turn around at the door and say, 'May I come and watch your television now and then?' Oh, wouldn't that be pathetic? But he won't kick you out. No, he won't. You walk right into the bedroom, and you open the second wife's closet. Take whatever clothes you like. That will give you an American wardrobe."

"Oh, I can't do that."

"You can! You can! Take First Sister-in-Law as your example." Their only brother had had a first wife in the village, but he took a second wife in Singapore, where he had gone to make his gold. Big Wife suffered during the Revolution. "The Communists will kill me," she wrote to her husband, "and you're having fun in Singapore." Little Wife felt so sorry for her, she reminded her husband that he owed it to Big Wife to get her out of China before it was too late. Little Wife saved the passage fare and did the paper work. But when Big Wife came, she chased Little Wife out of the house. There was nothing for their husband to do but build a second house, one for each wife and the children of each wife. They did get together, however, for yearly family portraits. Their sons' first and second wives were also in the pictures, first wives next to the husbands and second wives standing among the children. "Copy our sister-in-law," Brave Orchid instructed. "Make life unbearable for the second wife, and she'll leave. He'll have to build her a second house."

"I wouldn't mind if she stays," said Moon Orchid. "She can comb my hair and keep house. She can wash the dishes and serve our meals. And she can take care of the little boys." Moon Orchid laughed. Again it occurred to Brave Orchid that her sister wasn't very bright, and she had not gotten any smarter in the last thirty years.

"You must make it plain to your husband right at the start what you expect of him. That is what a wife is for – to scold her husband into becoming a good man. Tell him there will be no third wife. Tell him you may go visiting anytime you please. And I, the big sister, may visit your house for as long as I please. Let him know exactly how much money you expect for allowance."

"Should I ask for more or less money now that I'm here?"

"More, of course. Food costs more here. Tell him that your daughter, who is the oldest, must inherit his property. You have to establish these things at the start. Don't begin meek."

Sometimes Moon Orchid seemed to listen too readily – as if her sister were only talking-story. "Have you seen him in all these years?" she asked Brave Orchid.

"No. The last time I saw him was in China – with you. What a terrible, ugly man he must be not to send for you. I'll bet he's hoping you'd be satisfied with his money. How evil he is. You've had to live like a widow for thirty years. You're lucky he didn't have his second wife write you telling you he's dead."

"Oh, no, he wouldn't do that."

"Of course not. He would be afraid of cursing himself."

"But if he is so ugly and mean, maybe I shouldn't bother with him."

"I remember him," said her daughter. "He wrote me a nice letter."

"You can't remember him," said her mother. "You were an infant when he left. He never writes letters; he only sends money orders."

Moon Orchid hoped that the summer would wear away while her sister talked, that Brave Orchid would then find autumn too cold for travel. Brave Orchid did not enjoy traveling. She found it so nauseating that she was still recovering from the trip to San Francisco. Many of the children were home for the summer, and Moon Orchid tried to figure out which one was which. Brave Orchid had written about them in her letters, and Moon Orchid tried to match them up with the descriptions. There was indeed an oldest girl who was absent-minded and messy. She had an American name that sounded like "Ink" in Chinese. "Ink!" Moon Orchid called out; sure enough, a girl smeared with ink said, "Yes?" Then Brave Orchid worried over a daughter who had the mark of an unlucky woman; yes, there was certainly a girl with an upper lip as curled as Brigitte Bardot's. Moon Orchid rubbed this niece's hands and cold feet. There was a boy Brave Orchid said was thick headed. She had written that when he crawled as a baby his head was so heavy he kept dropping it on the floor. Moon Orchid did indeed see a boy whose head was big, his curls enlarging it, his eyebrows thick and slanted like an opera warrior's. Moon Orchid could not tell whether he was any less quick than the others. None of them was articulate or friendly. Brave Orchid had written about a boy whose oddity it was to stick pencil stubs in his ears. Moon Orchid sneaked up on the boys and lifted their hair to look for pencil stubs. "He hangs upside down from the furniture like a bat," his mother wrote. "And he doesn't obey." Moon Orchid didn't find a boy who looked like a bat, and no stubs, so decided that that boy must be the one in Vietnam. And the nephew with the round face and round eyes was the "inaccessible cliff." She immediately recognized the youngest girl, "the raging billows." "Stop following me around!" she shouted at her aunt. "Quit hanging over my neck!"

"What are you doing?" Moon Orchid would ask. "What are you reading?"

"Nothing!" this girl would yell. "You're breathing on me. Don't breathe on me."

It took Moon Orchid several weeks to figure out just how many children there were because some only visited and did not live at home. Some seemed to be married and had children of their own. The babies that spoke no Chinese at all, she decided, were the grandchildren.

None of Brave Orchid's children was happy like the two real Chinese babies who died. Maybe what was wrong was that they had no Oldest Son and no Oldest Daughter to guide them. "I don't see how any of them could support themselves," Brave Orchid said. "I don't see how anybody could want to marry them." Yet, Moon Orchid noticed, some of them seemed to have a husband or a wife who found them bearable.

"They'll never learn how to work," Brave Orchid complained.

"Maybe they're still playing," said Moon Orchid, although they didn't act playful.

"Say good morning to your aunt," Brave Orchid would order, although some of them were adults. "Say good morning to your aunt," she commanded every morning.

"Good morning, Aunt," they said, turning to face her, staring directly into her face. Even the girls stared at her — like cat-headed birds. Moon Orchid jumped and squirmed when they did that. They looked directly into her eyes as if they were looking for lies. Rude. Accusing. They never lowered their gaze; they hardly blinked.

"Why didn't you teach your girls to be demure?" she ventured.

"Demure!" Brave Orchid yelled. "They *are* demure. They're so demure, they barely talk."

It was true that the children made no conversation. Moon Orchid would try to draw them out. They must have many interesting savage things to say, raised as they'd been in the wilderness. They made rough movements, and their accents were not American exactly, but peasant like their mother's, as if they had come from a village deep inside China. She never saw the girls wear the gowns she had given them. The young, raging one, growled in her sleep, "Leave me alone." Sometimes when the girls were reading or watching television, she crept up behind them with a comb and tried to smooth their hair, but they shook their heads, and they turned and fixed her with those eyes. She wondered what they thought and what they saw when they looked at her like that. She liked coming upon them from the back to avoid being looked at. They were like animals the way they stared.

She hovered over a child who was reading, and she pointed at certain words. "What's that?" she tapped at a section that somebody had underlined or annotated. If the child was being patient, he said, "That's an important part."

"Why is it important?"

"Because it tells the main idea here."

"What's the main idea?"

"I don't know the Chinese words for it."

"They're so clever," Moon Orchid would exclaim. "They're so smart. Isn't it wonderful they know things that can't be said in Chinese?"

"Thank you," the child said. When she complimented them, they agreed with her! Not once did she hear a child deny a compliment.

"You're pretty," she said.

"Thank you, Aunt," they answered. How vain. She marveled at their vanity.

"You play the radio beautifully," she teased, and sure enough, they gave one another puzzled looks. She tried all kinds of compliments, and they never said, "Oh, no, you're too kind. I can't play it at all. I'm stupid. I'm ugly." They were capable children; they could do servants' work. But they were not modest.

"What time is it?" she asked, testing what kinds of minds they had, raised away from civilization. She discovered they could tell time very well. And they knew the Chinese words for "thermometer" and "library."

She saw them eat undercooked meat, and they smelled like cow's milk. At first she thought they were so clumsy, they spilled it on their clothes. But soon she decided they themselves smelled of milk. They were big and smelled of milk; they were young and had white hair.

When Brave Orchid screamed at them to dress better, Moon Orchid defended them, sweet wild animals that they were. "But they enjoy looking like furry animals. That's it, isn't it? You enjoy looking like wild animals, don't you?"

"I don't look like a wild animal!" the child would yell like its mother.

"Like an Indian, then. Right?"

"No!"

Moon Orchid stroked their poor white hair. She tugged at their sleeves and poked their shoulders and stomachs.

It was as if she were seeing how much it took to provoke a savage.

"Stop poking me!" they would roar, except for the girl with the cold hands and feet.

"Mm," she mused. "Now the child is saying, 'Stop poking me.'"

Brave Orchid put her sister to work cleaning and sewing and cooking. Moon Orchid was eager to work, roughing it in the wilderness. But Brave Orchid scolded her, "Can't you go any faster than that?" It infuriated Brave Orchid that her sister held up each dish between thumb and forefinger, squirted detergent on the back and front, and ran water without plugging up the drain. Moon Orchid only laughed when Brave Orchid scolded, "Oh, stop that with the dishes. Here. Take this dress and hem it." But Moon Orchid immediately got the thread tangled and laughed about that.

In the mornings Brave Orchid and her husband arose at 6 a.m. He drank a cup of coffee and walked downtown to open up the laundry. Brave Orchid made breakfast for the children who would take the first laundry shift; the ones going to summer school would take the afternoon and night shifts. She put her husband's breakfast into the food container that she had bought in Chinatown, one dish in each tier of the stack. Some mornings Brave Orchid brought the food to the laundry, and other days she sent it with one of the children, but the children let the soup slosh out when they rode over bumps on their bikes. They dangled the tiers from one handlebar and the rice kettle from the other. They were too lazy to walk. Now that her sister and niece were visiting, Brave Orchid went to the laundry later. "Be sure you heat everything up before serving it to your father," she yelled after her son. "And make him coffee after breakfast. And wash the dishes." He would eat with his father and start work.

She walked her sister and niece to the laundry by way of Chinatown. Brave Orchid pointed out the red, green, and gold Chinese school. From the street they could hear children's voices singing the lesson "I Am a Person of the Middle Nation." In front of one of the benevolent associations, a literate man was chanting the *Gold Mountain News*, which was taped to the window. The listening crowd looked at the pictures and said, "Aiaa."

"So this is the United States," Moon Orchid said. "It certainly looks different from China. I'm glad to see the Americans talk like us."

Brave Orchid was again startled at her sister's denseness. "These aren't the Americans. These are the overseas Chinese."

By the time they got to the laundry, the boiler was screaming hot and the machines were ready. "Don't touch or lean against any machine," Brave Orchid warned her sister. "Your skin would fry and peel off." In the midst of the presses stood the sleeve machine, looking like twin silver spaceships. Brave Orchid's husband fitted the shirt sleeves over it with a karate chop between the shoulder blades. "You mustn't back into that," said Brave Orchid.

"You should start off with an easy job," she said. But all the jobs seemed hard for Moon Orchid, who was wearing stockings and dress shoes and a suit. The buttons on the presses seemed too complicated for her to push – and what if she caught her hands or her head inside a press? She was already playing with the water jets dancing on springs from the ceiling. She could fold towels, Brave Orchid decided, and handkerchiefs, but there would be no clean dry clothes until afternoon. Already the temperature was going up.

"Can you iron?" Brave Orchid asked. Perhaps her sister could do the hand-finishing on the shirts when they came off the machines. This was usually Brave Orchid's husband's job. He had such graceful fingers, so good for folding shirts to fit the cardboard patterns that he had cut from campaign posters and fight and wrestling posters. He finished the shirts with a blue band around each.

"Oh, I'd love to try that," Moon Orchid said. Brave Orchid gave her sister her husband's shirts to practice on. She showed her how family clothes were marked with the ideograph "middle," which is a box with a line through its center. Moon Orchid tugged at the first shirt for half an hour, and she folded it crooked, the buttonholes not lined up with the buttons at all. When a customer came in, her ironing table next to the little stand with the tickets, she did not say "hello" but giggled, leaving the iron on the shirt until it turned yellow and had to be whitened with peroxide. Then she said it was so hot she couldn't breathe.

"Go take a walk," Brave Orchid said, exasperated. Even the children could work. Both girls and boys could sew. "Free Mending and Buttons," said the lettering on the window. The children could work all of the machines, even when they were little and had to stand on apple crates to reach them.

"Oh, I can't go out into Gold Mountain myself," Moon Orchid said.

"Walk back toward Chinatown," suggested Brave Orchid.

"Oh, come with me, please," Moon Orchid said.

"I have to work," said her sister. Brave Orchid placed an apple crate on the sidewalk in front of the laundry. "You sit out here in the cool air until I have a little time." She hooked the steel pole to the screw that unrolled the awning. "Just keep turning until the shadow covers the crate." It took Moon Orchid another half-hour to do this. She rested after every turn and left the pole hanging.

At noon, when the temperature inside reached one hundred and eleven degrees, Brave Orchid went out to the sidewalk and said, "Let's eat." She had heated the leftovers from breakfast on the little stove at the back of the laundry. In back there was also a bedroom for the nights when they finished packaging too tired to walk home. Then five or six people would crowd into the bed together. Some slept on the ironing tables, and the small children slept on the shelves. The shades would be pulled over the display windows and the door. The laundry would become a cozy new home, almost safe from the night footsteps, the traffic, the city outside. The boiler would rest, and no ghost would know there were Chinese asleep in their laundry. When the children were sick and had to stay home from school, they slept in that bedroom so that Brave Orchid could doctor them. The children said that the boiler, jumping up and down, bursting steam, flames shooting out the bottom, matched their dreams when they had a fever.

After lunch, Brave Orchid asked her husband if he and the children could handle the laundry by themselves. She wanted to take Moon Orchid out for some fun. He said that the load was unusually light today.

The sisters walked back to Chinatown. "We're going to get some more to eat," said Brave Orchid. Moon Orchid accompanied her to a gray building with a large storefront room, overhead fans turning coolly and cement floor cool underfoot. Women at round tables were eating black seaweed gelatin and talking. They poured Karo syrup on top of the black quivering mass. Brave Orchid seated Moon Orchid and dramatically introduced her, "This is my sister who has come to Gold Mountain to reclaim her husband." Many of the women were fellow villagers; others might as well have been villagers, together so long in California.

"Marvelous. You could blackmail him," the women advised. "Have him arrested if he doesn't take you back."

"Disguise yourself as a mysterious lady and find out how bad he is."

"You've got to do some husband beating, that's what you've got to do."

They were joking about her. Moon Orchid smiled and tried to think of a joke too. The large proprietress in a butcher's apron came out of the kitchen lugging tubs full of more black gelatin. Standing over the tables and smoking a cigarette, she watched her customers eat. It was so cool here, black and light-yellow and brown, and the gelatin was so cool. The door was open to the street, no passers-by but Chinese, though at the windows the venetian blinds slitted the sunlight as if everyone were hiding. Between helpings the women sat back, waving fans made out of silk, paper, sandalwood, and pandanus fronds. They were like rich women in China with nothing to do.

"Game time," said the proprietress, clearing the tables. The women had only been taking a break from their gambling. They spread ringed hands and mixed the ivory tiles click-clack for the next hemp-bird game. "It's time to go," said Brave Orchid, leading her sister outside. "When you come to America, it's a chance to forget some of the bad Chinese habits. A person could get up one day from the gambling table and find her life over." The gambling women were already caught up in their game, calling out good-byes to the sisters.

They walked past the vegetable, fish, and meat markets – not as abundant as in Canton, the carp not as red, the turtles not as old – and entered the cigar and seed shop. Brave Orchid filled her sister's thin hands with carrot candy, melon candy, and sheets of beef jerky. Business was carried out at one end of the shop, which was long and had benches against two walls. Rows of men sat smoking. Some of them stopped gurgling on their silver or bamboo water pipes to greet the sisters. Moon Orchid remembered many of them from the village; the cigar store owner, who looked like a camel, welcomed her. When Brave Orchid's children were young, they thought he was the Old Man of the North, Santa Claus.

As they walked back to the laundry, Brave Orchid showed her sister where to buy the various groceries and how to avoid Skid Row. "On days when you are not feeling safe, walk around it. But you can walk through it unharmed on your strong days." On weak days you notice bodies on the sidewalk, and you are visible to Panhandler Ghosts and Mugger Ghosts.

Brave Orchid and her husband and children worked hardest in the afternoon when the heat was the worst, all the machines hissing and thumping. Brave Orchid did teach her sister to fold the towels. She placed her at the table where the fan blew most. But finally she sent one of the children to walk her home.

From then on Moon Orchid only visited the laundry late in the day when the towels came out of the dryers. Brave Orchid's husband had to cut a pattern from cardboard so Moon Orchid could fold handkerchiefs uniformly. He gave her a shirt cardboard to measure the towels. She never could work any faster than she did on the first day.

The summer days passed while they talked about going to find Moon Orchid's husband. She felt she accomplished a great deal by folding towels. She spent the evening observing the children. She liked to figure them out. She described them aloud. "Now they're studying again. They read so much. Is it because they have enormous quantities to learn, and they're trying not to be savages? He is picking up his pencil and tapping it on the desk. Then he opens his book to page 168. His eyes begin to read. His eyes go back and forth. They go from left to right, from left to right." This makes her laugh. "How wondrous – eyes reading back and forth. Now he's writing his thoughts down. What's *that* thought?" she asked, pointing.

She followed her nieces and nephews about. She bent over them. "Now she is taking a machine off the shelf. She attaches two metal spiders to it. She plugs in the cord.

She cracks an egg against the rim and pours the yolk and white out of the shell into the bowl. She presses a button, and the spiders spin the eggs. What are you making?"

"Aunt, please take your finger out of the batter."

"She says, 'Aunt, please take your finger out of the batter,'" Moon Orchid repeated as she turned to follow another niece walking through the kitchen. "Now what's this one doing? Why, she's sewing a dress. She's going to try it on." Moon Orchid would walk right into the children's rooms while they were dressing. "Now she must be looking over her costumes to see which one to wear." Moon Orchid pulled out a dress. "This is nice," she suggested. "Look at all the colors."

"No, Aunt. That's the kind of dress for a party. I'm going to school now."

"Oh, she's going to school now. She's choosing a plain blue dress. She's picking up her comb and brush and shoes, and she's going to lock herself up in the bathroom. They dress in bathrooms here." She pressed her ear against the door. "She's brushing her teeth. Now she's coming out of the bathroom. She's wearing the blue dress and a white sweater. She's combed her hair and washed her face. She looks in the refrigerator and is arranging things between slices of bread. She's putting an orange and cookies in a bag. Today she's taking her green book and her blue book. And tablets and pencils. Do you take a dictionary?" Moon Orchid asked.

"No," said the child, rolling her eyeballs up and exhaling loudly. "We have dictionaries at school," she added before going out the door.

"They have dictionaries at school," said Moon Orchid, thinking this over. "She knows 'dictionary.'" Moon Orchid stood at the window peeping. "Now she's shutting the gate. She strides along like an Englishman."

The child married to a husband who did not speak Chinese translated for him, "Now she's saying that I'm taking a machine off the shelf and that I'm attaching two metal spiders to it. And she's saying the spiders are spinning with legs intertwined and beating the eggs electrically. Now she says I'm hunting for something in the refrigerator and – ha! – I've found it. I'm taking out butter – 'cow oil.' They eat a lot of cow oil,' she's saying."

"She's driving me nuts!" the children told each other in English.

At the laundry Moon Orchid hovered so close that there was barely room between her and the hot presses. "Now the index fingers of both hands press the buttons, and – kalump – the press comes down. But one finger on a button will release it – sssss – the steam lets loose. Sssst – the water squirts." She could describe it so well, you would think she could do it. She wasn't as hard to take at the laundry as at home, though. She could not endure the heat, and after a while she had to go out on the sidewalk and sit on her apple crate. When they were younger the children used to sit out there too during their breaks. They played house and store and library, their orange and apple crates in a row. Passers-by and customers gave them money. But now they were older, they stayed inside or went for walks. They were ashamed of sitting on the sidewalk, people mistaking them for beggars. "Dance for me," the ghosts would say before handing them a nickel. "Sing a Chinese song." And before they got old enough to know better, they'd dance and they'd sing. Moon Orchid sat out there by herself.

Whenever Brave Orchid thought of it, which was everyday, she said, "Are you ready to go see your husband and claim what is yours?"

"Not today, but soon," Moon Orchid would reply.

But one day in the middle of summer, Moon Orchid's daughter said, "I have to return to my family. I promised my husband and children I'd only be gone a few weeks. I should return this week." Moon Orchid's daughter lived in Los Angeles.

"Good!" Brave Orchid exclaimed. "We'll all go to Los Angeles. You return to your husband, and your mother returns to hers. We only have to make one trip."

"You ought to leave the poor man alone," said Brave Orchid's husband. "Leave him out of women's business."

"When your father lived in China," Brave Orchid told the children, "he refused to eat pastries because he didn't want to eat the dirt the women kneaded from between their fingers."

"But I'm happy here with you and all your children," Moon Orchid said. "I want to see how this girl's sewing turns out. I want to see your son come back from Vietnam. I want to see if this one gets good grades. There's so much to do."

"We're leaving on Friday," said Brave Orchid. "I'm going to escort you, and you will arrive safely."

On Friday Brave Orchid put on her dress-up clothes, which she wore only a few times during the year. Moon Orchid wore the same kind of clothes she wore every day and was dressed up. Brave Orchid told her oldest son he had to drive. He drove, and the two old ladies and the niece sat in the back seat.

They set out at gray dawn, driving between the grape trees, which hunched like dwarfs in the fields. Gnomes in serrated outfits that blew in the morning wind came out of the earth, came up in rows and columns. Everybody was only half awake. "A long time ago," began Brave Orchid, "the emperors had four wives, one at each point of the compass, and they lived in four palaces. The Empress of the West would connive for power, but the Empress of the East was good and kind and full of light. You are the Empress of the East, and the Empress of the West has imprisoned the Earth's Emperor in the Western Palace. And you, the good Empress of the East, come out of the dawn to invade her land and free the Emperor. You must break the strong spell she has cast on him that has lost him the East."

Brave Orchid gave her sister last-minute advice for five hundred miles. All her possessions had been packed into the trunk.

"Shall we go into your house together," asked Brave Orchid, "or do you want to go by yourself?"

"You've got to come with me. I don't know what I would say."

"I think it would be dramatic for you to go by yourself. He opens the door. And there you are – alive and standing on the porch with all your luggage. 'Remember me?' you say. Call him by his own name. He'll faint with shock. Maybe he'll say, 'No. Go away.' But you march right in. You push him aside and go in. Then you sit down in the most important chair, and you take off your shoes because you belong."

"Don't you think he'll welcome me?"

"She certainly wasn't very imaginative," thought Brave Orchid.

"It's against the law to have two wives in this country," said Moon Orchid. "I read that in the newspaper."

"But it's probably against the law in Singapore too. Yet our brother has two, and his sons have two each. The law doesn't matter."

"I'm scared. Oh, let's turn back. I don't want to see him. Suppose he throws me out? Oh, he will. He'll throw me out. And he'll have a right to throw me out, coming here, disturbing him, not waiting for him to invite me. Don't leave me by myself. You can talk louder than I can."

"Yes, coming with you would be exciting. I can charge through the door and say, 'Where is your wife?' And he'll answer, 'Why, she's right here.' And I'll say, 'This isn't your wife. Where is Moon Orchid? I've come to see her. I'm her first sister, and I've come to see that she is being well taken care of.' Then I accuse him of murderous things; I'd have him arrested – and you pop up to his rescue. Or I can take a look at his wife, and I say, 'Moon Orchid, how young you've gotten.' And he'll say, 'This isn't Moon Orchid.' And you come in and say, 'No. I am.' If nobody's home, we'll climb in a window. When they get back we'll be at home; you the hostess, and I your guest. You'll be serving me cookies and coffee. And when he comes in I'll say, 'Well, I see your husband is home. Thank you so much for the visit.' And you say, 'Come again anytime.' Don't make violence. Be routine."

Sometimes Moon Orchid got into the mood. "Maybe I could be folding towels when he comes in. He'll think I'm so clever. I'll get to them before his wife does." But the further they came down the great central valley – green fields changing to fields of cotton on dry, brown stalks, first a stray bush here and there, then thick – the more Moon Orchid wanted to turn back. "No. I can't go through with this." She tapped her nephew on the shoulder. "Please turn back. Oh, you must turn the car around. I should be returning to China. I shouldn't be here at all. Let's go back. Do you understand me?"

"Don't go back," Brave Orchid ordered her son. "Keep going. She can't back out now."

"What do you want me to do? Make up your minds," said the son, who was getting impatient.

"Keep going," said Brave Orchid. "She's come this far, and we can't waste all this driving. Besides, we have to take your cousin back to her own house in Los Angeles. We have to drive to Los Angeles anyway."

"Can I go inside and meet my grandchildren?"

"Yes," said her daughter.

"We'll see them after you straighten out things with your husband," said Brave Orchid.

"What if he hits me?"

"I'll hit *him*. I'll protect you. I'll hit him back. The two of us will knock him down and make him listen." Brave Orchid chuckled as if she were looking forward to a fight. But when she saw how terrified Moon Orchid was, she said, "It won't come to a fight. You mustn't start imagining things. We'll simply walk up to the door. If he answers, you'll say, 'I have decided to come live with you in the Beautiful Nation.' If *she* answers the door, you'll say, 'You must be Little Wife. I am Big Wife.' Why, you could even be generous. 'I'd like to see our husband, please,' you say. I brought my wig," said Brave Orchid. "Why don't you disguise yourself as a beautiful lady? I brought lipstick and powder too. And at some dramatic point, you pull off the wig and say, 'I am Moon Orchid.'"

"That is a terrible thing to do. I'd be so scared. I am so scared."

"I want to be dropped off at my house first," said the niece. "I told my family I'd be home to make lunch."

"All right," said Brave Orchid, who had tried to talk her niece into confronting her father five years ago, but all she had done was write him a letter telling him she was in Los Angeles. He could visit her, or she could visit him if he wanted to see her, she had suggested. But he had not wanted to see her.

When the car stopped in front of her daughter's house, Moon Orchid asked, "May I get out to meet my grandchildren?"

"I told you no," said Brave Orchid. "If you do that you'll stay here, and it'll take us weeks to get up our courage again. Let's save your grandchildren as a reward. You take care of this other business, and you can play with your grandchildren without worry. Besides, you have some children to meet."

"Grandchildren are more wonderful than children."

After they left the niece's suburb, the son drove them to the address his mother had given him, which turned out to be a skyscraper in downtown Los Angeles.

"Don't park in front," said his mother. "Find a side street. We've got to take him by surprise. We mustn't let him spot us ahead of time. We have to catch the first look on his face."

"Yes, I think I would like to see the look on his face."

Brave Orchid's son drove up and down the side streets until he found a parking space that could not be seen from the office building.

"You have to compose yourself," said Brave Orchid to her sister. "You must be calm as you walk in. Oh, this is most dramatic — in broad daylight and in the middle of the city. We'll sit here for a while and look at his building."

"Does he own that whole building?"

"I don't know. Maybe so."

"Oh, I can't move. My knees are shaking so much I won't be able to walk. He must have servants and workers in there, and they'll stare at me. I can't bear it."

Brave Orchid felt a tiredness drag her down. She had to baby everyone. The traffic was rushing, Los Angeles noon-hot, and she suddenly felt carsick. No trees. No birds. Only city. "It must be the long drive," she thought. They had not eaten lunch, and the sitting had tired her out. Movement would strengthen her; she needed movement. "I want you to stay here with your aunt while I scout that building," she instructed her son. "When I come back, we'll work out a plan." She walked around the block. Indeed, she felt that her feet stepping on the earth, even when the earth was covered with concrete, gained strength from it. She breathed health from the air, though it was full of gasoline fumes. The bottom floor of the building housed several stores. She looked at the clothes and jewelry on display, picking out some for Moon Orchid to have when she came into her rightful place.

Brave Orchid rushed along beside her reflection in the glass. She used to be young and fast; she was still fast and felt young. It was mirrors, not aches and pains, that turned a person old, everywhere white hairs and wrinkles. Young people felt pain.

The building was a fine one; the lobby was chrome and glass, with ashtray stands and plastic couches arranged in semicircles. She waited for the elevator to fill before she got in, not wanting to operate a new machine by herself. Once on the sixth floor she searched alertly for the number in her address book.

How clean his building was. The rest rooms were locked, and there were square overhead lights. No windows, though. She did not like the quiet corridors with carpets but no windows. They felt like tunnels. He must be very wealthy. Good. It would serve a rich man right to be humbled. She found the door with his number on it; there was also American lettering on the glass. Apparently this was his business office. She hadn't thought of the possibility of catching him at his job. Good thing she had decided to scout. If they had arrived at his house, they would not have found him. Then they would have had to deal with *her*. And she would have phoned him, spoiled the surprise, and gotten him on her side. Brave Orchid knew how the little wives maneuvered; her father had had two little wives.

She entered the office, glad that it was a public place and she needn't knock. A roomful of men and women looked up from their magazines. She could tell by their eagerness for change that this was a waiting room. Behind a sliding glass partition sat a young woman in a modern nurse's uniform, not a white one, but a light blue pantsuit with white trim. She sat before an elegant telephone and an electric typewriter. The wallpaper in her cubicle was like aluminum foil, a metallic background for a tall black frame around white paint with dashes of red. The wall of the waiting room was covered with burlap, and there were plants in wooden tubs. It was an expensive waiting room. Brave Orchid approved. The patients looked well dressed, not sickly and poor.

"Hello. May I help you?" said the receptionist, parting the glass. Brave Orchid hesitated, and the receptionist took this to mean that she could not speak English. "Just a moment," she said, and went into an inner room. She brought back another woman, who wore a similar uniform except that it was pink trimmed in white. This woman's hair was gathered up into a bunch of curls at the back of her head; some of the curls were fake. She wore round glasses and false eyelashes, which gave her an American look. "Have you an appointment?" she asked in poor Chinese; she spoke less like a Chinese than Brave Orchid's children. "My husband, the doctor, usually does not take drop-in patients," she said. "We're booked up for about a month." Brave Orchid stared at her pink-painted fingernails gesticulating, and thought she probably would not have given out so much information if she weren't so clumsy with language.

"I have the flu," Brave Orchid said.

"Perhaps we can give you the name of another doctor," said this woman, who was her sister-in-law. "This doctor is a brain surgeon and doesn't work with flu." Actually she said, "This doctor cuts brains," a child making up the words as she went along. She wore pink lipstick and had blue eyelids like the ghosts.

Brave Orchid, who had been a surgeon too, thought that her brother-in-law must be a clever man. She herself could not practice openly in the United States because the training here was so different and because she could never learn English. He was smart enough to learn ghost ways. She would have to be clever to outwit him. She needed to retreat and plan some more. "Oh, well, I'll go to another doctor, then," she said, and left.

She needed a new plan to get her sister and brother-in-law together. This nurse-wife was so young, and the office was so rich with wood, paintings, and fancy telephones, that Brave Orchid knew it wasn't because he couldn't get the fare together that he hadn't sent for his old wife. He had abandoned her for this modern, heartless girl. Brave Orchid wondered if the girl knew that her husband had a Chinese wife. Perhaps she should ask her.

But no, she mustn't spoil the surprise by giving any hints. She had to get away before he came out into the corridor, perhaps to go to one of the locked rest rooms. As she walked back to her sister, she noted corners and passageways, broom closets, other offices – ambush spots. Her sister could crouch behind a drinking fountain and wait for him to get thirsty. Waylay him.

"I met his second wife," she said, opening the car door.

"What's she like?" asked Moon Orchid. "Is she pretty?"

"She's very pretty and very young; just a girl. She's his nurse. He's a doctor like me. What a terrible, faithless man. You'll have to scold him for years, but first you need to sit up straight. Use my powder. Be as pretty as you can. Otherwise you won't be able to compete. You do have one advantage, however. Notice he has her be his worker. She is like a servant, so you have room to be the wife. She works at the office; you work at the house. That's almost as good as having two houses. On the other hand, a man's real partner is the hardest worker. You couldn't learn nursing, could you? No, I guess not. It's almost as difficult as doing laundry. What a petty man he turned out to be, giving up responsibility for a pretty face." Brave Orchid reached for the door handle. "Are you ready?"

"For what?"

"To go up there, of course. We're at his office, and I think we ought to be very direct. There aren't any trees to hide you, no grass to soften your steps. So, you walk right into his office. You make an announcement to the patients and the fancy nurses. You say, 'I am the doctor's wife. I'm going to see my husband.' Then you step to the inner door and enter. Don't knock on any doors. Don't listen if the minor wife talks to you. You walk past her without changing pace. When you see him, you say, 'Surprise!' You say, 'Who is that woman out there? She claims to be your wife.' That will give him a chance to deny her on the spot."

"Oh, I'm so scared. I can't move. I can't do that in front of all those people – like a stage show. I won't be able to talk." And sure enough, her voice was fading into a whisper. She was shivering and small in the corner of the seat.

"So. A new plan, then," said Brave Orchid, looking at her son, who had his forehead on the steering wheel. "You," she said. "I want you to go up to his office and tell your uncle that there has been an accident out in the street. A woman's leg has been broken, and she's crying in pain. He'll have to come. You bring him to the car."

"Mother."

"Mm," mused Brave Orchid. "Maybe we ought to put your aunt in the middle of the street, and she can lie down with her leg bent under her." But Moon Orchid kept shaking her head in trembling no's.

"Why don't you push her down in the intersection and pour ketchup on her? I'll run over her a little bit," said her son.

"Stop being silly," she said. "You Americans don't take life seriously."

"Mother, this is ridiculous. This whole thing is ridiculous."

"Go. Do what I tell you," she said.

"I think your schemes will be useless, Mother."

"What do you know about Chinese business?" she said. "Do as I say."

"Don't let him bring the nurse," said Moon Orchid.

"Don't you want to see what she looks like?" asked Brave Orchid. "Then you'll know what he's giving up for you."

"No. No. She's none of my business. She's unimportant."

"Speak in English," Brave Orchid told her son. "Then he'll feel he has to come with you."

She pushed her son out of the car. "I don't want to do this," he said.

"You'll ruin your aunt's life if you don't. You can't understand business begun in China. Just do what I say. Go."

Slamming the car door behind him, he left.

Moon Orchid was groaning now and holding her stomach. "Straighten up," said Brave Orchid. "He'll be here any moment." But this only made Moon Orchid groan louder, and tears seeped out between her closed eyelids.

"You want a husband, don't you?" said Brave Orchid. "If you don't claim him now, you'll never have a husband. Stop crying," she ordered. "Do you want him to see you with your eyes and nose swollen when that young so-called wife wears lipstick and nail polish like a movie star?"

Moon Orchid managed to sit upright, but she seemed stiff and frozen.

"You're just tired from the ride. Put some blood into your cheeks," Brave Orchid said, and pinched her sister's withered face. She held her sister's elbow and slapped the inside of her arm. If she had had time, she would have hit until the black and red dots broke out on the skin; that was the tiredness coming out. As she hit, she kept an eye on the rearview mirror. She saw her son come running, his uncle after him with a black bag in his hand. "Faster. Faster," her son was saying. He opened the car door. "Here she is," he said to his uncle. "I'll see you later." And he ran on down the street.

The two old ladies saw a man, authoritative in his dark western suit, start to fill the front of the car. He had black hair and no wrinkles. He looked and smelled like an American. Suddenly the two women remembered that in China families married young boys to older girls, who baby-sat their husbands their whole lives. Either that or, in this ghost country, a man could somehow keep his youth.

"Where's the accident?" he said in Chinese. "What is this? You don't have a broken leg."

Neither woman spoke. Brave Orchid held her words back. She would not let herself interfere with this meeting after long absence.

"What is it?" he asked. "What's wrong?" These women had such awful faces. "What is it, Grandmothers?"

"Grandmother?" Brave Orchid shouted. "This is your wife. I am your sister-in-law."

Moon Orchid started to whimper. Her husband looked at her. And recognized her. "You," he said. "What are you doing here?"

But all she did was open and shut her mouth without any words coming out.

"Why are you here?" he asked, eyes wide. Moon Orchid covered her face with one hand and motioned no with the other.

Brave Orchid could not keep silent. Obviously he was not glad to see his wife. "I sent for her," she burst out. "I got her name on the Red Cross list, and I sent her the plane ticket. I wrote her every day and gave her the heart to come. I told her how welcome she would be, how her family would welcome her, how her husband would welcome her. I did what you, the husband, had time to do in these last thirty years."

He looked directly at Moon Orchid the way the savages looked, looking for lies. "What do you want?" he asked. She shrank from his stare; it silenced her crying.

"You weren't supposed to come here," he said, the front seat a barrier against the two women over whom a spell of old age had been cast. "It's a mistake for you to be here. You can't belong. You don't have the hardness for this country. I have a new life."

"What about me?" whispered Moon Orchid.

"Good," thought Brave Orchid. "Well said. Said with no guile."

"I have a new wife," said the man.

"She's only your second wife," said Brave Orchid. "This is your real wife."

"In this country a man may have just one wife."

"So you'll get rid of that creature in your office?" asked Brave Orchid.

He looked at Moon Orchid. Again the rude American eyes. "You go live with your daughter. I'll mail you the money I've always sent you. I could get arrested if the Americans knew about you. I'm living like an American." He talked like a child born here.

"How could you ruin her old age?" said Brave Orchid.

"She has had food. She has had servants. Her daughter went to college. There wasn't anything she thought of that she couldn't buy. I have been a good husband."

"You made her live like a widow."

"That's not true. Obviously the villagers haven't stoned her. She's not wearing mourning. The family didn't send her away to work. Look at her. She'd never fit into an American household. I have important American guests who come inside my house to eat." He turned to Moon Orchid, "You can't talk to them. You can barely talk to me."

Moon Orchid was so ashamed, she held her hands over her face. She wished she could also hide her dappled hands. Her husband looked like one of the ghosts passing the car windows, and she must look like a ghost from China. They had indeed entered the land of ghosts, and they had become ghosts.

"Do you want her to go back to China then?" Brave Orchid was asking.

"I wouldn't wish that on anyone. She may stay, but I do not want her in my house. She has to live with you or with her daughter, and I don't want either of you coming here anymore."

Suddenly his nurse was tapping on the glass. So quickly that they might have missed it, he gestured to the old women, holding a finger to his mouth for just a moment: he had never told his American wife that he had a wife in China, and they mustn't tell her either.

"What's happening?" she asked. "Do you need help? The appointments are piling up."

"No. No," he said. "This woman fainted in the street. I'll be up soon."

They spoke to each other in English.

The two old women did not call out to the young woman. Soon she left. "I'm leaving too now," said the husband.

"Why didn't you write to tell her once and for all you weren't coming back and you weren't sending for her?" Brave Orchid asked.

"I don't know," he said. "It's as if I had turned into a different person. The new life around me was so complete; it pulled me away. You became people in a book I had read a long time ago."

"The least you can do," said Brave Orchid, "is invite us to lunch. Aren't you inviting us to lunch? Don't you owe us a lunch? At a good restaurant?" She would not let him off easily.

So he bought them lunch, and when Brave Orchid's son came back to the car, he had to wait for them.

Moon Orchid was driven back to her daughter's house, but though she lived in Los Angeles, she never saw her husband again. "Oh, well," said Brave Orchid. "We're all under the same sky and walk the same earth; we're alive together during the same moment." Brave Orchid and her son drove back north, Brave Orchid sitting in the back seat the whole way.

Several months went by with no letter from Moon Orchid. When she had lived in China and in Hong Kong, she had written every other week. At last Brave Orchid telephoned long distance to find out what was happening. "I can't talk now," Moon Orchid whispered. "They're listening. Hang up quickly before they trace you." Moon Orchid hung up on Brave Orchid before the minutes she had paid for expired.

That week a letter came from the niece saying that Moon Orchid had become afraid. Moon Orchid said that she had overheard Mexican ghosts plotting on her life. She had been creeping along the baseboards and peeping out windows. Then she had asked her daughter to help her find an apartment at the other end of Los Angeles, where she was now hiding. Her daughter visited her every day, but Moon Orchid kept telling her, "Don't come see me because the Mexican ghosts will follow you to my new hiding place. They're watching your house."

Brave Orchid phoned her niece and told her to send her mother north immediately, where there were no Mexicans, she said. "This fear is an illness," she told her niece. "I will cure her." ("Long ago," she explained to her children, "when the emperors had four wives, the wife who lost in battle was sent to the Northern Palace. Her feet would sink little prints into the snow.")

Brave Orchid sat on a bench at the Greyhound station to wait for her sister. Her children had not come with her because the bus station was only a five-block walk from the house. Her brown paper shopping bag against her, she dozed under the fluorescent lights until her sister's bus pulled into the terminal. Moon Orchid stood blinking on the stairs, hanging tightly to the railing for old people. Brave Orchid felt the tears break inside her chest for the old feet that stepped one at a time onto the cold Greyhound cement. Her sister's skin hung loose, like a hollowed frog's, as if she had shrunken inside it. Her clothes bagged, not fitting sharply anymore. "I'm in disguise," she said. Brave Orchid put her arms around her sister to give her body warmth. She held her hand along the walk home, just as they had held hands when they were girls.

The house was more crowded than ever, though some of the children had gone away to school; the jade trees were inside for the winter. Along walls and on top of tables, jade trees, whose trunks were as thick as ankles, stood stoutly, green now and without the pink skin the sun gave them in the spring.

"I am so afraid," said Moon Orchid.

"There is no one after you," said Brave Orchid. "No Mexicans."

"I saw some in the Greyhound station," said Moon Orchid.

"No. No, those were Filipinos." She held her sister's earlobes and began the healing chant for being unafraid. "There are no Mexicans after you," she said.

"I know. I got away from them by escaping on the bus."

"Yes, you escaped on the bus with the mark of the dog on it."

In the evening, when Moon Orchid seemed quieter, her sister probed into the cause of this trouble.

"What made you think anyone was after you?"

"I heard them talking about me. I snuck up on them and heard them."

"But you don't understand Mexican words."

"They were speaking English."

"You don't understand English words."

"This time, miraculously, I understood. I decoded their speech. I penetrated the words and understood what was happening inside."

Brave Orchid tweaked her sister's ears for hours, chanting her new address to her, telling her how much she loved her and how much her daughter and nephews and nieces loved her, and her brother-in-law loved her. "I won't let anything happen to you. I won't let you travel again. You're home. Stay home. Don't be afraid." Tears fell from Brave Orchid's eyes. She had whisked her sister across the ocean by jet and then made her scurry up and down the Pacific coast, back and forth across Los Angeles. Moon Orchid had misplaced herself, her spirit (her "attention," Brave Orchid called it) scattered all over the world. Brave Orchid held her sister's head as she pulled on her earlobe. She would make it up to her. For moments an attentiveness would return to Moon Orchid's face. Brave Orchid rubbed the slender hands, blew on the fingers, tried to stoke up the flickerings. She stayed home from the laundry day after day. She threw out the Thorazine and vitamin B that a doctor in Los Angeles had prescribed. She made Moon Orchid sit in the kitchen sun while she picked over the herbs in cupboards and basement and the fresh plants that grew in the winter garden. Brave Orchid chose the gentlest plants and made medicines and foods like those they had eaten in their village.

At night she moved from her own bedroom and slept beside Moon Orchid. "Don't be afraid to sleep," she said. "Rest. I'll be here beside you. I'll help your spirit find the place to come back to. I'll call it for you; you go to sleep." Brave Orchid stayed awake watching until dawn.

Moon Orchid still described aloud her nieces' and nephews' doings, but now in a monotone, and she no longer interrupted herself to ask questions. She would not go outside, even into the yard. "Why, she's mad," Brave Orchid's husband said when she was asleep.

Brave Orchid held her hand when she appeared vague. "Don't go away, Little Sister. Don't go any further. Come back to us." If Moon Orchid fell asleep on the sofa, Brave Orchid sat up through the night, sometimes dozing in a chair. When Moon Orchid fell asleep in the middle of the bed, Brave Orchid made a place for herself at the foot. She would anchor her sister to this earth.

But each day Moon Orchid slipped further away. She said that the Mexicans had traced her to this house. That was the day she shut the drapes and blinds and locked the doors. She sidled along the walls to peep outside. Brave Orchid told her husband that he must humor his sister-in-law. It was right to shut the windows; it kept her spirit from leaking away. Then Moon Orchid went about the house turning off the lights like during air raids. The house became gloomy; no air, no light. This was very tricky, the darkness a wide way for going as well as coming back. Sometimes Brave Orchid would switch on the lights, calling her sister's name all the while. Brave Orchid's husband installed an air conditioner.

The children locked themselves up in their bedrooms, in the storeroom and basement, where they turned on the lights. Their aunt would come knocking on the doors and say, "Are you all right in there?"

"Yes, Aunt, we're all right."

"Beware," she'd warn. "Beware. Turn off your lights so you won't be found. Turn off the lights before they come for us."

The children hung blankets over the cracks in the door-jambs; they stuffed clothes along the bottoms of doors. "Chinese people are very weird," they told one another.

Next Moon Orchid removed all the photographs, except for those of the grandmother and grandfather, from the shelves, dressers, and walls. She gathered up the family albums. "Hide these," she whispered to Brave Orchid. "Hide these. When they find me, I don't want them to trace the rest of the family. They use photographs to trace you." Brave Orchid wrapped the pictures and the albums in flannel. "I'll carry these far away where no one will find us," she said. When Moon Orchid wasn't looking, she put them at the bottom of a storage box in the basement. She piled old clothes and old shoes on top. "If they come for me," Moon Orchid said, "everyone will be safe."

"We're all safe," said Brave Orchid.

The next odd thing Moon Orchid did was to cry whenever anyone left the house. She held on to them, pulled at their clothes, begged them not to go. The children and Brave Orchid's husband had to sneak out. "Don't let them go," pleaded Moon Orchid. "They will never come back."

"They will come back. Wait and see. I promise you. Watch for them. Don't watch for Mexicans. This one will be home at 3:30. This one at 5:00. Remember who left now. You'll see."

"We'll never see that one again," Moon Orchid wept.

At 3:30 Brave Orchid would remind her, "See? It's 3:30; sure enough, here he comes." ("You children come home right after school. Don't you dare stop for a moment. No candy store. No comic book store. Do you hear?")

But Moon Orchid did not remember. "Who is this?" she'd ask. "Are you going to stay with us? Don't go out tonight. Don't leave in the morning."

She whispered to Brave Orchid that the reason the family must not go out was that "they" would take us in airplanes and fly us to Washington, D.C., where they'd turn us into ashes. Then they'd drop the ashes in the wind, leaving no evidence.

Brave Orchid saw that all variety had gone from her sister. She was indeed mad. "The difference between mad people and sane people," Brave Orchid explained to the children, "is that sane people have variety when they talk-story. Mad people have only one story that they talk over and over."

Every morning Moon Orchid stood by the front door whispering, whispering. "Don't go. The planes. Ashes. Washington, D.C. Ashes." Then, when a child managed to leave, she said, "That's the last time we'll see him again. They'll get him. They'll turn him into ashes."

And so Brave Orchid gave up. She was housing a mad sister who cursed the mornings for her children, the one in Vietnam too. Their aunt was saying terrible things when they needed blessing. Perhaps Moon Orchid had already left this mad old body, and it was a ghost bad-mouthing her children. Brave Orchid finally called her niece, who put Moon Orchid in a California state mental asylum. Then Brave Orchid opened up the windows and let the air and light come into the house again. She moved back into the bedroom with her husband. The children took the blankets and sheets down from the doorjambs and came back into the living room.

Brave Orchid visited her sister twice. Moon Orchid was thinner each time, shrunken to bone. But, surprisingly, she was happy and had made up a new story. She pranced like a child. "Oh, Sister, I am so happy here. No one ever leaves. Isn't that wonderful? We are all women here. Come. I want you to meet my daughters." She introduced Brave Orchid to each inmate in the ward – her daughters. She was especially proud of the pregnant ones. "My dear pregnant daughters." She touched the women on the head, straightened collars, tucked blankets. "How are you today, dear daughter?" "And, you know," she said to Brave Orchid, "we understand one another here. We speak the same language, the very same. They understand me, and I understand them." Sure enough, the women smiled back at her and reached out to touch her as she went by. She had a new story, and yet she slipped entirely away, not waking up one morning.

Brave Orchid told her children they must help her keep their father from marrying another woman because she didn't think she could take it any better than her sister had. If he brought another woman into the house, they were to gang up on her and play tricks on her, hit her, and trip her when she was carrying hot oil until she ran away. "I am almost seventy years old," said the father, "and haven't taken a second wife, and don't plan to now." Brave Orchid's daughters decided fiercely that they would never let men be unfaithful to them. All her children made up their minds to major in science or mathematics.

A SONG FOR A BARBARIAN REED PIPE

What my brother actually said was, "I drove Mom and Second Aunt to Los Angeles to see Aunt's husband who's got the other wife."

"Did she hit him? What did she say? What did he say?"

"Nothing much. Mom did all the talking."

"What did she say?"

"She said he'd better take them to lunch at least."

"Which wife did he sit next to? What did they eat?"

"I didn't go. The other wife didn't either. He motioned us not to tell."

"I would've told. If I was his wife, I would've told. I would've gone to lunch and kept my ears open."

"Ah, you know they don't talk when they eat."

"What else did Mom say?"

"I don't remember. I pretended a pedestrian broke her leg so he would come."

"There must've been more. Didn't Aunt get in one nasty word? She must've said something."

"No, I don't think she said anything. I don't remember her saying one thing."

In fact, it wasn't me my brother told about going to Los Angeles; one of my sisters told me what he'd told her. His version of the story may be better than mine because of its bareness, not twisted into designs. The hearer can carry it tucked away without it taking up much room. Long ago in China, knot-makers tied string into buttons and frogs, and rope into bell pulls. There was one knot so complicated that it blinded the knot-maker. Finally an emperor outlawed this cruel knot, and the nobles could not order it anymore. If I had lived in China, I would have been an outlaw knot-maker.

Maybe that's why my mother cut my tongue. She pushed my tongue up and sliced the frenum. Or maybe she snipped it with a pair of nail scissors. I don't remember her doing it, only her telling me about it, but all during childhood I felt sorry for the baby whose mother waited with scissors or knife in hand for it to cry — and then, when its mouth was wide open like a baby bird's, cut. The Chinese say "a ready tongue is an evil."

I used to curl up my tongue in front of the mirror and tauten my frenum into a white line, itself as thin as a razor blade. I saw no scars in my mouth. I thought perhaps I had had two frena, and she had cut one. I made other children open their mouths so I could compare theirs to mine. I saw perfect pink membranes stretching into precise edges that looked easy enough to cut. Sometimes I felt very proud that my mother committed such a powerful act upon me. At other times I was terrified — the first thing my mother did when she saw me was to cut my tongue.

"Why did you do that to me, Mother?"

"I told you."

"Tell me again."

"I cut it so that you would not be tongue-tied. Your tongue would be able to move in any language. You'll be able to speak languages that are completely different from one another. You'll be able to pronounce anything. Your frenum looked too tight to do those things, so I cut it."

"But isn't 'a ready tongue an evil'?"

"Things are different in this ghost country."

"Did it hurt me? Did I cry and bleed?"

"I don't remember. Probably."

She didn't cut the other children's. When I asked cousins and other Chinese children whether their mothers had cut their tongues loose, they said, "What?"

"Why didn't you cut my brothers' and sisters' tongues?"

"They didn't need it."

"Why not? Were theirs longer than mine?"

"Why don't you quit blabbering and get to work?"

If my mother was not lying she should have cut more, scraped away the rest of the frenum skin, because I have a terrible time talking. Or she should not have cut at all, tampering with my speech. When I went to kindergarten and had to speak English for the first time, I became silent. A dumbness – a shame – still cracks my voice in two, even when I want to say "hello" casually, or ask an easy question in front of the check-out counter, or ask directions of a bus driver. I stand frozen, or I hold up the line with the complete, grammatical sentence that comes squeaking out at impossible length. "What did you say?" says the cab driver, or "Speak up," so I have to perform again, only weaker the second time. A telephone call makes my throat bleed and takes up that day's courage. It spoils my day with self-disgust when I hear my broken voice come skittering out into the open. It makes people wince to hear it. I'm getting better, though. Recently I asked the postman for special-issue stamps; I've waited since childhood for postmen to give me some of their own accord. I am making progress, a little every day.

My silence was thickest – total – during the three years that I covered my school paintings with black paint. I painted layers of black over houses and flowers and suns, and when I drew on the blackboard, I put a layer of chalk on top. I was making a stage curtain, and it was the moment before the curtain parted or rose. The teachers called my parents to school, and I saw they had been saving my pictures, curling and cracking, all alike and black. The teachers pointed to the pictures and looked serious, talked seriously too, but my parents did not understand English. ("The parents and teachers of criminals were executed," said my father.) My parents took the pictures home. I spread them out (so black and full of possibilities) and pretended the curtains were swinging open, flying up, one after another, sunlight underneath, mighty operas.

During the first silent year I spoke to no one at school, did not ask before going to the lavatory, and flunked kindergarten. My sister also said nothing for three years, silent in the playground and silent at lunch. There were other quiet Chinese girls not of our family, but most of them got over it sooner than we did. I enjoyed the silence. At first it did not occur to me I was supposed to talk or to pass kindergarten. I talked at home and to one or two of the Chinese kids in class. I made motions and even made some jokes. I drank out of a toy saucer when the water spilled out of the cup, and everybody laughed, pointing at me, so I did it some more. I didn't know that Americans don't drink out of saucers.

I liked the Negro students (Black Ghosts) best because they laughed the loudest and talked to me as if I were a daring talker too. One of the Negro girls had her mother coil braids over her ears Shanghai-style like mine; we were Shanghai twins except that she was covered with black like my paintings. Two Negro kids enrolled in Chinese school, and the teachers gave them Chinese names. Some Negro kids walked me to school and home, protecting me from the Japanese kids, who hit me and chased me and stuck gum in my ears. The Japanese kids were noisy and tough. They appeared one day in kindergarten, released from concentration camp, which was a tic-tac-toe mark, like barbed wire, on the map.

It was when I found out I had to talk that school became a misery, that the silence became a misery. I did not speak and felt bad each time that I did not speak. I read aloud in first grade, though, and heard the barest whisper with little squeaks come out of my throat. "Louder," said the teacher, who scared the voice away again. The other Chinese girls did not talk either, so I knew the silence had to do with being a Chinese girl.

Reading out loud was easier than speaking because we did not have to make up what to say, but I stopped often, and the teacher would think I'd gone quiet again. I could not understand "I." The Chinese "I" has seven strokes, intricacies. How could the American "I," assuredly wearing a hat like the Chinese, have only three strokes, the middle so straight? Was it out of politeness that this writer left off strokes the way a Chinese has to write her own name small and crooked? No, it was not politeness; "I" is a capital and "you" is lower-case. I stared at that middle line and waited so long for its black center to resolve into tight strokes and dots that I forgot to pronounce it. The other troublesome word was "here," no strong consonant to hang on to, and so flat, when "here" is two mountainous ideographs. The teacher, who had already told me every day how to read "I" and "here," put me in the low corner under the stairs again, where the noisy boys usually sat.

When my second grade class did a play, the whole class went to the auditorium except the Chinese girls. The teacher, lovely and Hawaiian, should have understood about us, but instead left us behind in the classroom. Our voices were too soft or nonexistent, and our parents never signed the permission slips anyway. They never signed anything unnecessary. We opened the door a crack and peeked out, but closed it again quickly. One of us (not me) won every spelling bee, though.

I remember telling the Hawaiian teacher, "We Chinese can't sing 'land where our fathers died.'" She argued with me about politics, while I meant because of curses. But how can I have that memory when I couldn't talk? My mother says that we, like the ghosts, have no memories.

After American school, we picked up our cigar boxes, in which we had arranged books, brushes, and an inkbox neatly, and went to Chinese school, from 5:00 to 7:30 p.m. There we chanted together, voices rising and falling, loud and soft, some boys shouting, everybody reading together, reciting together and not alone with one voice. When we had a memorization test, the teacher let each of us come to his desk and say the lesson to him privately, while the rest of the class practiced copying or tracing. Most of the teachers were men. The boys who were so well behaved in the American school played tricks on them and talked back to them. The girls were not mute. They screamed and yelled during recess, when there were no rules; they had fist-fights. Nobody was afraid of children hurting themselves or of children hurting school property. The glass doors to the red and green balconies with the gold joy symbols were left wide open so that we could run out and climb the fire escapes. We played capture-the-flag in the auditorium, where Sun Yat-sen and Chiang Kai-shek's pictures hung at the back of the stage, the Chinese flag on their left and the American flag on their right. We climbed the teak ceremonial chairs and made flying leaps off the stage. One flag headquarters was behind the glass door and the other on stage right. Our feet drummed on the hollow stage. During recess the teachers locked themselves up in their office with the shelves of books, copybooks, inks from China. They drank tea and warmed their hands at a stove. There was no play supervision. At recess we had the school to ourselves, and also we could roam as far as we could go – downtown, Chinatown stores, home – as long as we returned before the bell rang.

At exactly 7:30 the teacher again picked up the brass bell that sat on his desk and swung it over our heads, while we charged down the stairs, our cheering magnified in the stairwell. Nobody had to line up.

Not all of the children who were silent at American school found voice at Chinese school. One new teacher said each of us had to get up and recite in front of the class, who were to listen. My sister and I had memorized the lesson perfectly. We said it to each other at home, one chanting, one listening. The teacher called on my sister to recite first. It was the first time a teacher had called on the second-born to go first. My sister was scared. She glanced at me and looked away; I looked down at my desk. I hoped that she could do it because if she could, then I would have to. She opened her mouth and a voice came out that wasn't a whisper, but it wasn't a proper voice either. I hoped that she would not cry, fear breaking up her voice like twigs underfoot. She sounded as if she were trying to sing though weeping and strangling. She did not pause or stop to end the embarrassment. She kept going until she said the last word, and then she sat down. When it was my turn, the same voice came out, a crippled animal running on broken legs. You could hear splinters in my voice, bones rubbing jagged against one another. I was loud, though. I was glad I didn't whisper. There was one little girl who whispered.

You can't entrust your voice to the Chinese, either; they want to capture your voice for their own use. They want to fix up your tongue to speak for them. "How much less can you sell it for?" we have to say. Talk the Sales Ghosts down. Make them take a loss.

We were working at the laundry when a delivery boy came from the Rexall drugstore around the corner. He had a pale blue box of pills, but nobody was sick. Reading the label we saw that it belonged to another Chinese family, Crazy Mary's family. "Not ours," said my father. He pointed out the name to the Delivery Ghost, who took the pills back. My mother muttered for an hour, and then her anger boiled over. "That ghost! That dead ghost! How dare he come to the wrong house?" She could not concentrate on her marking and pressing. "A mistake! Huh!" I was getting angry myself. She fumed. She made her press crash and hiss. "Revenge. We've got to avenge this wrong on our future, on our health, and on our lives. Nobody's going to sicken my children and get away with it." We brothers and sisters did not look at one another. She would do something awful, something embarrassing. She'd already been hinting that during the next eclipse we slam pot lids together to scare the frog from swallowing the moon. (The word for "eclipse" is *frog-swallowing-the-moon*.) When we had not banged lids at the last eclipse and the shadow kept receding anyway, she'd said, "The villagers must be banging and clanging very loudly back home in China."

("On the other side of the world, they aren't having an eclipse, Mama. That's just a shadow the earth makes when it comes between the moon and the sun."

"You're always believing what those Ghost Teachers tell you. Look at the size of the jaws!")

"Aha!" she yelled. "You! The biggest." She was pointing at me. "You go to the drugstore."

"What do you want me to buy, Mother?" I said.

"Buy nothing. Don't bring one cent. Go and make them stop the curse."

"I don't want to go. I don't know how to do that. There are no such things as curses. They'll think I'm crazy."

"If you don't go, I'm holding you responsible for bringing a plague on this family."

"What am I supposed to do when I get there?" I said, sullen, trapped. "Do I say, 'Your delivery boy made a wrong delivery'?"

"They know he made a wrong delivery. I want you to make them rectify their crime."

I felt sick already. She'd make me swing stinky censers around the counter, at the druggist, at the customers. Throw dog blood on the druggist. I couldn't stand her plans.

"You get reparation candy," she said. "You say, 'You have tainted my house with sick medicine and must remove the curse with sweetness.' He'll understand."

"He didn't do it on purpose. And no, he won't, Mother. They don't understand stuff like that. I won't be able to say it right. He'll call us beggars."

"You just translate." She searched me to make sure I wasn't hiding any money. I was sneaky and bad enough to buy the candy and come back pretending it was a free gift.

"Mymotherseztagimmesomecandy," I said to the druggist. Be cute and small. No one hurts the cute and small.

"What? Speak up. Speak English," he said, big in his white druggist coat.

"Tatatagimme somecandy."

The druggist leaned way over the counter and frowned. "Some free candy," I said. "Sample candy."

"We don't give sample candy, young lady," he said.

"My mother said you have to give us candy. She said that is the way the Chinese do it."

"What?"

"That is the way the Chinese do it."

"Do what?"

"Do things." I felt the weight and immensity of things impossible to explain to the druggist.

"Can I give you some money?" he asked.

"No, we want candy."

He reached into a jar and gave me a handful of lollipops. He gave us candy all year round, year after year, every time we went into the drugstore. When different druggists or clerks waited on us, they also gave us candy. They had talked us over. They gave us Halloween candy in December, Christmas candy around Valentine's day, candy hearts at Easter, and Easter eggs at Halloween. "See?" said our mother. "They understand. You kids just aren't very brave." But I knew they did not understand. They thought we were beggars without a home who lived in back of the laundry. They felt sorry for us. I did not eat their candy. I did not go inside the drugstore or walk past it unless my parents forced me to. Whenever we had a prescription filled, the druggist put candy in the medicine bag. This is what Chinese druggists normally do, except they give raisins. My mother thought she taught the Druggist Ghosts a lesson in good manners (which is the same word as "traditions").

My mouth went permanently crooked with effort, turned down on the left side and straight on the right. How strange that the emigrant villagers are shouters, hollering face to face. My father asks, "Why is it I can hear Chinese from blocks away? Is it that I understand the language? Or is it they talk loud?" They turn the radio up full blast to hear the operas, which do not seem to hurt their ears. And they yell over the singers that wail over the drums, everybody talking at once, big arm gestures, spit flying. You can see the disgust on American faces looking at women like that. It isn't just the loudness. It is the way Chinese sounds, chingchong ugly, to American ears, not beautiful like Japanese sayonara words with the consonants and vowels as regular as Italian. We make guttural peasant noise and have Ton Duc Thang names you can't remember. And the Chinese can't hear Americans at all; the language is too soft and western music unhearable. I've watched a Chinese audience laugh, visit, talk-story, and holler during a piano recital, as if the musician could not hear them. A Chinese-American, somebody's son, was playing Chopin, which has no punctuation, no cymbals, no gongs. Chinese piano music is five black keys. Normal Chinese women's voices are strong and bossy. We American-Chinese girls had to whisper to make ourselves American-feminine. Apparently we whispered even more softly than the Americans. Once a year the teachers referred my sister and me to speech therapy, but our voices would straighten out, unpredictably normal, for the therapists. Some of us gave up, shook our heads, and said nothing, not one word. Some of us could not even shake our heads. At times shaking my head no is more self-assertion than I can manage. Most of us eventually found some voice, however faltering. We invented an American-feminine speaking personality, except for that one girl who could not speak up even in Chinese school.

She was a year older than I and was in my class for twelve years. During all those years she read aloud but would not talk. Her older sister was usually beside her; their parents kept the older daughter back to protect the younger one. They were six and seven years old when they began school. Although I had flunked kindergarten, I was the same age as most other students in our class; my parents had probably lied about my age, so I had had a head start and came out even. My younger sister was in the class below me; we were normal ages and normally separated. The parents of the quiet girl, on the other hand, protected both daughters. When it sprinkled, they kept them home from school. The girls did not work for a living the way we did. But in other ways we were the same.

We were similar in sports. We held the bat on our shoulders until we walked to first base. (You got a strike only when you actually struck at the ball.) Sometimes the pitcher wouldn't bother to throw to us. "Automatic walk," the other children would call, sending us on our way. By fourth or fifth grade, though, some of us would try to hit the ball. "Easy out," the other kids would say. I hit the ball a couple of times. Baseball was nice in that there was a definite spot to run to after hitting the ball. Basketball confused me because when I caught the ball I didn't know whom to throw it to. "Me. Me," the kids would be yelling. "Over here." Suddenly it would occur to me I hadn't memorized which ghosts were on my team and which were on the other. When the kids said, "Automatic walk," the girl who was quieter than I kneeled with one end of the bat in each hand and placed it carefully on the plate. Then she dusted her hands as she walked to first base, where she rubbed her hands softly, fingers spread. She always got tagged out before second base. She would whisper-read but not talk. Her whisper was as soft as if she had no muscles. She seemed to be breathing from a distance. I heard no anger or tension.

I joined in at lunchtime when the other students, the Chinese too, talked about whether or not she was mute, although obviously she was not if she could read aloud. People told how *they* had tried *their* best to be friendly. *They* said hello, but if she refused to answer, well, they didn't see why they had to say hello anymore. She had no friends of her own but followed her sister everywhere, although people and she herself probably thought I was her friend. I also followed her sister about, who was fairly normal. She was almost two years older and read more than anyone else.

I hated the younger sister, the quiet one. I hated her when she was the last chosen for her team and I, the last chosen for my team. I hated her for her China doll hair cut. I hated her at music time for the wheezes that came out of her plastic flute.

One afternoon in the sixth grade (that year I was arrogant with talk, not knowing there were going to be high school dances and college seminars to set me back), I and my little sister and the quiet girl and her big sister stayed late after school for some reason. The cement was cooling, and the tetherball poles made shadows across the gravel. The hooks at the rope ends were clinking against the poles. We shouldn't have been so late; there was laundry work to do and Chinese school to get to by 5:00. The last time we had stayed late, my mother had phoned the police and told them we had been kidnapped by bandits. The radio stations broadcast our descriptions. I had to get home before she did that again. But sometimes if you loitered long enough in the schoolyard, the other children would have gone home and you could play with the equipment before the office took it away. We were chasing one another through the playground and in and out of the basement, where the playroom and lavatory were. During air raid drills (it was during the Korean War, which you knew about because every day the front page of the newspaper printed a map of Korea with the top part red and going up and down like a window shade), we curled up in this basement. Now everyone was gone. The playroom was army green and had nothing in it but a long trough with drinking spigots in rows. Pipes across the ceiling led to the drinking fountains and to the toilets in the next room. When someone flushed you could hear the water and other matter, which the children named, running inside the big pipe above the drinking spigots. There was one playroom for girls next to the girls' lavatory and one play-room for boys next to the boys' lavatory. The stalls were open and the toilets had no lids, by which we knew that ghosts have no sense of shame or privacy.

Inside the playroom the lightbulbs in cages had already been turned off. Daylight came in x-patterns through the caging at the windows. I looked out and, seeing no one in the schoolyard, ran outside to climb the fire escape upside down, hanging on to the metal stairs with fingers and toes.

I did a flip off the fire escape and ran across the school-yard. The day was a great eye, and it was not paying much attention to me now. I could disappear with the sun; I could turn quickly sideways and slip into a different world. It seemed I could run faster at this time, and by evening I would be able to fly. As the afternoon wore on we could run into the forbidden places – the boys' big yard, the boys' playroom. We could go into the boys' lavatory and look at the urinals. The only time during school hours I had crossed the boys' yard was when a flatbed truck with a giant thing covered with canvas and tied down with ropes had parked across the street. The children had told one another that it was a gorilla in captivity; we couldn't decide whether the sign said "Trail of the Gorilla" or "Trial of the Gorilla." The thing was as big as a house. The teachers couldn't stop us from hysterically rushing to the fence and clinging to the wire mesh. Now I ran across the boys' yard clear to the Cyclone fence and thought about the hair that I had seen sticking out of the canvas. It was going to be summer soon, so you could feel that freedom coming on too.

I ran back into the girls' yard, and there was the quiet sister all by herself. I ran past her, and she followed me into the girls' lavatory. My footsteps rang hard against cement and tile because of the taps I had nailed into my shoes. Her footsteps were soft, padding after me. There was no one in the lavatory but the two of us. I ran all around the rows of twenty-five open stalls to make sure of that. No sisters. I think we must have been playing hide-and-go-seek. She was not good at hiding by herself and usually followed her sister; they'd hide in the same place. They must have gotten separated. In this growing twilight, a child could hide and never be found.

I stopped abruptly in front of the sinks, and she came running toward me before she could stop herself, so that she almost collided with me. I walked closer. She backed away, puzzlement, then alarm in her eyes.

"You're going to talk," I said, my voice steady and normal, as it is when talking to the familiar, the weak, and the small. "I am going to make you talk, you sissy-girl." She stopped backing away and stood fixed.

I looked into her face so I could hate it close up. She wore black bangs, and her cheeks were pink and white. She was baby soft. I thought that I could put my thumb on her nose and push it bonelessly in, indent her face. I could poke dimples into her cheeks. I could work her face around like dough. She stood still, and I did not want to look at her face anymore; I hated fragility. I walked around her, looked her up and down the way the Mexican and Negro girls did when they fought, so tough. I hated her weak neck, the way it did not support her head but let it droop; her head would fall backward. I stared at the curve of her nape. I wished I was able to see what my own neck looked like from the back and sides. I hoped it did not look like hers; I wanted a stout neck. I grew my hair long to hide it in case it was a flower-stem neck. I walked around to the front of her to hate her face some more.

I reached up and took the fatty part of her cheek, not dough, but meat, between my thumb and finger. This close, and I saw no pores. "Talk," I said. "Are you going to talk?" Her skin was fleshy, like squid out of which the glassy blades of bones had been pulled. I wanted tough skin, hard brown skin. I had callused my hands; I had scratched dirt to blacken the nails, which I cut straight across to make stubby fingers. I gave her face a squeeze. "Talk." When I let go, the pink rushed back into my white thumbprint on her skin. I walked around to her side. "Talk!" I shouted into the side of her head. Her straight hair hung, the same all these years, no ringlets or braids or permanents. I squeezed her other cheek. "Are you? Huh? Are you going to talk?" She tried to shake her head, but I had hold of her face. She had no muscles to jerk away. Her skin seemed to stretch. I let go in horror. What if it came away in my hand? "No, huh?" I said, rubbing the touch of her off my fingers. "Say 'No,' then," I said. I gave her another pinch and a twist. "Say 'No.'" She shook her head, her straight hair turning with her head, not swinging side to side like the pretty girls'. She was so neat. Her neatness bothered me. I hated the way she folded the wax paper from her lunch; she did not wad her brown paper bag and her school papers. I hated her clothes – the blue pastel cardigan, the white blouse with the collar that lay flat over the cardigan, the homemade flat, cotton skirt she wore when everybody else was wearing flared skirts. I hated pastels; I would wear black always. I squeezed again, harder, even though her cheek had a weak rubbery feeling I did not like. I squeezed one cheek, then the other, back and forth until the tears ran out of her eyes as if I had pulled them out. "Stop crying," I said, but although she habitually followed me around, she did not obey. Her eyes dripped; her nose dripped. She wiped her eyes with her papery fingers. The skin on her hands and arms seemed powdery-dry, like tracing paper, onion skin. I hated her fingers. I could snap them like breadsticks. I pushed her hands down. "Say 'Hi,'" I said. "'Hi.' Like that. Say your name. Go ahead. Say it. Or are you stupid? You're so stupid, you don't know your own name, is that it? When I say, 'What's your name?' you just blurt it out, O.K.? What's your name?" Last year the whole class had laughed at a boy who couldn't fill out a form because he didn't know his father's name. The teacher sighed, exasperated, and was very sarcastic, "Don't you notice things? What does your mother call him?" she said. The class laughed at how dumb he was not to notice things. "She calls him father of me," he said. Even we laughed, although we knew that his mother did not call his father by name, and a son does not know his father's name. We laughed and were relieved that our parents had had the foresight to tell us some names we could give the teachers. "If you're not stupid," I said to the quiet girl, "what's your name?" She shook her head, and some hair caught in the tears; wet black hair stuck to the side of the pink and white face. I reached up (she was taller than I) and took a strand of hair. I pulled it. "Well, then, let's honk your hair," I said. "Honk. Honk." Then I pulled the other side – "ho-o-n-k" – a long pull; "ho-o-n-n-nk" – a longer pull. I could see her little white ears, like white cutworms curled underneath the hair. "Talk!" I yelled into each cutworm.

I looked right at her. "I know you talk," I said. "I've heard you." Her eyebrows flew up. Something in those black eyes was startled, and I pursued it. "I was walking past your house when you didn't know I was there. I heard you yell in English and in Chinese. You weren't just talking. You were shouting. I heard you shout. You were saying, 'Where are you?' Say that again. Go ahead, just the way you did at home." I yanked harder on the hair, but steadily, not jerking. I did not want to pull it out. "Go ahead. Say, 'Where are you?' Say it loud enough for your sister to come. Call her. Make her come help you. Call her name. I'll stop if she comes. So call. Go ahead."

She shook her head, her mouth curved down, crying. I could see her tiny white teeth, baby teeth. I wanted to grow big strong yellow teeth. "You do have a tongue," I said. "So use it." I pulled the hair at her temples, pulled the tears out of her eyes. "Say, 'Ow,'" I said. "Just 'Ow.' Say, 'Let go.' Go ahead. Say it. I'll honk you again if you don't say, 'Let me alone.' Say, 'Leave me alone,' and I'll let you go. I will. I'll let go if you say it. You can stop this anytime you want to, you know. All you have to do is tell me to stop. Just say, 'Stop.' You're just asking for it, aren't you? You're just asking for another honk. Well then, I'll have to give you another honk. Say, 'Stop.'" But she didn't. I had to pull again and again.

Sounds did come out of her mouth, sobs, chokes, noises that were almost words. Snot ran out of her nose. She tried to wipe it on her hands, but there was too much of it. She used her sleeve. "You're disgusting," I told her. "Look at you, snot streaming down your nose, and you won't say a word to stop it. You're such a nothing." I moved behind her and pulled the hair growing out of her weak neck. I let go. I stood silent for a long time. Then I screamed, "Talk!" I would scare the words out of her. If she had had little bound feet, the toes twisted under the balls, I would have jumped up and landed on them – crunch! – stomped on them with my iron shoes. She cried hard, sobbing aloud. "Cry, 'Mama,'" I said. "Come on. Cry, 'Mama.' Say, 'Stop it.'"

I put my finger on her pointed chin. "I don't like you. I don't like the weak little toots you make on your flute. Wheeze. Wheeze. I don't like the way you don't swing at the ball. I don't like the way you're the last one chosen. I don't like the way you can't make a fist for tetherball. Why don't you make a fist? Come on. Get tough. Come on. Throw fists." I pushed at her long hands; they swung limply at her sides. Her fingers were so long, I thought maybe they had an extra joint. They couldn't possibly make fists like other people's. "Make a fist," I said. "Come on. Just fold those fingers up; fingers on the inside, thumbs on the outside. Say something. Honk me back. You're so tall, and you let me pick on you.

"Would you like a hanky? I can't get you one with embroidery on it or crocheting along the edges, but I'll get you some toilet paper if you tell me to. Go ahead. Ask me. I'll get it for you if you ask." She did not stop crying. "Why don't you scream, 'Help'?" I suggested. "Say, 'Help.' Go ahead." She cried on. "O.K. O.K. Don't talk. Just scream, and I'll let you go. Won't that feel good? Go ahead. Like this." I screamed, not too loudly. My voice hit the tile and rang it as if I had thrown a rock at it. The stalls opened wider and the toilets wider and darker. Shadows leaned at angles I had not seen before. It was very late. Maybe a janitor had locked me in with this girl for the night. Her black eyes blinked and stared, blinked and stared. I felt dizzy from hunger. We had been in this lavatory together forever. My mother would call the police again if I didn't bring my sister home soon. "I'll let you go if you say just one word," I said. "You can even say, 'a' or 'the,' and I'll let you go. Come on. Please." She didn't shake her head anymore, only cried steadily, so much water coming out of her. I could see the two duct holes where the tears welled out. Quarts of tears but no words. I grabbed her by the shoulder. I could feel bones. The light was coming in queerly through the frosted glass with the chicken wire embedded in it. Her crying was like an animal's – a seal's – and it echoed around the basement. "Do you want to stay here all night?" I asked. "Your mother is wondering what happened to her baby. You wouldn't want to have her mad at you. You'd better say something." I shook her shoulder. I pulled her hair again. I squeezed her face. "Come on! Talk! Talk! Talk!" She didn't seem to feel it anymore when I pulled her hair. "There's nobody here but you and me. This isn't a classroom or a playground or a crowd. I'm just one person. You can talk in front of one person. Don't make me pull harder and harder until you talk." But her hair seemed to stretch; she did not say a word. "I'm going to pull harder. Don't make me pull anymore, or your hair will come out and you're going to be bald. Do you want to be bald? You don't want to be bald, do you?"

Far away, coming from the edge of town, I heard whistles blow. The cannery was changing shifts, letting out the afternoon people, and still we were here at school. It was a sad sound — work done. The air was lonelier after the sound died.

"Why won't you talk?" I started to cry. What if I couldn't stop, and everyone would want to know what happened? "Now look what you've done," I scolded. "You're going to pay for this. I want to know why. And you're going to tell me why. You don't see I'm trying to help you out, do you? Do you want to be like this, dumb (do you know what dumb means?), your whole life? Don't you ever want to be a cheerleader? Or a pompon girl? What are you going to do for a living? Yeah, you're going to have to work because you can't be a housewife. Somebody has to marry you before you can be a housewife. And you, you are a plant. Do you know that? That's all you are if you don't talk. If you don't talk, you can't have a personality. You'll have no personality and no hair. You've got to let people know you have a personality and a brain. You think somebody is going to take care of you all your stupid life? You think you'll always have your big sister? You think somebody's going to marry you, is that it? Well, you're not the type that gets dates, let alone gets married. Nobody's going to notice you. And you have to talk for interviews, speak right up in front of the boss. Don't you know that? You're so dumb. Why do I waste my time on you?" Sniffling and snorting, I couldn't stop crying and talking at the same time. I kept wiping my nose on my arm, my sweater lost somewhere (probably not worn because my mother said to wear a sweater). It seemed as if I had spent my life in that basement, doing the worst thing I had yet done to another person. "I'm doing this for your own good," I said. "Don't you dare tell anyone I've been bad to you. Talk. Please talk."

I was getting dizzy from the air I was gulping. Her sobs and my sobs were bouncing wildly off the tile, sometimes together, sometimes alternating. "I don't understand why you won't say just one word," I cried, clenching my teeth. My knees were shaking, and I hung on to her hair to stand up. Another time I'd stayed too late, I had had to walk around two Negro kids who were bonking each other's head on the concrete. I went back later to see if the concrete had cracks in it. "Look. I'll give you something if you talk. I'll give you my pencil box. I'll buy you some candy. O.K.? What do you want? Tell me. Just say it, and I'll give it to you. Just say, 'yes,' or, 'O.K.,' or, 'Baby Ruth.'" But she didn't want anything.

I had stopped pinching her cheek because I did not like the feel of her skin. I would go crazy if it came away in my hands. "I skinned her," I would have to confess.

Suddenly I heard footsteps hurrying through the basement, and her sister ran into the lavatory calling her name. "Oh, there you are," I said. "We've been waiting for you. I was only trying to teach her to talk. She wouldn't cooperate, though." Her sister went into one of the stalls and got handfuls of toilet paper and wiped her off. Then we found my sister, and we walked home together. "Your family really ought to force her to speak," I advised all the way home. "You mustn't pamper her."

The world is sometimes just, and I spent the next eighteen months sick in bed with a mysterious illness. There was no pain and no symptoms, though the middle line in my left palm broke in two. Instead of starting junior high school, I lived like the Victorian recluses I read about. I had a rented hospital bed in the living room, where I watched soap operas on t.v., and my family cranked me up and down. I saw no one but my family, who took good care of me. I could have no visitors, no other relatives, no villagers. My bed was against the west window, and I watched the seasons change the peach tree. I had a bell to ring for help. I used a bedpan. It was the best year and a half of my life. Nothing happened.

But one day my mother, the doctor, said, "You're ready to get up today. It's time to get up and go to school." I walked about outside to get my legs working, leaning on a staff I cut from the peach tree. The sky and trees, the sun were immense – no longer framed by a window, no longer grayed with a fly screen. I sat down on the sidewalk in amazement – the night, the stars. But at school I had to figure out again how to talk. I met again the poor girl I had tormented. She had not changed. She wore the same clothes, hair cut, and manner as when we were in elementary school, no make-up on the pink and white face, while the other Asian girls were starting to tape their eyelids. She continued to be able to read aloud. But there was hardly any reading aloud anymore, less and less as we got into high school.

I was wrong about nobody taking care of her. Her sister became a clerk-typist and stayed unmarried. They lived with their mother and father. She did not have to leave the house except to go to the movies. She was supported. She was protected by her family, as they would normally have done in China if they could have afforded it, not sent off to school with strangers, ghosts, boys.

We have so many secrets to hold in. Our sixth grade teacher, who liked to explain things to children, let us read our files. My record shows that I flunked kindergarten and in first grade had no IQ – a zero IQ. I did remember the first grade teacher calling out during a test, while students marked X's on a girl or a boy or a dog, which I covered with black. First grade was when I discovered eye control; with my seeing I could shrink the teacher down to a height of one inch, gesticulating and mouthing on the horizon. I lost this power in sixth grade for lack of practice, the teacher a generous man. "Look at your family's old addresses and think about how you've moved," he said. I looked at my parents' aliases and their birthdays, which variants I knew. But when I saw Father's occupations I exclaimed, "Hey, he wasn't a farmer, he was a . . ." He had been a gambler. My throat cut off the word – silence in front of the most understanding teacher. There were secrets never to be said in front of the ghosts, immigration secrets whose telling could get us sent back to China.

Sometimes I hated the ghosts for not letting us talk; sometimes I hated the secrecy of the Chinese. "Don't tell," said my parents, though we couldn't tell if we wanted to because we didn't know. Are there really secret trials with our own judges and penalties? Are there really flags in Chinatown signaling what stowaways have arrived in San Francisco Bay, their names, and which ships they came on? "Mother, I heard some kids say there are flags like that. Are there? What colors are they? Which buildings do they fly from?"

"No. No, there aren't any flags like that. They're just talking-story. You're always believing talk-story."

"I won't tell anybody, Mother. I promise. Which buildings are the flags on? Who flies them? The benevolent associations?"

"I don't know. Maybe the San Francisco villagers do that; our villagers don't do that."

"What do our villagers do?"

They would not tell us children because we had been born among ghosts, were taught by ghosts, and were ourselves ghost-like. They called us a kind of ghost. Ghosts are noisy and full of air; they talk during meals. They talk about anything.

"Do we send up signal kites? That would be a good idea, huh? We could fly them from the school balcony." Instead of cheaply stringing dragonflies by the tail, we could fly expensive kites, the sky splendid in Chinese colors, distracting ghost eyes while the new people sneak in. Don't tell. "Never tell."

Occasionally the rumor went about that the United States immigration authorities had set up headquarters in the San Francisco or Sacramento Chinatown to urge wetbacks and stowaways, anybody here on fake papers, to come to the city and get their files straightened out. The immigrants discussed whether or not to turn themselves in. "We might as well," somebody would say. "Then we'd have our citizenship for real."

"Don't be a fool," somebody else would say. "It's a trap. You go in there saying you want to straighten out your papers, they'll deport you."

"No, they won't. They're promising that nobody is going to go to jail or get deported. They'll give you citizenship as a reward for turning yourself in, for your honesty."

"Don't you believe it. So-and-so trusted them, and he was deported. They deported his children too."

"Where can they send us now? Hong Kong? Taiwan? I've never been to Hong Kong or Taiwan. The Big Six? Where?" We don't belong anywhere since the Revolution. The old China has disappeared while we've been away.

"Don't tell," advised my parents. "Don't go to San Francisco until they leave."

Lie to Americans. Tell them you were born during the San Francisco earthquake. Tell them your birth certificate and your parents were burned up in the fire. Don't report crimes; tell them we have no crimes and no poverty. Give a new name every time you get arrested; the ghosts won't recognize you. Pay the new immigrants twenty-five cents an hour and say we have no unemployment. And, of course, tell them we're against Communism. Ghosts have no memory anyway and poor eyesight. And the Han people won't be pinned down.

Even the good things are unspeakable, so how could I ask about deformities? From the configurations of food my mother set out, we kids had to infer the holidays. She did not whip us up with holiday anticipation or explain. You only remembered that perhaps a year ago you had eaten monk's food, or that there was meat, and it was a meat holiday; or you had eaten moon cakes or long noodles for long life (which is a pun). In front of the whole chicken with its slit throat toward the ceiling, she'd lay out just so many pairs of chopsticks alternating with wine cups, which were not for us because there were a different number from the number in our family, and they were set too close together for us to sit at. To sit at one of those place settings a being would have to be about two inches wide, a tall wisp of an invisibility. Mother would pour Seagram's 7 into the cups and, after a while, pour it back into the bottle. Never explaining. How can Chinese keep any traditions at all? They don't even make you pay attention, slipping in a ceremony and clearing the table before the children notice specialness. The adults get mad, evasive, and shut you up if you ask. You get no warning that you shouldn't wear a white ribbon in your hair until they hit you and give you the sideways glare for the rest of the day. They hit you if you wave brooms around or drop chopsticks or drum them. They hit you if you wash your hair on certain days, or tap somebody with a ruler, or step over a brother whether it's during your menses or not. You figure out what you got hit for and don't do it again if you figured correctly. But I think that if you don't figure it out, it's all right. Then you can grow up bothered by "neither ghosts nor deities." "Gods you avoid won't hurt you." I don't see how they kept up a continuous culture for five thousand years. Maybe they didn't; maybe everyone makes it up as they go along. If we had to depend on being told, we'd have no religion, no babies, no menstruation (sex, of course, unspeakable), no death.

I thought talking and not talking made the difference between sanity and insanity. Insane people were the ones who couldn't explain themselves. There were many crazy girls and women. Perhaps the sane people stayed in China to build the new, sane society. Or perhaps our little village had become odd in its isolation. No other Chinese, neither the ones in Sacramento, nor the ones in San Francisco, nor Hawaii speak like us. Within a few blocks of our house were half a dozen crazy women and girls, all belonging to village families.

There was the woman next door who was chatty one moment – inviting us children to our first "sky movie" – and shut up the next. Then we would see silver heat rise from her body; it solidified before our eyes. She made us afraid, though she said nothing, did nothing. Her husband threw the loudspeaker out the window and drove home fast in the middle of the show. She sat like stone in the front seat; he had to open the door for her and help her out. She slammed the door. After they went inside, we could hear doors slamming throughout their house. They did not have children, so it was not children slamming doors. The next day, she disappeared, and people would say she had been taken to Napa or Agnew. When a woman disappeared or reappeared after an absence, people whispered, "Napa." "Agnew." She had been locked up before. Her husband rented out the house and also went away. The last time he had left town, he had been single. He had gone back to China, where he had bought her and married her. Now while she was locked up in the asylum, he went, people said, to the Midwest. A year or two passed. He returned to Napa to drive her home. As a present, he had brought with him from the Midwest a child, half Chinese and half white. People said it was his illegitimate son. She was very happy to have a son to raise in her old age, although I saw that the boy hit her to get candy and toys. She was the one who died happy, sitting on the steps after cooking dinner.

There was Crazy Mary, whose family were Christian converts. Her mother and father had come to the Gold Mountain leaving Mary, a toddler, in China. By the time they made enough money to send for her, having replaced the horse and vegetable wagon with a truck, she was almost twenty and crazy. Her parents often said, "We thought she'd be grown but young enough to learn English and translate for us." Their other children, who were born in the U.S., were normal and could translate. I was glad that I was born nine months after my mother emigrated. Crazy Mary was a large girl and had a big black mole on her face, which is a sign of fortune. The black mole pulls you forward with its power; a mole at the back of the head pulls you back. She seemed cheerful, but pointed at things that were not there. I disliked looking at her; you never knew what you were going to see, what rictus would shape her face. Or what you would hear – growls, laughs. Her head hung like a bull's, and her eyes peeked at you out of her hair. Her face was a white blur because she was indoors so much and also because I tried not to look at her directly. She often had rice on her face and in her hair. Her mother cut her hair neatly around her ears, stubble at the back of her neck. She wore pajamas, a rough brown sweater buttoned crooked, and a big apron, not a work apron but a bib. She wore slippers, and you could see her thick ankles naked, her naked heels and tendons. When you went to her house, you had to keep alert because you didn't want her to come at you from around a corner, her hands loose. She would lurch out of dark corners; houses with crazy girls have locked rooms and drawn curtains. A smell came from her which would not have been unpleasant had it belonged to someone else. The house smelled of her, camphoraceous. Maybe they tied camphor on her pulse to cure her. Our mother used to tie dried prunes stuffed with camphor to our wrists. We got very embarrassed at school when the rags came loose and their contents fell out in clumps and grains. Crazy Mary did not improve, and so she too was locked up in the crazyhouse. She was never released. Her family said she liked it there.

There was a slough where our mother took us to pick orange berries. We carried them home in pots and bags to cook in an egg soup. It was not a wild slough, although tules, cattails and foxtails still grew, also dill, and yellow chamomile, fat and fuzzy as bees. People had been known to have followed the hobo paths and parted the tall stalks to find dead bodies – hobos, Chinese suicides, children. Red-winged blackbirds, whose shoulders were the same color as the berries, perched on a wood bridge, really a train trestle. When a train heaved across it, the black steam engine swollen to bursting like the boiler at the laundry, the birds flew up like Halloween.

We were not the only people who picked in the slough; a witchwoman also went there. One of my brothers named her Pee-A-Nah, which does not have a meaning. Of all the crazy ladies, she was the one who was the village idiot, the public one. When our mother was with us, she would chase the witchwoman away. We'd stand beside and behind our mother, who would say to her, "Leave us alone now" or "Good morning," and Pee-A-Nah would go away. But when we were by ourselves, she chased us. "Pee-A-Nah!" we'd scream. We'd run, terrified, along the hobo paths, over the trestle, and through the streets. Kids said she was a witch capable of witch deeds, unspeakable boilings and tearings apart and transformations if she caught us. "She'll touch you on the shoulder, and you'll not be you anymore. You'd be a piece of glass winking and blinking to people on the side-walk." She came riding to the slough with a broom between her legs, and she had powdered one cheek red and one white. Her hair stood up and out to the sides in dry masses, black even though she was old. She wore a pointed hat and layers of capes, shawls, sweaters buttoned at the throat like capes, the sleeves flying behind like sausage skins. She came to the slough not to harvest the useful herbs and berries the way we did, but to collect armfuls of cattails and tall grasses and tuber flowers. Sometimes she carried her broomstick horse like a staff. In the fall (she would be such a sight in the fall) she ran "faster than a swallow," her cattails popping seed, white seed puffs blowing after her, clouds of fairies dancing over her head. She streamed color and flapped in layers. She was an angry witch, not a happy one. She was fierce; not a fairy, after all, but a demon. She did run fast, as fast as a child, although she was a wrinkled woman, an outburst that jumped at us from bushes, between cars, between buildings. We children vowed that we would never run home if she came after one of us. No matter what she did to us, we had to run in the opposite direction from home. We didn't want her to know where we lived. If we couldn't outrun her and lose her, we'd die alone. Once she spotted my sister in our yard, opened the gate, and chased her up the stairs. My sister screamed and cried, banging on the door. Our mother let her in quickly, looking frightened as she fumbled at the latches to lock out Pee-A-Nah. My sister had to be chanted out of her screaming. It was a good thing Pee-A-Nah had a short memory because she did not find our house again. Sometimes when a bunch of tules and reeds and grasses mixed and blew and waved, I was terrified that it was she, that she was carrying them or parting them. One day we realized that we had not seen her for a while. We forgot her, never seeing her again. She had probably been locked up in the crazyhouse too.

I had invented a quill pen out of a peacock feather, but stopped writing with it when I saw that it waved like a one-eyed slough plant.

I thought every house had to have its crazy woman or crazy girl, every village its idiot. Who would be It at our house? Probably me. My sister did not start talking among nonfamily until a year after I started, but she was neat while I was messy, my hair tangled and dusty. My dirty hands broke things. Also I had had the mysterious illness. And there were adventurous people inside my head to whom I talked. With them I was frivolous and violent, orphaned. I was white and had red hair, and I rode a white horse. Once when I realized how often I went away to see these free movies, I asked my sister, just checking to see if hearing voices in motors and seeing cowboy movies on blank walls was normal, I asked, "Uh," trying to be casual, "do you talk to people that aren't real inside your mind?"

"Do I *what*?" she said.

"Never mind," I said fast. "Never mind. Nothing."

My sister, my almost-twin, the person most like me in all the world, had said, "*What*?"

I had vampire nightmares; every night the fangs grew longer, and my angel wings turned pointed and black. I hunted humans down in the long woods and shadowed them with my blackness. Tears dripped from my eyes, but blood dripped from my fangs, blood of the people I was supposed to love.

I did not want to be our crazy one. Quite often the big loud women came shouting into the house, "Now when you sell this one, I'd like to buy her to be my maid." Then they laughed. They always said that about my sister, not me because I dropped dishes at them. I picked my nose while I was cooking and serving. My clothes were wrinkled even though we owned a laundry. Indeed I was getting stranger every day. I affected a limp. And, of course, the mysterious disease I had had might have been dormant and contagious.

But if I made myself unsellable here, my parents need only wait until China, and there, where anything happens, they would be able to unload us, even me – sellable, marriageable. So while the adults wept over the letters about the neighbors gone berserk turning Communist ("They do funny dances; they sing weird songs, just syllables. They make us dance; they make us sing"), I was secretly glad. As long as the aunts kept disappearing and the uncles dying after unspeakable tortures, my parents would prolong their Gold Mountain stay. We could start spending our fare money on a car and chairs, a stereo. Nobody wrote to tell us that Mao himself had been matched to an older girl when he was a child and that he was freeing women from prisons, where they had been put for refusing the businessmen their parents had picked as husbands. Nobody told us that the Revolution (the Liberation) was against girl slavery and girl infanticide (a village-wide party if it's a boy). Girls would no longer have to kill themselves rather than get married. May the Communists light up the house on a girl's birthday.

I watched our parents buy a sofa, then a rug, curtains, chairs to replace the orange and apple crates one by one, now to be used for storage. Good. At the beginning of the second Communist five-year plan, our parents bought a car. But you could see the relatives and the villagers getting more worried about what to do with the girls. We had three girl second cousins, no boys; their great-grandfather and our grandfather were brothers. The great-grandfather was the old man who lived with them, as the river-pirate great-uncle was the old man who lived with us. When my sisters and I ate at their house, there we would be – six girls eating. The old man opened his eyes wide at us and turned in a circle, surrounded. His neck tendons stretched out. "Maggots!" he shouted. "Maggots! Where are my grandsons? I want grandsons! Give me grandsons! Maggots!" He pointed at each one of us, "Maggot! Maggot! Maggot! Maggot! Maggot! Maggot!" Then he dived into his food, eating fast and getting seconds. "Eat, maggots," he said. "Look at the maggots chew."

"He does that at every meal," the girls told us in English.

"Yeah," we said. "Our old man hates us too. What assholes."

Third Grand-Uncle finally did get a boy, though, his only great-grandson. The boy's parents and the old man bought him toys, bought him everything – new diapers, new plastic pants –

not homemade diapers, not bread bags. They gave him a full-month party inviting all the emigrant villagers; they deliberately hadn't given the girls parties, so that no one would notice another girl. Their brother got toy trucks that were big enough to climb inside. When he grew older, he got a bicycle and let the girls play with his old tricycle and wagon. My mother bought his sisters a typewriter. "They can be clerk-typists," their father kept saying, but he would not buy them a typewriter.

"What an asshole," I said, muttering the way my father muttered "Dog vomit" when the customers nagged him about missing socks.

Maybe my mother was afraid that I'd say things like that out loud and so had cut my tongue. Now again plans were urgently afoot to fix me up, to improve my voice. The wealthiest villager wife came to the laundry one day to have a listen. "You better do something with this one," she told my mother. "She has an ugly voice. She quacks like a pressed duck." Then she looked at me unnecessarily hard; Chinese do not have to address children directly. "You have what we call a pressed-duck voice," she said. This woman was the giver of American names, a powerful namer, though it was American names; my parents gave the Chinese names. And she was right: if you squeezed the duck hung up to dry in the east window, the sound that was my voice would come out of it. She was a woman of such power that all we immigrants and descendants of immigrants were obliged to her family forever for bringing us here and for finding us jobs, and she had named my voice.

"No," I quacked. "No, I don't."

"Don't talk back," my mother scolded. Maybe this lady was powerful enough to send us back.

I went to the front of the laundry and worked so hard that I impolitely did not take notice of her leaving.

"Improve that voice," she had instructed my mother, "or else you'll never marry her off. Even the fool half ghosts won't have her." So I discovered the next plan to get rid of us:

marry us off here without waiting until China. The villagers' peasant minds converged on marriage. Late at night when we walked home from the laundry, they should have been sleeping behind locked doors, not overflowing into the streets in front of the benevolent associations, all alit. We stood on tiptoes and on one another's shoulders, and through the door we saw spotlights open on tall singers afire with sequins. An opera from San Francisco! An opera from Hong Kong! Usually I did not understand the words in operas, whether because of our obscure dialect or theirs I didn't know, but I heard one line sung out into the night air in a woman's voice high and clear as ice. She was standing on a chair, and she sang, "Beat me, then, beat me." The crowd laughed until the tears rolled down their cheeks while the cymbals clashed – the dragon's copper laugh – and the drums banged like firecrackers. "She is playing the part of a new daughter-in-law," my mother explained. "Beat me, then, beat me," she sang again and again. It must have been a refrain; each time she sang it, the audience broke up laughing. Men laughed; women laughed. They were having a great time.

"Chinese smeared bad daughters-in-law with honey and tied them naked on top of ant nests," my father said. "A husband may kill a wife who disobeys him. Confucius said that." Confucius, the rational man.

The singer, I thought, sounded like me talking, yet everyone said, "Oh, beautiful. Beautiful," when she sang high.

Walking home, the noisy women shook their old heads and sang a folk song that made them laugh uproariously:

> Marry a rooster, follow a rooster.
> Marry a dog, follow a dog.
> Married to a cudgel, married to a pestle,
> Be faithful to it. Follow it.

I learned that young men were placing ads in the *Gold Mountain News* to find wives when my mother and father started answering them. Suddenly a series of new workers showed up at the laundry; they each worked for a week before they disappeared. They ate with us. They talked Chinese with my parents. They did not talk to us. We were to call them "Elder Brother," although they were not related to us. They were all funny-looking FOB's, Fresh-off-the-Boat's, as the Chinese-American kids at school called the young immigrants. FOB's wear high-riding gray slacks and white shirts with the sleeves rolled up. Their eyes do not focus correctly — shifty-eyed — and they hold their mouths slack, not tight-jawed masculine. They shave off their side-burns. The girls said *they'd* never date an FOB. My mother took one home from the laundry, and I saw him looking over our photographs. "This one," he said, picking up my sister's picture.

"No. No," said my mother. "This one," my picture. "The oldest first," she said. Good. I was an obstacle. I would protect my sister and myself at the same time. As my parents and the FOB sat talking at the kitchen table, I dropped two dishes. I found my walking stick and limped across the floor. I twisted my mouth and caught my hand in the knots of my hair. I spilled soup on the FOB when I handed him his bowl. "She can sew, though," I heard my mother say, "and sweep." I raised dust swirls sweeping around and under the FOB's chair — very bad luck because spirits live inside the broom. I put on my shoes with the open flaps and flapped about like a Wino Ghost. From then on, I wore those shoes to parties, whenever the mothers gathered to talk about marriages. The FOB and my parents paid me no attention, half ghosts half invisible, but when he left, my mother yelled at me about the dried-duck voice, the bad temper, the laziness, the clumsi-ness, the stupidity that comes from reading too much. The young men stopped visiting; not one came back. "Couldn't you just stop rubbing your nose?" she scolded. "All the village ladies are talking about your nose. They're afraid to eat our pastries because you might have kneaded the dough." But I couldn't stop at will anymore, and a crease developed across the bridge. My parents would not give up, though. "Though you can't see it," my mother said, "a red string around your ankle ties you to the person you'll marry. He's already been born, and he's on the other end of the string."

At Chinese school there was a mentally retarded boy who followed me around, probably believing that we were two of a kind. He had an enormous face, and he growled. He laughed from so far within his thick body that his face got confused about what the sounds coming up into his mouth might be, laughs or cries. He barked unhappily. He didn't go to classes but hung around the playgrounds. We suspected he was not a boy but an adult. He wore baggy khaki trousers like a man's. He carried bags of toys for giving to certain children. Whatever you wanted, he'd get it for you – brand-new toys, as many as you could think up in your poverty, all the toys you never had when you were younger. We wrote lists, discussed our lists, compared them. Those kids not in his favor gave lists to those who were. "Where do you get the toys?" I asked. "I . . . own . . . stores," he roared, one word at a time, thick tongued. At recess the day after ordering, we got handed out to us coloring books, paint sets, model kits. But sometimes he chased us – his fat arms out to the side; his fat fingers opening and closing; his legs stiff like Frankenstein's monster, like the mummy dragging its foot; growling; laughing-crying. Then we'd have to run, following the old rule, running away from our house.

But suddenly he knew where we worked. He found us; maybe he had followed us in his wanderings. He started sitting at our laundry. Many of the storekeepers invited sitting in their stores, but we did not have sitting because the laundry was hot and because it was outside Chinatown. He sweated; he panted, the stubble rising and falling on his fat neck and chin. He sat on two large cartons that he brought with him and stacked one on top of the other. He said hello to my mother and father, and then, balancing his heavy head, he lowered himself carefully onto his cartons and sat. My parents allowed this. They did not chase him out or comment about how strange he was. I stopped placing orders for toys. I didn't limp anymore; my parents would only figure that this zombie and I were a match.

I studied hard, got straight A's, but nobody seemed to see that I was smart and had nothing in common with this monster, this birth defect. At school there were dating and dances, but not for good Chinese girls. "You ought to develop yourself socially as well as mentally," the American teachers, who took me aside, said.

I told nobody about the monster. And nobody else was talking either; no mention about the laundry workers who appeared and disappeared; no mention about the sitter. Maybe I was making it all up, and queer marriage notions did not occur to other people. I had better not say a word, then. Don't give them ideas. Keep quiet.

I pressed clothes – baskets of giants' BVD's, long underwear even in summertime, T-shirts, sweat shirts. Laundry work is men's clothes, unmarried-men's clothes. My back felt sick because it was toward the monster who gave away toys. His lumpishness was sending out germs that would lower my IQ. His leechiness was drawing IQ points out of the back of my head. I maneuvered my work shifts so that my brothers would work the afternoons, when he usually came lumbering into the laundry, but he caught on and began coming during the evening, the cool shift. Then I would switch back to the afternoon or to the early mornings on weekends and in summer, dodging him. I kept my sister with me, protecting her without telling her why. If she hadn't noticed, then I mustn't scare her. "Let's clean house this morning," I'd say. Our other sister was a baby, and the brothers were not in danger. But the were-person would stalk down our street; his thick face smiled between the lettering on the laundry window, and when he saw me working, he shouldered inside. At night I thought I heard his feet dragging around the house, scraping gravel. I sat up to listen to our watchdog prowl the yard, pulling her long chain after her, and that worried me too. I had to do something about that chain, the weight of it scraping her neck fur short. And if she was walking about, why wasn't she barking? Maybe somebody was out there taming her with raw meat. I could not ask for help.

Every day the hulk took one drink from the watercooler and went once to the bathroom, stumbling between the presses into the back of the laundry, big shoes clumping. Then my parents would talk about what could be inside his boxes. Were they filled with toys? With money? When the toilet flushed, they stopped talking about it. But one day he either stayed in the bathroom for a long time or went for a walk and left the boxes unguarded. "Let's open them up," said my mother, and she did. I looked over her shoulder. The two cartons were stuffed with pornography – naked magazines, nudie postcards and photographs.

You would think she'd have thrown him out right then, but my mother said, "My goodness, he's not too stupid to want to find out about women." I heard the old women talk about how he was stupid but very rich.

Maybe because I was the one with the tongue cut loose, I had grown inside me a list of over two hundred things that I had to tell my mother so that she would know the true things about me and to stop the pain in my throat. When I first started counting, I had had only thirty-six items: how I had prayed for a white horse of my own – white, the bad, mournful color – and prayer bringing me to the attention of the god of the black-and-white nuns who gave us "holy cards" in the park. How I wanted the horse to start the movies in my mind coming true. How I had picked on a girl and made her cry. How I had stolen from the cash register and bought candy for everybody I knew, not just brothers and sisters, but strangers too and ghost children. How it was me who pulled up the onions in the garden out of anger. How I had jumped head-first off the dresser, not accidentally, but so I could fly. Then there were my fights at Chinese school. And the nuns who kept stopping us in the park, which was across the street from Chinese school, to tell us that if we didn't get baptized we'd go to a hell like one of the nine Taoist hells forever. And the obscene caller that phoned us at home when the adults were at the laundry. And the Mexican and Filipino girls at school who went to "confession," and how I envied them their white dresses and their chance each Saturday to tell even thoughts that were sinful. If only I could let my mother know the list, she – and the world – would become more like me, and I would never be alone again. I would pick a time of day when my mother was alone and tell her one item a day; I'd be finished in less than a year. If the telling got excruciating and her anger too bad, I'd tell five items once a week like the Catholic girls, and I'd still be through in a year, maybe ten months. My mother's most peaceful time was in the evenings when she starched the white shirts. The laundry would be clean, the gray wood floors sprinkled and swept with water and wet sawdust. She would be wringing shirts at the starch tub and not running about. My father and sisters and brothers would be at their own jobs mending, folding, packaging. Steam would be rising from the starch, the air cool at last. Yes, that would be the time and place for the telling.

And I wanted to ask again why the women in our family have a split nail on our left little toe. Whenever we asked our parents about it, they would glance at each other, embarrassed. I think I've heard one of them say, "She didn't get away." I made up that we are descended from an ancestress who stubbed her toe and fell when running from a rapist. I wanted to ask my mother if I had guessed right.

I hunkered down between the wall and the wicker basket of shirts. I had decided to start with the earliest item – when I had smashed a spider against the white side of the house: it was the first thing I killed. I said, clearly, "I killed a spider," and it was nothing; she did not hit me or throw hot starch at me. It sounded like nothing to me too. How strange when I had had such feelings of death shoot through my hand and into my body so that I would surely die. So I had to continue, of course, and let her know how important it had been. "I returned every day to look at its smear on the side of the house," I said. "It was our old house, the one we lived in until I was five. I went to the wall every day to look. I studied the stain." Relieved because she said nothing but only continued squeezing the starch, I went away feeling pretty good. Just two hundred and six more items to go. I moved carefully all the next day so as not to do anything or have anything happen to me that would make me go back to two hundred and seven again. I'd tell a couple of easy ones and work up to how I had pulled the quiet girl's hair and how I had enjoyed the year being sick. If it was going to be this easy, maybe I could blurt out several a day, maybe an easy one and a hard one. I could go chronologically, or I could work from easy to hard or hard to easy, depending on my mood. On the second night I talked about how I had hinted to a ghost girl that I wished I had a doll of my own until she gave me a head and body to glue together – that she hadn't given it to me of her own generosity but because I had hinted. But on the fifth night (I skipped two to reward myself) I decided it was time to do a really hard one and tell her about the white horse. And suddenly the duck voice came out, which I did not use with the family. "What's it called, Mother" – the duck voice coming out talking to my own mother – "when a person whispers to the head of the sages – no, not the sages, more like the buddhas but not real people like the buddhas (they've always lived in the sky and never turned into people like the buddhas) – and you whisper to them, the boss of them, and ask for things? They're like magicians? What do you call it when you talk to the boss magician?"

" 'Talking-to-the-top-magician,' I guess."

"I did that. Yes. That's it. That's what I did. I talked-to-the-top-magician and asked for a white horse." There. Said.

"Mm," she said, squeezing the starch out of the collar and cuffs. But I had talked, and she acted as if she hadn't heard.

Perhaps she hadn't understood. I had to be more explicit. I hated this. "I kneeled on the bed in there, in the laundry bedroom, and put my arms up like I saw in a comic book" – one night I heard monsters coming through the kitchen, and I had promised the god in the movies, the one the Mexicans and Filipinos have, as in "God Bless America," that I would not read comic books anymore if he would save me just this once; I had broken that promise, and I needed to tell all this to my mother too – "and in that ludicrous position asked for a horse."

"Mm," she said, nodded, and kept dipping and squeezing.

On my two nights off, I had sat on the floor too but had not said a word.

"Mother," I whispered and quacked.

"I can't stand this whispering," she said looking right at me, stopping her squeezing. "Senseless gabbings every night. I wish you would stop. Go away and work. Whispering, whispering, making no sense. Madness. I don't feel like hearing your craziness."

So I had to stop, relieved in some ways. I shut my mouth, but I felt something alive tearing at my throat, bite by bite, from the inside. Soon there would be three hundred things, and too late to get them out before my mother grew old and died.

I had probably interrupted her in the middle of her own quiet time when the boiler and presses were off and the cool night flew against the windows in moths and crickets. Very few customers came in. Starching the shirts for the next day's pressing was probably my mother's time to ride off with the people in her own mind. That would explain why she was so far away and did not want to listen to me. "Leave me alone," she said.

The hulk, the hunching sitter, brought a third box now, to rest his feet on. He patted his boxes. He sat in wait, hunching on his pile of dirt. My throat hurt constantly, vocal cords taut to snapping. One night when the laundry was so busy that the whole family was eating dinner there, crowded around the little round table, my throat burst open. I stood up, talking and burbling. I looked directly at my mother and at my father and screamed, "I want you to tell that hulk, that gorilla-ape, to go away and never bother us again. I know what you're up to. You're thinking he's rich, and we're poor. You think we're odd and not pretty and we're not bright. You think you can give us away to freaks. You better not do that, Mother. I don't want to see him or his dirty boxes here tomorrow. If I see him here one more time, I'm going away. I'm going away anyway. I am. Do you hear me? I may be ugly and clumsy, but one thing I'm not, I'm not retarded. There's nothing wrong with my brain. Do you know what the Teacher Ghosts say about me? They tell me I'm smart, and I can win scholarships. I can get into colleges. I've already applied. I'm smart. I can do all kinds of things. I know how to get A's, and they say I could be a scientist or a mathematician if I want. I can make a living and take care of myself. So you don't have to find me a keeper who's too dumb to know a bad bargain. I'm so smart, if they say write ten pages, I can write fifteen. I can do ghost things even better than ghosts can. Not everybody thinks I'm nothing. I am not going to be a slave or a wife. Even if I am stupid and talk funny and get sick, I won't let you turn me into a slave or a wife. I'm getting out of here. I can't stand living here anymore. It's your fault I talk weird. The only reason I flunked kindergarten was because you couldn't teach me English, and you gave me a zero IQ. I've brought my IQ up, though. They say I'm smart now. Things follow in lines at school. They take stories and teach us to turn them into essays. I don't need anybody to pronounce English words for me. I can figure them out by myself. I'm going to get scholarships, and I'm going away. And at college I'll have the people I like for friends. I don't care if their great-great-grandfather died of TB. I don't care if they were our enemies in China four thousand years ago. So get that ape out of here. I'm going to college. And I'm not going to Chinese school anymore. I'm going to run for office at American school, and I'm going to join clubs. I'm going to get enough offices and clubs on my record to get into college. And I can't stand Chinese school anyway; the kids are rowdy and mean, fighting all night. And I don't want to listen to any more of your stories; they have no logic. They scramble me up. You lie with stories. You won't tell me a story and then say, 'This is a true story,' or, 'This is just a story.' I can't tell the difference. I don't even know what your real names are. I can't tell what's real and what you make up. Ha! You can't stop me from talking. You tried to cut off my tongue, but it didn't work." So I told the hardest ten or twelve things on my list all in one outburst.

My mother, who is champion talker, was, of course, shouting at the same time. "I cut it to make you talk more, not less, you dummy. You're still stupid. You can't listen right. I didn't say I was going to marry you off. Did I ever say that? Did I ever mention that? Those newspaper people were for your sister, not you. Who would want you? Who said we could sell you? We can't sell people. Can't you take a joke? You can't even tell a joke from real life. You're not so smart. Can't even tell real from false."

"I'm never getting married, never!"

"Who'd want to marry you anyway? Noisy. Talking like a duck. Disobedient. Messy. And I know about college. What makes you think you're the first one to think about college? I was a doctor. I went to medical school. I don't see why you have to be a mathematician. I don't see why you can't be a doctor like me."

"I can't stand fever and delirium or listening to people coming out of anesthesia. But I didn't say I wanted to be a mathematician either. That's what the ghosts say. I want to be a lumberjack and a newspaper reporter." Might as well tell her some of the other items on my list. "I'm going to chop down trees in the daytime and write about timber at night."

"I don't see why you need to go to college at all to become either one of those things. Everybody else is sending their girls to typing school. 'Learn to type if you want to be an American girl.' Why don't you go to typing school? The cousins and village girls are going to typing school."

"And you leave my sister alone. You try that with the advertising again, and I'll take her with me." My telling list was scrambled out of order. When I said them out loud I saw that some of the items were ten years old already, and I had outgrown them. But they kept pouring out anyway in the voice like Chinese opera. I could hear the drums and the cymbals and the gongs and brass horns.

"You're the one to leave your little sisters alone," my mother was saying. "You're always leading them off some-where. I've had to call the police twice because of you." She herself was shouting out things I had meant to tell her – that I took my brothers and sisters to explore strange people's houses, ghost children's houses, and haunted houses blackened by fire. We explored a Mexican house and a red-headed family's house, but not the gypsies' house; I had only seen the inside of the gypsies' house in mind-movies. We explored the sloughs, where we found hobo nests. My mother must have followed us.

"You turned out so unusual. I fixed your tongue so you could say charming things. You don't even say hello to the villagers."

"They don't say hello to me."

"They don't have to answer children. When you get old, people will say hello to you."

"When I get to college, it won't matter if I'm not charming. And it doesn't matter if a person is ugly; she can still do schoolwork."

"I didn't say you were ugly."

"You say that all the time."

"That's what we're supposed to say. That's what Chinese say. We like to say the opposite."

It seemed to hurt her to tell me that — another guilt for my list to tell my mother, I thought. And suddenly I got very confused and lonely because I was at that moment telling her my list, and in the telling, it grew. No higher listener. No listener but myself.

"Ho Chi Kuei," she shouted. "Ho Chi Kuei. Leave then. Get out, you Ho Chi Kuei. Get out. I knew you were going to turn out bad. Ho Chi Kuei." My brothers and sisters had left the table, and my father would not look at me anymore, ignoring me.

Be careful what you say. It comes true. It comes true. I had to leave home in order to see the world logically, logic the new way of seeing. I learned to think that mysteries are for explanation. I enjoy the simplicity. Concrete pours out of my mouth to cover the forests with freeways and sidewalks. Give me plastics, periodical tables, t.v. dinners with vegetables no more complex than peas mixed with diced carrots. Shine floodlights into dark corners: no ghosts.

I've been looking up "Ho Chi Kuei," which is what the immigrants call us – Ho Chi Ghosts. "Well, Ho Chi Kuei," they say, "what silliness have you been up to now?" "That's a Ho Chi Kuei for you," they say, no matter what we've done. It was more complicated (and therefore worse) than "dog," which they say affectionately, mostly to boys. They use "pig" and "stink pig" for girls, and only in an angry voice. The river-pirate great-uncle called even my middle brother Ho Chi Kuei, and he seemed to like him best. The maggot third great-uncle even shouted "Ho Chi Kuei!" at the boy. I don't know any Chinese I can ask without getting myself scolded or teased, so I've been looking in books. So far I have the following translations for *ho* and/or *chi*: "centipede," "grub," "bastard carp," "chirping insect," "jujube tree," "pied wag-tail," "grain sieve," "casket sacrifice," "water lily," "good frying," "non-eater," "dustpan-and-broom" (but that's a synonym for "wife"). Or perhaps I've romanized the spelling wrong and it is *Hao* Chi Kuei, which could mean they are calling us "Good Foundation Ghosts." The immigrants could be saying that we were born on Gold Mountain and have advantages. Sometimes they scorn us for having had it so easy, and sometimes they're delighted. They also call us "Jook Sing," or "Bamboo Nodes." Bamboo nodes obstruct water.

I like to look up a troublesome, shameful thing and then say, "Oh, is that all?" The simple explanation makes it less scary to go home after yelling at your mother and father. It drives the fear away and makes it possible someday to visit China, where I know now they don't sell girls or kill each other for no reason.

Now colors are gentler and fewer; smells are antiseptic. Now when I peek in the basement window where the vil-lagers say they see a girl dancing like a bottle imp, I can no longer see a spirit in a skirt made of light, but a voiceless girl dancing when she thought no one was looking. The very next day after I talked out the retarded man, the huncher, he disappeared. I never saw him again or heard what became of him. Perhaps I made him up, and what I once had was not Chinese-sight at all but child-sight that would have disappeared eventually without such struggle. The throat pain always returns, though, unless I tell what I really think, whether or not I lose my job, or spit out gaucheries all over a party. I've stopped checking "bilingual" on job applications. I could not understand any of the dialects the interviewer at China Airlines tried on me, and he didn't understand me either. I'd like to go to New Society Village someday and find out exactly how far I can walk before people stop talking like me. I continue to sort out what's just my childhood, just my imagination, just my family, just the village, just movies, just living.

Soon I want to go to China and find out who's lying – the Communists who say they have food and jobs for everybody or the relatives who write that they have not the money to buy salt. My mother sends money she earns working in the tomato fields to Hong Kong. The relatives there can send it on to the remaining aunts and their children and, after a good harvest, to the children and grandchildren of my grandfather's two minor wives. "Every woman in the tomato row is sending money home," my mother says, "to Chinese villages and Mexican villages and Filipino villages and, now, Vietnamese villages, where they speak Chinese too. The women come to work whether sick or well. 'I can't die,' they say, 'I'm supporting fifty,' or 'I'm supporting a hundred.' "

What I'll inherit someday is a green address book full of names. I'll send the relatives money, and they'll write me stories about their hunger. My mother has been tearing up the letters from the youngest grandson of her father's third wife. He has been asking for fifty dollars to buy a bicycle. He says a bicycle will change his life. He could feed his wife and

children if he had a bicycle. "We'd have to go hungry ourselves," my mother says. "They don't understand that we have
ourselves to feed too." I've been making money; I guess it's
my turn. I'd like to go to China and see those people and find
out what's a cheat story and what's not. Did my grandmother
really live to be ninety-nine? Or did they string us along all
those years to get our money? Do the babies wear a Mao button like a drop of blood on their jumpsuits? When we overseas Chinese send money, do the relatives divide it evenly
among the commune? Or do they really pay 2 percent tax
and keep the rest? It would be good if the Communists were
taking care of themselves; then I could buy a color t.v.

Here is a story my mother told me, not when I was
young, but recently, when I told her I also talk-story. The
beginning is hers, the ending, mine.

In China my grandmother loved the theater (which
I would not have been able to understand because of my sev-
enth-grade vocabulary, said my mother). When the actors
came to the village and set up their scaffolding, my grandmother bought a large section up front. She bought enough
room for our entire family and a bed; she would stay days and
nights, not missing even the repeating scenes.

The danger was that the bandits would make raids on
households thinned out during performances. Bandits followed the actors.

"But, Grandmother," the family complained, "the bandits
will steal the tables while we're gone." They took the chairs to
plays.

"I want every last one of you at that theater," my grandmother raved. "Slavegirls, everybody. I don't want to watch
that play by myself. How can I laugh all by myself? You
want me to clap alone, is that it? I want everybody there.
Babies, everybody."

"The robbers will ransack the food."

"So let them. Cook up the food and take it to the theater. If you're so worried about bandits, if you're not going to concentrate on the play because of a few bandits, leave the doors open. Leave the windows open. Leave the house wide open. I order the doors open. We are going to the theater without worries."

So they left the doors open, and my whole family went to watch the actors. And sure enough, that night the bandits struck – not the house, but the theater itself. "Bandits aa!" the audience screamed. "Bandits aa!" the actors screamed. My family ran in all directions, my grandmother and mother holding on to each other and jumping into a ditch. They crouched there because my grandmother could run no farther on bound feet. They watched a bandit loop a rope around my youngest aunt, Lovely Orchid, and prepare to drag her off. Suddenly he let her go. "A prettier one," he said, grabbing somebody else. By daybreak, when my grandmother and mother made their way home, the entire family was home safe, proof to my grandmother that our family was immune to harm as long as they went to plays. They went to many plays after that.

I like to think that at some of those performances, they heard the songs of Ts'ai Yen, a poetess born in A.D. 175. She was the daughter of Ts'ai Yung, the scholar famous for his library. When she was twenty years old, she was captured by a chieftain during a raid by the Southern Hsiung-nu. He made her sit behind him when the tribe rode like the haunted from one oasis to the next, and she had to put her arms around his waist to keep from falling off the horse. After she became pregnant, he captured a mare as his gift to her. Like other captive soldiers until the time of Mao, whose soldiers volunteered, Ts'ai Yen fought desultorily when the fighting was at a distance, and she cut down anyone in her path during the madness of close combat. The tribe fought from horseback, charging in a mass into villages and encampments. She gave birth on the sand; the barbarian women were said to be able to birth in the saddle. During her twelve-year stay with the barbarians, she had two children. Her children did not speak Chinese. She spoke it to them when their father was out of the tent, but they imitated her with senseless singsong words and laughed.

The barbarians were primitives. They gathered inedible reeds when they camped along rivers and dried them in the sun. They dried the reeds tied on their flagpoles and horses' manes and tails. Then they cut wedges and holes. They slipped feathers and arrow shafts into the shorter reeds, which became nock-whistles. During battle the arrows whistled, high whirling whistles that suddenly stopped when the arrows hit true. Even when the barbarians missed, they terrified their enemies by filling the air with death sounds, which Ts'ai Yen had thought was their only music, until one night she heard music tremble and rise like desert wind. She walked out of her tent and saw hundreds of the barbarians sitting upon the sand, the sand gold under the moon. Their elbows were raised, and they were blowing on flutes. They reached again and again for a high note, yearning toward a high note, which they found at last and held – an icicle in the desert. The music disturbed Ts'ai Yen; its sharpness and its cold made her ache. It disturbed her so that she could not concentrate on her own thoughts. Night after night the songs filled the desert no matter how many dunes away she walked. She hid in her tent but could not sleep through the sound. Then, out of Ts'ai Yen's tent, which was apart from the others, the barbarians heard a woman's voice singing, as if to her babies, a song so high and clear, it matched the flutes. Ts'ai Yen sang about China and her family there. Her words seemed to be Chinese, but the barbarians understood their sadness and anger. Sometimes they thought they could catch barbarian phrases about forever wandering. Her children did not laugh, but eventually sang along when she left her tent to sit by the winter campfires, ringed by barbarians.

After twelve years among the Southern Hsiung-nu, Ts'ai Yen was ransomed and married to Tung Ssu so that her father would have Han descendants. She brought her songs back from the savage lands, and one of the three that has been passed down to us is "Eighteen Stanzas for a Barbarian Reed Pipe," a song that Chinese sing to their own instruments. It translated well.

CHINA MEN

CONTENTS

For Tom, George, Norman, and Joe Hong
and Earll and Joseph Kingston

Once upon a time, a man, named Tang Ao, looking for the Gold Mountain, crossed an ocean, and came upon the Land of Women. The women immediately captured him, not on guard against ladies. When they asked Tang Ao to come along, he followed; if he had had male companions, he would've winked over his shoulder.

"We have to prepare you to meet the queen," the women said. They locked him in a canopied apartment equipped with pots of makeup, mirrors, and a woman's clothes. "Let us help you off with your armor and boots," said the women. They slipped his coat off his shoulders, pulled it down his arms, and shackled his wrists behind him. The women who kneeled to take off his shoes chained his ankles together.

A door opened, and he expected to meet his match, but it was only two old women with sewing boxes in their hands. "The less you struggle, the less it'll hurt," one said, squinting a bright eye as she threaded her needle. Two captors sat on him while another held his head. He felt an old woman's dry fingers trace his ear; the long nail on her little finger scraped his neck. "What are you doing?" he asked. "Sewing your lips together," she joked, blackening needles in a candle flame. The ones who sat on him bounced with laughter. But the old women did not sew his lips together. They pulled his ear-lobes taut and jabbed a needle through each of them. They had to poke and probe before puncturing the layers of skin correctly, the hole in the front of the lobe in line with the one in back, the layers of skin sliding about so. They worked the needle through – a last jerk for the needle's wide eye ("needle's nose" in Chinese). They strung his raw flesh with silk threads; he could feel the fibers.

The women who sat on him turned to direct their attention to his feet. They bent his toes so far backward that his arched foot cracked. The old ladies squeezed each foot and broke many tiny bones along the sides. They gathered his toes, toes over and under one another like a knot of ginger root. Tang Ao wept with pain. As they wound the bandages tight and tighter around his feet, the women sang footbinding songs to distract him: "Use aloe for binding feet and not for scholars."

During the months of a season, they fed him on women's food: the tea was thick with white chrysanthemums and stirred the cool female winds inside his body; chicken wings made his hair shine; vinegar soup improved his womb. They drew the loops of thread through the scabs that grew daily over the holes in his earlobes. One day they inserted gold hoops. Every night they unbound his feet, but his veins had shrunk, and the blood pumping through them hurt so much, he begged to have his feet re-wrapped tight. They forced him to wash his used bandages, which were embroidered with flowers and smelled of rot and cheese. He hung the bandages up to dry, streamers that drooped and draped wall to wall. He felt embarrassed; the wrappings were like underwear, and they were his.

One day his attendants changed his gold hoops to jade studs and strapped his feet to shoes that curved like bridges. They plucked out each hair on his face, powdered him white, painted his eyebrows like a moth's wings, painted his cheeks and lips red. He served a meal at the queen's court. His hips swayed and his shoulders swiveled because of his shaped feet. "She's pretty, don't you agree?" the diners said, smacking their lips at his dainty feet as he bent to put dishes before them.

* * *

In the Women's Land there are no taxes and no wars. Some scholars say that that country was discovered during the reign of Empress Wu (A.D. 694-705), and some say earlier than that, A.D. 441, and it was in North America.

On Fathers

Waiting at the gate for our father to come home from work, my brothers and sisters and I saw a man come hastening around the corner. Father! "BaBa!" "BaBa!" We flew off the gate; we jumped off the fence. "BaBa!" We surrounded him, took his hands, pressed our noses against his coat to sniff his tobacco smell, reached into his pockets for the Rainbo notepads and the gold coins that were really chocolates. The littlest ones hugged his legs for a ride on his shoes. And he laughed a startled laugh. "But I'm not your father. You've made a mistake." He took our hands out of his pockets. "But I'm not your father." Looking closely, we saw that he probably was not. We went back inside the yard, and this man continued his walk down our street, from the back certainly looking like our father, one hand in his pocket. Tall and thin, he was wearing our father's two-hundred-dollar suit that fit him just right. He was walking fast in his good leather shoes with the wingtips.

Our mother came out of the house, and we hung on to her while she explained, "No, that wasn't your father. He did look like BaBa, though, didn't he? From the back, almost exactly." We stood on the sidewalk together and watched the man walk away. A moment later, from the other direction, our own father came striding toward us, the one finger touching his hat to salute us. We ran again to meet him.

THE FATHER FROM CHINA

Father, I have seen you lighthearted:

"Let's play airplane," you said. "I'll make you a toy air-plane." You caught between your thumb and finger a dragonfly. You held it by the abdomen. Its fast wings blurred, but when its motor paused, I saw that the wings were networks of cellophane. Its head bulged with eyes, below which the rest of its face was crowded. "You hold it," you said. Around its belly you slipped a lasso of thread, which you tightened, crinkled its shell, pinched a waist, and the tail bent downward slightly. Then you tied the other end of the string around my finger, and said, "Let go." The tying hadn't hurt it one bit; the dragonfly whirled up and flew in circles at the extent of the string, which I pulled toward me and cast away, controlling my pet airplane. It flew lower, and I turned with it not to get entangled. Suddenly the dragonfly dropped and dangled, but all we had to do was shake it, and it flew again. After a while, though I poked and prodded, it did not go any more. You watched for five more dragonflies to alight until each sister and brother had had a turn.

Upon hearing about the sage of the Ming period who shook himself and turned into a red dragonfly, I remembered our airplane, which was not red. The sunlight had iridized the black into blues and greens.

On summer nights, when we picked new routes home from the laundry through the Stockton streets, crickets covered the sidewalks and the lighted windows. Bats flew between the buildings, and some got hit by cars; we examined them, spread their wings, looked at their teeth and furry countenances. The bats wafted like burned paper in the searchlights, which lit up tightrope walkers who had strung wires from the tallest rooftops and walked with no nets to and from the courthouse dome. On garbage nights, we children ran ahead and rummaged the department store bins for treasures; in trade, you left our garbage, a bag here and a bag on the next block. But usually we didn't walk the long way on Main Street; we went through Chinatown, Tang People's Street, gray and quiet except for the clicking of gamblers who had left a window open. Then we passed the Japanese's closed-up house, nobody home for years, and the Filipino Lodge, where we sat on the benches that were held up by tree bark growing over their edges; the Filipinos had gone in for the night. On our own front porch, you snapped on the light, and the moths came swarming. "It's a Hit-lah," you said, swatting one with your newspaper. "Hit-lah," we shouted, and attacked the moths, killed them against the walls and railings, "*Hit*-lah!" and a hit on the first syllable. They were plain no-color butterflies. We killed Hitler moths every summer of The War. It was interesting to grow older and find out that only we called them that, and outside the family, things have other names.

But usually you did not play. You were angry. You scared us. Every day we listened to you swear, "Dog vomit. Your mother's cunt. Your mother's smelly cunt." You slammed the iron on the shirt while muttering, "Stink pig. Mother's cunt." Obscenities. I made a wish that you only meant gypsies and not women in general.

You were tricked twice by gypsies. One unwrapped her laundry right there on the counter. She shook out her purple and rose cloths, held them up, and said, "You've torn my best dress. Oh, look. And the blouse, too. Nothing left but rags. And the skirts. Torn to pieces. Mangled. You'll have to pay for them, you know. Replace them. Oh, my new expensive tablecloth. You're going to have to give me money for

new clothes. A wardrobe. Come on. Pay up now. Pay. Pay."
She wiggled her fingers through the holes. She had brought
dustrags, of course.

"No," you said. "Your clothes be old," you said.

The gypsy strewed her clean, pressed rags and rushed out,
but she returned with a sister gypsy – and a cop. The two
gypsies talked hard, their earrings leaping with the movements of their jaws. The fan and air-conditioner circulated
the smell of their winged hairdos. The policeman, whose
navy blue bulk expanded to fill the room, metal and wood
clunking, kept saying, "Small claims court." Deportation. So
you paid, rang up the No Sale on the cash register and paid.
Twice.

"I knew she was up to something," MaMa shouted.
"Remember when I sorted her bag, I said, 'How do the
gypsies afford to have rags laundered?' I could tell that that
Romany demoness was up to no good. She and that other
one who acted as witness concocted a big story in English
for the police. And you couldn't speak English well enough
to counteract it. Fell for it twice. You fell for it twice."

"Kill your Romany mother's cunt," you said between
your clenched teeth. "Kill your Romany demoness mother's
cunt dead." There is a Cantonese word that sounds almost
like "grandmother," po, and means a female monster that
looms and sags. In the storeroom were a black bag and a
white bag, which we never opened. They were big enough
for us children to climb like hills and we called them Black
Bag Po and White Bag Po. You called the gypsies those names
too. "Old bags," you muttered. "Gypsy bag. Smelly pig bag.
Sow. Stink pig. Bag cunt."

When the gypsy baggage and the police pig left, we were
careful not to be bad or noisy so that you would not turn on
us. We knew that it was to feed us you had to endure demons
and physical labor.

You screamed wordless male screams that jolted the house

upright and staring in the middle of the night. "It's BaBa," we children told one another. "Oh, it's only BaBa again." MaMa would move from bed to bed. "That was just BaBa having a dream. Bad dreams mean good luck." She would leave us puzzling, then what do good dreams mean?

Worse than the swearing and the nightly screams were your silences when you punished us by not talking. You rendered us invisible, gone. MaMa told us to say Good Morning to you whether or not you answered. You kept up a silence for weeks and months. We invented the terrible things you were thinking: That your mother had done you some unspeakable wrong, and so you left China forever. That you hate daughters. That you hate China.

You complained about holiday dumplings: "Women roll dough to knead out the dirt from between their fingers. Women's fingernail dirt." Yet you did eat them. MaMa said, though, that you only lately began eating pastries. "Eating pastries is eating dirt from women's fingernails and from between their fingers." As if women had webs. Finger jams.

MaMa pays you back, with her tomato and potato wages, the money she sends to China. "They're my relatives," she says, "not his."

You say with the few words and the silences: No stories. No past. No China.

You only look and talk Chinese. There are no photographs of you in Chinese clothes nor against Chinese landscapes. Did you cut your pigtail to show your support for the Republic? Or have you always been American? Do you mean to give us a chance at being real Americans by forgetting the Chinese past?

You are a man who enjoys plants and the weather. "It's raining," you said in English and in Chinese when the California drought broke. "It's raining." You make us inordinately happy saying a simple thing like that. "It rains."

What I want from you is for you to tell me that those

curses are only common Chinese sayings. That you did not mean to make me sicken at being female. "Those were only sayings," I want you to say to me. "I didn't mean you or your mother. I didn't mean your sisters or grandmothers or women in general."

I want to be able to rely on you, who inked each piece of our own laundry with the word *Center*, to find out how we landed in a country where we are eccentric people.

On New Year's eve, you phone the Time Lady and listen to her tell the minutes and seconds, then adjust all the clocks in the house so their hands reach midnight together. You must like listening to the Time Lady because she is a recording you don't have to talk to. Also she distinctly names the present moment, never slipping into the past or sliding into the future. You fix yourself in the present, but I want to hear the stories about the rest of your life, the Chinese stories. I want to know what makes you scream and curse, and what you're thinking when you say nothing, and why when you do talk, you talk differently from Mother.

I take after MaMa. We have peasant minds. We see a stranger's tic and ascribe motives. I'll tell you what I suppose from your silences and few words, and you can tell me that I'm mistaken. You'll just have to speak up with the real stories if I've got you wrong.

My father was born in a year of the Rabbit, 1891 or 1903 or 1915. The first year of the Republic was 1911. In one of his incarnations, one of the Buddhas was a rabbit; he jumped alive into a fire to feed the hungry.

BaBa was the youngest and the smartest of four brothers. They put their ears to the door of the room where he was being born. At midday the midwife came out carrying a basin of blood; and they did not understand how a baby could be constructed with so much blood left over.

The oldest brother, Dai Bak, Big Uncle, said, "Get some

boxes and chairs and come with me." The brothers balanced the teaks and pines in a stack under their parents' window and climbed it like acrobats. By the time they reached the curved sill, the baby had been born. They saw its foot sticking out of a bundle tied to the hook of the rice scale. The baby's bottom plumped out the white cloth. Their mother and father were laughing, and laughed harder when they saw the boys at the window. "BiBi has arrived," their father announced, and simultaneously they heard a baby's cry come from the dumpling, the *dim sum*, the little heart. The brothers clutched one another, they cheered, jumped up and down. " 'Jump like a squirrel,' " they sang. " 'Bob like a blue jay, tails in the air, tails in the air.' A baby is born. A baby is born." They scrambled down and ran inside to have a look at him. They hung over the headboard, knelt by the bedside, put their heads next to the baby's on their mother's pillow. All day the brothers smiled when they saw one another and the baby.

Grandmother, Ah Po, said, "Your little brother is different from any of you. Your generation has no boy like this one. Come. Look." She unwrapped the baby to show how skinny he was. She uncurled his fists, and his brothers touched the wrinkles inside, looked at their own wrinkles. "Look at the length of his hands and fingers," said Ah Po. "This kind of hand was made for holding pens. This is the boy we'll prepare for the Imperial Examinations." The other boys were built like horses and oxen, made for farmwork. Ah Po let them each sit on the bed and hold the baby in his lap. They felt big and important. Dai Bak, the oldest, remembered also holding the other two; curious how each brother had felt different in his arms, this one so light. "Now when you go out to play, you have a baby to strap on your back," he said to the brother who, up to then, had been the youngest. Grandfather stood at the foot of the bed and was dumfounded that he had four sons, all in his old age.

At the baby's one-month birthday party, Ah Po gave him the Four Valuable Things: ink, inkslab, paper, and brush. The other children had only gotten money. She put the brush in his right fist. Villagers and relatives praised the way he waved it about. Eating bowls of chicken-feet-and-sweet-vinegar soup and pigs'-feet-and-sweet-vinegar soup, they said good words for the future. Ah Po shaved her baby's head except for the crown, though it was only baby fuzz he had growing on his head. The house was ashine with lights and lucky with oranges.

Third Uncle, Sahm Bak, waited until the baby was tucked away in his parents' bedroom for a nap. Then he ducked into that room and pressed himself against the wall so as not to be spotted from the guest hall, the doors never shut in this house. He dropped to his knees, crawled quickly behind and under furniture, and reached the bed. He grabbed two hand-fuls of the quilt and hoisted himself up, his chubby legs kick-ing. He saw the baby asleep, curled in a nest of blankets in the middle of the bed. Sahm Bak delighted in drawing the cur-tains and hiding inside the layers of canopy and mosquito netting; this high bed was his flying boat to the moon, a secret room, a stage for plays, night in the middle of the day. He stood up, captain of his flying boat, and walked over to his baby brother. His feet sank into the quilts. He was wear-ing a pair of leather shoes his father had brought back from the Gold Mountain. The shoes were too big for him, but he had stuffed the toes. He pushed and pulled the baby free of the blankets, then he jumped on its stomach. The baby was not as soft as the quilts. The unexpected bones and the over-size shoes made Sahm Bak fall. The baby began to cry. Sahm Bak got to his feet quickly. He had to hurry before the noise brought the adults running. He jumped up and down, up and down on the baby's stomach, so bouncy. The baby let out a squeal each time the shoes depressed his stomach. When the adults arrived, the baby was not squalling any more, but was blue. Since being hit and scolded on a birthday would be bad luck, Sahm Bak had to wait until the next day for his punishment; Dai Bak, who should have been more alert watching his brothers, would have to be punished too. The adults sent the guests hastily home with red eggs and ginger to "fill their hands."

For years afterwards, Ah Po would say, "You were so bad, you stomped on him for hours."

"I don't remember doing that," her third son said. "Do you remember my doing that?" he asked you, BaBa.

"No," you said. "I don't remember either."

Sometimes Sahm Bak pretended he was a baby, quietly nudging himself onto his mother's lap, but when she noticed him, she put him on the floor and picked up BaBa, her BiBi, her lap baby. She loved him so much, she licked the snot from his nose.

Grandfather, Ah Goong, plowed fields hour after hour alone, inching along between earth and sky. To amuse himself, he sang girls' songs in an old man's falsetto. He wished for a happy daughter he could anticipate seeing in the evenings after work; she would sing for him and listen to him sing. He tied his ox near some water and took a walk about the village to find out what the neighbors were doing. One family he often visited had had a baby due at the same time as our family. After seeing what he himself had gotten, he went to find out what they'd gotten. His mouth and throat, his skin puckered all over with envy. He discovered why to be envious is "to guzzle vinegar." Theirs was the loveliest dainty of a baby girl. She lay ignored in a yam basket. He gazed at her and sang to her until he had to leave, should he fall farther behind in his plowing. The next time he visited, he brought her a red ribbon, which he fashioned into a bow and arranged by her ear. He laughed at the air it gave her. She wore rags, which sent waves of delicious pity coursing through him. "Poor girl," he said. "Poor, poor girl."

The day his third son stomped on the baby, Ah Goong sneaked away from the commotion. He scooped up party food on the way out. He went to the girl's house. He tucked red packets of money in her faded shirt, no special red dress for her today, no new red jacket, no tiger shoes nor hat with eight boy dolls for tassels. Her family offered him shredded carrots, scant celebration. How sorry he felt for her, how he loved her. She cried, squeezing bitty tears out of her shut lids. His heart and his liver filled with baby tears. Love filled his heart and his liver. He piled grapefruits and oranges in a pyramid for her. He tarried so long that he had to use the outhouse, but he carefully weighed his shit on the outhouse scales so that these neighbors could return a like amount to his fields.

He cut a reed from the New Year narcissus and blew tunes between his thumbs. Though the snowpeas would be fewer at harvest, he brought the girl their blossoms, pinks with purple centers, light blues with dark blue centers, the vine flowering variously as if with colors of different species. She chewed on the flowers and pulled the tendrils apart in her chubby hands. Extravagance. In the summer he fanned her with a sandalwood fan; he rubbed its ribs with sandpaper, and with one pass, the air thickened with memories of Hawai'i, which is the Sandalwood Mountains. In the autumn the two of them would rattle dry peapods.

"It's only a girl," her parents kept saying. "Just a girl."

"Yes," said Ah Goong. "Pretty little sister. Pretty miss."

Away from her he detached a fuzzy green melon from its nest and tucked it for a moment inside his sweater next to his heart. Whenever he had to leave her, he felt the time until he would see her again extend like an unplowed field, the sun going down and a long country night to come. No, he would not endure it.

He went home and put on the brown greatcoat that he had bought in San Francisco. "Where are you going with that coat in this weather?" asked Ah Po, who did not follow him about the house because of her bound feet; the three maids who fanned her and helped her walk were working in the kitchen. When she walked unassisted or with one maid, she touched the walls gracefully with thumb and little finger spread, index and middle fingers together, fourth finger down. "I'll just take a peek at the baby," he said, "then go out." He picked up his wife's baby and hid him inside his greatcoat. If you had been a little older, BaBa, you might have felt proud, singled out for an excursion that made Ah Goong dance down the road, a bright idea in his head.

He ran into the neighbor's house and unwrapped the baby, first the greatcoat, then the diapers to show the family that this doggy really was a boy. "Since you want a boy and I want a girl," he said, "let's strike a bargain. Let's trade." The family was astounded. They would have let him buy the girl if only he'd asked. They would have had to give her away eventually anyhow. And here was this insane man who did not know the value of what he had. What a senile fool. Take him up on it before he comes to his senses. As if his son's boyness were not enough, he pointed out his attributes. "This boy will be very intelligent," he said. "He's got scholar's hands. And look what a smart forehead he has. He'll win a name for you at the Imperial Examinations. He's very skinny and eats hardly any food."

"Yes, we'll take him," said the neighbors. Ah Goong placed the girl inside his greatcoat. He did not remove the boy's fancy clothes, the gold necklace, the new shoes, nor the jade bracelet that signified that you would not have to do physical labor. He hurried out before her family could change their minds. His heart beat that they would reclaim her at the last minute. The girl wore no jewelry, but with his soul he adopted her, full diapers and all.

He walked slowly, adoring the peachy face. He sat by the side of the road to look at her. He counted her pink toes and promised that no one would break them. He tickled her under the chin. She would make his somber sons laugh. Kindness would soon soften the sides of their mouths. They would kneel to listen to her funny requests. They would beguile her with toys they'd make out of feathers and wood. "I'll make you a doll," he promised her. "I'll buy you a doll." And surely his wife would get used to her soon. The walk home was the nicest time. He showed her, his daughter, how the decorative plants grow wild and the useful plants in rows. "Flower," he said, pointing. "Tree." He rested by the stream for her to listen to its running.

At home, he walked directly to the crib and tucked her in. He drew the quilt over her as a disguise. Then he hung up his greatcoat and returned to the crib, gave the quilt a pat. She was a well-behaved baby and made no noise. He kept strolling past the crib. His happiness increased in her vicinity. "My heart and my liver" he called her. (*Sweetheart* is an English word that emigrants readily learn.)

Ah Po heard the sniffing and squeaking of a baby waking up. She swayed over to the crib. The baby noises sounded unfamiliar. She screamed when she saw the exchanged baby.

Ah Goong came running. "What's wrong? What's wrong?" he asked.

"What is this? Where's my baby?" Ah Po yelled.

"It's all right." He patted the baby. "Everything's all right. He's at the neighbors'. They'll take good care of him."

"What neighbors?" she yelled. "What's he doing at the neighbors'? Whose is this ugly thing?"

"Oh, no, she isn't ugly. Look at her." He picked her up.

"Where's my baby? You crazy old man. You're insane. You idiot. You dead man."

"The neighbors have him. I brought this one back in his place." He held his little girl. "All we have are boys. We need a girl."

"You traded our son for a girl? How could you? Who has my son? Oh, it's too late. It's too late." She thrust her arms as far as she could reach; she bent her torso from side to side, backward and forward, a woman six feet tall on toy feet. "Take me to that family," she cried. "We're trading back." Lunging her weight at Ah Goong, who hunched his shoulders and caved in his chest to protect the baby, she pushed him out the door. She walked in back of him, shoving him while hanging on to his shoulder. She was not used to dashing about on the roads. "I'm coming to rescue you, BiBi. Your mother's coming." Ah Goong clung to his baby as if she were holding him up. "Dead man," Ah Po raged, "trading a son for a slave. Idiot." He led her to the neighbors' house, weeping as he walked. "Dead demon." The villagers lined the road to look at Grandfather and Grandmother making fools of themselves.

Ah Po scolded the girl's family. "Cheating the greedy pig, huh? Thieves. Swindlers. Taking advantage of an idiot. Cheaters. Trying to catch a pig, are you? Did you really think you'd get away with it? Pig catchers. A girl for a boy. A girl for a boy." The family hung their heads.

She pulled the girl out of Ah Goong's arms and shoved her at an older child. Her own baby she snatched and held tight. She sent for her sedan chair and waited for it in the road. She carried her son herself all the way home, not letting Ah Goong touch her baby, not letting him ride. He hardly saw the road for his tears. Poor man.

Perhaps it was that very evening and not after the Japanese bayoneted him that he began taking his penis out at the dinner table, worrying it, wondering at it, asking why it had given him four sons and no daughter, chastising it, asking it whether it were yet capable of producing the daughter of his dreams. He shook his head and clucked his tongue at it.

When he saw what a disturbance it caused, he laughed, laughed in Ah Po's irked face, whacked his naked penis on the table, and joked, "Take a look at *this* sausage."

When BiBi was walking upright instead of "in cow position" on all fours, his second brother, Ngee Bak, walked him to the fields. "Come on, BiBi," he said, taking his hand. "Let's go look at what shoots came up overnight." He slowed his steps for the toddler, but walking the veering way children walk, the two boys often turned around and went back the way they came, each one following the other here and there, lifting rocks, prodding bugs, squatting to part the grass and thrill at the small live movements. But a plan kept reappearing in Ngee Bak's mind so that they did eventually arrive at the rice field, which looked like a lake on fire with rows of doubling green flames.

"Isn't it beautiful?" said Ngee Bak, who threw a pebble at the water in front of BiBi. Waterdrops spattered his knees, and laughter gurgled up inside his chest like ripples and like the waterdrops. With both hands, he plucked stones out of the dam. He threw one rock after another and loved the giggles that splashed happily out of his mouth. Then he pushed the mud and rice straw and rocks aside and jumped into the water, kicked it, watched the rings spread and fade. He touched the shoots, grasped them, and pulled, such a satisfying loosening and snapping of roots from the earth. He collected the green rice in his pockets.

Meanwhile, Ngee Bak ran tattletaling to the house, "Come quick. Hurry. Look. Look. Look at BiBi."

Grandfather and Grandmother lifted him out of the water and ordered their oldest son, "Go cut a switch." Dai Bak did not climb a tree for a fresh switch; he hunted in the faggots for a brittle branch that had fallen during a winter storm. He trimmed off the twigs. He knelt at his parents' feet and knocked his forehead on the ground.

"Please beat me, Father and Mother, to teach me a lesson," he requested.

They took turns hitting him across the back and shoulders, not his head because they did not want to damage his brains. "This – will – teach – you – to – teach – your – younger – brother – to – watch – his – younger – brother," a switch with each word. They administered what Tu Fu called "the beating by which he remembered his guilt." There was sap in the branch yet.

"Thank you, Father and Mother," he said when they were done whipping. BiBi and Ngee Bak stood nearby and watched. The two of them listened, thankful he wasn't the oldest, who has the duty of setting a good example. (We American children heard too, and resolved not to "return" to China.)

Instead of acrobatics and shuttlecock, he liked studying. Ah Po kept her boy close. She sewed little scholar's caps and scholar's gowns. She used the leftover black scraps for knee patches on her other sons' pants. Even before BiBi could talk, she fed and lodged itinerant scholars, who stayed the night or week to read to him. They drew giant words and held them over his crib. "How intelligent he looks," they told her. When he was old enough for regular lessons, his brothers sometimes came inside from their chores to rest on the floor at the tutor's feet. Ah Po did not stop them, did not chase them back out. If they overheard some learning, all the better; they would have it to ponder during their years in the fields. Soon the farming brothers' heads nodded; when they suddenly jerked awake, it embarrassed them that the tutor might have seen them bored. One by one they withdrew to slop pigs, draw water, feed chickens before it grew too dark for chickens to eat, dumb fowls.

BaBa was also very good at gambling, but he won so often that his brothers would not play with him. "It's not fair," they complained. "He memorizes the cards and tiles."

"He's lucky," Ah Po bragged, her eyes and her rings glittering as if she were sweeping in the winnings herself. "Lucky."

So instead of gambling in the evenings, BaBa "hummed" poems. He practiced his handwriting at his own corner of the gambling table, which was also the dining table. The words he wrote were as large as his chest, the word *heart* bigger than his own heart, the word *man* almost as big as himself. He had to stand on a chair to write so big, "playing with big words" like the nine-year-old Tu Fu, who wrote enough words "to fill a hard-bottomed bag." A humming came from him continually.

The three older brothers founded a clubhouse inside a grape arbor. By excluding one, they made a secret society. Under the jagged leaves, the three brothers peeked at their little brother kneeling in the dirt. He was scratching the ground with a stick. "He's writing," they whispered. "Even outdoors he's writing. Let's torture him." They scurried out of the vines and circled him while they sang "The Song of the Man of the Green Hill." They schemed that if their mother saw them from the house, she'd think they were only playing with him. " 'Poetry addict, poetry addict,' " they sang. " 'Poetry addict won't work for rice, shoulders a hoe but forgets to till. Poetry addict won't comb his hair, defends his home with a rusty sword. Poetry addict rude to guests, out of food and forgets to eat. He won't loosen tongue to bring about the fall of seventy cities.' " He scribbled on the ground until his brothers wearied and left him alone.

One autumn morning, when he was about fourteen years old, he left the village to take the qualifying test for the last Imperial Examination ever given. Instead of taking a boat, he walked beneath the trees, useful for inspiration, their branches like open arms forking smaller and smaller until the topmost branches spread into fingers reaching and gesturing, posing and pointing in the wind. The branches formed words too, as did the skeins of geese. "The snow goose of ambition stirs its wings," Tu Fu had said on his way to the tests. "I ride the great snow goose of my ambition." The geese flew with wingtips pointing. The farther BaBa walked from the village, the larger the world grew. He sat by a stream at noon and hummed a poem that ordered the sounds of water.

Toward evening he passed a hermitage with door open and no hermit inside; he passed an inn, and farmhouses where rich families were lighting lanterns. The owls flew with fanning wings into the twilight. He spread his bedroll in a reaped field. The wooden pillow under his neck lifted his thick braid, which Grandmother had woven tight to last for days, and it trailed on the ground. No trees obstructed the simple sky, no building or mountain; no hair blew in his face. He saw only sky, which made him feel simultaneously very big and very small, like one of the stars, like an eye. Each time he awoke, he could tell by the moon's place how long he had slept, and how unevenly.

No one moment was the dawn, but ten thousand blending moments, each one a dawn. The sun edging up did not begin the morning; it was somehow always at its center.

Noticing the foreign ways of fencing, terracing, and ricking, he walked two days. Within sight of the building that had been erected centuries ago specially for examinations, he threw away his village clothes, which were not proper clothing but wrappings and rags, and donned a black silk robe. He walked through the doorposts – fresh red posters on left and right: TO BEGIN THE YEAR, TELL ABOUT THE GREATNESS OF CHINA. MAY ALL THE EARTH'S PEOPLE DRINK WINE. And above the door: COME AND GO IN PEACE, which is a common blessing. So this was the Dragon's Gate, and he was a carp ready to run the falls.

He entered a courtyard, where scholars quietly conversed, not a one of them loud and scolding like the villagers. As he wandered among them, he heard them talk about what happened in books as if it were real. They were a different race from the splay-fingered village men, whose most imaginative talk was about the Gold Mountain. The scholars sprang riddles on one another. One would describe a situation or a relationship and the others, by calculating geomancy, rhymes, metaphors, puns, and radicals and other sections of words, guessed which ideograph it made. They clapped hands and laughed when somebody hit on the answer. Explaining to the ones who didn't get it, they opened their left palms and drew invisible calligraphy on them with the long, tapering index fingers of their right hands.

The camaraderie ended when an official stood at an inner door and called them out of the courtyard one by one. At mid-afternoon, he shouted the name BaBa had invented for himself on the occasion of taking the tests. (His baby name was like Shy Cutie, which would not do here.) It was the first time he heard his adult name said aloud by someone else. If another scholar had answered to that name, one or the other would have renamed himself on the spot, in case the name did not have enough power for two people. An official led BaBa to a cell, where he asked him to undress. The official looked over his naked body for notes written on the skin, combed through his long hair for hidden papers, cut open the seams and hems of his clothes. "I'll bring your dinner at six," he said, and took away BaBa's bedroll and everything in it.

BaBa sat on the cot, sat at the table. He would have enjoyed the luxury of having a window, though he did not need daylight or moonlight to study by. With hands folded behind his back, he paced, brushing the floor with the balls of his feet, and sang his memorizations. A jailer brought food, returned for the utensils, gave him back his bedroll, and locked him up "until time for the first test," he said. He left a teapot, around which BaBa held his hands and caught the rich heat that arose. He decided to stay awake all night. The tea lasted a short while. Fireflies in a jar would have given an appearance of warmth. Back in the village he had read by their light. Steam must have been issuing from his mouth and nose, but he could not see it. Huddling in a blanket, his knees against his chest, he perched on the straight-backed chair, but the blanket turned into a nest for sleeping, and he had to discard it. Muttering the texts, he gave voice and breath to word after word. His attention was a flame; when he saw it turn into a firefly, shrinking, going out, he almost fell off the chair with alarm; for a moment or longer he had fallen asleep. He tried propping himself up by the elbows. His eyes closed, and shapes and colors began turning into dreams. He tried holding his eyelids open with his fingers, but in the dark they might as well have been closed. He understood the blue-eyed Buddha-who-cut-off-his-eyelids. He stood on the chair and stretched – and felt a hook or a ring in a beam directly overhead. So there it was; of course, the poets said it would be there. He looped the end of his pigtail into the ring and tied it tight. Then he sat in his chair to study some more. When he dozed, his own hair jerked his head back up. Hours later, when the pull on his scalp no longer kept him alert, he opened the table drawer, where he found an awl. Like the poets whose blood had been wiped off it, he jabbed the awl into his thigh, held it there, and studied on. At the worst dark of the night, he needed neither ring nor awl. "Aiya!" Out of the disembodying dark came screams of men already driven mad, footsteps, scufflings, someone yelling, "Ah Ma. Ah Ma." The poets say that men have used the ring to hang themselves.

At last an official unlocked the cell to give him breakfast. He searched him again before escorting him to a testing room, where a panel of scholars sat at a long table. BaBa stood with his face to the wall and his hands clasped behind him. In this position he recited by heart from the Three Character Classics, the Five Classics (*The Book of Changes*, *The Book of History*, *The Book of Poetry*, *The Book of Propriety*, *The Spring and Autumn Annals*), and the Thirteen Classics by Confucius's disciples; the examiners also threw in some five-word poems. He had been afraid that nothing would come out of his mouth, but once the first words, many of which he had kept ready on his tongue, broke forth, the rest came tumbling out, like water, like grain. The judges wrote numbers beside his new name. When he returned to the cell, he felt lighter. On the second evening he reached the last word of the last book. He fell asleep that night without having to study for the first time in years.

On the third morning an official returned his Four Valuable Things. He set brushes, ink, inkslab, and paper on the table horizontally and vertically, aligned the papers' edges parallel to the table's edges. He sat with spine straight and ground the ink blacker and blacker. The blacker his ink, the more patient the man – the Genie of the Ink, who is no bigger than a fly, will land in it. A proctor entered and handed BaBa the topics to write about, and locked the door on his way out. His hand hollow as if fingers curled around a walnut, an actual walnut when he was a child, BaBa held the pen perpendicular, ready. So he was to write alone in a cell instead of among candidates sitting together in a hall. Poets warned about fake walls and blinds behind which established scholars hid and made fun of the candidates – the old men taking the test for the twentieth time and the young men tapping their feet and scratching as they conned words. The ceilings and walls of the cell seemed opaque enough. He concentrated on remembering the text. Knowledge fell into place, moved from head, from heart, down his arm and out the fingers to converge at the tip of the brush. At a downward pull, he made the first mark in the upper left side of the first word. The heel of his hand steady on the table, he drew the strong deliberate stem, then with a shake he quickened a branch. His fingers lifted on the thin strokes, pulling the brush up for tapering, and pressed down for the heavier, thicker lines, a flick the hook at the bottom. He worked for three days, building each word from top to bottom, left to right, water strokes, dots for flames, tailing gondolas for the boat words, never going back for repairs. He wrote in many styles including The Beauty Adorns Her Hair with Blossoms and The Maid Apes Her Mistress. The seven-hundred-word essays were geometries that demonstrated his knowledge of philosophy and, because this was modern times, of international politics. He dared one poem in the grass style and, with a new brush, one humorous poem that darted down the page like swifts in a clear sky.

He waited for three days to hear his rank among the scholars, who talked about winning and losing. They were at leisure. It was too late to study any more and too early to begin studying for the next try three years hence. Failing wasn't such a shame. Kai Li-shih hid in the gambling houses but became a poet nevertheless. Tu Fu, the Earthly Poet, sang about how he failed his third, fifth, and sixth tries, and about failing on his fortieth birthday. He had even failed a special test arranged in his honor. And he had come from eleven generations of scholars. (BaBa was the only one as far back as the family knew. We were a family of eighty pole fighters and no scholars.) Though the ignorant villagers would tease and mock, there was an honorable tradition of failing the exams. The emperors gave special honorary degrees for perseverance to eighty- and ninety-year-olds who had tried their whole lives. Ah, but winning, a scholar would become one of the philosophers who rules China; everyone would hear of him, everyone would want to befriend him. All things good come to the mandarin scholar. His ancestors would receive titles and degrees. (His descendants would not get anything, and so save the government expenses and trouble.)

BaBa did not win the top honors; he would have had an easier life then and not come to the Gold Mountain. He did not "fly" to Canton or Peiping. He must have been a Learned Scholar or a Righteous Worthy; he won the job of village teacher. Our family painted the rooftree red and trimmed the windows with green and gold.

His new name brought him enough luck, and so he kept it; the name he has now is that name: Think Virtue, my father's name. I hesitate to tell it; I don't want him traced and deported. Even MaMa rarely calls him by name and not this one but other vocatives, like So-and-so's Father. Friends call him Uncle or Brother or Teacher. Anyway, a translation, Think Virtue, is nothing like this name; the English words are like fiction, that is, their sounds are dissimilar from the Chinese sounds. Nobody would call anyone else by a translation, Think Virtue his written name anyway. He is still disguised. Think Virtue – *think* is an ideograph combining the radicals for *field* and *heart*, and *virtue* also has the root *heart* in it; his name looks like two valentines and is not as cerebral as it appears in English.

So he had once had three free days. He spent them talking to the other scholars, making friends, singing, touring the capital. Counting the days walking, you had seven free days.

My maternal grandparents or "outside grandmother" and "outside grandfather" – one of the words in *maternal grandparents* the same as in *foreigner* or *barbarian* – these "outsiders" tracked BaBa down by following the invisible red string that ties his ankle to MaMa's. Year by year the string grew shorter.

The outside grandparents had four daughters, and so one of this grandmother's habits whenever she heard of an interesting boy or young man was to count him. Using the poor people's divining method, she took a pinchful of rice, said his name, and counted the grains to see if she had picked an odd or even number, carefully dropping each speck back into the rice box. Odd meant Yes, this boy was her daughter's true husband; even meant No, wrong boy; *four* sounds like *die*. In addition to counting rice, she confirmed the results by paying an expensive blind fortuneteller to touch a list of young men's names, and he picked out her future son-in-law. He also used the yarrow sticks and the tortoise shell and told the wedding date.

Then these outsiders sent spies to find out if their prospective son-in-law was deformed or leprous or mad or poor or ugly. His family sent counterspies. Some families bribed the neighbors to bruit it about how good looking, intelligent, rich, and good humored their son or daughter was. But BaBa's and MaMa's families did not have to lie; he and she were exceptionally smart, the proof being their literacy. The outside grandfather, like the real one, was an unusual man in that he valued girls; he taught all his daughters how to read and write. The families had about the same amounts of money, earned by the generations going-out-on-the-road to the Gold Mountain.

On her third to the last evening at home, MaMa dressed in white. A lucky old woman, who had a good woman's long life, helped her wash her hair, though this being modern days she only sprinkled water on her head. Dressed in white, MaMa sat behind her bedcurtains to sing-and-weep. "Come and hear the bride cry," the village women invited one another. "Hurry. Hurry. The bride's started singing-and-crying." "Listen. Listen. The bride's singing. The bride's weeping." They sat around the bed to listen as if they were at the opera. The girl children sat too; they would learn the old and new songs. The women called out ideas: "Cry about the years your mother held you prisoner." "And you're ransomed at last." "Scold your mother for not finding you your husband sooner."

"Give me a rifle to shoot my mother down," MaMa wailed. "Mother, you've kept me working at your house. You've hidden me from my husband and family. Mother, I'm leaving you now. I'm aiming my rifle at your stomach and shooting you down."

"Oh-h-h," exclaimed the women. "She's the best crying bride I've ever heard." The drummers banged. The bride's mother stood against the wall and smiled proudly.

"Cry for widows and orphans," the guests suggested. "Cry for boys and men drafted into armies." "And leaving for the Gold Mountain." She cried-and-sang about the three times her father left for the Gold Mountain and how he brought back two stepmothers. "They fried dumplings for their own babies and spattered oil on my feet," she sang. "And my bridegroom will go too out-on-the-road and send me photographs of an old man."

"Sing for a husband for the spinsters." "Sing for a husband for my older sister," said pretty younger sisters who could not jump over the old maids.

"Pull a barrel on top of you, and cry over how heavy a man is." The women cackled at that one.

"Cry for going hungry."

"The men don't make enough money for spending all those years away."

"Scold them for enjoying the barbarian lands more than home." "Scold unfaithful men." "Make up a song for scolding a man when he comes back."

"My husband will pick a plum," she sang. "He'll pick a plum blossom as I become a prune."

The women punctuated her long complaints with clangs of pot lids for cymbals. The rhymes made them laugh. MaMa wailed, her eyes wet, and sang as she laughed and cried, mourned, joked, praised, found the appropriate old songs and invented new songs in melismata of singing and keening. She sang for three evenings. The length of her laments that ended in sobs and laughter was wonderful to hear.

The bridegroom's family sent three thousand wedding cakes, two thousand of the expensive bought kind and one thousand of the homemade cheap kind. They sent either one thousand pigs or one pig and the price of a thousand pigs. The outside grandparents parceled the cakes and hunks of crackly orange-skin pork among their friends and relatives, gave some each evening to the women who came to hear the crying-and-singing, and also sent it by messengers throughout the village.

On the morning of the fourth day, MaMa dressed in her black wedding coat with the embroidered flowers and birds. ("I'm going to order wedding coats from Hong Kong for you," she says. "No. No, thanks," we say.) Layers of veiling hung from her headdress; no one could see her face. Men carried the bridal palanquin through the streets, where a band of dancers and beggars, "the flowery ones," who cannot be turned away on a wedding day, followed. "She rides like a queen above the men," said the wedding guests. "The men are kidnapping her," they also said. Her palanquin was called a "bridge." She would go no more to her parents' house except as a visitor; the visit a woman makes to her parents is a metaphor for rarity.

In the middle of the courtyard of her new home, she sat on a round wicker tray. Another lucky old woman lifted the veil in back and combed her hair, but actually only touched it with a comb, her hair being already dressed. The wedding guests gasped, wanting to reach out and stop the comb; they had also been uneasy at the hairwashing and at hearing the bad words, *death*, *army*, *rifle*, and at seeing the woman riding above the men. There was a suspense, a shock to see the bride dressed in funeral white, to see her feet and butt touch the winnower, which touches food, and to watch the burning of the paper horses like a funeral. The wedding guests held still, waited, then exhaled, laughed, and shouted.

Then the bride went inside the house to meet the groom. Being a very clever bride and having been coached by the married women, when the wedding guests pulled aside the bedcurtains and she saw him for the first time — sitting in his bed "like a Buddha statue," she said; that is, "like a *fut*" – she leapt up on the bed and sat facing him so closely that there was no room for her to kowtow. She quickly served him the tea; the kowtowing-to-the-husband part of the ceremony was skipped.

You were sitting there on your bed when out of nowhere jumped this veiled woman. Your family had reminded you, "Be sure to make her bow her head," but she was already pouring tea while the wedding guests threw popcorn, which fell like a warm snowfall, covering the quilt, landing on her headdress, and catching in your long sleeves. In the kitchen more corn popped like distant gunfire.

Bride and groom arose from the cloud of popcorn and went to the family hall, where Grandfather and Grandmother sat in the two best chairs. The new couple kneeled at their feet and served them tea while they said lucky words about long life and many children and much money. The mother-in-law gave the daughter-in-law jewelry. The bride's sisters served dry tea to the women in the groom's family; dry tea is a cupful of cookie crumbs.

Finally at the feast, the groom and his brothers walked from table to table to drink an entire glass of whiskey at each toast. The bride and her sisters walked to each table to pour and drink tea; the wedding guests loaded her tray with red money. Serving with both hands, she displayed her arms, covered from wrists to elbows with gold and jade bracelets, the right arm showing his family's gifts, the left arm her family's. Many of the bracelets were chains of American quarter eagle gold pieces. Catenaries of gold necklaces strung with gold coins, jade hearts, and gold words adorned her neck. She also wore a gold ring in the shape of two clasping hands that Grandfather had brought from the Gold Mountain.

After the guests left, the bride and groom went to their room, which was fluffy with popcorn, and he saw her face for the first time.

* * *

BaBa made a living by being the village teacher. Every day at sunrise, he called the roll in a name chant, which was a sort of hexameter, each student's name filling half a line. Staggering the lessons, he began the older boys copying their textbook and told the six- and seven-year-olds, "Repeat after me." He read Lesson One to them many times, the children chorusing line by line. They copied it while he read a more advanced lesson with an older group.

At 9 a.m. everyone went home for breakfast, which was recess. There was no need for other rest; reading and writing are rest, mere sitting. When all the boys were copying at once, BaBa walked up and down between tables, corrected a brush hold, switched a pen from left hand to right hand, straightened a paper and a spine. He kept a rod tucked under his arm. All seemed to go well the first few days, the students obedient enough, though when sweeping out the schoolhouse he found piles of chewed sunflower seeds in corners.

In the evening, after marking the copybooks, which were almost all poor, he began working on a project he had thought up to give his students an advantage in their education. Instead of having them buy handwriting patterns printed in Canton, he would make one for each boy, using that boy's own special words, including his father's name, which some shy or backward villagers did not tell their children. He ruled sturdy pieces of paper into squares and filled each square with a word that was the epitome of a particular kind of stroke or radical. The students would insert these master sheets into the transparent sleeves of their tracing booklets and follow the lines of their teacher's excellent handwriting. He would finish two or three patterns an evening until every student had one.

Worries, like roosters crowing in the dark, woke BaBa hours before he needed to go to school. He stared at the ceiling, listened, listed things to do, waited until his father and brothers, silent like thieves, stealing an extra hour from the night, got up and walked to the fields, and the women went to the well to catch the first water of dawn, the Glory of the Well, good for the skin. Before sunrise, he walked to the schoolhouse; the closer he came, the louder the birds, whose wakening sounded like children's voices. To his horror, children's voices, their laughter, and the scrape and thud of furniture came from the schoolhouse. A small boy at the door sprang up as he recognized his teacher. The boy ran inside, where scurrying, talking – a door slammed – scuttling stopped completely upon BaBa's entrance. The students were supposed to be studying during the hour before the teacher's arrival, their loud studious voices to accompany the farmers' walk to the fields. The whole village must have heard the chaos. He did not know which boys to punish; they were now chanting the last lines of their various lessons.

When he explained things in the common language, the students should have marveled that they had a teacher who knew the meanings of the texts and not just the rote. Today he would explain some of the "parallelisms" – how the directions, the elements, the humors, the architecture of emperors' palaces and commoners' houses, the weather, the trees, the members of families, the hours of the day, the centuries, the dynasties of China, the winds, all have their correspondences one to another. For example, pre-dawn is the time of the unborn child and of bulbs in the earth. Mid-winter, midnight, and old age are times of sleep and death and harvest in the barns. The students ought to know that at that very moment, they were at a mid-morning in spring, youth, a growing time. It was a year of Approach, when a good man is inexhaustible in his will to learn and teach. He recited the poem that had won first place at the Imperial Examinations: "'Escaping the fire, the second grandfather ran with the pig in his arms, and the fifth son carried the sheep.' The numbers, the relatives, the animals all have important meanings," he said. "The winner explained that he was describing an actual fire at his house."

Eyes blinked and glazed. Heads nodded and jerked. Boys flipped their pigtails over the tops of their heads and unbraided the ends; they hid their sleeping eyes behind the hair. At any moment, they would awaken and go into uproar again. BaBa retreated. "Read aloud after me," he said, quitting explanations. Sometimes the boys shouted out the end of a line. He liked them for doing that, though it was just an outburst against tedium. When their voices dwindled, he looked at the clock; there was half an hour to fill. "Read aloud by yourselves," he said. Without his leading them, they straggled and faltered; the smartest boy heard himself solo, and stopped. So he diverted them to chanting the multiplication tables until breakfast. Once he placed the rod across the shoulders of a boy who snored aloud. The rod transmitted a sense of his corporeity, the skin, the muscles, the two wing bones.

BaBa could not eat breakfast, and both his mother and my mother said, "You have to eat. You can't use your brain all day without food." He paced, then had to go to school again.

"Writing," he taught, "isn't painting. Get enough ink on the brush to complete a stroke in one movement. Don't go back to fill in. No backward painting. If you don't have enough ink, use the dry brush technique, a very advanced method." He handed out the one-of-a-kind patterns he had made. "What do we do with the patterns we spent money on?" the students asked. While the younger students one by one stood beside his desk and read aloud, out of the corners of his eyes he saw a writer splotch his paper; another took dab after dab to form one stroke; another outlined a word and colored it in; another dribbled ink in the wide part of a word, then spread it out. Heavy hands moving from right to left smeared columns of writing.

At mid-afternoon, he told the students that they had been working so hard, he would treat them: he'd give them the first line of a couplet, and they could finish it almost any way they pleased. He read many examples in order to inspire them. But boredom drained their eyes. The word *poetry* had hit them like a mallet stunning cattle. As he recited, two boys were whispering; he needed to reprimand them, knock their heads together right now, but a scolding would interrupt the poem. He pressed onward, his face stiff, eyes glowering, ruining the mood of the poem, his lips mouthing the words. "Now I'll give you a first line that establishes the season and place," he said. "You find the second line. You can write about an animal, a plant, a battle strategy, the climate, a cloud, a finger of the hand, a tree, a feeling, a color, a political rank, a condition of the soil, whatever. You can write about a boat; there are many different kinds."

"Go ahead. Start now," he said when the boys continued to stare.

"What do you want us to do?" asked a boy who had been sighing and yawning throughout the assignment.

"Could you explain that again?" asked another boy, exasperated, rolling his eyes at the teacher's ineptness.

He had fallen into talking about the parallels they hadn't understood earlier, but it was too late; dropping a lesson once started spoils a teacher's authority.

"I don't get it." "We don't understand you." "You don't explain clearly."

"Take a guess," he suggested. "Taking a guess is the same as making up a story."

"That doesn't make sense." "We don't understand." "You're making things up because you don't know the answers."

A flash of lightning broke red across the room. He grit his teeth. He wanted to kill. "Finish the couplet," he said.

"What's that?"

A blood vessel must have broken in his temple, and the red lightning was the blood spurted across his eyes.

"Could you repeat your half of the poem?" someone asked.

"Could you repeat the assignment?" said someone else, whom he ignored.

Controlling his face, he repeated the start of the couplet, and what poetry had been in the line was a mortification in his mouth.

"Explain," said the students.

The boys spoke in the brute vulgate, and he saw that he had made a bad mistake translating literature into the common speech. The students had lost respect for him; if he were so smart, he would not speak like them. Scorn curled their lips and lifted their eyebrows. "Explain," they demanded without standing up for recognition.

The opening line was not even a complex one, very colloquial: "At mid-morning in late spring, when walking west —"

"What?" "What did he say?" The students had not seen his anger, then; it had not shown on his face. They would otherwise not act so dumb. "Explain that again."

Their previous teacher must have spent school time drinking tea and reading novels.

"How do you write *clear* and *bright*?" At last, one of the boys was getting down to work, though he had forgotten two of the simplest and most commonly used ideographs in the language. BaBa wrote the words invisibly on his table. "Slower," said the boy. BaBa wrote with ink on paper. "How do you write *wood*?" the boy asked. BaBa wrapped his hand around the boy's and wrote the tree-like word. "See?" BaBa said. "It looks like a tree." The word written by two people's hands wiggled with impatience and with not wanting to show impatience, the little hand pulling one way and the big hand another.

BaBa kept hearing furtive motion behind him. Just you wait until I give your parents your report cards, he thought. I'll show you. You'll be sorry. ("In China parents beat children for getting beaten by the teacher," said the adults.)

He whirled and hit a boy on the arm. "Work!" he shouted. Neither the boy whose hand he guided nor the one he hit said "Thank you, Teacher."

At last he decided that they had sweated enough over the couplet, which they should have closed instantly. He had meant it as a recreation, a break in the work, just for fun. The boys were forcing him to turn literature into a weapon against them.

During the tracing hour, their heavy heads lolled like cows' heads toward whatever insect of distraction alit. Some boys drew pictures of animals. The younger children squirmed from one buttock to the other, wriggling to join the girls and baby boys playing outside.

At last the day ended. The students could not possibly have reached the last sentence in unison, but all together they closed their books at 4 p.m. as if they had been dismissed. Mid-sentence, mid-word, they slapped their books shut and tricked their teacher into saying, "Well, you may go." Then they charged out the door without bidding "Thank you, Teacher" or "Good afternoon, Teacher."

Suddenly the school was quiet. A dusty peace settled. BaBa sat down at his desk. The greased paper in the windows soaked up the afternoon sun in brownish stains. Most "desks" were only pieces of furniture the farmers could spare. A few show-offs had given their sons heirloom tables knotty with carvings. It was a small room after all, not an unwieldy size. He sprinkled water on the floor and swept it clean – gobs of sunflower seeds again in the corner. He smoothed out the paper wads and read them. He poured the dustpan of sweepings into the stove. Long strands of shedded hair snapped in the fire. As he walked about the room, everything he touched became well ordered. He would oil new paper for the windows, perhaps white paper rather than brown so the students could see better. He would bring a hammer and nails and other tools tomorrow. He would build a fence around the school and dig a garden. Then the students might not want so much to escape. Leaving the door open for light and air, he graded papers and recorded the low grades in a ledger.

His wife was watching for him in the road when he came home late. "I thought you'd been kidnapped by bandits," she said. "It's dangerous to be out after dark. Where would we get the money to ransom you?" He went immediately to dinner. Perhaps the student he hit would have felt it more if he ate better. He was losing weight teaching.

He dreamed that he was teaching mathematics but the numbers did not come out right. The correct answer wavered and changed by itself into an impossible figure; digits kept switching places. The students were yelling, "What's the answer, Teacher?" He abandoned the calculations and, rod raised, went chasing after them. They laughed when he hit them. The rod seemed to press giggles out of them. They hid under their tables. They jumped through the paper windows. "QUIET!" he screamed. He screamed lessons, morals, stories, poems, songs, but the students kept playing and fighting. Parents and the district principal peeked in the holes in the windows and saw that he could not teach. "Go away!" he screamed, and woke himself up.

There came to be small difference between his day life and the nightmares. The students ran amok. They stole vegetables from the neighboring gardens; they played war; they staged shows on top of the tables. He tried locking the door on the late boys and got some satisfaction from their shadows bobbing and passing like puppets at the windows, but they worried him when they disappeared. Where did they go? The school looked like a crazy house, like a Sung

Dynasty painting of a classroom showing kids putting boxes over one another's heads, drawing cartoons of their teacher, lying on their backs and spinning chairs and tables with their feet.

As the year went on, BaBa made a habit of staying at school during breakfast so that he would not have to wrench himself away from home twice in one morning. He used the rest period to read his own books before he forgot how. Someone had to enjoy reading in this school. The students ruined his eating; they ruined his sleep. They spoiled the songs of birds. And they were taking his books and calligraphy from him too – no time now for his own reading, no time to practice his own writing. Teaching was destroying his literacy. He was spending his brains picking out flaws and poring over them. School was the very opposite of reading and writing. The books that he taught had lost their subtlety and life, puns dead from slow explanations, philosophy reduced to saws. He could not read without thinking up test questions and paraphrases. He shrank poems to fit the brains of peasant children, who were more bestial than animals; when he used to plow, the water buffalo had let him prop a book between its horns.

One day when the students were throwing paper at one another, he walked over to a wad of it, the students watching, picked it up, and put it inside his desk drawer. He opened a book that had no connection whatsoever to school and read it. There were indeed a few students who took up their own books and read, did as he did; for a while on that one day, he taught by example, which, according to sages, is the most powerful way of teaching. Silently he unfurled a scroll and wrote as he pleased while all around him the class fell apart.

A boy got up from his desk and, since the teacher did not scold him, walked around him, pulled monkey faces, and peered in his ear. Egged on by the others, the wild boy jostled his teacher's elbow; his writing broke into a black smear. He stood up, knocking over the chair, which fell with a silencing bang. The students hushed. He seized the rod – the brush rolling down the scroll – and hit the boy, not carefully on the back but anywhere. The boy rolled up into a ball. BaBa hit harder, but the blows fell as if landing on a cushion. He struck almost as hard as he could, but there was an inconclusiveness. Perhaps if the boy had screamed louder when he hit harder, or if he could himself feel the pain, then he would have had satisfaction. If only the boy would properly kneel. If he could hit with all his might. Suddenly he stopped; it felt like beating a doll. Like a Japanese sensei, he ordered the boy to kneel with his head on the ground just outside the open door, where everyone could see him in shame, but when BaBa checked the doorway, the boy had run away.

"Why do we need to write?" the students asked. "We can pay letter writers." "We aren't going to starve," they said. "We'll go to sea and pick up the free gold on the Gold Mountain."

During the next two years, BaBa had two babies; they closed up the circle of children who harried his day. The boy and girl did keep his wife busy though; she had them to dote on.

BaBa did not learn how hard and often students have to be hit to make them polite. He shot them with an imaginary pistol; he stabbed them with an imaginary knife. Sometimes while standing in front of the bad boys, he pointed the imaginary pistol at his own head, and blew it open; then they would see the insides of his skull and know what their hate had done. He also imagined lifting his arms and flying over their heads, out the door, and into the sky; then they would want to learn how he did it. If the Imperial Examinations had not been canceled, he might have tried for a job away from children, become not a magistrate refereeing quarrels but a scribe or a bookkeeper. Mental work was harder than physical work, although it was not exactly the mind that teaching strained. He yearned for the fields with their quiet surprises, which he had plowed around – the nest with eggs from which he had felt the warmth rise, the big mushroom with nibbles around its crown and the mouse dead underneath, a volunteer lily when the field had been sown to rice.

Grading papers night after night for years, BaBa became susceptible to the stories men told, which were not fabulations like the fairy tales and ghost stories told by women. The Gold Mountain Sojourners were talking about plausible events less than a century old. Heroes were sitting right there in the room and telling what creatures they met on the road, what customs the non-Chinese follow, what topsy-turvy land formations and weather determine the crops on the other side of the world, which they had seen with their own eyes. Nuggets cobbled the streets in California, the loose stones to be had for the stooping over and picking them up. Four Sojourners whom somebody had actually met in Hong Kong had returned from the Gold Mountain in 1850 with three thousand or four thousand American gold dollars each. These four men verified that gold rocks knobbed the rivers; the very dirt was atwinkle with gold dust. In their hunger the men forgot that the gold streets had not been there when they'd gone to look for themselves.

One night of a full moon, BaBa neglected to grade papers, and joined the talking men and listening women. His oldest brother, Dai Bak, who had already traveled to Cuba and back, told how fish the size of long squash fell with the rain. "In Cuba the sky rains fish – live, edible fish. Fish *this* big fell on the roofs and sidewalks. Their tails and fins were flipping. Thick gray fish, little orange and yellow ones, all different species of fish. I caught a rainbow fish in my frying pan. We had to shovel them off the roofs before the sun rotted them."

"Isn't Havana a seaport?" BaBa asked. "Isn't Cuba an

island? Couldn't it have happened that a tornado sucked the seas up into the air, and water fell back down like rain on the land, fish and seaweed and all?"

"No. We were inland, and it wasn't salt water but fresh water sprinkling in raindrops. In fact, they were freshwater trout that fell. And it wasn't storming. I saw fish fall. It rains fish in Cuba." Everyone believed Dai Bak, since he was older than BaBa.

Most of the men had already been to the Gold Mountain and did not ask as at the beginning of going-out-on-the-road, "Does it rain, then, on the other side of the world?"

"I saw plains covered with cattle from horizon to horizon," said Grandfather. "The cowboys herd thousands of head of cattle, not one cowboy leading one cow on a rope like here."

"On the Gold Mountain, a man eats enough meat at one meal to feed a family for a month," said Great Grandfather. "Yes, slabs of meat." The hungrier the family got, the bigger the stories, the more real the meat and the gold.

Grandfather also said, "The Gold Mountain is lonely. You could get sick and almost die, and nobody come to visit. When you're well, you climb out of your basement again, and nobody has missed you." "Idiot," shouted Grandmother. "What do you know? Don't listen to the idiot. Crazy man. Only an idiot would bring up a bad luck story like that tonight." They acted as if he hadn't said it.

Great Grandfather said, "In Hawai'i the papayas are so big, the children scoop out the seeds and carve faces and light candles inside the shell. The candles grow on trees. You can make black ink from the nuts of that same tree."

"Don't sign contracts," he said. "Go as free working men. Not 'coolies.'" He undid his shirt and showed a white scar that was almost lost in his wrinkles. "We're men, not boy apprentices."

"America – a peaceful country, a free country." America. The Gold Mountain. The Beautiful Nation.

The night grew late. The men talking-story, lighting chains of cigarettes, and drinking wine, did not need to sleep in order to have dreams. "Let me show you. Let me show you. My turn. My turn." Even the ones who had only explored the world as far as Canton and Hong Kong had stories. Second Uncle, Ngee Bak, dressed in his Western suit, grabbed an old man's cane and strutted straight through the house. "My name is John Bullyboy," he said, imitating a foreign walk and talk, stiff-legged and arrogant, big nostrils in the air, cane swishing about and hitting chinamen and dogs. He did not swerve for shit in his path. Those playing blindmen bumped into the English demon and knocked him over. The women scolded, "Do we have to remind you that you have to work in the morning? You're making so much noise, you're waking the babies." But the men talked on, and the women went to bed self-righteous and angry; *they* would rise early to feed the chickens and the children; *they* were not childish like men. But the women couldn't sleep for the rumbling laughter, and returned, not to be left out. Grandmother brought out the gold that Great Great Grandfather, Great Grandfather, Grandfather, and the uncles had earned. Hardly diluted by alloys, it gave off red glints in the lantern light. The family took turns hefting the gold, which was heavier than it looked; its density was a miracle in the hand. A chain lowering into the palm coiled and folded on its links like a gold snake. Grandmother boiled gold and they drank the water for strength. Gold blood ran in their veins. How could they not go to the Gold Mountain again, which belonged to them, which they had invented and discovered?

Suddenly a knocking pounded through the house. Someone with a powerful hand was at the front gate in the middle of the night. Talk stopped. Everyone reached for a weapon – a cleaver, a hammer, a scythe. They blew out lights and listened for breathing and footsteps. A lookout shouted down from the coign door, "It's Kau Goong." Great Uncle.

"Kau Goong's come home." They threw open doors. The children were up now too. "Huh!" In strode Kau Goong, Grandmother's brother, an incarnation of a story hero, returning during a night of stories, a six–foot-tall white gorilla with long hair and white eyebrows that pointed upward like an owl's, his mouth jutting like an ape's, saying "Huh!" "Huh! Here I am," he roared. "I've come back." He threw down his bags. "Help yourselves! Ho!" His sister's relatives scrambled for the gifts. Nobody asked where he had won these prizes. He threw off his coat and unbuckled pistols and silver knives. While the family emptied the bags, he cleaned his guns, twirled the cylinders, blew and sighted through the bullet chambers and bores. In better times, he had walked unarmed up to rich people and taken their money. He was the biggest man in the known world, and there was no law.

"It just so happened," said Ah Po, "that when you were on your journey, pirates boarded a passenger boat going upriver and one going downriver, and sacked them both. I'm glad you're safe." Ransoms had been collected and paid.

"Dangerous times," said Kau Goong. He shook his head. "Sixty dollars for an old lady." "Yes, sixty dollars for an old lady." This was a family saying, meaning nobody was safe from kidnappers.

The family divided up used shoes, a coat, a blanket, and some lunches. "These old shoes hardly replace all the loot the bandits took from us," said Ah Po. "You'll have to look harder for those raiders. The last time they came here, I peeked from my hiding place up on the roof, and at that very moment, the full moon shone on a bandit's face. It was a Mah from Duck Doo. Let's raid their village and take our stuff back. Revenge."

Too few boats were plying the rivers. Kau Goong had boarded them as far as the ocean and also far inland, and had found no money, jewels, or silks. "Is this all?" said Ah Po.

"We need to go-out-on-the-road again," Kau Goong roared. "We need to go to the Gold Mountain." And since the Chinese word for "need" and "want" and "will" is one and the same word, he was also saying, "We want to go-out-on-the-road again. We will go to the Gold Mountain."

"Every man who leaves must reach the Gold Mountain, and every man must come home to Han Mountain," said Grandmother and Mother, unable to stop the emigration, and hoping that saying something would make it so. The men reassured them that, of course, they were Sojourners only, that they meant to come back, not settle in America with new wives. "Didn't I return last time? And the time before that?" they said; "I'm a Gold Mountain Sojourner, only a tourist," and kept other possibilities secret from women.

"One last time out-on-the-road," said the oldest men.

No infant cried out, no fireball flashed a warning, no careless eater dropped a dish or a chopstick, no sick neighbor knocked asking for medicine, no deer or rooster called in the moonlight, no cloud passed over the full moon. Crickets continued chirping. Nothing unusual happened; all remained in continuance. So, omens favorable, one of the grandfathers said, "Write a list of the men going-out-on-the-road."

BaBa set down the date, which was in 1924, and listed: Grandfather, Second Grandfather, Third Grandfather, Fourth Grandfather, Great Uncle, First Uncle, Second Uncle, and Third Uncle. After Third Uncle's name, he wrote his own name. He wanted to taste the rain fish; he wanted to pocket some gold. He wanted to say good-bye to the students. "You'll have to find a new teacher; I'm going to the Gold Mountain." He would quit school in the middle of a lesson.

"I'll get a legal visa," he said. Words of anguish came up from Ah Po, "But you're only a boy."

The travelers teased him. "Hoo! So he thinks he can walk about the West posing as a scholar." "He'll saunter up to the Immigration Demon and say, 'I'm an academician. Hand over my visa.'" "They'll clap him in jail for lying." "How are you going to prove that you're a scholar? Open up your skull and show them your brains?" "Just because he's skinny and too weak for physical labor, he thinks the white demons will say he's obviously a scholar. But they can't tell a teacher's body from a laborer's body."

"I have a diploma."

"Huh. He thinks they make laws to search out scholars to teach them and rule them. Listen, stupid, nobody gets to be classified 'Scholar.' You can't speak English, you're illiterate, no scholar, no visa. 'Coolie.' Simple test."

A kinder uncle reminded him of a father's advice to his son. "'Son, books can't be turned into food when you're hungry, nor into clothes when you're cold.'"

At the request of the women, he wrote lists of things to bring back from the Gold Mountain: Dunhill lighters, Rolex wristwatches, Seth Thomas clocks, Parker pens, Singer sewing machines, glass window panes, davenports, highboys, pianos.

"You'll make a lot of money," said MaMa. "You'll come home rich. You'll fly. You'll show them."

The next day the families unburied their documents — visas, passports, re-entry permits, American birth certificates, American citizenship papers — and distributed them. BaBa and Sahm Bak, Third Uncle, beginners, let it out that they were interested in purchasing papers and that they were willing to be adopted by Gold Mountain Sojourners who were legal citizens of the United States of America. These Americans had declared the birth of a new son for every year they had been visiting in China and thereby made "slots" for many "paper sons." When a Sojourner retired from going-out-on-the-road or died, he made another slot. Somebody took his place. The last owner of papers taught their buyer the details about the house, the farm, the neighborhood, the family that were nominally his now. A Test Book accompanied the papers; the Sojourners who had traveled on that set of papers had recorded the questions the Immigration Demons had asked, and how they had answered. The men preparing to go wandered in the fields and among the mud huts and great houses of the village, chanting these facts to a beat, rhymed them, quizzed one another. They ate sturgeon for mental prowess. They paid big fees to memory experts, and it was like in the old days when the Jesuit priest Matteo Ricci taught how to study for the Imperial Examinations, which were no more. BaBa read Test Books to their new owners, who repeated the words to memorize another man's life, a consistent life, an American life.

BaBa would go with two sets of papers: bought ones and his own, which were legal and should get him into the Gold Mountain according to American law. But his own papers were untried, whereas the fake set had accompanied its owners back and forth many times. These bought papers had a surname which was the same as our own last name – unusual luck: he would be able to keep the family name. He would carry his diplomas, and if they did not work, he would produce the fake papers.

Our family calculated money for passage. They mortgaged a field and also borrowed fifteen hundred dollars from the neighbor in the front house and another fifteen hundred dollars from the neighbor in the back house. (This three thousand dollars must have been in Chinese money.) They promised high interest, and it was also understood that our family, including the descendants, even after the monetary repayment of the debt, would show gratitude to those families, wherever their descendants, forever.

Husbands and wives exchanged stories to frighten one another. The men told about a husband who smeared his cheating wife with honey and tied her naked on an ant hill. The women told how there was once a queen, who, jealous of the king's next wife, had this other woman's arms and legs cut off and her eyes, tongue, and ears cut out. She shoved her through the hole of the outhouse, then showed her to the king, who looked down and said, "What's that?" "It's the human pig," said the queen. The wives, of course, agreed with the American antimiscegenation laws; the men would have to come home, and also they would have to be faithful, preferably celibate.

The villagers unfolded their maps of the known world, which differed: turtles and elephants supported the continents, which were islands on their backs; in other cartographies, the continents were mountains with China the middle mountain, Han Mountain or Tang Mountain or the Wah Republic, a Gold Mountain to its west on some maps and to its east on others. Yet the explorers who had plotted routes to avoid sea monsters and those who had gone in the directions the yarrow fell had found gold as surely as the ones with more scientific worlds. They had met one another as planned in Paris or Johannesburg or San Francisco.

"Bali," said a very great grandfather, pointing at the fabulous island where the holy monkeys live. He had seen the monkeys dance. Hou Yin the Monkey God lives on Bali. A generation of great grandfathers had gone there and brought back wives. Others had remained and turned into monkeys.

"Not me," said First Uncle, Dai Bak. "No big cities in Bali. The money is in the big cities now. I'm going to San Francisco."

"Chicago," said Second Uncle, Ngee Bak. "Right in the middle of North America."

"Canada," said Third Uncle, Sahm Bak. "I hear it's easier to get into Canada."

"I'm going as a worker if I can't go as a teacher," BaBa said. His brothers laughed at him. Those frail hands lifting sledgehammers?

"Don't go," said Ah Po. "You're never coming back." And then she wept, having spoken his life.

The band of Gold Mountain travelers walked to the ocean. Almost a troop themselves, they were not challenged by bandits, rebels, government or warlord armies, or by demons, to whom China belonged now. At the waterfront, the oldest men dickered in demon language for ships, "How much? Dollars? No, too much." BaBa was glad that he was the youngest and had go-betweens.

BaBa never told us about sailing on a ship. He did not say whether he went as a carpenter or crewman or passenger from Canton or Macao or Hong Kong. Did masts and riggings, sails, smokestacks, and bridges block the sky, and at night did the ship's lights wash out the stars? Or could he stand on the deck and again see the sky without anything in the way? He would have had suitcases full of dried food. He would have brought seeds of every kind of vegetable.

The ship docked in Cuba, where the surf foamed like the petticoats of the dancing ladies. This part of the journey was legal. For money, BaBa rolled cigarettes and cigars ("Mexican cigarettes") and worked in the sugarcane fields. He did not see any rain of fish, but promises would be kept on the Gold Mountain mainland.

I tell everyone he made a legal trip from Cuba to New York. But there were fathers who had to hide inside crates to travel to Florida or New Orleans. Or they went in barrels and boxes all the way up the coast to New York harbor. BaBa may have been in charge of addressing those crates, marking them "Fragile" in Chinese and English and Spanish. Yes, he may have helped another father who was inside a box.

* * *

I think this is the journey you don't tell me:

The father's friends nailed him inside a crate with no conspicuous air holes. Light leaked through the slats that he himself had fitted together, and the bright streaks jumped and winked as the friends hammered the lid shut above his head. Then he felt himself being lifted as in a palanquin and carried to a darker place. Nothing happened for hours so that he began to lose his bearings – whether or not he was in a deep part of the ship where horns and anchor chains could not be heard, whether or not there had already been a pulling away from land, a plunging into the ocean, and this was steady speed. The father sat against a corner and stretched each limb the diagonal of the box, which was a yard by a yard by a yard. He had padded the bottom with his bedding and clothes. He had stuffed dried food, a jar of water, and a chamber pot in a bag. The box contained everything. He felt caught.

Various futures raced through his mind: walking the plank, drowning, growing old in jail, being thrown overboard in chains, flogged to tell where others were hiding, hung by the neck, returned to China – all things that happened to caught chinamen.

Suddenly – a disturbance – a giant's heart came to life; the ship shook and throbbed. A pulse had started up, and his box vibrated with it. He thought he could hear men running and calling. He must be near the engine room or a deck, near people.

The father's thoughts reached out as if stretching in four directions – skyward, seaward, back toward land, and forward to the new country. Oh, he did yearn for the open sea. The nerves in his chest and legs jumped with impatience. In the future he had to walk on deck the entire voyage, sleep on it, eat there.

He ought to have brought a knife to cut holes in the wood, or at least to carve more lines into the grain. He wanted to look out and see if his box had dropped overboard and was floating atop water, a transparency that ought not to be able to bear weight; he could have been immersed and this wooden air bubble hanging at a middle depth, or falling through the whale waters. People said that a Dragon King ruled an underwater city in the Yellow River; what larger oceanic unknown – tortoises twenty feet across, open-mouthed fish like the marine monster that swallowed the sutras – swam alongside or beneath him. What eels, sharks, jellies, rays glided a board's-width away? He heard the gruff voices of water lizards calling for the night rain. He must not be afraid; it was sea turtles and water lizards that had formed a bridge for King Mu of Chou.

Because of fear, he did not eat nor did he feel hungry. His bowels felt loose and bladder full, but he squeezed shut ass and sphincter against using the chamber pot. He slept and woke and slept again, and time seemed long and forever. Rocking and dozing, he felt the ocean's variety – the peaked waves that must have looked like pines; the rolling waves, round like shrubs, the occasional icy mountain; and for stretches, lulling grasslands.

He heard voices, his family talking about gems, gold, cobbles, food. They were describing meat, just as they had his last evenings home. "They eat it raw." "All you can eat." The voices must have been the sounds of the ocean given sense by his memory. They were discussing a new world. "Skyscrapers tall as mountains." He would fly an aeroplane above the skyscrapers tall as mountains. "They know how to do things there; they're very good at organization and machinery. They have machines that can do anything." "They'll invent robots to do all the work, even answer the door." "All the people are fat." "They're honest. If they say they'll do something, they do it. A handshake is enough." "They arrive for appointments at the very moment they say they will." "They wrap everything – food, flowers, clothes.

You can use the paper over again. Free paper bags." "And westward, there are wild horses. You can eat them or ride them." It alarmed him when the strange talk did not cease at his concentration. He was awake, not dozing, and heard mouth noises, sighs, swallows, the clicking and clucking of tongues. There were also seas when the waves clinked like gold coins, and the father's palm remembered the peculiar heaviness of gold. "Americans are careless; you can get rich picking over what they drop." "Americans are forgetful from one day to the next." "They play games, sports; grown men play ball like children." "All you have to do is stay alert; play a little less than they do, use your memory, and you'll become a millionaire." "They have swimming pools, elevators, lawns, vacuum cleaners, books with hard covers, X-rays." The villagers had to make up words for the wonders. "Something new happens every day, not the same boring farming."

The sea invented words too. He heard a new language, which might have been English, the water's many tongues speaking and speaking. Though he could not make out words, the whispers sounded personal, intimate, talking him over, sometimes disapproving, sometimes in praise of his bravery.

"It's me. It's me." A solid voice. Concrete words. "I'm opening the box." It was the smuggler, who squeaked the nails out and lifted the lid. He helped the father climb out of the box with firm and generous hands. "You're safe to come out and walk," he said. The size of the room outside the box seemed immense and the man enormous. He brought fresh food from the dining room and fresh water and he talked to the father.

Suddenly they heard a march of footsteps, the leather heels of white demons. Coming steadily toward them. The two men gave each other a look, parted, and ran between the hallways of cargo, ducked behind crates. The door clanked open, shut, and the father heard the footsteps nearing. He made out the sounds of two people pacing, as if searching for a stowaway. Crouched like a rabbit, he felt his heart thud against his own thigh. He heard talking and fervently wished to know whether they were discussing stowaways. He looked for other places to dart, but the crates, lashed with rope, towered above him in straight stacks. He was in a wedge with an opening like a cracked door. The cargo room was small after all, a mere closet, and he could not step from aisle to aisle without being seen; his footsteps would echo on the metal floor. If only there were portholes to jump through or tarpaulins to hide under.

The white demons' voices continued. He heard them speak their whispery language whose sentences went up at the end as if always questioning, sibilant questions, quiet, quiet voices. The demons had but to walk this far and see into the wedge. His friend, the smuggler, could say, "I came to check the ropes," or "The captain ordered me to take inventory." Or "I'm looking for stowaways, and I found one," and deliver him up. But there were no explanations for him, a stowaway chinaman. He would not be able to talk convincingly; he would have to fight. He hardly breathed, became aware of inadequate shallow breaths through his nose.

Then, so close to his face he could reach out and touch it, he saw a white trouser leg turn this way and that. He had never seen anything so white, the crease so sharp. A shark's tooth. A silver blade. He would not get out of this by his own actions but by luck.

Then, blessedness, the trouser leg turned once more and walked away.

He had not been caught. The demons had not looked down. After a time of quiet, the two hiders called to each other and came out hysterical with relief. Oh, they had the luck of rich men. The trousers had practically brushed his face.

"It's time to go back in your box," said the smuggler. A moment before, the father had thought it would be a joy to be back in, but as the lid shut on him again, reluctance almost overwhelmed him. He did not visit outside of the box again. He rode on, coming to claim the Gold Mountain, his own country.

The smuggler came occasionally and knocked a code on the wood, and the stowaway father signaled back. Thus he knew that he had not been forgotten, that he had been visited. This exchange of greetings kept him from falling into the trance that overtakes animals about to die.

At last the smuggler let him out; the ship had docked at a pier in New York. He motioned the father up hatches, across empty decks, around corners to an unguarded gangway. He would not have to swim past patrol boats in the dark. "Come. Come. Hurry," the smuggler guided him. He staggered along on cramped legs; the new air dizzied him. As they were saying good-bye, the smuggler said, "Look," and pointed into the harbor. The father was thrilled enough to see sky and skyscrapers. "There." A gray and green giantess stood on the gray water; her clothes, though seeming to swirl, were stiff in the wind and the moving sea. She was a statue, and she carried fire and a book. "Is she a goddess of theirs?" the father asked. "No," said the smuggler, "they don't have goddesses. She's a symbol of an idea." He was glad to hear that the Americans saw the idea of Liberty so real that they made a statue of it.

The father walked off the ship and onto the Gold Mountain. He disciplined his legs to step confidently, as if they belonged where they walked. He felt the concrete through his shoes. The noise and size of New York did not confuse him; he followed a map that his kinsmen had drawn so clearly that each landmark to Chinatown seemed to be waiting to welcome him. He went to the Extending Virtue Club, where people from his own village gave him a bed in a basement; it could have been a grocery shelf or an ironing table or the floor under a store counter. To lie stretched out on any part of the Gold Mountain was a pleasure to him.

Of course, my father could not have come that way. He came a legal way, something like this:

Arriving in San Francisco Bay, the legal father was detained for an indefinite time at the Immigration Station on Angel Island, almost within swimming distance of San Francisco. In a wooden house, a white demon physically examined him, poked him in the ass and genitals, looked in his mouth, pulled his eyelids with a hook. This was not the way a father ought to have been greeted. A cough tickled his chest and throat, but he held it down. The doctor demon pointed to a door, which he entered to find men and boys crowded together from floor to ceiling in bunkbeds and on benches; they stood against the walls and at the windows. These must be the hundred China Men who could enter America, he thought. But the quota was one hundred a year, not one hundred per day, and here were packed more than one hundred, nearer two hundred or three. A few people made room for him to set down his suitcases. "A newcomer. Another newcomer," they called out. A welcome party made its way to him. "I'm the president of the Self-Governing Association," one of them was telling him in a dialect almost like his. "The most important rule we have here is that we guard one another's chances for immigration." He also asked for dues; the father gave a few dimes toward buying newspapers and phonograph records, an invention that he had never heard before. "Now you're eligible to vote," said the president, who then said that he had won his office by having been on the island the longest, three and a half years. The legal father's heart sank, and rose again; there must be something wrong with this man, not a good man, a criminal to be jailed for so long. "Do you want to spend money on a rubber ball? Vote Yes or No." The legal father voted No. How odd it would be to say to these men, "Play ball. Go ahead. Play with it," as if they were boys and could play. Even the boys wouldn't play. Who can be that lighthearted? He wasn't really going to stay here for more than a day or two, was he? He made his way across the room. Some of the men were gambling, others exercising, cutting one another's hair, staring at their feet or folded hands or the floor. He saw two men handcuffed to each other. Readers chanted San Francisco newspapers, *Young China* and *Chinese World*. The legal father, who was skillful and lucky, joined a game and won forty silver dollars, and gave away one for the rubber ball. He learned who was being deported and who was serving a year's sentence before deportation.

A bell went off like a ship's alarm, but it was a dinner bell. The father followed the others to a dining hall. About ten women were coming out. They were the first women he had seen since China, and they already belonged to husbands. He did not know that he had come to a country with no women. The husbands and wives talked quickly as the guards pushed them past one another. The father saw the man ahead of him hold hands with a woman for a moment and – he saw it – pass her a note. She dropped it. She knelt and, fixing her shoe with one hand, snatched the piece of paper with the other. A big white matron grabbed her arm and took the paper. Though these people were all strangers, the father joined the men who surrounded the matron. They wrested the paper from her and tore it up. The legal father ate some of the shreds. That was the last time the men's and women's mealtimes overlapped. There seemed to be no other immediate consequences; perhaps denial of entry would be the punishment.

The China Men who worked in the kitchen brought food cooked and served in buckets. "Poison," the prisoners grumbled. "A couple of years ago," said the president of the

Self-Governing Association, "the demons tried to starve us to death. They were taking the food money for themselves. If it weren't for us rioting, you newcomers wouldn't be eating so much today. We faced bayonets for this food." The legal father wasn't sure he would've wanted any more of the slop they were eating.

The men spent the long days rehearsing what they would say to the Immigration Demon. The forgetful men fingered their risky notes. Those who came back after being examined told what questions they had been asked. "I had to describe all the streets in my village." "They'll ask, 'Do you have any money?' and 'Do you have a job?'" "They've been asking those questions all this week," the cooks and janitors confirmed. "What's the right answer?" asked the legal fathers. "Well, last week they liked 'No job' because it proves you were an aristocrat. And they liked 'No money' because you showed a willingness to work. But this week, they like 'Yes job' and 'Yes money' because you wouldn't be taking jobs away from white workers." The men groaned, "Some help." The demons did not treat people of any other race the way they did Chinese. The few Japanese left in a day or two. It was because their emperor was strong.

Footsteps walked across the ceiling, and bedsprings squeaked above their heads. So there were more of them locked on the second floor. "The women are up there," the father was told. Diabolical, inauspicious beginning – to be trodden over by women. "Living under women's legs," said the superstitious old-fashioned men from the backward villages. "Climbed over by women." It was bad luck even to walk under women's pants on clotheslines. No doubt the demons had deliberately planned this humiliation. The legal father decided that for a start in the new country, he would rid himself of Chinese superstitions; this curse would not count.

He read the walls, which were covered with poems. Those who could write protested this jailing, this wooden house (*wood* rhyming with *house*), the unfair laws, the emperor too weak to help them. They wrote about the fog and being lonely and afraid. The poets had come to a part of the world not made for honor, where "a hero cannot use his bravery." One poet was ready to ride his horse to do mighty American deeds but instead here he sat corraled, "this wooden house my coffin." The poets must have stayed long to carve the words so well. The demons were not going to free him, a scholar, then. Some were not poems exactly but statements. "This island is not angelic." "It's not true about the gold." One man blamed "the Mexican Exclusion Laws" for his imprisonment. The writers were anonymous; no official demon could trace them and penalize them. Some signed surname and village, but they were still disguised; there were many of that name from that village, many men named Lee from Toi Sahn, many a Hong of Sun Woi, and many a Three District Man and Four District No Such Man. There were dates of long stays.

Night fell quickly; at about four o'clock the fog poured down the San Francisco hillsides, covered the bay, and clouded the windows. Soon the city was gone, held fast by black sea and sky. The fog horns mourned. San Francisco might have been a figment of Gold Mountain dreams.

The legal father heard cries and thumps from someone locked in a separate shed. Words came out of the fog, the wind whipping a voice around the Island. "Let me land. Let me out. Let me land. I want to come home."

In the middle of one night when he was the only man awake, the legal father took out his Four Valuable Things, and using spit and maybe tears to mix the ink, he wrote a poem on the wall, just a few words to observe his stay. He wrote about wanting freedom. He did not sign his name; he would find himself a new American name when he landed. If the U.S. government found out his thoughts on freedom, it might not let him land. The next morning the readers sang the new poem for the others to hear. "Who wrote this wonderful poem during the night?" they asked, but the father modestly did not say.

For one another's entertainment, the men rehearsed and staged skits, puppet shows, and heroic parts of operas. They juggled fruit, bottles, and the new rubber ball. The father, who was traveling with the adventures of Yüeh Fei, the Patriot, in six volumes, read aloud the part where Yüeh Fei's mother carved on his back four words: FIRST − PROTECT MY NATION. He held up for all to see the illustrations of warriors in battle. He also carried the poems of Li Po, the best poet, the Heavenly Poet, the Great White Light, Venus. The father sang about a sentry stopping Li Po from entering a city. Li Po was drunk as usual and riding a mule. He refused to give his name to the sentry, but wrote a daring poem that he was a man from whose mouth the emperor had wiped the drool; the emperor's favorite wife had held his inkslab. The impressed sentry granted him entrance. This poem heartened the men; they laughed and clapped at Li Po's cleverness and the sentry's recognition of him and poetry.

"What is a poem exactly?" asked an illiterate man, a Gold Mountain Sojourner who had spent twenty years in America and was on his way back to his family. "Let me give it a try," he said. "A short poem: 'On the Gold Mountain, I met black men black like coal.' Is that a poem?" The literate men were delighted. "Marvelous," they said. "Of course, it's a poem." "A simile. A simile. Yes, a poem." The legal father liked it so much, he remembered it forever.

The legal father learned many people's thoughts because he wrote their letters. They told their wives and mothers how wonderful they found the Gold Mountain. "The first place I came to was The Island of Immortals," they told him to write. "The foreigners clapped at our civilized magnificence when we walked off the ship in our brocades. A fine welcome. They call us 'Celestials.'" They were eating well;

soon they would be sending money. Yes, a magical country. They were happy, not at all frightened. The Beautiful Nation was glorious, exactly the way they had heard it would be. "I'll be seeing you in no time." "Today we ate duck with buns and plum sauce," which was true on days when the China Men in San Francisco sent gifts.

Every day at intervals men were called out one by one. The legal father kept himself looking presentable. He wore his Western suit and shined shoes, constantly ready.

One morning the barracks awoke to find a man had hanged himself. He had done it from a railing. At first he looked as if he had been tortured, his legs cut off. He had tied his legs bent at the knees like an actor or beggar playing a man with no legs, and hung himself by pushing over his chair. His body had elongated from hanging all night. The men looked through his papers and found X's across them. When new arrivals looked for beds, nobody told them that a dead, hung man had slept in that one.

Also, the rumor went, a woman upstairs had killed herself by sharpening a chopstick and shoving it through her ear. Her husband had sent for her, and she did not understand why he did not come to take her home.

At last came the legal father's turn to be interrogated. He combed his hair again. He said his good-byes. Inside the interrogation room were several white demons in formal wear; the legal father gauged by the width of lapels and ties that his own suit was not quite stylish. Standing beside the table was a Chinese-looking soldier in American uniform and a demon soldier in the same uniform. This Chinese American was the interpreter. The legal father sat opposite the interrogators, who asked his name, his village, where he was born, his birth date – easy questions.

"Can you read and write?" the white demon asked in English and the Chinese American asked in Cantonese.

"Yes," said the legal father.

But the secretary demon was already writing No since he obviously couldn't, needing a translator.

"When did you cut off your pigtail?" asked the translator.

"In 1911," said the legal father. It was a safe answer, the year he would have picked anyway, not too early before the Republic nor too late, not too revolutionary nor too reactionary. Most people had cut their hair in 1911. He might have cut it for fashion as much as for revolution.

"Do you have relatives who are American citizens?"

The janitor, a China Man, who just then entered the room with dustpan and broom, nodded.

"Yes."

"Who?"

"My grandfather is an American. My father is an American. So I'm an American, also my three older brothers and three uncles – all Americans."

Then came the trap questions about how many pigs did they own in 1919, whether the pig house was made out of bricks or straw, how many steps on the back stoop, how far to the outhouse, how to get to the market from the farm, what were the addresses of the places his grandfather and father and brothers and uncles had lived in America. The interrogators liked asking questions with numbers for answers. Numbers seemed true to them. "Quick. How many windows do you have in your house?" "How many times did your grandfather return to the United States?" "Twice." "Twice?" "Yes, twice. He was here once and returned twice. He was here three times altogether. He spent half his life in America and half in China." They looked into his eyes for lies. Even the Chinese American looked into his eyes, and they repeated his answers, as if doubting them. He squelched an urge to change the answers, elaborate on them. "Do you have any money?" "Yes." "How much?" He wondered if they would charge him higher fees the more money he reported. He decided to tell the truth; lying added traps. Whether or not he spoke the truth didn't matter anyway; demons were capricious. It was up to luck now.

They matched his answers to the ones his relatives and fellow villagers gave. He watched the hands with yellow hair on their backs turn the copies of his grandfather's and father's papers.

They told him to go back to the jail, where he waited for more weeks. The next time he was called to be examined – *searched* the Chinese word – they asked again, "What American relatives do you have?"

"My grandfather and father," he said again, "and also my three brothers and three uncles."

"Your grandfather's papers are illegal," the Chinese American translated. "And your father is also an illegal alien." One by one the demons outlawed his relatives and ancestors, including a Gold Rush grandfather, who had paid a bag of gold dust to an American Citizenship Judge for papers. "There are no such things as Citizenship Judges," said the Immigration Demon and put an X across the paper that had been in the family for seventy-five years. He moved on to ask more trap questions, the directions the neighbors' houses faced and the number of water buffaloes in 1920, and sent him back to the barracks.

He waited again. He was examined again, and since he had an accurate memory, he told them the same number of pigs as the last two times, the same number of water buffaloes (one), the same year of cutting his queue, and at last they said, "You may enter the United States of America." He had passed the American examination; he had won America. He was not sure on what basis they let him in – his diploma, his American lineage (which may have turned out to be good after all), his ability to withstand jailing, his honesty, or the skill of his deceits.

This legal father then worked his way across the continent to New York, the center of America.

* * *

Ed, Woodrow, Roosevelt, and Worldster held their bowls to their mouths and shoveled as fast as they could, chewing crackly pork and pressed duck in one bite, gulping while jabbing from the center dishes without choosiness. They raced as if food were scarce and one of them would be left the runt pig. Woodrow picked up the soup tureen and drank directly from it. "Uh. Uh," the others protested, but didn't stop gulping to say "You're cheating."

Worldster threw down his bowl and chopsticks, spit the bones "p-foo" out on the table, knocked back his shot of whiskey, jumped up – his orange crate hit the floor with a bang – and shouted, "I won. I won."

But Woodrow, the soup drinker, ran out the door. "Last one to leave the table loses," he said.

"You're still chewing and swallowing," Worldster yelled.

"Okay," said Ed. "Okay, I lose." His friends cheered him as he leaned back and sipped his whiskey. "That was a four-and-a-half-minute dinner," he said, looking at his new gold watch. "It's a record." They gave their record a cheer.

The last one to finish eating did the dishes. While the others returned to work in the front of the laundry, Ed set a kettle to boil, unfolded his newspaper, lit a Lucky Strike, the brand he had chosen, and poured another glass of whiskey and a cup of coffee. Reading while drinking and smoking was one of the great pure joys of existence. He read that a Gold Mountain Sojourner, upon returning to his village, had gotten bilked by relatives, most of whom he had never met before. They had flocked to him. They tricked him with an intricate scheme for investing in a bogus Hong Kong housing project for refugees. Another Sojourner put his life savings into a bank that the entire village had set up just to get his money. The Sojourners were quoted as saying they were coming back to America.

Ed scraped the dishes onto the tablecloth, which was layers of newspapers. Then he rolled up the top layer; the table was instantly clean and already covered for the next meal. He sudsed the dishes with laundry soap and put them in a drainer. From the whistling tea kettle, he poured boiling water on them; the water was so hot, the dishes dried before his eyes. It was a method he remembered the slaves in China using. Dishwashing just took common sense; women had made such a to-do about it. The Gold Mountain was indeed free: no manners, no traditions, no wives.

When he joined his partners doing the ironing, his favorite part of laundry work, they were planning "the weekend."

"I want to go tea dancing," said Worldster, "and take driving lessons." He had a thick moustache and tried to look like Clark Gable.

"Let's see the Statue of Liberty at night," said Woodrow, who vowed that he would make a million bucks by 1935.

"I want to go on a date," said Roosevelt, who was looking for a medical school that gave night classes. "A weekend date with a Rockette," he said in English.

"I know where *City Lights* is playing," said Ed. "Also *Little Miss Marker*. You know, someday, when the people from the future see the movies, they'll think people today walked and moved like Charlie Chaplin." Oh, it was wonderful; for a dime the ushers let you stay all day through the intermissions, and the shows ran again and again. "Every Saturday night is a party in this country." Customers were picking up the big bundles – cash for the weekend.

Ed placed shirt after shirt on the stack that was growing beside his ironing board. Friends were fairer than brothers; there was an equality. When Tu Fu left his village, friends cared for him; "we swore brotherhood for eternity," he wrote. How good life was. Ed was young, and he was in New York with three new true friends who sang at their work.

They were singing the Rainy Alley Poet, who lived in Paris and followed black hair in the rain: "'I will follow that gleam though stumbling in the haze, the twilight like a bubble of rose rising in the wine glass, and let my nostalgic eyes become ensnared in memory dark as her hair.' "

"Aiya," breathed Woodrow. "True love. True life. The free pursuit of happiness."

"Aiya. That's me," said Roosevelt, " 'ensnared in memory dark as her hair,' except it should be blonde hair. 'Ensnared in memory yellow as her hair!' "

They sang Wang Tu Ching, a Sojourner, who had done all the wonderful things that a young man ought to do in Paris – having affairs, getting French girls pregnant. " 'Oh, this endless journey home. I am Chinese, and must not expect happiness but tears and sacrifice. Farewell, Latin Quarter, chestnut trees, bookstalls along the Seine.' " " 'Latin Quarter, chestnut trees,' " Ed repeated.

" 'I'm madly in love with Europe,' " they sang, " 'where I played my reed flute on an empty stomach.' " This was a song by Ai Ch'ing, a fellow Kwangtung man.

They sang an old poet, too, Yüan Mei, who had advocated educating women and written from a woman's point of view: " 'For years I've been imagining a boat/Shooting over the waves as fast as any bird/But never taking the traveler away from friends/Always carrying the traveler back to his home.' "

"Oh, that's beautiful," said Roosevelt. He rested under the fan and smoked a cigarette with tears in his eyes. "That's how I feel." The men were thinking not about one another but of lifelong friends.

"And listen to this one," said Ed. "The first wife welcomes her man home: 'If it were not for Second Wife, you would not come home. She is your plum blossom.' "

"Oh, oh," moaned the lonesome men. "Welcomed home by two wives."

They worked very late at night, and after a while did not sing or talk. The two fans whirred, blowing the calendars, the monthly calendars swinging on the walls, and the pages of the daily calendars riffling. Ed's legs ached. At about eleven o'clock, he spoke the bitter verses of "The Laundry Song," by Wen I-to of Chicago:

> *A piece, two pieces, three pieces —*
> *Wash them clean,*
> *Four pieces, five pieces, six —*
> *Iron them smooth.*

No, they were not going to be welcomed home by wives; they would stay here working forever. He thumped his iron on the accents.

> *Years pass and I let drop but one homesick tear.*
> *A laundry lamp burns at midnight.*
> *The laundry business is low, you say,*
> *Washing out blood that stinks like brass —*
> *Only a Chinaman can debase himself so.*
> *But who else wants to do it? Do you want it?*
> *Ask for the Chinaman. Ask the Chinaman.*

The other men were so tired, they only grunted in agreement. At midnight they switched off the lights in the windows, turned the Open sign around to Closed, and pulled down the shades. They worked without interruptions from customers, then made the ironing tables into beds.

Under his desk lamp, Ed did the accounts on his abacus and wrote down the profits in ledgers. Woodrow, who had bought a Kodak with a part of his million, took a picture of him. "You can send this to your wife and tell her you study a lot," he said. When Ed finished the bookkeeping, the others were asleep. In the quiet of the night, he practiced his calligraphy by writing down modern poems for his friends to paste on the walls over their ironing tables. He wrote a letter to his wife, and went to bed.

On Saturday Ed and Woodrow went to Fifth Avenue to shop for clothes. With his work pants, Ed wore his best dress shirt, a silk tie, gray silk socks, good leather shoes with pointed toes, and a straw hat. At a very good store, he paid two hundred dollars cash for a blue and gray pinstripe suit, the most expensive suit he could find. In the three-way mirror, he looked like Fred Astaire. He wore the suit out of the store. Woodrow took a picture of him dancing down the New York Public Library steps next to one of the lions. "I don't see why you have to spend all this money on clothes," said Woodrow, whose entire wardrobe came from the unclaimed laundry. He was the one who had written the sign in English: WE WILL NOT BE RESPONSIBLE FOR CLOTHES UNCLAIMED AFTER 30 DAYS. He shot his cuffs and said, "You must admit I look pretty swanky in these secondhand outfits." The two of them strolled Fifth Avenue and caught sight of themselves in windows and hubcaps. They looked all the same Americans.

Suddenly a band of white demons came up from behind them. One picked off Ed's straw hat and kicked its lid through. Before Ed and Woodrow could decide what to do for the shame on China Men, they saw the whites stomp on other whites' hats. "It must be a custom," said Ed.

That afternoon, the partners trimmed one another's hair with their barber's shears and electric hair clippers. They copied Ed's professional haircut, parted in the middle and the two sides lifted just so in "pompadours." Then all four gentlemen went to a tearoom. Ed regretted having to check his gray felt hat at the door. It looked good with his new suit. Girls liked the way he cocked his head and looked at them sideways with his hat brim tilted at a smart angle. The hatcheck girl also sold them strips of tickets for ten cents apiece. The hostess escorted them to a table, where they ordered cookies, open-faced raw cucumber sandwiches, strawberry parfaits, and tea. They nibbled carefully at their sandwiches, chewed with their mouths shut, sipped tea, and dabbed their lips even though they had not slobbered or made crumbs. They looked around at the couples to decide which dancing girls they were going to ask. "Look at the legs on that one," said Roosevelt. "She must be a Rockette."

"The main difference between them and us Tang People," Woodrow observed, "is the shape of their nostrils, which are oval instead of small, neat, and round like ours."

They were saying those things in Chinese, so weren't being rude. They were sophisticated New York gentlemen, and knew more about American manners than white people. "When I was a waiter," said Worldster, "there were hick tourists who tipped us after every course. Every time we came to the table they tipped us." Since the music took so long stopping, he went over to a couple, tapped the white man on the shoulder, and cut in. "What's your name, sweetheart?" he said like in the movies.

The others waited until the orchestra stopped, then stood and walked out onto the dance floor. "Dance with me?" Ed asked, holding out his tickets. "Sure," the blonde dancing girl of his choice said, smiling, taking several tickets, which was a compliment; he would get to dance with her a lot. He smiled back and said, "Sure." The music did not start up right away. "You like come my table after you dance with me?" he invited. "Of course," she said. "You speak English very well," she said. "Thank you," he said. "You be very beautiful. Pretty. You be pretty. I like you." "How nice," she said. "Thank you. You're very handsome. You're good looking. Do you understand *handsome*?" "Sure. Of course. How nice. Thank you." A fox-trot started, and he put out his hand; she put her hand in it, and he led her, his feet in their new leather shoes, glissading across the waxed wood floor. He saw himself and her in the mirrors, and they looked like the movies. He guided her a little closer with the intimate hand at her waist. He looked down at the gold eyebrows and curving eyelashes and her blue eyes. He pulled their two clasped hands closer so that her gold hair brushed his hand. Her hair was fine and soft, not like hair at all. He dared a dip, and her wonderful hair rippled near the floor and swung back against his other hand. When the music stopped, she said, "You're a very good dancer." "And handsome too?" he asked. She laughed with her beautiful lipsticked mouth.

The others had also brought their blondes over to the table under the potted palm, and they ate the sandwiches, drank tea, and smoked cigarettes. "Is he really a Chinese prince?" Worldster's girl asked. "What's 'prince'?" asked Ed. "A king's son," she said. "A king's son," said Worldster in Chinese. "Oh, yes," said Ed, "in China, we all be prince with so much money. Too much money. But. Now we all the same Americans."

They danced until they had no more tickets. And they danced with as many different blondes as they pleased. And Ed was so handsome that some danced with him for free, vied with one another to dance with him. He became bold enough to ask the friendliest blonde, one who had been studying his eyes, his high cheekbones, and neat nose, who had made him unbutton his sleeve and hold his tan arm against her pink arm, "You like come home with me? Please?"

"No, honey," she said. "No."

Not one of the four of them told any blonde that they were married and were fathers. "See you next week," they said, learning new ways to say good-bye. "See ya." "So long."

On Sunday they rode the ferry boat to Coney Island. Woodrow asked a blonde to take pictures of the four friends with their arms on the railing and their black hair flying in the wind. At the beach, a bathing beauty photographed them in their bathing suits, nobody wearing a jockstrap, which might not yet have come into fashion. Ed had bought a beach robe, "which is different from a bedroom robe," he explained. He sent many pictures to his wife, including one of himself sitting on the sand with his arms around his knees and his sweat shirt tied around his neck; he was smiling and looking out to sea.

On another weekend, Worldster, who had taken flying lessons, rented an aeroplane and invited each of his friends up into the sky. (*Friends* in Chinese connotes play, good times, and youth.) "We're men of the Twentieth Century," he lectured as Ed marveled at the speed and height. "We're modern men, and have to learn to make use of the new machines." He explained how to move the plane right and left and up and down, then said, "You try it," and let go of the controls. Ed flew over rivers, trees, and houses, raced cars, and made the plane go back up when it fell into air pockets. They circled the airport and waggled their wings at Roosevelt and Woodrow down there.

Ed sent his wife pictures of himself in the cockpit; he wore a white scarf flying behind him, goggles, and a leather skullcap with flaps over the ears. He also sent several shots of the plane in the air, an insect against the white sky.

Woodrow bought a car, and Roosevelt a motorcycle. Each of the four friends stood by the car for his picture. They also took pictures of one another leaning into curves on the motorcycle. Ed did not pass the driver's test but drove anyway. "You can drive without a license here," he wrote to people in China. "It's a free country."

In the spring, Ed sent his wife a picture of the four partners with their arms around one another's shoulders, laughing next to a Keep Off the Grass sign. He was wearing another two-hundred-dollar suit, a navy blue one, and a shirt with French cuffs, which closed with gold cuff links. For a winter picture, he sat on a rock in Central Park in his new gray greatcoat and jaunty hat and leather gloves lined with rabbit fur.

In his quiet time at night, he mounted the photographs in a fine leather album. With his first spending money, he had bought a postcard of the Statue of Liberty, the album, picture mounts, white ink, and a pen with a steel nib. He pasted that postcard in his expensive album, then added the other pictures.

Ed's wife wrote often and sometimes sent lichee, which she had picked from the three trees that Ed's father had planted and the twenty trees that Ed's brother had planted. When would he return to plant lichee trees?

Then she wrote that their two children had died. What should she do? "I think you ought to come back right now," she said.

He did much worrying, and hit upon a plan. He would not end his American life but show her how to live one. "Here's what you have to do if I'm to bring you to America," he wrote, though there was a law against her. "I will bring you to America on one condition, and that is, you get a Western education. I'll send you money, which you must only spend on school, not on food or clothes or jewelry or relatives. Leave the village. Go to Hong Kong or Canton and enroll in a Western scientific school. A science school. Get a degree. Send it to me as evidence you are educated, and I'll send you a ship ticket. And don't go to a school for classical literature. Go to a scientific school run by white people. And when you get your degree, I'll send for you to come here to the United States." He would figure out later how to accomplish that.

When next she wrote, she had enrolled in medical school; she was writing him from there. As years passed and sometimes she became discouraged with how long her education was taking and how difficult the work, he wrote encouragement: "If you don't get that degree, I'll not send for you. We will never see each other again." He did not want an ignorant villager for his American wife.

So much time went by, he saved another two hundred dollars, which he spent on a gray suit and a Countess Mara tie.

At last she mailed him her diploma. He spent another few years saving passage money, and fifteen years after they had last seen one another, he sent for her. Applying for her, he risked having his citizenship again scrutinized. She would enter legally and gracefully, no question of asking a lady to ride the sea in a box or to swim to an unwatched shore.

At dinner one evening, he announced to his partners, "I've sent for my wife, who will be here in January." They were so surprised that they stopped their eating race.

"How did you save enough money?" Worldster asked.

"I guess you'll be moving to your own apartment," said Roosevelt.

"Why do you want to do that?" asked Woodrow.

After writing letters for fifteen years, Ed and his wife ended their correspondence. They were near each other, she on Ellis Island, where there was no mail, and he on Manhattan. When he saw her on the ferry, she was standing surrounded by bundles and bags, no child tugging her coat and no baby in her arms. He recognized her, though she was older. Her hair was slicked against her head with a bun in back, a proper married-lady hairdo. In spite of the law against her, she was landing, her papers in order. Her immigration verified the strength of his citizenship.

"Here you are," he said. "You've come."

"You look like a foreigner," she said. "I can barely recognize you."

"Was it a rough journey?" he asked.

"It was terrible," she exclaimed. "The Japanese were right behind me. When I tried to board the ship from Canton to Hong Kong, the man acted as if my papers were wrong and asked for a seventy-five-dollar bribe. So I ran to another gangplank and found out seventy-five dollars wasn't policy at all; this man wanted a hundred dollars. I had to run back to the first entrance. Then I paid another hundred to get off the ship. It was the last ship out of Canton before the Japanese took the harbor. And I was so seasick, I vomited the whole way across the Atlantic. And what a questioning I got on the Island. They asked me what year you had cut your queue, and a workman shook his head, hawked, and spat. It was a signal. So I said, 'I don't know.' On my way to be locked up again, I said to that workman, 'That was a delicious bun you gave me. Thank you. I hope you bring me another if you have more.' Get it? It was a code I made up, meaning, 'Thank you for giving me the right answer. Please give me more help.' Oh, I was so scared. If it weren't for him I might not be here."

"Don't worry any more," said Ed. "That's over now. Don't worry any more." Her big eyes had lines aound them. "That's all over now," he said.

"I had to build roads," she said. "Since your father is too crazy to work, and you were away, I had to pay the labor tax for two men. Your father followed me and wept on the road when I left."

"Never mind now," he said. "That's all over now."

They rode the subway to the room he had rented in preparation for her coming. He taught her the name of the the subway stop for the laundry. "Easu Bu-odd-way Su-ta-son," she repeated. "That's good," he said. "Remember that, and you can't get lost."

She unpacked jars of seeds. "But we aren't farmers any more," he said. "I'll plant in tin cans and put them out here on the fire escape," she said. "You'll see how many vegetables we can grow in cans."

She showed him a piece of cloth. "Do you recognize this?" she asked. "The Japanese were right behind me, and I had time to take just one keepsake – the trimming on the bed canopy." She had ripped it off and shoved it in her purse.

She unfolded it. "This is the only thing we have left from China," she said. "The heirloom." A red phoenix and a red dragon played across the strip of linen; the Chinese words down one end and English words across the top said, "Good morning." She had cross-stitched it herself.

"You could write English even then," he teased her, "and getting ready to come here." "I didn't know what it said," she demurred, "I only copied it from a needlework book."

He took her shopping and bought her a black crepe dress with a bodice of white lace ruffles and buttons of rhinestone and silver. "You look very pretty," he told her. They bought a black coat with a fur collar and a little black-eyed animal head over her shoulder, high heels, silk stockings, black kid gloves, and a picture hat with a wide, wide brim and silk fluttery ribbon. They strolled in their finery along Fifth Avenue. "I washed all these windows," he told her. "When I first came here, I borrowed a squeegee and rags and a bucket, and walked up and down this street. I went inside each store and asked if they wanted the windows washed. The white foreigners aren't so hard to get along with; they nod to mean Yes and shake their heads to mean No, the same as anybody." New York glittered and shined with glass. He had liked pulling the water off the panes and leaving brief rainbows. While working, he had looked over the displays of all the wonderful clothes to own and wear. He had made the money to pool for starting the laundry. "In the spring," he promised her, "we'll buy you white cotton gloves."

"On the first day of autumn," he told her, "New Yorkers stomp on one another's straw hats. I wear my gray felt one as soon as summer's over. I save the straw for spring. I'm not extravagant. You ought to put your earrings in the safe deposit box at the bank. Pierced ears look a little primitive in this country." He also told her to buy makeup at a drugstore. "American people don't like oily faces. So you ought to use some powder. It's the custom. Also buy some rouge. These foreigners dislike yellow skin."

She also bought a long black rat of hair to roll her own hair over for an upswept hairdo. At a beauty parlor, she had her wavy hair cut and curled tighter with a marcel. She washed, ironed, and wrapped her silk pants and dresses and never wore them again.

He took her to see the Statue of Liberty. They climbed the ladder, she in high heels, up the arm to the torch, then the stairs to the crown. "Now we're inside her chin. This part must be the nose." From the windows of the crown, he showed her his city.

They also went to the top of the Empire State Building, took the second elevator to the very top, the top of the world. Ed loved the way he could look up at the uncluttered sky. They put money in the telescopes and looked for the laundry and their apartment. "So I have been on the tallest building in the world," she said. "I have seen everything. Wonderful. Wonderful. Amazing. Amazing."

"Yes," he said. "Everything's possible on the Gold Mountain. I've danced with blondes." "No, really?" she said. "You didn't. You're making that up, aren't you? You danced with demonesses? I don't believe it."

Her favorite place to go was the free aquarium, "the fish house," where all manner of creatures swam. Walking between the lighted tanks, she asked, "When do you think we'll go back to China? Do you think we'll go back to China?" "Shh," he said. "Shh." The electric eels glowed in their dark tank, and the talking fish made noises. "There are bigger fish in China," she said.

They went to the movies and saw *Young Tom Edison* with Mickey Rooney. They both liked the scene where the mother took Eh-Da-Son into the barn, but only pretended to thrash him; she faked the slaps and crying and scolding to fool the strict father, the father "the severe parent," according to Confucius, and the mother "the kind parent." ("My bones, my flesh, father and mother," said Tu Fu.) After the movie, Ed explained to his wife that this cunning, resourceful, successful inventor, Edison, was who he had named himself after. "I see," she said. "Eh-Da-Son. Son as in *sage* or *immortal* or *saint*."

They also saw a movie where a big man bridged two mountain peaks with his prone body. He held on to one cliff of a chasm with his fingers and the other with his toes. Hundreds of little people walked across on him.

The four partners no longer had to race to get out of doing the dishes. Ed's wife shopped and cooked. She bought a tiered food carrier, filled each pot with a different accompaniment to rice, and carried it and a pot of soup hot through the subway to the laundry. The first day she did this, she got off at the wrong stop in the underground city. She went from white ghost to white ghost shouting over the trains, which sounded like the Japanese bombing, "Easu Bu-odd-way Su-ta-son?" And a conductor said, "Of course. East Broadway Station. Go that way."

"He understood me," she proudly told the men. "I can speak English very well." She set the table with her home-made meal so they didn't get to buy restaurant take-out food any more. And they did not race but had manners. "Tell me how you started this laundry," she said. Woodrow described their Grand Opening. "Our friends sent stands of flowers tied in wide red ribbons, on which your husband wrote good words in gold ink. We exploded firecrackers out on the sidewalk, right out there on Mott Street. And then the customers came." "Working for ourselves, we can close whenever we please and go do as we like," Ed said.

The partners did not tell her that they hardly ever celebrated holidays. They had learned that holidays do not appear with the seasons; the country does not turn festive just because a rubric day appears on the calendar. The cooking women, the shopping and slicing and kneading and chopping women brought the holidays. The men let holidays pass. If they did not go to the bother of keeping it, a holiday was another free day. It was that free a country. They could neglect attending the big public celebrations such as those at the benevolent associations and New Year's eve at Times Square, and no one minded. Neglecting the planting and harvest days made no difference in New York. No neighbors looked askance. And there were no godly repercussions. They had no graves to decorate for the memorial days of Clarity and Brightness. They did arrange cotton snow, reindeer, a stable scene, and a Santa Claus in the laundry window at Christmas. "We don't want them to break our window or not bring their laundry," Ed explained. His wife brought back the holidays. She made the holidays appear again.

Her arrival ended Ed's independent life. She stopped him from reading while eating. She'd learned at the school of Western medicine, she said, that doing those two actions at once divides the available blood between brain and stomach; one should concentrate. She kept telling Ed to cut down on his smoking. She polished his World's Fair copper souvenir ashtray clean. She cut new covers from brown wrapping paper and shirt cardboards for his books, and resewed the bindings. He inked the new covers with the titles, authors, and volume numbers.

When the partners took the couple to a restaurant, the men wiped their chopsticks and bowls with napkins. "That doesn't really clean them, you know," she said. "All you're doing is wiping the germs around. Germs are little animals invisible to the naked eye." "That must be a superstition from your village, a village superstition," said Worldster. "You ought to give up village superstitions in America." The next day she brought her microscope to the laundry and showed them the germs under their fingernails and on their tongues and in the water.

At one of their dinners, Worldster handed papers to Woodrow and Roosevelt, and the three of them started discussing business.

"What is this?" said Ed.

"Deeds for the business," said Worldster, "contracts for the partnership."

"Where's mine?" said Ed. "What contracts? Why contracts all of a sudden?"

"Where's his?" asked his wife.

"You weren't at the meeting," said Worldster.

"Since when did we have to have contracts?" Ed asked. "We had a spoken partnership. We shook hands. We gave one another our word."

"We wrote it down too," said Worldster. "I guess you have the status of an employee."

"I don't see why you didn't show up for the meeting," said Roosevelt.

"This is all perfectly legal," said Woodrow. "Look – registered with the demon courts." It was in English. There wasn't anything Ed could do. They had ganged up on him and swindled him out of his share of the laundry. "You were always reading when we were working," somebody said.

"What are we going to do?" said his wife, the lines around her eyes and mouth deepening.

"Don't worry," he said. "I've been planning for us to go to California anyway."

So the two of them took a train across the United States, stopping in Chicago to visit some relatives – they saw more of the United States than they had ever seen of China – and went to live in California, which some say is the real Gold Mountain anyway.

Many times it has happened that a young man walks along a mountain road far from home. He may have passed the Imperial Examinations ("entered the toad palace on the moon") or failed. If he failed, he would be singing a song, "What Does the Scholar Do with His Bagful of Books After Failing?" Or he may not have been a student at all but a farmer at market overnight − or an artisan, whose wife will be pleased with the good money he made on pots or rugs or shoes. Or he carries a satisfying batch of cotton or silk on his back and is heading into town. On the nooning day, sun and leaves dapple his face with shadows and golden coins. The fine road opens before him coming around turns and over rises. Grass and water above and below him, he glimpses the road ahead threading the mountains. Some of the one hundred kinds of birds that fly the sky and nest the earth let him see them, and even the phoenix seems to hover near. A music accompanies him. Released for this day from his past and future, the young traveler feels his freedom. His walk is loose. He cocks his head; the music is real. He laughs at its cacophony, which blasts any worries out of his head. He sings melodies that wind like ribbons into the vistas. His conducting hands lift notes out of the air, stroke them, and let them go. Long streams drop down mountains. Beyond mountains, still higher mountains rise until the peaks fade from human sight. He is climbing a dragon's spine. Green-black trees twist overhead, taller than distant mountains. The man is the size of the far trees.

Suddenly it starts to rain. The naked drought-dwarfs with the one eye on top of their heads run for cover. Thunder and lightning close out the day. The trees howl, bend to earth, and snap back as if giants were stepping on them in their run downhill. The grass flattens against the ground. The wind, though it's only the wind, whips up a sense of danger in him, and the young man hurries along, hoping for a shrine to use as shelter. When he begins to despair of finding any such signs of other people having come this way, a big house appears in the woods, and simultaneously the smell of a strong flower fills his head. Lightning reveals him knocking at the unfamiliar emblems on the outer gate; thick passion flower vines like elephant trunks twist around the carved and lacquered pillars.

The storm dies for a moment as if listening to his knocks. The forms and colors of the clouds change rapidly. A gold, silver, and pink mist covers the house.

An old servant answers, and dogs charge out, barking at him. Sometimes, though, the beautiful lady lives there alone and comes to the gate herself. She is the most beautiful woman he has ever seen. She must have come from the West Lake region, land of the most beautiful women in the world. (Kwangtung women are the second most beautiful.) "Enter, stranger," she says, and later he remembers that the cheerless wind again quieted, the guard dogs subsided, and he heard her voice. In the garden, lumps of peacocks squat on the branches of swaying, laden trees. He follows her on a long path to the inner door; he walks under a horizontal scroll of mountains and sea. The red paper surely means a good house; a spirit woman or a fox would not have it, would she? Walking on through the cool rooms, he follows her retreating back. She is wearing a light-colored dress, her hair a black tail alive down the middle. She turns one corner after another until he wonders if he can find his way out alone. She finally enters a small room and faces him. "Change your wet clothes," she says in a voice that sings. "I'll return with more food." On a stool by the fire he finds clothing and slippers, which fit him. A tureen of hot soup sits on a table, and one bowl has already been poured. The tea steeps. How lucky am I, he thinks; a stranger is owed no more than a drink of water.

"Please eat with me." Her voice startles him because he did not hear her return to the room. She is dressed in the old style. (No matter what year this is, China is old enough for there to have been an old style.) She wears the combs with the long prongs. Her eyebrows are moth's wings joined at the center, and her eyes are like bronze bells with brights and deeps.

Holding her right sleeve with her left hand, she uncovers the complex dishes – duck in sheets, embryonic chicks in soup and in cakes, minces, and stuffings. Steam rises as if a mirage of food floated on the table. The meal lasts for a long while. He sucks bones thoroughly of marrow. He pushes an almond sliver over all the taste buds in his mouth, the ones along the upper gums, the lower gums, the ones under his tongue, and the corners of his cheeks. Then he bolts meat and rice. He gorges; he indulges his appetite. Food seems to reappear, the bowls bottomless. She pours tea and gives him the tiny cup with her own hands. He accepts it carefully so that his fingers do not oafishly touch hers. He feeds like an aristocrat.

If he knows ceramics and manners, he picks up a piece of tableware and says, "How beautiful." "Yes, hold it up to the light and see the glow," she says. The orange of the firelight suffuses the porcelain. He hears a deer cry outside. She ignores it. She is looking into his face, and her mouth forms a delightful O. She touches his wrist. "Tell me a story about your life," she says. As he talks, feeding her admiration, he understands that he is a special man. Up to now he was only filling his work-habituated hands with the clay from the least fertile part of his land; he made utensils, but she calls him an artist. If he is a failed student, he has his poems to sing to her, and she comforts him so that he is almost glad he lost at the exams. If he won, then what triumph – a position in government service and a beautiful woman – the beginning of a run of victories.

If he is a cobbler, she asks him to sew a pair of shoes for her, challenging him to do it before the storm abates. From the suede she brings him, he cuts pieces as symmetrical as butterflies. Until now he frugally used scraps from the winter coats. After finishing the seams, he nimbly works flowers into the tops and sides. He kneels before her chair, where she sits enthroned, and she steps into the shoes. Her tiny feet in each of his palms, he has the impression that he is holding a fairy dancing on his hands. "I can give you your wishes," she is saying. "I can give you time to study, money to buy gold thread and rare glazes." He laughs, "Spoken like a woman who never has to work. I wish never to have to work at all." What a strange woman. If he were a farmer, would she give him a shovel or a bag of manure as a present?

A farmer whose wife and babies are waiting for him would mean to stay only until the rain stops, only until the end of the slow night. He would memorize each moment and the scrolls and the furniture and the food; his wife would enjoy hearing about this lucky night.

His wife is waiting at home, cooking roots and bark for the children, the adopted daughter or son, the widower uncle, the old folks with no teeth. She is a brave cooking wife. She has never had a romantic dinner for two. He'll have to ask her if she can manage without sweating so, and he doesn't like the calluses on her hands and feet either.

The young husband should have hinted for some leftovers to bring home to his dying grandparents and hungry parents and toilsome wife. When he found out there was going to be free food, he could have sent the rich woman's servant to fetch his family. Instead he feeds like a zoo animal, a pet.

Toward the end of the meal, he asks, "Do you live here alone?"

"I'm a widow," she says, and he feels all the erotic things the words *young widow* arouse in men.

As if she expected just him and no other, his hostess brings him the very fruits, the very poem, the very game he likes best. "I'll leave when the storm flags," he says. "I'll leave after the winning point." The storm heightens. She wins a game, and he wins a game; they have to play again. She tells him the long, long story of how she came to be a young widow. Tears magnify her eyes and brim on the lids, the prisms breaking and melting, wetting the pink cheekbones, the white cheeks, the corners of her mouth. When she talks, the words give her mouth such shapes that he cannot cease watching it. His wife's tears were no more interesting than his own tears; her nose turned red when she cried. One more fascination, and yet one more holds him. Through the windows, there gleams weather fit for travel, but he stays. He becomes drowsy. He will see his wife the next day, for lunch at the latest.

For breakfast the beautiful widow feeds him more foods he has never eaten before, shows him more things he has only known in stories. When he asks if he can pack a few leftovers for his wife, she looks at him gravely, and says, "Let me give you a better present. You must take a lasting gift from me. Tell me about your work, and I can show you how to improve it and make lots of money." She says "lots of money" as if she were a girl imitating adult talk, guessing at his grown-up concerns. She seems to have come from a world where the inhabitants do not use money. She brings glazes in textures, blues, and greens the potter has not been able to mix, mounds of white lamb's wool to the weaver, paper with deer and willow and mountain watermarks to the poet, rolls of leather and cloth, threads like skeins of rainbows to the cobbler and tailor. To try the new substances, his hands begin their familiar work. They move smoothly now, not encountering bumps or tangles, knots, or nodes. The slips run exactly. Then, of course, he has to wait for the kiln to fire, the ink to dry, the glue to set. The embroidery artist has begun stitching the first of the one hundred birds, that is, two hundred birds, a pair of each kind, composed about a tree. Then, time to eat. Then, time to go to bed again, too late to travel. He should have observed the custom of refusing gifts.

The morning light shows his work to him; he sees in what he has done the possibility of the lightest, smallest shoe, the true poem, the embroidery or painting of the phoenix. He may fathom at this moment how many more pieces he has to make before the masterpiece. He bows to the years he must remain at his work. Each piece draws him on to the next one. Days go by. Nights.

And it is not only the work that holds him but the woman. If he is a tailor, he sews for her; the clothes are her size, and he does not mind that she cannot sew or cook, or that she sometimes laughs inappropriately. With clean tools and rich materials to choose from, he does the most elegant work of his life. He has a new life, a new quotidian. He does not forget the old life, but he remembers it like a bedtime story heard as a child. The beautiful lady pleases him easily; she disappears for a part of each day so that he can work. The student writes his poem about her and looks forward to her listening to it. The potter dedicates his vases to her. He used to make them for his wife, but that was not the same. At first he is very happy. The beautiful lady gives him enough to eat, robes, music from nowhere. "Love me," she says. "I love you," she says. "Do you love me?" Like a salt plum, she makes his mouth water. He and his wife never talked about loving each other. Now whenever he conjures up thoughts about his family, he sees their black and white portraits. "I love you," she says, and he loves this stranger more than mother and father.

But one day there seems a surplus of pots, shoes, scrolls. The embroidery artist has finished his two hundredth bird. When he has completed this much, doesn't he usually go to market?

The beautiful lady, braceleted up to her elbows like a bride, draws her eyebrows and the line connecting them with special care. She feeds him and charms him.

"Tell me you've been happy here," she says. "Tell me you are happy."

"I have been happy here. I have never been happier than here with you. Why are you crying? Why are you looking like that?"

"Stay with me today."

"I'll be gone for just a few hours." Or "I'll be back in just a few days."

"I love this scroll. Let me have it. Don't sell it." "And these shoes." She says, "I love this cup, its lines, its design, its handle. Let me keep it," pulling things out of his pack.

"But I've already given you the best pieces. These are for market."

"But you don't need to go to market any more," she says.

He says, "I don't need to study any more. I'm ready to take the examination again."

"It's harvest time," he says. Or "Time for the planting."

She puts on the same dress she wore when he first saw her. She brings festive food as for Sweethearts' Day, but when he finishes eating, he takes up his pack. "I have to find out," says the student, "if I can beat this year's crop of scholars." Suddenly he yearns for air that does not smell feverish with gardenias. She kneels at his feet and begs him to stay. Perhaps it is now that the deer cries. She stands, opens her robe, opens it like wings, and wraps him inside, enclosing him against her naked body, reminding him how unwifely her breasts and thighs are, how helplessly her body works as his touches it.

Unable to remain joined, connected, he breaks from her, and leaves.

On the road, breathing dizzies him. The sky looks as big as it is. He has been seeing window-framed pieces of it for too long. Its immensity dazzles him – blue without end.

His appearance startles the townspeople, who run, pretending they are late for something important, not looking back. Dogs slink from him. He could leave his bundles on the street and no thief would touch them because of the phosphorescence that would rub off like contagious death. Children point at him, and the mothers hit them and rush them away. Confusedly, he arranges his wares on the ground in wait for shoppers. The vendors on either side of him and the letter writers across the way dismantle their tables and awnings; not discussing it, they leave quickly. Even with no competition, he cannot lure any customers. He picks up his goods and stumbles to a better location.

This young man must have had a good family and a loyal village because as he wanders like a ghost, a villager from his former life grabs him. "Brother Brother," calls the fellow villager, and the sounds of "Brother Brother" are like a rooster's crow in the morning. "What's wrong? What's happened to you? Where have you been all this time? We've missed you. Aiya! Look at you. You're so thin. Have you been ill? Why, I can feel your bones. What black bags under your eyes, and why do you let your hair hang like this? Here, let me braid it for you. You shouldn't be traveling when you're sick. Let me see you home." The villager puts his arms around the young man. The familiar is so comforting that he sobs.

His friend guides him along the mountain road toward the home village. They are like two bugs in the landscape. The nearby oaks are gnarling and the far pines standing straight. The trees hold gray antlers high, already budded with leaves. Midway home, the young man stops. He seems to hear something, and though he stares straight ahead, the whites under his irises show. Marionette strings pull him into the tall grass. He remembers a beautiful lady he met in a previous incarnation or a dream last night.

The closer he comes to where the house had been, the more the home village becomes the dream. "Look," says his friend. "A grave."

Where a front door stood is the marker for a noble-woman's grave. The rain and wind have not quite rubbed the dates and the strange emblems off. She has been dead for years, centuries.

Fear burns along the young man's spine, and he runs from the lonely spot where no paths meander, no house looms, no peacocks or dogs stalk among the lilac trees. His friend dashes after him, not to be left by himself at the grave.

The young man walks home with his fellow villager. Sun, air, wind chase away his memory of nightingales singing and night-blooming cereus. The young husband returns to his family. The hero's home has its own magic.

Fancy lovers never last.

THE GREAT GRANDFATHER OF THE SANDALWOOD MOUNTAINS

About a year ago, I mailed fifty dollars to China to a cousin who is black, they say, and not strictly a cousin. "You don't have to send anything," my mother said several times. "It's entirely up to you," which, of course, it wasn't; we'd already been asked. Like his father before him, my maternal grandfather had brought a third wife back from his third trip West, Bali or Hawai'i or South America or Africa. They had one black boy child, who is MaMa's half-brother. He grew up and got married and now has a son, the cousin to whom I sent the fifty dollars. He had written saying that a bicycle costs fifty dollars, and that it would change his life to own one. "I'll make sure in my letter," said MaMa, "to specify that it was you who sent it." "It doesn't matter," I said. "You don't have to do that." I don't want anybody attached to me forever with gratitude.

A few weeks later, a letter came from my black "uncle," the bicycle cousin's father. "Why did you send him money and me nothing?" he wrote. "I'm the father. I deserve the money. If you don't send me my money, I'm going to kill him." Even though they are black Chinese Red Communists living on the other side of the world, and even though they are poor, I do not believe he meant that. He must have only threatened to use his son as a hostage because he thinks us so entirely foreign we would be susceptible to such a threat; he was appealing to us Americans in a language we'd understand. "Furthermore," he said, "you have disrupted the economy and technology of the commune. Send fifty dollars in reparations." We don't feel an obligation to send him anything.

But in case he means what he said and Communists are as wild as the stories about them, I won't tell the name of our village. I don't want anybody arresting my uncle for extortion or confiscating the bicycle. The Chinese American newspapers list names of tourists from the United States and Hong Kong who disappear visiting China.

I am glad to see that the black grandmother ended up with a son and a grandson who are articulate. When she came to China she "jabbered like a monkey," but no one answered her. "Who knows what she was saying anyway?" She fell mute.

Many men on my mother's side of the family, even today, even the young men in countries where polygamy has been outlawed, have two wives, two houses, two families. The men in the past had three wives. The first wife, of course, was the important one; the others were "for love."

At a party in Honolulu, I met a dancer just returned from China, where she studied for six months. (Her aunt in China danced the Dark Haired Girl's part in *The White Haired Girl*.) She visited her ancestral village, Chung Sahn, where Sun Yat Sen was born, where the ancestors of most Chinese Americans in Hawai'i came from. She said that all the people were housed and fed. Her uncle's house had been divided into apartments, and he lived in one of them. "Were very many killed during the Revolution – I mean, Liberation?" I asked. She said No. "Nobody in my family," she said. I said, "Most of the men in our family were killed. The relatives write letters asking for money and bicycles." She said, "There are remote parts of the country where people are still ignorant, greedy, and lazy."

A physicist wrote me a letter about his trip to China; he visited his ancestral village, which, it so happens, is also my ancestral village. He had been born there, but emigrated to America as a child. After lecturing at Beijing University, he was given a Volkswagen. Dressed like one of the people and speaking both Mandarin and Cantonese, he traveled about freely. When he arrived at the village, he saw houses from his childhood; the ones that had belonged to families that had sent men to the United States had been decorated with expensive tiles. He met a woman whom he recognized from his childhood as an aunt and went home with her. An automobile and some electrical kitchen appliances were rusting in the yard, stuff brought back from the Gold Mountain; there was no gasoline or electricity in the village. A young man was sitting idle by the door; he was some kind of a cousin. "Stay for dinner," the aunt invited the physicist, but the young man said rudely, "He's too busy to have dinner." The physicist ate at the communal dining room; the commune people also showed him around. Though the land in this area was more fertile than in most other parts of China, he found the farmers less eager to meet production quotas. In the middle of the work day, young men sat talking about how someday soon they would move to the Gold Mountain, where their ancestors, American pioneers, had gone for hundreds of years. The physicist felt that indeed there was something different about the people in our village.

I'd like to go to China if I can get a visa and – more difficult – permission from my family, who are afraid that applying for a visa would call attention to us: the relatives in China would get in trouble for having American capitalist connections, and we Americans would be put in relocation camps during the next witch hunt for Communists. Should I be able to convince my family about the good will of normalization, it's not the Great Wall I want to see but my ancestral village. I want to talk to Cantonese, who have always been revolutionaries, nonconformists, people with fabulous imaginations, people who invented the Gold Mountain. I want to discern what it is that makes people go West and turn into Americans. I want to compare China, a country I made up, with what country is really out there.

I have gone east, that is, west, as far as Hawai'i, where I have stood alongside the highway at the edge of the sugar-cane and listened for the voices of the great grandfathers. But the cane is merely green in the sunlight; the tassels waving in the wind make no blurry fuzzy outlines that I can construe as a message from them. The dirt and sun are red and not aglitter with gold motes like in California. Red and green do not readily blend, nothing lurking in the overlaps to bend the eyes. The winds blowing in the long leaves do not whisper words I hear. Yet the rows and fields, organized like conveyor belts, hide murdered and raped bodies; this is a dumping ground. Old Filipino men die in abandoned sheds. Mushrooms and marijuana grow amidst the cane, irrigated by the arches of vaulting water. People with friends on the mainland steal long-distance calls on the field telephones.

Driving along O'ahu's windward side, where sugarcane grew in my great grandfathers' day, I like looking out at the ocean and seeing the pointed island offshore, not much bigger than a couple of houses, nothing else out in that ocean to catch the eye – Mokoli'i Island, but nobody calls it that. I had a shock when I heard it's also named Chinaman's Hat. I had only encountered that slurred-together word in taunts when walking past racists. (They would be the ones loafing on a fence, and they said the chinaman was sitting on a fence ". . . trying to make a dollar out of fifty cents.") But Hawai'i people call us Paké, which is their way of pronouncing Bak-ah, Uncle. They even call Chinese women Paké.

When driving south, clockwise, there is an interesting optical illusion. At a certain point in the road, the sky is covered with Chinaman's Hat, which bulges huge, near. The closer you drive toward what seems like a mountain, the farther it shrinks away until there it is, quite far off, an island, a brim and crown on the water.

At first, I did not say Chinaman's Hat; I didn't call the island anything. "You see the island that looks like a Chinaman's hat?" locals ask, and visitors know right away which one they mean.

I swam out to Chinaman's Hat. We walked partway in low tide, then put on face masks. Once you open your eyes in the water, you become a flying creature. Schools of fish – zebra fish, rainbow fish, red fish – curve with the currents, swim alongside and away; balloon fish puff out their porcupine quills. How unlike a dead fish a live fish is. We swam through spangles of silver-white fish, their scales like sequins. Sometimes we entered cold spots, deserts, darkness under clouds, where the sand churned like gray fog, and sometimes we entered golden chambers. There are summer forests and winter forests down there. Sea cucumbers, holothurians, rocked side to side. A sea turtle glided by and that big shell is no encumbrance in the water. We saw no sharks, though they spawn in that area, and pilot fish swam ahead in front of our faces. The shores behind and ahead kept me unafraid.

Approaching Chinaman's Hat, we flew around and between a group of tall black stones like Stonehenge under-water, and through there, came up onto the land, where we rested with arms out holding on to the island. We walked among the palm trees and bushes that we had seen from the other shore. Large white birds were nesting on the ground under these bushes. We hurried to the unseen side of the island. Even such a tiny island has its windward and leeward. On the ocean side, we found a cave, a miniature pirate's cove with a finger of ocean for its river, a beach of fine yellow sand, a blowhole, brown and lavender cowry shells, not broken, black live crabs side-stepping and red dead crabs drying in the red sun, a lava rock shelf with tide pools as warm as baths and each one with its ecology. A brown fish with a face like a cartoon cow's mugged at me. A white globule quivered, swelled, flipped over or inside out, stretched and turned like a human being getting out of bed, opened and opened; two arms and two legs flexed, and feathery wings, webbing the arms and the legs to the body, unfolded and flared; its thighs tapered to a graceful tail, and its ankles had tiny wings on them – like Mercury; its back was muscled like a comic book superhero's – blue and silver metallic leotards outlined with black racing stripes. It's a spaceman, I thought. A tiny spaceman in a spacesuit. Scooping these critters into another tide pool, I got into theirs, and lying in it, saw nothing but sky and black rock, the ocean occasionally flicking cold spit.

At sunset we built a campfire and sat around it inside a cleft in the hillside. We cooked and ate the fish we caught. We were climbing along a ledge down to the shore, holding on to the face of the island in the twilight, when a howling like wolves, like singing, came rising out of the island. "Birds," somebody said. "The wind," said someone else. But the air was still, and the high, clear sound wound through the trees. It continued until we departed. It was, I know it, the island, the voice of the island singing, the sirens Odysseus heard.

The Navy continues to bomb Kaho'olawe and the Army blasts the green skin off the red mountains of O'ahu. But the land sings. We heard something.

It's a tribute to the pioneers to have a living island named after their work hat.

I have heard the land sing. I have seen the bright blue streaks of spirits whisking through the air. I again search for my American ancestors by listening in the cane.

Ocean people are different from land people. The ocean never stops saying and asking into ears, which don't sleep like eyes. Those who live by the sea examine the driftwood and glass balls that float from foreign ships. They let scores of invisible imps loose out of found bottles. In a scoop of salt water, they revive the dead blobs that have been beached in storms and tides: fins, whiskers, and gills unfold; mouths, eyes, and colors bloom and spread. Sometimes ocean people are given to understand the newness and oldness of the world; then all morning they try to keep that boundless joy like a little sun inside their chests. The ocean also makes its people know immensity.

They wonder what continents contain the ocean on its other side, what people live there. Hong Kong off the coast tugged like a moon at the Cantonese; curiosity had a land mass to fasten upon, and beyond Hong Kong, Taiwan, step by step a leading out. Cantonese travel, and they gamble.

But China has a long round coastline, and the northern people enclosed Peiping, only one hundred miles from the sea, with walls and made roads westward across the loess. The Gulf of Chihli has arms, and beyond, Korea, and beyond that, Japan. So the ocean and hunger and some other urge made Cantonese people explorers and Americans.

Bak Goong, Great Grandfather, came to Hawai'i at the invitation of the Royal Hawaiian Agricultural Society. Their agent, who had been born in our district and spoke like us, came straight into the village and talked about how he got to be a recruiter. Even today the family trusts any insurance, encyclopedia, or gadget salesman who talks like us, our language a music that charms away common sense. The family knew the growing habits of cane; a stand grew in the courtyard. Convoys used to relay lichee and sugarcane from Canton to the Imperial palace. A few times a year, on a holiday or a birthday, Grandmother cut a stalk and divided it into small chunks, one for each person. The sweet taste affected Bak Goong. The recruiter told his fellow villagers, Chinese were the first sugarmakers in Hawai'i; they brought the first millstones and vats in 1802. "Right now," said the agent, "we're offering free passage, free food, free clothing, and housing. In fact, we're advancing you six dollars. Here. See. I have six dollars right here. Here, Grandma. We'll let Po Po hold it; she can return it to me if she wants to. Couldn't you use six dollars before you've even begun to work? You repay it with just six weeks' work. After six weeks, clear profit. Figure it out. You're joining us at a lucky time. The pay just went up again. You're getting an instant raise. We need every kind of labor. You inexperienced kids can be house servants for two dollars a month. Now, once you secure this fine job, you'll want to protect it, right? You're thinking, What if I get to the Sandalwood Mountains, and they fire me? Well, listen to this. We can't fire you. We protect you against firing. We can't fire you because you sign this three-year contract, and for more protection, this five-year contract." "Mm," said the family. "Of course, there'll be some hardships, but that's life, isn't it? You'll be traveling with a shipload of fellow Chinese, with whom you'll be sharing free housing. You'll have people to discuss things with. We're giving you a dormitory just like going to college. And did you know that the Sandalwood Mountains are very close to the Gold Mountain? You get free passage as far as the Sandalwood Mountains, where you can stay as long as you want, and you invest a little of your profits in passage to California. You'll get there before the Gold Rush is over. Why, in Hawai'i, you're already halfway there. Figure: You start with nothing. You already have six dollars' advance. Three years from today, home with riches."

Impressed by the agent's homely dialect, his suit, his title, and his philosophic bent, Bak Goong muttered what Confucius taught on the occasion of breaking a promise to his captors, "'Heaven doesn't hear an oath which is forced on one,'" and made his X.

He told his family that he would be back in three years. Traveling alone, he watched armies march or straggle by, close calls, he on a cliff, an army in the ravine; he behind a waterfall, an army drinking at the river; he flattened like a shadow on the earth, an army silhouetted against the moon. He spied British demons with big noses and guns. He was walking on dangerous and sick land. In the north, the Yellow River had reversed its course overnight; it reared up, coiled in the air, and slapped down backwards to run the other way, south instead of north. It troughed new watercourses and flooded four provinces before settling on its route. Winds collided. The Yangtze also flooded. Eels hung from ceilings, and red worms curled inside wells and jars. Migrating from lakes of drowned crops and trees, farmers came to fields of dust where drought cracked the ground, the land was burned, and there were no fishing boats on the rivers. New monsters were appearing on the earth, barbarians everywhere; the British demons opened the seaports to opium and soldiers. A crazy Cantonese (whose name is pronounced like our own last name but isn't the same at all), either fooling the Jesus demons or deranged by Christian education, taught that Mary had given two virgin births, Jesus and himself. With a sister and two brothers, Jesus Christ's Younger Brother led sixteen provinces and the Taiping, the army of the Great Peace, the Long Hairs, in revolt against the emperor and his British and French armies. The Shao Lin, an order of fighting monks, famous for their battles against the Manchus, were emerging again. The Manchus had burned the Shao Lin Temple, but their five Founding Fathers had escaped by hiding under a bridge (Pagoda and Bridge their symbols), then trained successors, who were the teachers of the monks fighting for the Great Peace. The Miao tribes and the Nien were also uprising, as were the Moslems of Yunan. The magnetic poles of the world had switched; gravity itself had come loose. China was changing again, as it does every thirty years in small cycles and every hundred years in large cycles.

Bak Goong recognized a century-size upheaval; he shook his head and walked away, turned his back and walked away.

He arrived in Canton without being conscripted, and signed on a schooner as a crewman to make extra money while traveling. He would jump ship in Hawai'i if he wasn't allowed to quit there.

The Chinese who had sailed before him had painted a sea bird on the side of the ship, which protected it from storms. His first free moment he lowered himself on a rope and painted eyes on the bow. He tied poles and lines to the rails and caught fish. The ocean was a bowl with horizon all around. Lucky to be a crewman.

He met all manner of men, broad faced and sharp faced Han Men, tall dark ones, white ones, little ones like the Japanese. One group spoke the language so queerly that he laughed out loud. He imitated their *thl* sound blown out of the mouth with big, airy cheeks and spit. "One, two, three, *four*." Sputtering and spitting as he shouted out the *four*, which has that *thl*, he called out the rhythm for lifting and hauling. "Do you come from near our village?" a man from the *thl* village asked. "Yes, I also come from the *Four* Districts," said Bak Goong. He mimicked men with staccato consonants and a lone northerner who spoke a soft dialect like English, and he would have talked to the Englishmen too except that he could not hear their sliding, slippery little voices out of the fronts of their pursed mouths. "Their asses must be as tight as their mouths," he said out loud right in front of them.

The Chinese passengers were locked belowdeck though they were not planning to escape. Their fresh air was the whiff and stir when crewmen exchanged the food buckets for the vomit and shit buckets. Some men brought their pigs, which slept under the bottom bunks. The beds looked like stacks of coffins in a death house. "Here we are," said Bak Goong, who had to sleep in this hold too, "emigrating with our pigs our only family."

He gave advice to the boys who were away from their mothers for the first time. "You'll be a rich man in three years," he said. "Three years is forever for a kid, but for a man in his thirties like me, the years pass too quickly. Don't you notice how one year passes faster than the last? The first year abroad will be the worst; then we'll wish that time would slow up for our lives to last longer." (He talked about time as going from up to down, last week being the "upper week" and next week the "lower week," time a sort of ladder that one descends.)

"Be quiet, Dog Vomit," somebody hollered. "Shut up and let me sleep."

"Don't say 'vomit,'" somebody else groaned.

"Try laughing," said Bak Goong. "I'll bet you can't laugh and vomit at the same time." *Laugh* is another word that has the *thl* combination in that queer dialect. "And as for the dark," he advised the children, "it makes the room feel larger, doesn't it?"

"Tobacco shit stops the seasickness," said an opium smoker, who passed his pipe.

"No, no, shit cures colds, not seasickness."

"Let's try it for seasickness."

"Your mother's cunt. You make this room smoky, and I'll throw up all over you."

The berths, come to think of it, were also stacked like beds in an opium house. "Is opium bitter?" asked Bak Goong. "It's not addicting if you just try it once, right?" The tempted men had a discussion on exactly which pipe – the twelfth? the hundredth? – addicted, and how often – once a week? five times a day? once a month? – an addict smoked. "It takes two years of smoking three times a day to learn the opium habit," an addict said confidently.

So Bak Goong gave a tobacco shit man some money and smoked. The silver and wooden water pipes gurgled like rivers; the bowl pipes drew airily. Bak Goong leaned against the wall, and the meaning of life and time and what he was doing on this ship all became clear to him; even his vomity feeling fell into its place in the scheme of the universe. His thoughts branched and flowed and branched again and connected like rivers, veins, roads, ships' lanes. New ideas sparked, and he caught his breath when he saw their connections to old ideas. Circles wheeled by, whirled concentrically, and stilled into a simple light. The bald heads of monks, who sit in circles, bowed toward the center like a hand, a lotus flower, or wood sorrel closing. The world's people arranged themselves in parades, palaces, windows, roads, stadiums, attempting to form this bond. These men in the hold were trying to circumnavigate the world. Men build bridges and streets when there is already an amazing gold electric ring connecting every living being as surely as if we held hands, flippers and paws, feelers and wings. Though he was leaving his good wife and his village, they were connected to him by a gold net or a light; it shimmered when the people and other creatures moved about. Even the demons abovedeck let out a glow. Bak Goong thought he understood the Tao, which is everywhere and in everything, even in our excrement, which is why opium is shit. It seemed that he would have to bring his mind hard to bear in order to discriminate between sleeping and waking, work and play, yours and mine. Wars were laughable; how could a human being remember which side he was on? Fear gives us red to brighten the world, and meanings are for decoration. "Is this true?" he asked, and answered, "Yes." Everything was true. He was Lao Tse's great thinker, who can embrace opposing thoughts at the same moment. He loved the strangers around him as much as he loved his family. He closed his eyes and saw islands in the sea or planets in space or lakes he could dive into or observe. Suffering, happiness, hurt children were similar dots. He felt wise. But after enjoying his wisdom for a while, he noticed that there had been all along a weight or a rock at the bottom of his well-being, the familiar nag of tasks to do. The opium must be wearing off soon; was there a last question he wanted to ask it? "How am I going to withstand pain, plain physical hurt?" An accidental cut could make him say, "I can't bear it." He dug his nails into his arm. How could he take lonely inevitable death? What about death with pain, pain unto death? That his body felt content now did not mean that it had learned a sufficient lesson in the habit of well-being. An urge to touch the ground with bare feet came over him, not to have floorboards or shoes between him and earth. What if his body had to undergo deliberate torture, for example? "Don't hurt," he answered himself, or opium, the reminder, answered him. "Don't give pain. Don't take pain." The ring of light was disbanding, slivers of it returning to the various separate bodies of flesh and bone. How not to take pain? How to have no pain? "Be able," he said. "Be capable." Capable. Opium was merely a rest from constant pain. He said aloud, repeating, "Be capable," to remember this answer for use later when these unwordable feelings were gone. "I am a capable man. An able man," he said, and did feel a touch of dreariness at this mundane answer. He wrapped himself in his quilt and patted his money belt to feel his sugarcane contract crackle. "No pain. Don't give pain. Don't take pain." He did not smoke opium again on the journey because he did not want to become an addict or to spend money.

After three months at sea, Bak Goong smelled in the wind a sweetness like a goddess visiting. Whenever the hatches and doors opened in the right combinations, the men below also smelled it. "It's sandalwood," Bak Goong said, looking for land on the horizon. The smell of boxes and chests of drawers, statues, castanets and fans, incenses and powders must have inspired him to come here. Chinese had followed that essence to India, where sandalwood grew in phoenix-shaped roots in the caves of lions, and to Persia, where it congealed in the Eastern Ocean as a cicada. And now they followed sandalwood to its home here.

One day Bak Goong opened the hatches for the men below, who stumbled through the passageways and up ladders to the topdeck, where they blinked in the sunlight. A demon from shore counted and recounted the China Men. There were three or four fewer live ones than when they began the journey. The demon strung a tab about each neck. Bak Goong climbed down to the longboat, past the weeds that had grown like skirts on the ship's sides.

On shore among crates, burlap bags, barrels, haystacks, they waited for their bosses, some of whom were China Men. The men with no papers signed anything that was handed them; most made a cross like the ideograph *ten*; "The Word Ten," they called their signatures. A pair of horses, which delighted Bak Goong, pulled a wagon to the dock, but only a few workers rode to those fields close enough to Honolulu to be reached by roads. Bak Goong's group was to walk, led by a demon boss on a horse. He bade good-byes to friends he had made on the ship. Walking after rolling on the sea confused his legs, but with his seabag across his back, he edged quickly to the front of the group. He buffered himself in case the demon used his whip on men.

They walked out of the town and up a mountain road so narrow that the demon dismounted and led the horse. The trail led upward among banana trees. Bak Goong ate bananas to his heart's content, throwing away the peels instead of scraping their insides and eating the fibers; there were that many bananas, hands of them, overripe fruit rotting on the ground. He ate fruit and nuts he had never seen before. And mangos like in China. He wished he could give his wife some. With a handful of rice a day, he could live here without working. Five-petaled flowers spun from the trees, pink stars, white stars, yellow stars, striped red and white stars. At one beautiful spot, white trumpet flowers hung above his head like hats. He walked on ground royally carpeted with jacaranda. When the sun became hot, a tall rain fell and made two rainbows across the sky, the colors of the top one in the opposite order of the bottom one. "Aiya," said the men. "Beautiful. Beautiful." "Is that a good omen or a bad omen?" "How does it happen?" "It has to be a good omen." The rainbows moved ahead of them. Before they became too wet, the rain stopped; the sun and breeze dried them. Bak Goong memorized all this to tell his wife.

He sucked in deep breaths of the Sandalwood Mountain air, and let it fly out in a song, which reached up to the rims of volcanoes and down to the edge of the water. His song lifted and fell with the air, which seemed to breathe warmly through his body and through the rocks. The clouds and frigate birds made the currents visible, and the leaves were loud. If he did not walk heavy seated and heavy thighed like a warrior, he would float away, snuggle into the wind, and let it slide him down to the ocean, let it make a kite, a frigate bird, a butterfly of him. He would dive head first off the mountain, glide into the airstreams thick with smells, and curve into the ocean. From this mountaintop, ocean before him and behind him, he saw the size of the island. He sang like the heroes in stories about wanderers and exiles, poets and monks and monkeys, and princes and kings out for walks. His arias unfurled and rose in wide, wide arcs.

The men passed a hutment of grass shacks with long yellow thatch weathered and fine, rippling and ruffling in the breeze like the hair of blonde ladies. Roofs had fallen, and the frames showed like bones. The doorways were empty. They did not see brown people come and go.

They descended another side of the mountain and walked along the sea all day, and at last came to the place where they were to work. They had arrived in the middle of the workday, and were to start at once. There was no farm, no sugarcane ready to tend. It was their job to hack a farm out of the wilderness, which they were to level from the ocean to the mountain. To do this, Bak Goong was given a machete, a saw, an ax, and a pickax. The green that had looked like grass at a distance was a tangle of trees so thick that they shut out sunlight. Leaves grew only on their tops and bent backs. They were not tall trees, branch having wrestled branch into a knot that gnarled for miles. It may have been one tree that had replanted itself tighter and tighter. A criminal dropped into the midst of the webwork would be imprisoned forever. Beginning anywhere, Bak Goong chopped into the edge of this strange forest. He could not take hold of the branches because of the thorns on them. Dust shook down. Coughing, alarmed at how quickly he grew hot, tired, and thirsty in the intervals between the water-and-tea man's rounds, he shook a silver ball from the flat glass bottle he carried in his pocket and swallowed it for thirst. He gave pills to the boys working on either side of him. Though he chopped, hacked, and sawed with all his might, the knot of trees did not seem smaller. Black birds with flashes of white wings flew easily straight through the maze.

After work, though he could get sick and die from mixing cold water with hot sweat – open pores draw in the cold – he ran with the others into the ocean, and let it wash him. In the water rushing away from him, he held on to his body and mind with effort. The horizon seemed to be up in the air. He would have gone to sleep right there on the beach, but the ones who had arrived earlier had established an eating system. "Eh, China Man, come eat," the China Men invited. They had already organized the food, decided who would cook and on what terms. "Eh, China Man, come eat," Bak Goong imitated their English. So he got to sit down to a good dinner on plank tables. They passed around candy before dinner; it was a regular welcome party. The few Hawaiian workers passed around salt. Chinese take a bit of sugar to remind them in times of bitter struggle of the sweetness of life, and Hawaiians take a few grains of salt on the tongue because it tastes like the sea, like the earth, like human sweat and tears. Some fishermen and surfers and a demon traveler also ate with them, as did the other great grandfather, Bak Sook Goong, who was not yet related. (They would have called one another Bak and Sook in any case – Uncles.) These strangers ate like a family, drank from the same soup tureen, ate from the same plates of accompaniments to the rice. They did not gobble directly from the center dishes to the mouth but first touched the meat or vegetable to the rice. Bak Goong was lucky to have fallen among the civilized in the wild Sandalwood Mountains. He ate chunks of coconut wet in its milk and the fruit they had gathered on the way that morning. The hot tea on the hot day cooled him.

In the talk-story time after dinner, young men gave advice to young men. There were no old men in the Sandalwood Mountains. "Mind your own business, and work like an ox." "Don't gamble." "Keep your machete sharp, and hold it like so when you smell a demon near you." "Wrap your queue around your head or tuck it inside your shirt." "If you have the opium habit, you can ask for your wages by the week." Bak Goong congratulated himself on what a good ear he had; he could understand much of what these unusual men were saying. He had traveled to the middle of the ocean and was getting along with the people he found. He spoke to the most foreign, barbarous-looking China Men. When a storyteller lost him with apocopations, he wondered whether a puff of opium would help him understand language more clearly, but "No," he said politely, "I'd not be able to repay you." The men who had come earlier also said that the plantation had a rule that they not talk at work, but this rule was so absurd, he thought he must have misheard tones.

He lay down out in the open. The sights of the day unreeled behind his eyelids – the ocean jumping with silver daggers, fronds shredding in wind, twin rainbows, spinning flowers, the gray mass of the maze tree like all the roads of many lives. How was he to marvel adequately, voiceless? He needed to cast his voice out to catch ideas. I wasn't born to be silent like a monk, he thought, then promptly said. "If I knew I had to take a vow of silence," he added, "I would have shaved off my hair and become a monk. Apparently we've taken a vow of chastity too. Nothing but roosters in this flock."

The next morning at 5 a.m., he was again standing before the fist of trees. The dimness of shapes gave the coming day many possibilities until the sun delineated the pleached trees, the mountains, and another day of toil. He worked for that day and the next and the next without saying anything, but got angry, chopping as if cutting arms and legs. He withstood the hours; he did the work well, but the rule of silence wrought him up whenever a demon rode by. He wanted to talk about how he sawed through trunks and the interlocked branches held the trees upright. He suddenly had all kinds of things to say. He wanted to tell the men who worked beside him about the rewards to look forward to, for example, chewing cane for breakfast; the fibers would clean their teeth like a toothbrush. "You go out on the road to find adventure," he wanted to say, "and what do you find but another farm where the same things happen day after day. Work. Work. Work. Eat. Eat. Eat. Shit and piss. Sleep. Work. Work." He axed a limb at each word. "Actually, I like being bored," he would have said. "Nothing bad is happening, no useless excitement." He wanted to discuss mutes and kings who rip out tongues by the roots.

And one day – he could not help it – he sang about the black mountains reddening and how mighty was the sun that shone on him in this enchanted forest and on his family in China. The sweep of the ocean was so wide, he watched the sun rise and set in it. In the heat of noon, he wished he could shoot out the sun, like Prince I, who dropped nine suns with his bow and arrows. The demons paid his singing no mind.

317

They must have thought he was singing a traditional song when he was really commenting and planning.

"I've solved the talking," he sang to his fellow workers. "If that demon whips me, I'll catch the whip and yank him off his horse, crack his head like a coconut. In an emergency a human being can do miracles – fly, swim, lift mountains, throw them. Oh, a man is capable of great feats of speed and strength."

There was a bang or crack next to his ear. The demon was recoiling his whip. "Shut up, Paké." He heard distinct syllables out of the white demon's moving mouth. "Shut up. Go work. Chinaman, go work. You stay go work. Shut up." He caught every word, which surprised him so much, he forgot to grab the whip. He labored on, muttering, "Shut up. Shut up, you." He found a cut on his shoulder.

The men tried burning instead of cutting the trees. They set fires in the red heat of the sun. Bak Goong felt the fire was the same as his anger; his anger was this size and this red. But only the dead branches and leaves burned. Cutting the burned trees, the men became sooted black. To make them work faster, the demons had a trick of telling the slowest man that he was sick and had to take the day off without pay.

On their own time, after 5 p.m., the workers built two huts for bunkhouses, each with wooden beds laid head to foot one above another like the shelves on ships. They arranged gourds and vines, buckets, and hats on the verandas, which they kept adding to the huts. Bak Goong wove a hammock, and it was as comfortable as his mother's lap.

At the very end of the day, the men exchanged remedies. They scraped one another's backs with spoons to get rid of rheumatism and arthritis. For heat sickness they scraped necks with the edge of a coin cooled in water, the square hole in the middle of the coin giving a good grip. They slapped the insides of one another's elbows and knees, where tiredness collects. They soaked cuts and sores, and rubbed bruises with tobacco and whiskey. Some exercised, and Bak Goong learned some kung fu movements and also some ways of breathing that would strengthen his body and sharpen his brain. They nursed runaways who had escaped from other work camps. Bak Goong showed his scarring shoulder and said, "I will talk again. Listen for me." Boys put rocks under their pillows to stop crying at night. Several people not from the same village believed in "passing fear over fire," which means lifting one who has been badly frightened and passing him over a fire. Some "passed rice over hearts" and some "over heads." Everybody thought that his way of doing things was the way all Chinese were supposed to do them.

Bak Goong worried that he had overlooked a trick clause in his contract and that he would not be paid at all; this was some kind of a slave labor camp. But pay day came. When the demon handed him his money Bak Goong counted it in front of him in Chinese and in business ("pidgin") English. He came out short. "Too little," he complained, holding up his fingers. "Too little bit money. Are you trying to catch a pig?" he asked, which means to cheat, to take advantage of a greedy person.

The paymaster demon said, "Shut up, you. You shut up," clapping a hand over his own mouth several times. Bak Goong had been fined for talking. And sick men had been docked for every day they had been lying lazy in bed. Those who had not recovered from crossing the ocean got an accounting of how much they owed for food and lodging plus passage. The strong workers had money subtracted for broken tools.

The men cursed as they reckoned their pay. "Dead man." "Rotten corpse afloat." "Corpse on the roadside." "Hunchback with a turtle on his back," that is "Cuckold." "Your mother's ass." "Your mother's cunt." "They take my piss and shit away from me to feed their fields. Take my shit." "Eat my shit and piss. Drink piss, white monster. Eat shit." Bak Goong turned his ass at the pig catcher demon's face. He was finding out that the dollar a week wasn't the minimum wage but the maximum to strive for, that hoeing paid less than other jobs. The China Man accountant told them their wages were reduced until the plantation made a bigger profit. If Bak Goong did not give any dinner parties, did not drink or smoke or gamble, he would bring home maybe a hundred dollars after three years. The big talk about a thousand dollars must have been about men who came home old to die after scrimping for thirty years and more.

One day, like a knight rescuing a princess, Bak Goong broke clear through the thicket. The demons bought bullocks; they had longer horns than water buffaloes. He yoked them to the stumps, which they yanked out. But the Hawaiians quit rather than help pull the boulders out of the earth. The remaining workers plowed around groups of big rocks in the middle of the fields. They were the first human beings to dig into this part of the island and see the meat and bones of the red earth. After rain, the mud ran like blood. The maze tree and woodrose sprouted behind the plows.

A team of six men including Bak Goong was sent to a plantation farther up the coast where cane already stood like a green army; the tassels were called "arrows." On the same day as he cleared land, he cut cane twice as tall as a man. The cane and rice growers were trying out the seasons. The workers stripped the long leaves like shucking corn. Dust shook loose, and they breathed it even through their kerchiefs. They cut the stalks close to the ground. The new men tasted the cane in which the sap was running warm. They cut the tips beneath the top three nodes for seed cane. There were seeds in the arrows, but it was faster to plant the nodes. The men seemed small and few wading among the sticky mounds.

The wagoners, who had a good job, drove the cane to the sugar mill on a route along the sea. It was crushed into molasses and boiled into sugar, for which the world was developing an insatiable hunger as for opium.

Bak Goong and his team brought the seed cane and a few bottles of rum back. The land was ready to be sown. They bagged the slips in squares of cloth tied over their shoulders. Flinging the seed cane into ditches, Bak Goong wanted to sing like a farmer in an opera. When his bag was empty, he stepped into the furrow and turned the seed cane so the nodes were to the sides, nodes on either side of the stick like an animal's eyes. He filled the trenches and patted the pregnant earth.

The work changed from watering season to hoeing season. He weeded the ivy that wrapped and would choke the young cane, the ratoons. The vines pulled like rubber. Using a short hoe, he knelt to uproot them, and carried the weeds to the fires at the ends of the rows else they take root where they fell. He worked even in the rain lest he lose money. Then there was a stripping season when he peeled the plants so they would use their strength to make sugar instead of leaves.

The next harvest, the men invented a burning season when they set the cane on fire to burn off the outer leaves instead of stripping by hand. They chose a dry and moderately windy day. Like a savage, Bak Goong ran with brands, torching the cane along the border. During the night watches, fires like furry red beasts lurked and occasionally roared into the black sky, showing it endless, nothing illuminated but smoke as high as the flames climbed. In the day the smoke curled like white snakes in the directions of the winds. Demons in white suits walked gingerly inspecting the char. Then there was clearing and planting, the hoeing, and harvest, and the planting season again.

The cough that had begun when he cut trees and stripped leaves worsened because of breathing the hot sweet smoke and because of the hoeing in the rains. On the hottest days, the coughing made his nose bleed. He stuffed rags in his nostrils and kept working. The blood clotted in the back of his throat, and he spit out gouts. He hawked and spat to entertain the men and to disgust the demons. His cough did come in handy. When the demons howled to work faster, faster, he coughed in reply. The deep, long, loud coughs, barking and wheezing, were almost as satisfying as shouting. He let out scolds disguised as coughs. When the demon beat his horse and dust rose from its brown flanks, he coughed from his very depths. All Chinese words conveniently a syllable each, he said, "Get – that – horse – dust – away – from – me – you – dead – white – demon. Don't – stare – at – me – with – those – glass – eyes. I – can't – take – this – life." He felt better after having his say. He did not even mind the despair, which dispelled upon his speaking it. The suicides who walked into the ocean or jumped off the mountains were not his kindred.

At night the very thought of dust tickled his lungs. In order to sleep, he imagined his lungs warming and becoming two red diamonds.

If the moisture and soil had been natural to cane, the men would not have had to work so hard coaxing it, leading water to it. The weather and soil were just good enough for cane to require constant nursing and effort. There was a scarcity of animals on the island too, and of laborers.

Whenever Bak Goong looked up from the work, the mountains were there above him. They rose, sheer green walls without slope like great stage curtains that could part or rise, and then he would see behind them what really runs the world, whether the gods' faces are kind or evil. The beings on either side of the curtains would have a look at one another – surprise – before they shut again. Perhaps the gods did fly this far from China and landed on this island for a rest in mid-ocean. Perhaps China Men attracted them. On a gray day, the mountains looked like Chinese mountains. But usually they were stark, bright green curtains. After a rainstorm, waterfalls dropped like silver scrolls down each fold. Bak Goong said, "Aiya!" in wonder. He counted over twenty waterfalls before his eyes.

For recreation, because he was a farmer and as antidote for the sameness of the cane, he planted a garden near the huts. Planting as if in his old village, which was like this island in weather and red dirt, he even grew flowers, for which there was no edible use whatsoever. "It's a regular park with coppices and flowers," he said. He ticked off in a chant the cuttings, seeds, and bulbs he had brought across the ocean – pomelo, kumquat, which is "golden luck," tangerines, citron also known as five fingers and Buddha's hand, ginger, bitter melon and other kinds of melon, squashes, peas, beans, narcissus, orchids, and chrysanthemums. To see how his plants had grown and changed overnight gave him eagerness, a reason, and curiosity for getting out of bed in the morning. The transplants another gardener had given him would be standing up. Tomatoes the size of pinheads would have appeared in the centers of the yellow flowers. His orange tree would have grown a pair of balls. He took his morning piss in his garden. He garnered and ate thinnings for breakfast. "Harvest," he said with one skinny luffa in his hand. For free, he found mushrooms, full-blown white domes and orange puffs in the grass and fluted wooden ears in the trees. He let at least one of each kind of plant go to seed and collected their generations. Harvest gave him a happy sense of order. "Li Shih Min," he informed the others, "established such order in his kingdom that criminals came out of jail for harvests and returned for the winter executions."

On their "day offu," the China Men went into Honolulu to spend their pay. They could ride cane and mill wagons as far as they had built roads, and they walked until there was another road, where they could catch another wagon for a few cents more. A family could eat for a week on that fare. They dressed for town in their black silk suits and yellow straw boaters with the black band and forked streamers; their braids hung between the swallowtails. "I'm going to town," Bak Goong sang and sang *town* as if Honolulu were his own village. A family man, he walked the entire way and reached town by noon. He went directly to the general store, where he bought a money order for his wife and dictated a letter about how well and lighthearted he was in this Sandalwood paradise. The leftover money was his to keep or spend on careful gambling (more for the companionship than the money), a restaurant meal with a shot of whiskey, and a yearly picture taken at the photo studio. Unlike Bak Sook Goong, the other great grandfather, he did not spend money on Sandalwood Mountain women. He wandered about on the wooden sidewalks creaking underfoot and sat in the stores. "Come in and sit awhile," the store owners said as if inviting him into their own houses in China, and he was a real uncle or brother.

Most of the men were young enough to have their entire lives changed on a day off. A farmer could come to town, change his name, and become a merchant. Bak Goong met men who had forgotten the names of their Chinese family or the name and location of their Chinese village. They kept shaking their heads when he named village after village. They had lost a last piece of paper or a letter with the address on it. The gambling men played with fate for a new life. They bought chances. It was no work at all to throw the dice, flip a card, or pick a word in the pigeon lottery. In one Sunday, a lucky man could buy a farm or take a ship home or to California, stand up from the gambling table and walk to the harbor. Or he could sign his years away, mortgage his labor and future, not go home yet, ever. Two poor men gamble and one becomes a rich man. The other becomes a fleaman. A day in town was full of possibilities.

The other great grandfather, Bak Sook Goong, did not spend much of his time off with the men. One day off, when following a stream, he heard the voices and laughter of women, and from behind bushes, saw them in a pool at the foot of a waterfall. Some naked women were bathing. Nude women sitting on the rocks were weaving flowers and leaves into crowns for their drying hair. They were singing, and laughed at the ends of lines, so he knew it had to be a lascivious song. And one of them was looking at him, into his eyes. Instead of covering herself, she held his gaze and washed herself here and there. Then she said something, and the women tugged him out of hiding. They made him bathe with them. "But this is just like stories," he told them, though they did not understand everything he said. "Let me sing you one." He stood garlanded and sang to them about a prince on horseback who came upon naked sisters bathing and singing. "Sun and water double and touch, double and touch," he sang. "Wash up here – and here – and wash down there." He did the movements as he sang, and the beautiful women understood and laughed. The end of that song was that the prince had burst out laughing, and the sisters covered themselves and vanished, but these women asked him to have a picnic with them.

"Come eat, Brother," they said in English. "Sit, Brother. You stay eat. Stay eat, Brother." As he ate with them serving him, he was reminded that this was the right way for a man to live, and how much he missed his family, which was a family of women, two wives and many daughters, also many slaves. He turned to the woman who had looked so boldly at him. "I come live with you?" he asked. "Let me come live with you."

"Yes," she said. "You come live with me." He became the godfather of many Hawaiian children. "Paké godfather," they called him.

When the China Men asked Bak Sook Goong how his family was doing, they continued to mean the one in China, and he answered that way too. After work and on days off, he went to his Hawaiian village.

Bak Goong, meanwhile, helped build a dragon for the many New Years to come. He collected metal and glass shards, seashells, and wood shavings, which he glued and sewed into scales. Once a month, he brought his dragon section to town and added it to the tail, which grew very layered and long. When the clothes he had brought from China and the new clothes he had bought here turned into rags, he worked them into the dragon. The island dragon was more splendid than any village dragon he had left behind. None of the men had seen a longer dragon in China. "This is the longest dragon in the world," they said. Only the men who regularly practiced kung fu were dragon dancers. They argued about which postures and moves were the correct kung fu. They had been taught by different teachers in contradicting traditions. On New Year's the dragon in its fierce dance undulated like the Pacific Ocean, coiled and twisted, leapt and stepped nimbly among the firecrackers. Bak Goong had his picture taken inside the dragon, not in motion but stretched out straight, the dancers' feet in white socks aligned in front of the wooden sidewalks.

Bak Goong spoke kindly and happily at the beginning of the New Year, saying only good things. But some aggravation would make him swear, and no year was perfect.

Once he saw five humpback whales on their New Year's birthing journey pass like spouting islands, backs like wet rocks, alive with moss and lichen. A wind blew leaves across the beach.

In 1856 every great grandfather on every island gave some of his money to throw a Grand Ball for the Sandalwood Mountain king and queen's wedding. Neither Bak Goong nor Bak Sook Goong went to it, but they were represented by wealthy China Men. "He practices quadrilles alone in front of a mirror in his room at night," the plain men gossiped. The ball was held at the courthouse. Four white demons, named with Chinese names and dressed in mandarin gowns, acted as hosts. The queen danced the opening quadrille with a real China Man, the king with a demoness. Six whole sheep and one hundred and fifty chickens were eaten. The China Men's Ball was the most elegant ever held in Hawai'i. The newspapers praised the China Men for their dancing and generosity; a ball was not above their comprehension. Great grandmothers were to understand that their husbands did not spend $3,700 on a Grand Ball to dance with the blonde Jesus demonesses or the princesses of the wild people but to prove their civility.

When Bak Goong needed to get off this rock of an island, he sat at an edge of the ocean where he often watched the sun pop out on his left, and later drop back in on his right. One moonless night the winds blowing from Kona met the winds blowing trade, and the air was still; the fronds hung silent. Two people were standing in the black water halfway between him and the horizon, halfway between the sky and earth. A yellow light shown from them; their random movements repeated in series, a dance. They revolved in the only brightness, and stopped, hands and feet held like Balinese temple dancers. Time moved at their rate of motion. It was either two people or one Hindoo with four arms. He heard music draw out into one long note. The waves going in and out forever was the same as no motion at all. The ocean remains the same basic water. Flesh does not evolve into the necessary iron. He yearned for the sun to blast out of the ocean. He sat for hours in the exact center of eternity.

Then it all started up again; the couple on the water stirred. A fisherman and woman suddenly came out of the sea and walked toward him. "Want to see our catch?" He could barely answer for staring at their ordinary faces.

Between the time the Hindoo danced and these two stood beside him, he had seen streaming up to him rows of shining people; they had had wings flapping light and bare feet and hands glowing. It had been bright as day.

"You like fish, Brother?" "You like fish, Uncle?" said the human voices coming from flesh and blood bodies. The light was contained in lanterns the man and woman were carrying and also came from the rising moon. The two figures were only an elderly Hawaiian couple he had met before; they had been nightfishing. They handed him a fish, "Eh, you like fish?" and walked away along the beach.

Later when he heard people say they had seen the torches of the dead warriors who walk across the water, he would say, "You saw the Hawaiians nightfishing or checking their lobster traps." But when someone said, "Those are the Hawaiians nightfishing," Bak Goong, a fanciful, fabulous man, said, "It may be dead Hawaiian warriors walking." If a human being crossed the path of the walkers, he could die on the spot, but Bak Goong said that he knew for a fact that this was not true. He mustn't sit so long looking at the ocean, he resolved. The opium must have had a permanent effect; he would not take any more. He asked the tobacco shit men, "How can you tell it hasn't changed you once and for all? Could everything have become permanently exaggerated?" Now that he was in a new land, who could tell what normal was?

Among the cane weeds, he found a new, free opiate: a mushroom with a speckled brown cap that turned purple when picked. It tasted of earth and must, but he did not see much new vision; perhaps he had seen all there was to see. He did not eat it again. Nor did he chew the wood whose Hawaiian name sounded like *ka fa*, "fake flower" in Cantonese. So he had smoked opium, eaten mushroom, and gambled, but he would not become an opium addict or mushroom addict or gambler. He was a talk addict.

On another day off, he got lost while exploring and came upon abandoned huts he had not seen before. The doors and windows gaped. Some huts only had a hole for crawling in and out of. The stones, however, had not tumbled down but sat stacked one on top of another in god shapes or human shapes — he did not know what they meant. There were no rocks wrapped in fresh ti leaves. In case it had been measles or smallpox that had emptied the village, he did not go inside any house.

Suddenly out of the air and lifting the hair on the back of his neck like the wind lifting the grass on the roofs came a howling that was high and long. It's a bird, he reasoned. It's crying in flight. That's why the notes come now here, now there. It's wild dogs on the hillside. But it grew louder and in it he heard sobs, the lamentation of old men and children, thousands of souls wailing in separate voices. He could not make out the quivering words, or it was a language he did not know. "Ghosts," his wife would have said. I'm imagining this, he thought. It's really wild dogs. Or wolves. They sounded hungry. He felt like weeping in sympathy; sorrow filled his chest, but he kept the tears back not to blind himself as he ran out of the village.

A woman standing by the last hut called to him. "This way. This way," she said. "You hear?" he asked. "Yes," she said, but the noise stopped. She stood under plumeria, the star flower, the deadman's flower that grows in graveyards. The hut behind her had been mended, the earth around it swept. She touched his arm; he felt a tiredness come from her and weight his arm. His face nodded toward hers, his head heavy and helpless. Though no icy breath came from her mouth, his chicken skin was proof of the supernatural nearby, and he left quickly, rudely. When he looked back, she had gone inside her hut.

He entered town in an unfamiliar place with the sun setting and no wagons in sight. A police demon stopped him, but English phrases had flown out of his mind. The police demon was about to arrest him, runaway chinamen a menace now, but just then Bak Goong saw a young countryman across the street, someone who could help him. "Sook-ah," he called out. "Sook-ah," that is, "Hey, Father's Younger Brother." "Sook-ah."

"Sugar?" said the police demon. "Sugar plantation? You better hurry. The wagon is leaving soon." He pointed with his nightstick to a street that jumped into recognition. Bak Goong returned on the last wagon.

Old men laugh with tears in their eyes every time they hear or tell the "sugar" story. Another way it goes is like this: A China Man enters a grocery store, where he wants to buy some sugar for New Year's day. But at the counter he can't think of the word. Luckily, a young man walks past the door. "Sook-ah," the older man calls, and the grocer demon gets him a bag of sugar, a good omen for the New Year.

On days off, it was safest to stay on the plantation. There was entertainment to be had without spending money. It was a recreation to sleep like winter gods. Peddlers came bringing medicines and toiletries; they talked-story and talked stink about people on the other plantations. The pesky missionary Jesus demons also came nosing and sniffing out Hawaiians and China Men even in the remote valleys. They were like the wandering persuaders in China. Some workers walked about with them, whispering and nodding. Converts got extra days off on demon holidays. "I'm just a pig catcher," they said as they dressed up for church, where they ate free food, "and you get to go inside demon houses." Bak Goong went to Christian church once or twice, but they talked "baptism," and he quit. He asked the converts, "Who's the pig that got caught?" They didn't even talk like China Men any more, the salt gone from their speech. "Thank God," they said instead of "Your mother's cunt."

Jesus demonesses with pale eyebrows and gold eyelashes visited on a Sunday. They spoke a well-intoned Cantonese, which sounded disincarnated coming out of their white faces. They said they had lived in China and respected Chinese. They wanted to come in and talk-story. Fingers in black books, they took peeks to see what to say next.

Bak Goong walked about the room to look at these strange women from various angles. No rudeness seemed to discomfit them; when any of the men did some interesting Chinese antic, they complimented him or did not notice. They handed out presents – candy, clothes, toothpaste, combs, soaps, medicines, Jesus pictures, which were grisly cards with a demon nailed to a cross, probably a warning about what happened to you if you didn't convert. In China, Bak Goong had seen pictures of soldiers eating Christians, whose meat looked like drumsticks. The briny men asked the Jesus demonesses, "Would you administer this medicine to me?" They grinned lewdly at one another, but the demonesses did not see Chinese facial expressions. The men brushed up against their yellow hair, reached behind and touched it. They talked about what was under the long dresses; no lady would understand anyway.

A mischievousness came into the room. Bak Goong brewed tea for the ladies. "It's the custom to drink it all," he said, scooping sugar into the cups. The sugar made the demonesses thirstier, and they asked for more tea. The men asked for more stories so that the women stayed and stayed. The listeners did like the one about the baby being born and the childless wise men searching for him and finding him. "Speak English," Bak Goong requested. If anybody talked long enough in a foreign language and he heard enough, he understood. At last the ladies got up one at a time, and everyone knew they were going to the outhouse to piss.

Later the men rolled on the floor laughing. Bak Goong told the origin of the joke they'd played: "The Story of Chan

Moong Gut and the Gambling Wives," he announced, and clanged his pot-lid cymbals. "Chan invited all the rich women to his house to play cards while their husbands were at work. He lured them with prizes and pastries. He served them syrup with just a little water. The sweetness made the ladies drink tea and go to the urine bucket continually. No, no, don't laugh yet. There's more. There's more. Chan Moong Gut had wet the rim of the bucket with red paint. That night their husbands beat the ladies. 'What man did you allow to paint a red ring around your ass?' the husbands hollered. They spanked their wives' asses redder. Wait till the white demonesses' husbands see their asses." The men drew rings with lascivious fingers. "You're going to hell," said the demon convert China Men. "Straight to hell, you demons."

Bak Goong told more stories about Chan Moong Gut, Fortunate Dream Chan, a trickster who never worked but lived by his wits gambling and catching pigs. He used to put chicken shit at the bottom of the rice for the blindman. When the blindman ate past the nicely mounded top, he said, "Oh, how wonderfully seasoned. How kind to put sauce in my rice."

"Every morning Chan would shit on his neighbor's doorstep. The first couple of days the neighbor stepped in it when he went out. After that, he opened the door cautiously and cleaned it up, cursing all the while. Chan Moong Gut arranged that this neighbor would run into him at market. Chan was boasting what an undauntable appetite he had. 'I can eat anything,' he said, tricking the people around him into buying him food. They were wagering on how much and how fast he could eat. He was good at sleight of hand, and was hiding food in his clothes. The neighbor thought of a bet, and he set the terms himself instead of letting wily Chan do it. 'I'll bet,' said the neighbor, 'that you can't eat whatever appears on my doorstep tomorrow morning.' Chan Moong Gut took the bet. Instead of shitting on the step, however, he arranged bananas dipped in brown sugar sauce. The neighbor could barely stand to look, but he felt gratified watching Chan hold his nose and weep as he ate shit. He was glad to give Chan the money and believed that he had caught a pig." People with the name Chan have asked storytellers to change the trickster's name, or to forget those stories in America.

It wasn't right that Bak Goong had to save his talking until after work when stories would have made the work easier. He grew the habit of clamping his mouth shut in a line, and the sun baked that expression on him. If he opened his mouth, words might tumble forth like coral out of the surf; spit would spout like lava. He still hacked at the cane while coughing: "Take – that – white – demon. Take – that. Fall – to – the – ground – demon. Cut – you – into – pieces. Chop – off – your – legs. Die – snake. Chop – you – down – stinky – demon." His sentences shortened, angry pellets that shot out of him.

He woke one morning and felt a yang wind blow too hot through his body. He forced himself to sit up, not to be left behind among the sick, who were one-third of the workers. He rolled out of bed, stood, and fell. The healthier men were heading out into the humid day. He pulled himself up and dropped into his bunk. Asleep, again and again he seemed to jump out of bed, run sluggishly about gathering his clothes and tools, run through thick air in search of the fields, hear the demon boss in wait for him saying, "Late. You late, Paké," only to wake up and find that nothing had been done, no shoes put on, no breakfast eaten. He slept while the gecko lizards tsked-tsked-tsked at his sloth. He slept while a mushroom grew in a corner of the hut. His garden did not cajole him out of bed.

Each time he awoke, he was lying among the sick men, some breathing with clogged lungs like his, some doubled up holding their stomachs, cripples soaking their limbs. A few men looked bodily healthy but did not move. Somebody seemed to be piling dry leaves near the door and lighting them.

In his fever, he yearned so hard for his family that he felt he appeared in China. He reached out his arms and said, "Wife. Wife, I'm home." But she said, "What are you doing here? What are you doing here without the money? Moneyless and bodiless, you better go back to the Sandalwood Mountains. Go back and pick up your money and your body. Go back where you belong. Go now." He tried to talk to her, but his tongue was heavy and his throat blocked. He awoke certain that he had to cure himself by talking whenever he pleased.

Yin, the cool, was returning a little. Raindrops plunked loudly on the banana and ti leaves. It was what the Hawaiians called a cane-tapping rain. He chuckled with the geckos, their fingers and toes spread like little suctioning stars on the walls and ceilings, where they waited to flick at bugs. They were so sly playing dead, but through their translucent skins he saw their blue hearts beating and their organs swallowing. He shouted to make them leap to the ground. When they hid, he heard their clucking and chuckling. He had learned to recognize some of them individually. He told the sick men around him, "You can't die because then your poor wife will miss you, your family will go hungry awaiting your pay, and your mother will be uncertain forever what became of you. If there were only yourself, you would have the luxury of dying. Uncles and Brothers, I have diagnosed our illness. It is a congestion from not talking. What we have to do is talk and talk."

He lurched out to the rain barrel, poured water down his back and splashed it on his face. His wife would have scolded him for drinking cold water, a Sandalwood Mountain habit he was acquiring. He was carrying water to the sicker men when a demon galloped toward him, boss and horse both with cavernous nostrils wide open. Bak Goong turned toward the fields. The demon pushed sick men out the door. He pulled a boy by the hair. Bak Goong could tell he was saying, "Aha! I caught you malingering, you fake, lazy, sneaky chinaman." He pointed the whip toward the cane. "Go work, Paké. No stay sick." The demons had changed their rules again, no longer sending stragglers back to the huts. Bak Goong put his left arm around the stalks and leaned his face and body against them while his right arm swung at the feet of the cane. He neither sang nor spoke. Unhealthily, he wet handkerchiefs and plastered them on his head.

That evening, he talked an apt story to the silenced men, who had heard it already in the long ago place where there had been mothers and children: "Old Uncles and Young Uncles, I have an appropriate story to tell. It cannot be left unsaid." He recalled a land arranged in layers like clouds or stages, where animals, common men and women, kings and gods held adventures. "Bak-ah, Sook-ah, a long time ago in China, there lived a king who would have given his kingdom for a son. Powerful but childless, sonless, yearning to be a father, he bought ponies of various sizes for his someday son to ride as he grew. He would trot behind his father on tours of the kingdom. Together they would shoot arrows, snare rabbits, and catch fish. Longing to hold his own son to his chest, he felt envious looking at ordinary fathers. He read tea leaves and oil wicks looking for a son. But at last, when his wish was granted and his own only boy was born, the queen and the midwives hesitated to show him the new prince. 'Is it a boy?' he asked. 'It is a boy, isn't it?' He pushed aside the blanket and saw that on either side of the bald head, the prince had little pointed furry ears like a kitten's. 'Oh, no,' said the king. 'Cat ears. The prince has cat ears. We order everyone present never to tell that the prince has cat ears. Keep our secret. Don't tell the people.'

335

"So the years went by; the prince grew into noble perfection except for the kitty ears. The queen combed his long hair over them. Only in appearance were the ears strange; the prince heard as clearly as anyone else. The subjects exclaimed over his handsomeness. The king never mentioned the cat ears, and so the secret grew large inside his chest and mouth.

"One day when the boy was almost grown, the king could not hold the secret inside himself any more. He walked alone in a winter field, where he scooped out a hole. He shouted into it, 'The king's son has cat ears. The king's son has cat ears.' He shouted until he was empty of his secret, and satisfied, relieved, he pushed the dirt back into the hole and stamped it down.

"In the spring, grass grew in that field, and when the wind blew through it, the people heard words. The sounds swelled through the summer, enunciated until the people knew for sure what the tall grass and the wind said louder and louder: 'The king's son has cat ears. The king's son has cat ears.' It grew into a song. 'The king's son has cat ears.' The news spread throughout the land. It made the people laugh to hear it."

The listening men thought how they would love their baby boy even if he had cat ears; he'd be even cuter with cat ears. They would brag as they handed out red eggs to the other unfamilied men, who would come to visit the baby. "See?" the fathers would say. "Cat ears. Bet you've never seen anything like them." "Eh, Father," the other China Men would say enviously. "A father, are you?" They'd make much of giving the baby red money.

The next day the men plowed, working purposefully, but they dug a circle instead of straight furrows. They dug a wide hole. They threw down their tools and flopped on the ground with their faces over the edge of the hole and their legs like wheel spokes.

"Hello down there in China!" they shouted. "Hello, Mother." "Hello, my heart and my liver."

"I miss you." "What are you doing right now?" "Happy birthday. Happy birthday for last year too."

"I've been working hard for you, and I hate it."

"Sometimes I forget my family and go to clubs. I drink all night." "I lost all the money again." "I've become an opium addict." "I don't even look Chinese any more." "I'm sorry I ate it all by myself."

". . . and I fell to my knees at the sight of twenty waterfalls." "I saw only one sandalwood tree."

They said any kind of thing. "Blonde demoness." "Polynesian demoness."

"I'm coming home by and by." "I'm not coming home." "I'm staying here in the Sandalwood Mountains."

"I want to be home," Bak Goong said.

"I'm bringing her home," said Bak Sook Goong.

They had dug an ear into the world, and were telling the earth their secrets.

"I want home," Bak Goong yelled, pressed against the soil, and smelling the earth. "I want my home," the men yelled together. "I want home. Home. Home. Home. Home."

Talked out, they buried their words, planted them. "Like cats covering shit," they laughed.

"That wasn't a custom," said Bak Goong. "We made it up. We can make up customs because we're the founding ancestors of this place."

They made such a noise that the demons could have come charging upon them and the hole fill with the sounds of battle. But the demons hid, the China Men so riled up, who knows what they were up to?

From the day of the shout party, Bak Goong talked and sang at his work, and did not get sent to the punishment fields. In cutting season, the demons no longer accompanied the knife-wielding China Men into deep cane.

Soon the new green shoots would rise, and when in two years the cane grew gold tassels, what stories the wind would tell.

Bak Goong, the great grandfather with a good memory, kept his promises and so chose to go back to China. Bak Sook Goong also went back, though the king and queen of the Sandalwood Mountains had ruled that a China Man who married a Hawaiian would be called Hawaiian, and many another Paké godfather stayed. Bak Sook Goong brought his Sandalwood Mountain wife back with him. She would become sister of his other two wives. He would abandon none of them. So these two great grandfathers made their lives of a piece.

As you know, any plain person you chance to meet can prove to be a powerful immortal in disguise come to test you.

Li Fu-yen told a story about Tu Tzu-chun, who lived from A.D. 558 to 618, during the Northern Chou and Sui dynasties. Tu's examiner was a Taoist monk, who made him rich twice, and twice Tu squandered his fortune though it took him two lifetimes to do so. The third time the Taoist gave him money, he bought a thousand li of good land, plowed it himself, seeded it, built houses, roads, and bridges, then welcomed widows and orphans to live on it. With the left-over money, he found a husband for each spinster and a wife for every bachelor in his family, and also paid for the weddings. When he met the Taoist again, he said, "I've used up all your money on the unfortunates I've come across."

"You'll have to repay me by working for me," said the Taoist monk. "I need your help on an important difficult task." He gave Tu three white pills. "Swallow these," he said, pouring him a cup of wine. "All that you'll see and feel will be illusions. No matter what happens, don't speak; don't scream. Remember the saying 'Hide your broken arms in your sleeves.'"

"How easy," said Tu as he swallowed the pills in three gulps of wine. "Why should I scream if I know they're illusions?"

Level by level he descended into the nine hells. At first he saw oxheads, horsefaces, and the heads of generals decapitated in war. Illusions. Only illusions, harmless. He laughed at the heads. He had seen heads before. Soon fewer heads whizzed through the dark until he saw no more of them.

Suddenly his wife was being tortured. Demons were cutting her up into pieces, starting with her toes. He heard her scream; he heard her bones crack. He reminded himself that she was an illusion. *Illusion*, he thought. She was ground into bloodmeal.

Then the tortures on his own body began. Demons poured bronze down his throat and beat him with iron clubs and chains. They mortar-and-pestled and packed him into a pill.

He had to walk over mountains of knives and through fields of knives and forests of swords. He was killed, his head chopped off, rolling into other people's nightmares.

He heard gods and goddesses talking about him, "This man is too wicked to be reborn a man. Let him be born a woman." He saw the entrance of a black tunnel and felt tired. He would have to squeeze his head and shoulders down into that enclosure and travel a long distance. He pushed head first through the entrance, only the beginning. A god kicked him in the butt to give him a move on. (This kick is the reason many Chinese babies have a blue-gray spot on their butts or lower backs, the "Mongolian spot.") Sometimes stuck in the tunnel, sometimes shooting helplessly through it, he emerged again into light with many urgent things to do, many messages to deliver, but his hands were useless baby's hands, his legs wobbly baby's legs, his voice a wordless baby's cries. Years had to pass before he could regain adult powers; he howled as he began to forget the cosmos, his attention taken up with mastering how to crawl, how to stand, how to walk, how to control his bowel movements.

He discovered that he had been reborn a deaf-mute female named Tu. When she became a woman, her parents married her to a man named Lu, who at first did not mind. "Why does she need to talk," said Lu, "to be a good wife? Let her set an example for women." They had a child. But years later, Lu tired of Tu's dumbness. "You're just being stubborn," he said, and lifted their child by the feet. "Talk, or I'll dash its head against the rocks." The poor mother held her hand to her mouth. Lu swung the child, broke its head against the wall.

Tu shouted out, "Oh! Oh!" – and he was back with the Taoist, who sadly told him that at the moment when she had said, "Oh! Oh!" the Taoist was about to complete the last step in making the elixir for immortality. Now that Tu had broken his silence, the formula was spoiled, no immortality for the human race. "You overcame joy and sorrow, anger, fear, and evil desire, but not love," said the Taoist, and went on his way.

On Mortality Again

The last deed of Maui the Trickster, the Polynesian demigod who played jokes, pushed the sky higher, roped the sun with braided pubic hair from his mother, pulled the land up out of the ocean, and brought fire to earth, was to seek immortality for men and women by stealing it from Hina of the Night. He instructed the people, the beasts, the birds, and the elements to be silent. Hunters walked through forests and fishermen waited in this same silence. In silence the snarer caught birds alive, plucked the few red feathers, and released them; the seer read the clouds, heard spirits and did not disturb them. Children learned and worked silently. There was a chant that could hardly be discerned from silence. Maui dived into the ocean, where he found great Hina asleep. Through her vagina like a door, he entered her body. He took her heart in his arms. He had started tunneling out feet first when a bird, at the sight of his legs wiggling out of the vagina, laughed. Hina awoke and shut herself, and Maui died.

THE GRANDFATHER OF THE SIERRA
NEVADA MOUNTAINS

The trains used to cross the sky. The house jumped and dust shook down from the attic. Sometimes two trains ran parallel going in opposite directions; the railroad men walked on top of the leaning cars, stepped off one train onto the back of the other, and traveled the opposite way. They headed for the caboose while the train moved against their walk, or they walked toward the engine while the train moved out from under their feet. Hoboes ran alongside, caught the ladders, and swung aboard. I would have to learn to ride like that, choose my boxcar, grab a ladder at a run, and fling myself up and sideways into an open door. Elsewhere I would step smoothly off. Bad runaway boys lost their legs trying for such rides. The train craunched past – pistons stroking like elbows and knees, the coal cars dropping coal, cows looking out between the slats of the cattlecars, the boxcars almost stringing together sentences – Hydro-Cushion, Georgia Flyer, Route of the Eagle – and suddenly sunlight filled the windows again, the slough wide again and waving with tules, for which the city was once named; red-winged blackbirds and squirrels settled. We children ran to the tracks and found the nails we'd placed on them; the wheels had flattened them into knives that sparked.

Once in a while an adult said, "Your grandfather built the railroad." (Or "Your grandfathers built the railroad." Plural and singular are by context.) We children believed that it was that very railroad, those trains, those tracks running past our house; our own giant grandfather had set those very logs into the ground, poured the iron for those very spikes with the big heads and pounded them until the heads spread like that, mere nails to him. He had built the railroad so that trains would thunder over us, on a street that inclined toward us. We lived on a special spot of the earth, Stockton, the only city on the Pacific coast with three railroads – the Santa Fe, Southern Pacific, and Western Pacific. The three railroads intersecting accounted for the flocks of hoboes. The few times that the train stopped, the cows moaned all night, their hooves stumbling crowdedly and banging against the wood.

Grandfather left a railroad for his message: We had to go somewhere difficult. Ride a train. Go somewhere important. In case of danger, the train was to be ready for us.

The railroad men disconnected the rails and took the steel away. They did not come back. Our family dug up the square logs and rolled them downhill home. We collected the spikes too. We used the logs for benches, edged the yard with them, made bases for fences, embedded them in the ground for walkways. The spikes came in handy too, good for paperweights, levers, wedges, chisels. I am glad to know exactly the weight of ties and the size of nails.

Grandfather's picture hangs in the dining room next to an equally large one of Grandmother, and another one of Guan Goong, God of War and Literature. My grandparents' similarity is in the set of their mouths; they seem to have hauled with their mouths. My mouth also feels the tug and strain of weights in its corners. In the family album, Grandfather wears a greatcoat and Western shoes, but his ankles show. He hasn't shaved either. Maybe he became sloppy after the Japanese soldier bayoneted his head for not giving directions. Or he was born slow and without a sense of direction.

The photographer came to the village regularly and set up a spinet, potted trees, an ornate table stacked with hardbound books of matching size, and a backdrop with a picture of paths curving through gardens into panoramas; he lent his subjects dressy ancient mandarin clothes, Western suits, and hats. An aunt tied the fingers of the lame cousin to a book, the string leading down his sleeve; he looks like he's carrying it. The family hurried from clothes chests to mirrors without explaining to Grandfather, hiding Grandfather. In the family album are group pictures with Grandmother in the middle, the family arranged on either side of her and behind her, second wives at the ends, no Grandfather. Grandmother's earrings, bracelets, and rings are tinted jade green, everything and everybody else black and white, her little feet together neatly, two knobs at the bottom of her gown. My mother, indignant that nobody had readied Grandfather, threw his greatcoat over his nightclothes, shouted, "Wait! Wait!" and encouraged him into the sunlight. "Hurry," she said, and he ran, coat flapping, to be in the picture. She would have slipped him into the group and had the camera catch him like a peeping ghost, but Grandmother chased him away. "What a waste of film," she said. Grandfather always appears alone with white stubble on his chin. He was a thin man with big eyes that looked straight ahead. When we children talked about overcoat men, exhibitionists, we meant Grandfather, Ah Goong, who must have yanked open that greatcoat – no pants.

MaMa was the only person to listen to him, and so he followed her everywhere, and talked and talked. What he liked telling was his journeys to the Gold Mountain. He wasn't smart, yet he traveled there three times. Left to himself, he would have stayed in China to play with babies or stayed in the United States once he got there, but Grandmother forced him to leave both places. "Make money," she said. "Don't stay here eating." "Come home," she said.

Ah Goong sat outside her open door when MaMa worked. (In those days a man did not visit a good woman alone unless married to her.) He saw her at her loom and came running with his chair. He told her that he had found a wondrous country, really gold, and he himself had gotten two bags of it, one of which he had had made into a ring. His wife had given that ring to their son for his wedding ring. "That ring on your finger," he told Mother, "proves that the Gold Mountain exists and that I went there."

Another of his peculiarities was that he heard the crackles, bangs, gunshots that go off when the world lurches; the gears on its axis snap. Listening to a faraway New Year, he had followed the noise and come upon the blasting in the Sierras. (There is a Buddhist instruction that that which is most elusive must, of course, be the very thing to be pursued; listen to the farthest sound.) The Central Pacific hired him on sight; chinamen had a natural talent for explosions. Also there were not enough workingmen to do all the labor of building a new country. Some of the banging came from the war to decide whether or not black people would continue to work for nothing.

Slow as usual, Ah Goong arrived in the spring; the work had begun in January 1863. The demon that hired him pointed up and up, east above the hills of poppies. His first job was to fell a redwood, which was thick enough to divide into three or four beams. His tree's many branches spread out, each limb like a little tree. He circled the tree. How to attack it? No side looked like the side made to be cut, nor did any ground seem the place for it to fall. He axed for almost a day the side he'd decided would hit the ground. Halfway through, imitating the other lumberjacks, he struck the other side of the tree, above the cut, until he had to run away. The tree swayed and slowly dived to earth, creaking and screeching like a green animal. He was so awed, he forgot what he was supposed to yell. Hardly any branches broke; the tree sprang, bounced, pushed at the ground with its arms. The limbs did not wilt and fold; they were a small forest, which he chopped. The trunk lay like a long red torso; sap ran from its cuts like crying blind eyes. At last it stopped fighting. He set the log across sawhorses to be cured over smoke and in the sun.

He joined a team of men who did not ax one another as they took alternate hits. They blew up the stumps with gunpowder. "It was like uprooting a tooth," Ah Goong said. They also packed gunpowder at the roots of a whole tree. Not at the same time as the bang but before that, the tree rose from the ground. It stood, then plunged with a tearing of veins and muscles. It was big enough to carve a house into. The men measured themselves against the upturned white roots, which looked like claws, a sun with claws. A hundred men stood or sat on the trunk. They lifted a wagon on it and took a photograph. The demons also had their photograph taken.

Because these mountains were made out of gold, Ah Goong rushed over to the root hole to look for gold veins and ore. He selected the shiniest rocks to be assayed later in San Francisco. When he drank from the streams and saw a flash, he dived in like a duck; only sometimes did it turn out to be the sun or the water. The very dirt winked with specks.

He made a dollar a day salary. The lucky men gambled, but he was not good at remembering game rules. The work so far was endurable. "I could take it," he said.

The days were sunny and blue, the wind exhilarating, the heights godlike. At night the stars were diamonds, crystals, silver, snow, ice. He had never seen diamonds. He had never seen snow and ice. As spring turned into summer, and he lay under that sky, he saw the order in the stars. He recognized constellations from China. There — not a cloud but the Silver River, and there, on either side of it — Altair and Vega, the Spinning Girl and the Cowboy, far, far apart. He felt his heart breaking of loneliness at so much blue-black space between star and star. The railroad he was building would not lead him to his family. He jumped out of his bedroll. "Look! Look!" Other China Men jumped awake. An accident? An avalanche? Injun demons? "The stars," he said. "The stars are here." "Another China Man gone out of his mind," men grumbled. "A sleepwalker." "Go to sleep, sleepwalker." "There. And there," said Ah Goong, two hands pointing. "The Spinning Girl and the Cowboy. Don't you see them?" "Homesick China Man," said the China Men and pulled their blankets over their heads. "Didn't you know they were here? I could have told you they were here. Same as in China. Same moon. Why not same stars?" "Nah. Those are American stars."

Pretending that a little girl was listening, he told himself the story about the Spinning Girl and the Cowboy: A long time ago they had visited earth, where they met, fell in love, and married. Instead of growing used to each other, they remained enchanted their entire lifetimes and beyond. They were too happy. They wanted to be doves or two branches of the same tree. When they returned to live in the sky, they were so engrossed in each other that they neglected their work. The Queen of the Sky scratched a river between them with one stroke of her silver hairpin – the river a galaxy in width. The lovers suffered, but she did devote her time to spinning now, and he herded his cow. The King of the Sky took pity on them and ordered that once each year, they be allowed to meet. On the seventh day of the seventh month (which is not the same as July 7), magpies form a bridge for them to cross to each other. The lovers are together for one night of the year. On their parting, the Spinner cries the heavy summer rains.

Ah Goong's discovery of the two stars gave him something to look forward to besides meals and tea breaks. Every night he located Altair and Vega and gauged how much closer they had come since the night before. During the day he watched the magpies, big black and white birds with round bodies like balls with wings; they were a welcome sight, a promise of meetings. He had found two familiars in the wilderness: magpies and stars. On the meeting day, he did not see any magpies nor hear their chattering jaybird cries. Some black and white birds flew overhead, but they may have been American crows or late magpies on their way. Some men laughed at him, but he was not the only China Man to collect water in pots, bottles, and canteens that day. The water would stay fresh forever and cure anything. In ancient days the tutelary gods of the mountains sprinkled corpses with this water and brought them to life. That night, no women to light candles, burn incense, cook special food, Grandfather watched for the convergence and bowed. He saw the two little stars next to Vega – the couple's children. And bridging the Silver River, surely those were black flapping wings of magpies and translucent-winged angels and faeries. Toward morning, he was awakened by rain, and pulled his blankets into his tent.

The next day, the fantailed orange-beaked magpies returned. Altair and Vega were beginning their journeys apart, another year of spinning and herding. Ah Goong had to find something else to look forward to. The Spinning Girl and the Cowboy met and parted six times before the railroad was finished.

When cliffs, sheer drops under impossible overhangs, ended the road, the workers filled the ravines or built bridges over them. They climbed above the site for tunnel or bridge and lowered one another down in wicker baskets made stronger by the lucky words they had painted on four sides. Ah Goong got to be a basketman because he was thin and light. Some basketmen were fifteen-year-old boys. He rode the basket barefoot, so his boots, the kind to stomp snakes with, would not break through the bottom. The basket swung and twirled, and he saw the world sweep underneath him; it was fun in a way, a cold new feeling of doing what had never been done before. Suspended in the quiet sky, he thought all kinds of crazy thoughts, that if a man didn't want to live any more, he could just cut the ropes or, easier, tilt the basket, dip, and never have to worry again. He could spread his arms, and the air would momentarily hold him before he fell past the buzzards, hawks, and eagles, and landed impaled on the tip of a sequoia. This high and he didn't see any gods, no Cowboy, no Spinner. He knelt in the basket though he was not bumping his head against the sky. Through the wickerwork, slivers of depths darted like needles, nothing between him and air but thin rattan. Gusts of wind spun the light basket. "Aiya," said Ah Goong. Winds came up under the basket, bouncing it. Neighboring baskets swung together and parted. He and the man next to him looked at each other's faces. They laughed. They might as well have gone to Malaysia to collect bird nests. Those who had done high work there said it had been worse; the birds screamed and scratched at them. Swinging near the cliff, Ah Goong stood up and grabbed it by a twig. He dug holes, then inserted gunpowder and fuses. He worked neither too fast nor too slow, keeping even with the others. The basketmen signaled one another to light the fuses. He struck match after match and dropped the burnt matches over the sides. At last his fuse caught; he waved, and the men above pulled hand over hand hauling him up, pulleys creaking. The scaffolds stood like a row of gibbets. Gallows trees along a ridge. "Hurry, hurry," he said. Some impatient men clambered up their ropes. Ah Goong ran up the ledge road they'd cleared and watched the explosions, which banged almost synchronously, echoes booming like war. He moved his scaffold to the next section of cliff and went down in the basket again, with bags of dirt, and set the next charge.

This time two men were blown up. One knocked out or killed by the explosion fell silently, the other screaming, his arms and legs struggling. A desire shot out of Ah Goong for an arm long enough to reach down and catch them. Much time passed as they fell like plummets. The shreds of baskets and a cowboy hat skimmed and tacked. The winds that pushed birds off course and against mountains did not carry men. Ah Goong also wished that the conscious man would fall faster and get it over with. His hands gripped the ropes, and it was difficult to let go and get on with the work. "It can't happen twice in a row," the basketmen said the next trip down. "Our chances are very good. The trip after an accident is probably the safest one." They raced to their favorite basket, checked and double-checked the four ropes, yanked the strands, tested the pulleys, oiled them, reminded the pulleymen about the signals, and entered the sky again.

Another time, Ah Goong had been lowered to the bottom of a ravine, which had to be cleared for the base of a trestle, when a man fell, and he saw his face. He had not died of shock before hitting bottom. His hands were grabbing at air. His stomach and groin must have felt the fall all the way down. At night Ah Goong woke up falling, though he slept on the ground, and heard other men call out in their sleep. No warm women tweaked their ears and hugged them. "It was only a falling dream," he reassured himself.

Across a valley, a chain of men working on the next mountain, men like ants changing the face of the world, fell, but it was very far away. Godlike, he watched men whose faces he could not see and whose screams he did not hear roll and bounce and slide like a handful of sprinkled gravel.

After a fall, the buzzards circled the spot and reminded the workers for days that a man was dead down there. The men threw piles of rocks and branches to cover bodies from sight.

The mountainface reshaped, they drove supports for a bridge. Since hammering was less dangerous than the blowing up, the men played a little; they rode the baskets swooping in wide arcs; they twisted the ropes and let them unwind like tops. "Look at me," said Ah Goong, pulled open his pants, and pissed overboard, the wind scattering the drops. "I'm a waterfall," he said. He had sent a part of himself hurtling. On rare windless days he watched his piss fall in a continuous stream from himself almost to the bottom of the valley.

One beautiful day, dangling in the sun above a new valley, not the desire to urinate but sexual desire clutched him so hard he bent over in the basket. He curled up, overcome by beauty and fear, which shot to his penis. He tried to rub himself calm. Suddenly he stood up tall and squirted out into space. "I am fucking the world," he said. The world's vagina was big, big as the sky, big as a valley. He grew a habit: whenever he was lowered in the basket, his blood rushed to his penis, and he fucked the world.

Then it was autumn, and the wind blew so fiercely, the men had to postpone the basketwork. Clouds moved in several directions at once. Men pointed at dust devils, which turned their mouths crooked. There was ceaseless motion; clothes kept moving; hair moved; sleeves puffed out. Nothing stayed still long enough for Ah Goong to figure it out. The wind sucked the breath out of his mouth and blew thoughts from his brains. The food convoys from San Francisco brought tents to replace the ones that whipped away. The baskets from China, which the men saved for high work, carried cowboy jackets, long underwear, Levi pants, boots, earmuffs, leather gloves, flannel shirts, coats. They sewed rabbit fur and deerskin into the linings. They tied the wide brims of their cowboy hats over their ears with mufflers. And still the wind made confusing howls into ears, and it was hard to think.

The days became nights when the crews tunneled inside the mountain, which sheltered them from the wind, but also hid the light and sky. Ah Goong pickaxed the mountain, the dirt filling his nostrils through a cowboy bandanna. He shoveled the dirt into a cart and pushed it to a place that was tall enough for the mule, which hauled it the rest of the way out. He looked forward to cart duty to edge closer to the entrance. Eyes darkened, nose plugged, his windy cough

worse, he was to mole a thousand feet and meet others digging from the other side. How much he'd pay now to go
swinging in a basket. He might as well have gone to work in
a tin mine. Coming out of the tunnel at the end of a shift, he
forgot whether it was supposed to be day or night. He blew
his nose fifteen times before the mucus cleared again.

The dirt was the easiest part of tunneling. Beneath the
soil, they hit granite. Ah Goong struck it with his pickax, and
it jarred his bones, chattered his teeth. He swung his sledgehammer against it, and the impact rang in the dome of his
skull. The mountain that was millions of years old was locked
against them and was not to be broken into. The men teased
him, "Let's see you fuck the world now." "Let's see you fuck
the Gold Mountain now." But he no longer felt like it.
"A man ought to be made of tougher material than flesh," he
said. "Skin is too soft. Our bones ought to be filled with
iron." He lifted the hammer high, careful that it not pull him
backward, and let it fall forward of its own weight against the
rock. Nothing happened to that gray wall; he had to slam
with strength and will. He hit at the same spot over and over
again, the same rock. Some chips and flakes broke off. The
granite looked everywhere the same. It had no softer or
weaker spots anywhere, the same hard gray. He learned to
slide his hand up the handle, lift, slide and swing, a circular
motion, hammering, hammering, hammering. He would
bite like a rat through that mountain. His eyes couldn't see;
his nose couldn't smell; and now his ears were filled with the
noise of hammering. This rock is what is real, he thought.
This rock is what real is, not clouds or mist, which make
mysterious promises, and when you go through them are
nothing. When the foreman measured at the end of twenty-
four hours of pounding, the rock had given a foot. The
hammering went on day and night. The men worked eight
hours on and eight hours off. They worked on all eighteen
tunnels at once. While Ah Goong slept, he could hear the

sledgehammers of other men working in the earth. The steady banging reminded him of holidays and harvests; falling asleep, he heard the women chopping mincemeat and the millstones striking.

The demons in boss suits came into the tunnel occasionally, measured with a yardstick, and shook their heads. "Faster," they said. "Faster. Chinamen too slow. Too slow." "Tell us we're slow," the China Men grumbled. The ones in top tiers of scaffolding let rocks drop, a hammer drop. Ropes tangled around the demons' heads and feet. The cave China Men muttered and flexed, glared out of the corners of their eyes. But usually there was no diversion – one day the same as the next, one hour no different from another – the beating against the same granite.

After tunneling into granite for about three years, Ah Goong understood the immovability of the earth. Men change, men die, weather changes, but a mountain is the same as permanence and time. This mountain would have taken no new shape for centuries, ten thousand centuries, the world a still, still place, time unmoving. He worked in the tunnel so long, he learned to see many colors in black. When he stumbled out, he tried to talk about time. "I felt time," he said. "I saw time. I saw world." He tried again, "I saw what's real. I saw time, and it doesn't move. If we break through the mountain, hollow it, time won't have moved anyway. You translators ought to tell the foreigners that."

Summer came again, but after the first summer, he felt less nostalgia at the meeting of the Spinning Girl and the Cowboy. He now knew men who had been in this country for twenty years and thirty years, and the Cowboy's one year away from his lady was no time at all. His own patience was longer. The stars were meeting and would meet again next year, but he would not have seen his family. He joined the others celebrating Souls' Day, the holiday a week later, the fourteenth day of the seventh month. The supply wagons from San Francisco and Sacramento brought watermelon, meat, fish, crab, pressed duck. "There, ghosts, there you are. Come and get it." They displayed the feast complete for a moment before falling to, eating on the dead's behalf.

In the third year of pounding granite by hand, a demon invented dynamite. The railroad workers were to test it. They had stopped using gunpowder in the tunnels after avalanches, but the demons said that dynamite was more precise. They watched a scientist demon mix nitrate, sulphate, and glycerine, then flick the yellow oil, which exploded off his fingertips. Sitting in a meadow to watch the dynamite detonated in the open, Ah Goong saw the men in front of him leap impossibly high into the air; then he felt a shove as if from a giant's unseen hand − and he fell backward. The boom broke the mountain silence like fear breaking inside stomach and chest and groin. No one had gotten hurt; they stood up laughing and amazed, looking around at how they had fallen, the pattern of the explosion. Dynamite was much more powerful than gunpowder. Ah Goong had felt a nudge, as if something kind were moving him out of harm's way. "All of a sudden I was sitting next to you." "Aiya. If we had been nearer, it would have killed us." "If we were stiff, it would have gone through us." "A fist." "A hand." "We leapt like acrobats." Next time Ah Goong flattened himself on the ground, and the explosion rolled over him.

He never got used to the blasting; a blast always surprised him. Even when he himself set the fuse and watched it burn, anticipated the explosion, the bang − *bahng* in Chinese − when it came, always startled. It cleaned the crazy words, the crackling, and bingbangs out of his brain. It was like New Year's, when every problem and thought was knocked clean out of him by firecrackers, and he could begin fresh. He couldn't worry during an explosion, which jerked every head to attention. Hills flew up in rocks and dirt. Boulders turned over and over. Sparks, fires, debris, rocks, smoke burst up, not at the same time as the boom (*bum*) but before that – the sound a separate occurrence, not useful as a signal.

The terrain changed immediately. Streams were diverted, rockscapes exposed. Ah Goong found it difficult to remember what land had looked like before an explosion. It was a good thing the dynamite was invented after the Civil War to the east was over.

The dynamite added more accidents and ways of dying, but if it were not used, the railroad would take fifty more years to finish. Nitroglycerine exploded when it was jounced on a horse or dropped. A man who fell with it in his pocket blew himself up into red pieces. Sometimes it combusted merely standing. Human bodies skipped through the air like puppets and made Ah Goong laugh crazily as if the arms and legs would come together again. The smell of burned flesh remained in rocks.

In the tunnels, the men bored holes fifteen to eighteen inches deep with a power drill, stuffed them with hay and dynamite, and imbedded the fuse in sand. Once, for extra pay, Ah Goong ran back in to see why some dynamite had not gone off and hurried back out again; it was just a slow fuse. When the explosion settled, he helped carry two-hundred-, three-hundred-, five-hundred-pound boulders out of the tunnel.

As a boy he had visited a Taoist monastery where there were nine rooms, each a replica of one of the nine hells. Lifesize sculptures of men and women were spitted on turning wheels. Eerie candles under the suffering faces emphasized eyes poked out, tongues pulled, red mouths and eyes, and real hair, eyelashes, and eyebrows. Women were split apart and men dismembered. He could have reached out and touched the sufferers and the implements. He had dug and dynamited his way into one of these hells. "Only here there are eighteen tunnels, not nine, plus all the tracks between them," he said.

One day he came out of the tunnel to find the mountains white, the evergreens and bare trees decorated, white tree sculptures and lace bushes everywhere. The men from snow country called the icicles "ice chopsticks." He sat in his basket and slid down the slopes. The snow covered the gouged land, the broken trees, the tracks, the mud, the campfire ashes, the unburied dead. Streams were stilled in mid-run, the water petrified. That winter he thought it was the task of the human race to quicken the world, blast the freeze, fire it, redden it with blood. He had to change the stupid slowness of one sunrise and one sunset per day. He had to enliven the silent world with sound. "The rock," he tried to tell the others. "The ice." "Time."

The dynamiting loosed blizzards on the men. Ears and toes fell off. Fingers stuck to the cold silver rails. Snowblind men stumbled about with bandannas over their eyes. Ah Goong helped build wood tunnels roofing the track route. Falling ice scrabbled on the roofs. The men stayed under the snow for weeks at a time. Snowslides covered the entrances to the tunnels, which they had to dig out to enter and exit, white tunnels and black tunnels. Ah Goong looked at his gang and thought, If there is an avalanche, these are the people I'll be trapped with, and wondered which ones would share food. A party of snowbound barbarians had eaten the dead. Cannibals, thought Ah Goong, and looked around. Food was not scarce; the tea man brought whiskey barrels of hot tea, and he warmed his hands and feet, held the teacup to his nose and ears. Someday, he planned, he would buy a chair with metal doors for putting hot coal inside it. The magpies did not abandon him but stayed all winter and searched the snow for food.

The men who died slowly enough to say last words said, "Don't leave me frozen under the snow. Send my body home. Burn it and put the ashes in a tin can. Take the bone jar when you come down the mountain." "When you ride the fire car back to China, tell my descendants to come for me." "Shut up," scolded the hearty men. "We don't want to hear about bone jars and dying." "You're lucky to have a body to bury, not blown to smithereens." "Stupid man to hurt yourself," they bawled out the sick and wounded. How their wives would scold if they brought back deadmen's bones. "Aiya. To be buried here, nowhere." "But this is somewhere," Ah Goong promised. "This is the Gold Mountain. We're marking the land now. The track sections are numbered, and your family will know where we leave you." But he was a crazy man, and they didn't listen to him.

Spring did come, and when the snow melted, it revealed the past year, what had happened, what they had done, where they had worked, the lost tools, the thawing bodies, some standing with tools in hand, the bright rails. "Remember Uncle Long Winded Leong?" "Remember Strong Back Wong?" "Remember Lee Brother?" "And Fong Uncle?" They lost count of the number dead; there is no record of how many died building the railroad. Or maybe it was demons doing the counting and chinamen not worth counting. Whether it was good luck or bad luck, the dead were buried or cairned next to the last section of track they had worked on. "May his ghost not have to toil," they said over graves. (In China a woodcutter ghost chops eternally; people have heard chopping in the snow and in the heat.) "Maybe his ghost will ride the train home." The scientific demons said the transcontinental railroad would connect the West to Cathay. "What if he rides back and forth from Sacramento to New York forever?" "That wouldn't be so bad. I hear the cars will be like houses on wheels." The funerals were short. "No time. No time," said both China Men and demons. The railroad was as straight as they could build it, but no ghosts sat on the tracks; no strange presences haunted the tunnels. The blasts scared ghosts away.

When the Big Dipper pointed east and the China Men detonated nitroglycerine and shot off guns for the New Year, which comes with the spring, these special bangs were not as loud as the daily bangs, not as numerous as the bangs all year. Shouldn't the New Year be the loudest day of all to obliterate the noises of the old year? But to make a bang of that magnitude, they would have to blow up at least a year's supply of dynamite in one blast. They arranged strings of chain reactions in circles and long lines, banging faster and louder to culminate in a big bang. And most importantly, there were random explosions – surprise. Surprise. SURPRISE. They had no dragon, the railroad their dragon.

The demons invented games for working faster, gold coins for miles of track laid, for the heaviest rock, a grand prize for the first team to break through a tunnel. Day shifts raced against night shifts, China Men against Welshmen, China Men against Irishmen, China Men against Injuns and black demons. The fastest races were China Men against China Men, who bet on their own teams. China Men always won because of good teamwork, smart thinking, and the need for the money. Also, they had the most workers to choose teams from. Whenever his team won anything, Ah Goong added to his gold stash. The Central Pacific or Union Pacific won the land on either side of the tracks it built.

One summer day, demon officials and China Man translators went from group to group and announced, "We're raising the pay – thirty-five dollars a month. Because of your excellent work, the Central Pacific Railroad is giving you a four-dollar raise per month." The workers who didn't know better cheered. "What's the catch?" said the smarter men. "You'll have the opportunity to put in more time," said the railroad demons. "Two more hours per shift." Ten-hour shifts inside the tunnels. "It's not ten hours straight," said the demons. "You have time off for tea and meals. Now that you have dynamite, the work isn't so hard." They had been working for three and a half years already, and the track through the Donner Summit was still not done.

The workers discussed the ten-hour shift, swearing their China Man obscenities. "Two extra hours a day – sixty hours a month for four dollars." "Pig catcher demons." "Snakes." "Turtles." "Dead demons." "A human body can't work like that." "The demons don't believe this is a human body. This is a chinaman's body." To bargain, they sent a delegation of English speakers, who were summarily noted as trouble-makers, turned away, docked.

The China Men, then, decided to go on strike and demand forty-five dollars a month and the eight-hour shift. They risked going to jail and the Central Pacific keeping the pay it was banking for them. Ah Goong memorized the English, "Forty-five dollars a month – eight-hour shift." He practiced the strike slogan: "Eight hours a day good for white man, all the same good for China Man."

The men wrapped barley and beans in ti leaves, which came from Hawai'i via San Francisco, for celebrating the fifth day of the fifth month (not May but mid-June, the sum-mer solstice). Usually the way the red string is wound and knotted tells what flavors are inside – the salty barley with pickled egg, or beans and pork, or the gelatin pudding. Ah Goong folded ti leaves into a cup and packed it with food. One of the literate men slipped in a piece of paper with the strike plan, and Ah Goong tied the bundle with a special pat-tern of red string. The time and place for the revolution against Kublai Khan had been hidden inside autumn moon-cakes. Ah Goong looked from one face to another in admira-tion. Of course, of course. No China Men, no railroad. They were indispensable labor. Throughout these mountains were brothers and uncles with a common idea, free men, not coolies, calling for fair working conditions. The demons were not suspicious as the China Men went gandying up and down the tracks delivering the bundles tied together like lines of fish. They had exchanged these gifts every year. When the summer solstice cakes came from other camps, the recipients cut them into neat slices by drawing the string through them. The orange jellies, which had a red dye stick inside soaked in lye, fell into a series of sunrises and sunsets. The aged yolks and the barley also looked like suns. The notes gave a Yes strike vote. The yellow flags to ward off the five evils – centipedes, scorpions, snakes, poisonous lizards, and toads – now flew as banners.

The strike began on Tuesday morning, June 25, 1867. The men who were working at that hour walked out of the tunnels and away from the tracks. The ones who were sleeping slept on and rose as late as they pleased. They bathed in streams and shaved their moustaches and wild beards. Some went fishing and hunting. The violinists tuned and played their instruments. The drummers beat theirs at the punchlines of jokes. The gamblers shuffled and played their cards and tiles. The smokers passed their pipes, and the drinkers bet for drinks by making figures with their hands. The cooks made party food. The opera singers' falsettos almost perforated the mountains. The men sang new songs about the railroad. They made up verses and shouted Ho at the good ones, and laughed at the rhymes. Oh, they were madly singing in the mountains. The storytellers told about the rise of new kings. The opium smokers when they roused themselves told their florid images. Ah Goong sifted for gold. All the while the English-speaking China Men, who were being advised by the shrewdest bargainers, were at the demons' headquarters repeating the demand: "Eight hours a day good for white man, all the same good for China Man." They had probably negotiated the demons down to nine-hour shifts by now.

The sounds of hammering continued along the tracks and occasionally there were blasts from the tunnels. The scabby white demons had refused to join the strike. "Eight hours a day good for white man, all the same good for China Man," the China Men explained to them. "Cheap John Chinaman," said the demons, many of whom had red hair. The China Men scowled out of the corners of their eyes.

On the second day, artist demons climbed the mountains to draw the China Men for the newspapers. The men posed bare-chested, their fists clenched, showing off their arms and backs. The artists sketched them as perfect young gods reclining against rocks, wise expressions on their handsome noble-nosed faces, long torsos with lean stomachs, a strong arm extended over a bent knee, long fingers holding a pipe, a rope of hair over a wide shoulder. Other artists drew faeries with antennae for eyebrows and brownies with elvish pigtails; they danced in white socks and black slippers among mushroom rings by moonlight.

Ah Goong acquired another idea that added to his reputation for craziness: The pale, thin Chinese scholars and the rich men fat like Buddhas were less beautiful, less manly than these brown muscular railroad men, of whom he was one. One of ten thousand heroes.

On the third day, in a woods – he would be looking at a deer or a rabbit or an Injun watching him before he knew what he was seeing – a demon dressed in a white suit and tall hat beckoned him. They talked privately in the wilderness. The demon said, "I Citizenship Judge invite you to be U. S. citizen. Only one bag gold." Ah Goong was thrilled. What an honor. He would accept this invitation. Also what advantages, he calculated shrewdly; if he were going to be jailed for this strike, an American would have a trial. The Citizenship Judge unfurled a parchment sealed with gold and ribbon. Ah Goong bought it with one bag of gold. "You vote," said the Citizenship Judge. "You talk in court, buy land, no more chinaman tax." Ah Goong hid the paper on his person so that it would protect him from arrest and lynching. He was already a part of this new country, but now he had it in writing.

The fourth day, the strikers heard that the U. S. Cavalry was riding single file up the tracks to shoot them. They argued whether to engage the Army with dynamite. But the troops did not come. Instead the cowardly demons blockaded the food wagons. No food. Ah Goong listened to the optimistic China Men, who said, "Don't panic. We'll hold out forever. We can hunt. We can last fifty days on water." The complainers said, "Aiya. Only saints can do that. Only magic men and monks who've practiced." The China Men refused to declare a last day for the strike.

The foresighted China Men had cured jerky, fermented wine, dried and strung orange and grapefruit peels, pickled and preserved leftovers. Ah Goong, one of the best hoarders, had set aside extra helpings from each meal. This same quandary, whether to give away food or to appear selfish, had occurred during each of the six famines he had lived through. The foodless men identified themselves. Sure enough, they were the shiftless, piggy, arrogant type who didn't worry enough. The donors scolded them and shamed them the whole while they were handing them food: "So you lived like a grasshopper at our expense." "Fleaman." "You'll be the cause of our not holding out long enough." "Rich man's kid. Too good to hoard." Ah Goong contributed some rice crusts from the bottoms of pans. He kept how much more food he owned a secret, as he kept the secret of his gold. In apology for not contributing richer food, he repeated a Mohist saying that had guided him in China: " 'The superior man does not push humaneness to the point of stupidity.' " He could hear his wife scolding him for feeding strangers. The opium men offered shit and said that it calmed the appetite.

On the fifth and sixth days, Ah Goong organized his possessions and patched his clothes and tent. He forebore repairing carts, picks, ropes, baskets. His work-habituated hands arranged rocks and twigs in designs. He asked a reader to read again his family's letters. His wife sounded like herself except for the polite phrases added professionally at the beginnings and the ends. "Idiot," she said, "why are you taking so long? Are you wasting the money? Are you spending it on girls and gambling and whiskey? Here's my advice to you: Be a little more frugal. Remember how it felt to go hungry. Work hard." He had been an idle man for almost a week. "I need a new dress to wear to weddings. I refuse to go to another banquet in the same old dress. If you weren't such a spendthrift, we could be building the new courtyard where we'll drink wine among the flowers and sit about in silk gowns all day. We'll hire peasants to till the fields. Or lease them to tenants, and buy all our food at market. We'll have clean fingernails and toenails." Other relatives said, "I need a gold watch. Send me the money. Your wife gambles it away and throws parties and doesn't disburse it fairly among us. You might as well come home." It was after one of these letters that he had made a bonus investigating some dud dynamite.

Ah Goong did not spend his money on women. The strikers passed the word that a woman was traveling up the railroad and would be at his camp on the seventh and eighth day of the strike. Some said she was a demoness and some that she was a Chinese and her master a China Man. He pictured a nurse coming to bandage wounds and touch foreheads or a princess surveying her subjects; or perhaps she was a merciful Jesus demoness. But she was a pitiful woman, led on a leash around her waist, not entirely alive. Her owner sold lottery tickets for the use of her. Ah Goong did not buy one. He took out his penis under his blanket or bared it in the woods and thought about nurses and princesses. He also just looked at it, wondering what it was that it was for, what a man was for, what he had to have a penis for.

There was rumor also of an Injun woman called Woman Chief, who led a nomadic fighting tribe from the eastern plains as far as these mountains. She was so powerful that she had four wives and many horses. He never saw her though.

The strike ended on the ninth day. The Central Pacific announced that in its benevolence it was giving the workers a four-dollar raise, not the fourteen dollars they had asked for. And that the shifts in the tunnels would remain eight hours long. "We were planning to give you the four-dollar raise all along," the demons said to diminish the victory. So they got thirty-five dollars a month and the eight-hour shift. They would have won forty-five dollars if the thousand demon workers had joined the strike. Demons would have listened to demons. The China Men went back to work quietly. No use singing and shouting over a compromise and losing nine days' work.

There were two days that Ah Goong did cheer and throw his hat in the air, jumping up and down and screaming Yippee like a cowboy. One: the day his team broke through the tunnel at last. Toward the end they did not dynamite but again used picks and sledgehammers. Through the granite, they heard answering poundings, and answers to their shouts. It was not a mountain before them any more but only a wall with people breaking through from the other side. They worked faster. Forward. Into day. They stuck their arms through the holes and shook hands with men on the other side. Ah Goong saw dirty faces as wondrous as if he were seeing Nu Wo, the creator goddess who repairs cracks in the sky with stone slabs; sometimes she peeks through and human beings see her face. The wall broke. Each team gave the other a gift of half a tunnel, dug. They stepped back and forth where the wall had been. Ah Goong ran and ran, his boots thudding to the very end of the tunnel, looked at the other side of the mountain, and ran back, clear through the entire tunnel. All the way through.

He spent the rest of his time on the railroad laying and bending and hammering the ties and rails. The second day the China Men cheered was when the engine from the West and the one from the East rolled toward one another and touched. The transcontinental railroad was finished. They Yippee'd like madmen. The white demon officials gave speeches. "The Greatest Feat of the Nineteenth Century," they said. "The Greatest Feat in the History of Mankind," they said. "Only Americans could have done it," they said, which is true. Even if Ah Goong had not spent half his gold on Citizenship Papers, he was an American for having built the railroad. A white demon in top hat tap-tapped on the gold spike, and pulled it back out. Then one China Man held the real spike, the steel one, and another hammered it in.

While the demons posed for photographs, the China Men dispersed. It was dangerous to stay. The Driving Out had begun. Ah Goong does not appear in railroad photographs. Scattering, some China Men followed the north star in the constellation Tortoise the Black Warrior to Canada, or they kept the constellation Phoenix ahead of them to South America or the White Tiger west or the Wolf east. Seventy lucky men rode the Union Pacific to Massachusetts for jobs at a shoe factory. Fifteen hundred went to Fou Loy Company in New Orleans and San Francisco, several hundred to plantations in Mississippi, Georgia, and Arkansas, and sugarcane plantations in Louisiana and Cuba. (From the South, they sent word that it was a custom to step off the sidewalk along with the black demons when a white demon walked by.) Seventy went to New Orleans to grade a route for a railroad, then to Pennsylvania to work in a knife factory. The Colorado State Legislature passed a resolution welcoming the railroad China Men to come build the new state. They built railroads in every part of the country – the Alabama and Chattanooga Railroad, the Houston and Texas Railroad, the Southern Pacific, the railroads in Louisiana and Boston, the Pacific Northwest, and Alaska. After the Civil War, China Men banded the nation North and South, East and West, with crisscrossing steel. They were the binding and building ancestors of this place.

Ah Goong would have liked a leisurely walk along the tracks to review his finished handiwork, or to walk east to see the rest of his new country. But instead, Driven Out, he slid down mountains, leapt across valleys and streams, crossed plains, hid sometimes with companions and often alone, and eluded bandits who would hold him up for his railroad pay and shoot him for practice as they shot Injuns and jack-rabbits. Detouring and backtracking, his path wound back and forth to his railroad, a familiar silver road in the wilderness. When a train came, he hid against the shaking ground in case a demon with a shotgun was hunting from it. He picked over camps where he had once lived. He was careful to find hidden places to sleep. In China bandits did not normally kill people, the booty the main thing, but here the demons killed for fun and hate. They tied pigtails to horses and dragged chinamen. He decided that he had better head for San Francisco, where he would catch a ship to China.

Perched on hillsides, he watched many sunsets, the place it was setting, the direction he was going. There were fields of grass that he tunneled through, hid in, rolled in, dived and swam in, suddenly jumped up laughing, suddenly stopped. He needed to find a town and human company. The spooky tumbleweeds caught in barbed wire were peering at him, waiting for him; he had to find a town. Towns grew along the tracks as they did along rivers. He sat looking at a town all day, then ducked into it by night.

At the familiar sight of a garden laid out in a Chinese scheme – vegetables in beds, white cabbages, red plants, chives, and coriander for immortality, herbs boxed with boards – he knocked on the back door. The China Man who answered gave him food, the appropriate food for the nearest holiday, talked-story, exclaimed at how close their ancestral villages were to each other. They exchanged information on

how many others lived how near, which towns had Chinatowns, what size, two or three stores or a block, which towns
to avoid. "Do you have a wife?" they asked one another. "Yes.
She lives in China. I have been sending money for twenty
years now." They exchanged vegetable seeds, slips, and cuttings, and Ah Goong carried letters to another town or
China.

Some demons who had never seen the likes of him gave
him things and touched him. He also came across lone
China Men who were alarmed to have him appear, and,
unwelcome, he left quickly; they must have wanted to be the
only China Man of that area, the special China Man.

He met miraculous China Men who had produced families out of nowhere – a wife and children, both boys and
girls. "Uncle," the children called him, and he wanted to stay
to be the uncle of the family. The wife washed his clothes,
and he went on his way when they were dry.

On a farm road, he came across an imp child playing in
the dirt. It looked at him, and he looked at it. He held out a
piece of sugar; he cupped a grassblade between his thumbs
and whistled. He sat on the ground with his legs crossed, and
the child climbed into the hollow of his arms and legs. "I
wish you were my baby," he told it. "My baby." He was very
satisfied sitting there under the humming sun with the baby,
who was satisfied too, no squirming. "My daughter," he said.
"My son." He couldn't tell whether it was a boy or a girl. He
touched the baby's fat arm and cheeks, its gold hair, and
looked into its blue eyes. He made a wish that it not have to
carry a sledgehammer and crawl into the dark. But he would
not feel sorry for it; other people must not suffer any more
than he did, and he could endure anything. Its mother came
walking out into the road. She had her hands above her like a
salute. She walked tentatively toward them, held out her
hand, smiled, spoke. He did not understand what she said
except "Bye-bye." The child waved and said, "Bye-bye,"

crawled over his legs, and toddled to her. Ah Goong continued on his way in a direction she could not point out to a
posse looking for a kidnapper chinaman.

Explosions followed him. He heard screams and went on,
saw flames outlining black windows and doors, and went
on. He ran in the opposite direction from gunshots and the
yell – *eeha awha* – the cowboys made when they herded
cattle and sang their savage songs.

Good at hiding, disappearing – decades unaccounted for
– he was not working in a mine when forty thousand chinamen were Driven Out of mining. He was not killed or kidnapped in the Los Angeles Massacre, though he gave money
toward ransoming those whose toes and fingers, a digit per
week, and ears grotesquely rotting or pickled, and scalped
queues, were displayed in Chinatowns. Demons believed
that the poorer a chinaman looked, the more gold he had
buried somewhere, that chinamen stuck together and would
always ransom one another. If he got kidnapped, Ah Goong
planned, he would whip out his Citizenship Paper and show
that he was an American. He was lucky not to be in
Colorado when the Denver demons burned all chinamen
homes and businesses, nor in Rock Springs, Wyoming, when
the miner demons killed twenty-eight or fifty chinamen.
The Rock Springs Massacre began in a large coal mine
owned by the Union Pacific; the outnumbered chinamen
were shot in the back as they ran to Chinatown, which the
demons burned. They forced chinamen out into the open
and shot them; demon women and children threw the
wounded back in the flames. (There was a rumor of a good
white lady in Green Springs who hid China Men in the
Pacific Hotel and shamed the demons away.) The hunt went
on for a month before federal troops came. The count of
the dead was inexact because bodies were mutilated and
pieces scattered all over the Wyoming Territory. No white
miners were indicted, but the government paid $150,000 in

reparations to victims' families. There were many family men, then. There were settlers – abiding China Men. And China Women. Ah Goong was running elsewhere during the Drivings Out of Tacoma, Seattle, Oregon City, Albania, and Marysville. The demons of Tacoma packed all its chinamen into boxcars and sent them to Portland, where they were run out of town. China Men returned to Seattle, though, and refused to sell their land and stores but fought until the army came; the demon rioters were tried and acquitted. And when the Boston police imprisoned and beat 234 chinamen, it was 1902, and Ah Goong had already reached San Francisco or China, and perhaps San Francisco again.

In Second City (Sacramento), he spent some of his railroad money at the theater. The main actor's face was painted red with thick black eyebrows and long black beard, and when he strode onto the stage, Ah Goong recognized the hero, Guan Goong; his puppet horse had red nostrils and rolling eyes. Ah Goong's heart leapt to recognize hero and horse in the wilds of America. Guan Goong murdered his enemy – crash! bang! of cymbals and drum – and left his home village – sad, sad flute music. But to the glad clamor of cymbals entered his friends – Liu Pei (pronounced the same as Running Nose) and Chang Fei. In a joyful burst of pink flowers, the three men swore the Peach Garden Oath. Each friend sang an aria to friendship; together they would fight side by side and live and die one for all and all for one. Ah Goong felt as warm as if he were with friends at a party. Then Guan Goong's archenemy, the sly Ts'ao Ts'ao, captured him and two of Liu Pei's wives, the Lady Kan and the Lady Mi. Though Ah Goong knew they were boy actors, he basked in the presence of Chinese ladies. The prisoners traveled to the capital, the soldiers waving horsehair whisks, signifying horses, the ladies walking between horizontal banners, signifying palanquins. All the prisoners were put in one bedroom, but Guan Goong stood all night outside the door with a lighted candle in his hand, singing an aria about faithfulness. When the capital was attacked by a common enemy, Guan Goong fought the biggest man in one-to-one combat, a twirling, jumping sword dance that strengthened the China Men who watched it. From afar Guan Goong's two partners heard about the feats of the man with the red face and intelligent horse. The three friends were reunited and fought until they secured their rightful kingdom.

Ah Goong felt refreshed and inspired. He called out Bravo like the demons in the audience, who had not seen theater before. Guan Goong, the God of War, also God of War and Literature, had come to America – Guan Goong, Grandfather Guan, our own ancestor of writers and fighters, of actors and gamblers, and avenging executioners who mete out justice. Our own kin. Not a distant ancestor but Grandfather.

In the Big City (San Francisco), a goldsmith convinced Ah Goong to have his gold made into jewelry, which would organize it into one piece and also delight his wife. So he handed over a second bag of gold. He got it back as a small ring in a design he thought up himself, two hands clasping in a handshake. "So small?" he said, but the goldsmith said that only some of the ore had been true gold.

He got a ship out of San Francisco without being captured near the docks, where there was a stockade full of jailed chinamen; the demonesses came down from Nob Hill and took them home to be servants, cooks, and baby-sitters.

Grandmother liked the gold ring very much. The gold was so pure, it squished to fit her finger. She never washed dishes, so the gold did not wear away. She quickly spent the railroad money, and Ah Goong said he would go to America again. He had a Certificate of Return and his Citizenship Paper.

But this time, there was no railroad to sell his strength to. He lived in a basement that was rumored to connect with tunnels beneath Chinatown. In an underground arsenal, he held a pistol and said, "I feel the death in it." "The holes for the bullets were like chambers in a beehive or wasp nest," he said. He was inside the earth when the San Francisco Earthquake and Fire began. Thunder rumbled from the ground. Some say he died falling into the cracking earth. It was a miraculous earthquake and fire. The Hall of Records burned completely. Citizenship Papers burned, Certificates of Return, Birth Certificates, Residency Certificates, passenger lists, Marriage Certificates – every paper a China Man wanted for citizenship and legality burned in that fire. An authentic citizen, then, had no more papers than an alien. Any paper a China Man could not produce had been "burned up in the Fire of 1906." Every China Man was reborn out of that fire a citizen.

Some say the family went into debt to send for Ah Goong, who was not making money; he was a homeless wanderer, a shiftless, dirty, jobless man with matted hair, ragged clothes, and fleas all over his body. He ate out of garbage cans. He was a louse eaten by lice. A fleaman. It cost two thousand dollars to bring him back to China, his oldest sons signing promissory notes for one thousand, his youngest to repay four hundred to one neighbor and six hundred to another. Maybe he hadn't died in San Francisco, it was just his papers that burned; it was just that his existence was outlawed by Chinese Exclusion Acts. The family called him Fleaman. They did not understand his accomplishments as an American ancestor, a holding, homing ancestor of this place. He'd gotten the legal or illegal papers burned in the San Francisco Earthquake and Fire; he appeared in America in time to be a citizen and to father citizens. He had also been seen carrying a child out of the fire, a child of his own in spite of the laws against marrying. He had built a railroad out of sweat, why not have an American child out of longing?

The Laws

The United States of America and the Emperor of China cordially recognize the inherent and inalienable right of man to change his home and allegiance, and also the mutual advantage of the free migration and emigration of their citizens and subjects respectively from the one country to the other for purposes of curiosity, of trade, or as permanent residents. ARTICLE V OF THE BURLINGAME TREATY, SIGNED IN WASHINGTON, D.C., JULY 28, 1868, AND IN PEKING, NOVEMBER 23, 1869

The First Years: 1868, the year of the Burlingame Treaty, was the year 40,000 miners of Chinese ancestry were Driven Out. The Fourteenth Amendment, adopted in that same year, said that naturalized Americans have the same rights as native-born Americans, but in 1870 the Nationality Act specified that only "free whites" and "African aliens" were allowed to apply for naturalization. Chinese were not white; this had been established legally in 1854 when Chan Young unsuccessfully applied for citizenship in Federal District Court in San Francisco and was turned down on grounds of race. (He would have been illegal one way or another anyway; the Emperor of China did not give permission for any of his subjects to leave China until 1859.) Debating the Nationality Act,

Congressmen declared that America would be a nation of "Nordic fiber."

1878: California held a Constitutional Convention to settle "the Chinese problem." Of the 152 delegates, 35 were not American citizens but Europeans. The resulting constitution, voted into existence by a majority party of Working Men and Grangers, prohibited Chinese from entering California. New state laws empowered cities and counties to confine them within specified areas or to throw them out completely. Shipowners and captains were to be fined and jailed for hiring or transporting them. (This provision was so little respected that the American merchant marine relied heavily on Chinese seamen from the Civil War years to World War I.) "Mongolians, Indians, and Negroes" were barred from attending public schools. The only California fishermen forced to pay fishing and shellfish taxes were the Chinese, who had brought shrimp nets from China and started the shrimp, abalone, and lobster industries. (The taxes were payable monthly.) Those Chinese over eighteen who were not already paying a miner's tax had to pay a "police tax," to cover the extra policing their presence required. Though the Chinese were filling and leveeing the San Joaquin Delta for thirteen cents a square yard, building the richest agricultural land in the world, they were prohibited from owning land or real estate. They could not apply for business licenses. Employers could be fined and jailed for hiring them. No Chinese could be hired by state, county, or municipal governments for public works. No "Chinese or Mongolian or Indian" could testify in court "either for or against a white man."

At this time San Francisco supplemented the anti-Chinese state laws with some of its own: a queue tax, a "cubic air ordinance" requiring that every residence have so many cubic feet of air per inhabitant, a pole law prohibiting the use of carrying baskets on poles, cigar taxes, shoe taxes, and laundry taxes.

Federal courts declared some of the state and city laws unconstitutional, and occasionally citizens of a county or city repealed an especially punitive ordinance on the grounds that it was wrong to invite the Chinese to come to the United States and then deny them a livelihood. The repealed laws were often reenacted in another form.

1880: The Burlingame Treaty was modified. Instead of being free, the immigration of Chinese laborers to the United States would be "reasonably limited." In return (so as not to bring about limits on American entry into China), the American government promised to protect Chinese from lynchings.

1881: The Burlingame Treaty was suspended for a period of twenty years. (Since 1881 there has been no freedom of travel between China and the United States.) In protest against this suspension and against the refusal to admit Chinese boys to U.S. Army and Naval academies, China ordered scholars studying in the United States to return home. The act suspending the treaty did have two favorable provisions: all Chinese already resident in the United States in 1882 could stay; and they were permitted to leave and reenter with a Certificate of Return.

1882: Encouraged by fanatical lobbying from California, the U.S. Congress passed the first Chinese Exclusion Act. It banned the entrance of Chinese laborers, both skilled and unskilled, for ten years. Anyone unqualified for citizenship could not come in − and by the terms of the Nationality Act of 1870, Chinese were not qualified for citizenship. Some merchants and scholars were granted temporary visas.

1884: Congress refined the Exclusion Act with An Act to Amend an Act. This raised fines and sentences and further defined "merchants" to exclude "hucksters, peddlers, or those engaged in taking, draying, or otherwise preserving shell or other fish for home consumption or exportation."

1888: The Scott Act, passed by Congress, again forbade the entry of Chinese laborers. It also declared that Certificates of Return were void. Twenty thousand Chinese were trapped outside the United States with now-useless reentry permits. Six hundred returning travelers were turned back at American ports. A Chinese ambassador, humiliated by immigration officers, killed himself. The law decreed that Certificates of Residence had to be shown on demand; any Chinese caught without one was deported.

1889: Chinese pooled money to fight the various Exclusion Acts in the courts. They rarely won. In *Chae Chan Ping* v. *The United States*, Chae Chan Ping argued for the validity of his Certificate of Return. The Supreme Court ruled against him, saying that "regardless of the existence of a prior treaty," a race "that will not assimilate with us" could be excluded when deemed "dangerous to . . . peace and security . . . . It matters not in what form aggression and encroachment come, whether from the foreign nation acting in its national character or from vast hordes of its people crowding in upon us." Moreover, said the Court, "sojourners" should not "claim surprise" that any Certificates of Return obtained prior to 1882 were "held at the will of the government, revocable at any time, at its pleasure."

1892: The Geary Act extended the 1882 Exclusion Act for another ten years. It also decreed that Chinese caught illegally in the United States be deported after one year of hard labor.

Chinese Americans formed the Equal Rights League and the Native Sons of the Golden State in order to fight disenfranchisement bills. Chinese Americans demanded the right to have their citizenship confirmed before traveling abroad.

1893: In *Yue Ting* v. *The United States*, the U.S. Supreme Court ruled that Congress had the right to expel members of a race who "continue to be aliens, having taken no steps toward becoming citizens, and incapable of becoming such under the naturalization laws."This applied only to Chinese; no other race or nationality was excluded from applying for citizenship.

1896: A victory. In *Yick Wo* v. *Hopkins*, the U.S. Supreme Court overturned San Francisco safety ordinances, saying that they were indeed designed to harass laundrymen of Chinese ancestry.

1898: Another victory.The Supreme Court decision in *The United States* v. *Wong Kim Ark* stated that a person born in the United States to Chinese parents is an American.This decision has never been reversed or changed, and it is the law on which most Americans of Chinese ancestry base their citizenship today.

1900: Deciding *The United States* v. *Mrs. Cue Lim*, the Supreme Court ruled that wives and children of treaty merchants – citizens of China, aliens traveling on visas – were allowed to come to the United States.

1904: The Chinese Exclusion Acts were extended indefinitely, and made to cover Hawai'i and the Philippines as well as the continental United States. The question of exclusion was not debated in Congress; instead, the measure passed as a rider on a routine appropriations bill. China boycotted American goods in protest.

1906: The San Francisco Board of Education ordered that all Chinese, Japanese, and Korean children be segregated in an Oriental school. President Roosevelt, responding to a protest from the Japanese government, persuaded the Board of Education to allow Japanese to attend white schools.

1917: Congress voted that immigrants over sixteen years of age be required to pass an English reading test.

1924: An Immigration Act passed by Congress specifically excluded "Chinese women, wives, and prostitutes." Any American who married a Chinese woman lost his citizenship; any Chinese man who married an American woman caused her to lose her citizenship. Many states had also instituted antimiscegenation laws. A Supreme Court case called *Chang Chan et al. v. John D. Nagle* tested the law against wives; Chang Chan et al. lost. For the first time, the 1924 Immigration Act distinguished between two kinds of "aliens": "immigrants" were admitted as permanent residents with the opportunity to become citizens eventually; the rest – scholars, merchants, ministers, and tourists – were admitted on a temporary basis and were not eligible for citizenship. The number of persons allowed in the category of immigrant was set by law at one-sixth of one percent of the total population of that ancestry in the United States as of the 1920 census. The 1920 census had the lowest count of ethnic Chinese in this country since 1860. As a result, only 105 Chinese immigrants were permitted each year.

In *Cheuno Sumchee v. Nagle*, the Supreme Court once again confirmed the right of treaty merchants to bring their wives to the United States. This was a right that continued to be denied to Chinese Americans.

1938: A Presidential proclamation lifted restriction on immigration for Chinese and nationals of a few other Asian countries. The Chinese were still ineligible for citizenship, and the quota was "100."

1943: The United States and China signed a treaty of alliance against the Japanese, and Congress repealed the Exclusion Act of 1882. Immigration continued to be limited to the 1924 quota of 105, however, and the Immigration and Nationalization Service claimed to be unable to find even that many qualified Chinese. A "Chinese" was defined as anyone with more than 50 percent Chinese blood, regardless of citizenship or country of residence. At this time Japanese invaders were killing Chinese civilians in vast numbers; it is estimated that more than 10 million died. Chinese immigration into the United States did not rise.

1946: Congress passed the War Bride Act, enabling soldiers to bring Japanese and European wives home, then enacted a separate law allowing the wives and children of Chinese Americans to apply for entry as "non-quota immigrants." Only now did the ethnic Chinese population in the United States begin to approach the level of seventy years previous. (When the first Exclusion Act was passed in 1882, there were some 107,000 Chinese here; the Acts and the Driving Out steadily reduced the number to fewer than 70,000 in the 1920s.)

1948: The Refugee Act passed by Congress this year applied only to Europeans. A separate Displaced Persons Act provided that for a limited time – 1948 to 1954 – ethnic Chinese already living in the United States could apply for citizenship. During the postwar period, about 10,000 Chinese were permitted to enter the country under individual private bills passed by Congress. Confidence men, like the Citizenship Judges of old, defrauded hopeful Chinese by promising to acquire one of these bills for $1,500.

1950: After the Chinese Communist government took over in 1949, the United States passed a series of Refugee Relief Acts and a Refugee Escapee Act expanding the number of "non-quota immigrants" allowed in. As a condition of entry, the Internal Security Act provided that these refugees swear they were not Communists. (Several hundred "subversives or anarchists" of various races were subsequently deported; some were naturalized citizens who were "denaturalized" beforehand.)

1952: The Immigration and Nationality Act denied admission to "subversive and undesirable aliens" and made it simpler to deport "those already in the country." Another provision of this act was that for the first time Chinese women were allowed to immigrate under the same conditions as men.

1954: Ruling on *Mao* v. *Brownell*, the Supreme Court upheld laws forbidding Chinese Americans to send money to relatives in China. Before the Communist Revolution, there were no such restrictions in effect; Chinese Americans sent $70 million during World War II. Nor could they send money or gifts through CARE, UNESCO, or church organizations, which provided only for non-Communist countries.

1957: The Refugee Relief Act of 1953 expired in 1956 and was followed by the Act of 1957, which provided for the distribution of 18,000 visas that had remained unused.

1959: Close relatives, including parents, were allowed to enter.

1960: A "Fair Share Refugee Act" allowed certain refugees from Communist and Middle Eastern countries to enter. Close to 20,000 people who were "persecuted because of race, religion, or political beliefs" immigrated before this act was repealed in 1965, when a new act allowed the conditional entry of 10,200 refugees annually.

1962: A Presidential directive allowed several thousand "parolees" to enter the United States from Hong Kong. Relatives of citizens and resident aliens were eligible. President Kennedy gave Congress a special message on immigration, saying, "It is time to correct the mistakes of the past."

1965: A new Immigration and Nationality Act changed the old quota system so that "national origin" no longer means "race" but "country of birth." Instead of being based on a percentage of existing ethnic populations in the United States, quotas were reallocated to countries – 20,000 each. But this did not mean that 20,000 Chinese immediately could or did come to the United States. Most prospective immigrants were in Hong Kong, a British colony. Colonies received 1 percent of the mother country's allotment: only 200. "Immediate relatives," the children, spouses, and parents of citizens, however, could enter without numerical limitations. Also not reckoned within the quota limitations were legal residents returning from a visit abroad.

1968: Amendments to the Immigration and Nationality Act provided that immigrants not be allocated by race or nation but by hemispheres, with 120,000 permitted to enter from the Western Hemisphere and 170,000 from the Eastern Hemisphere. This act limits immigration from the Western Hemisphere for the first time in history. The 20,000-per-country quota remained in effect for the Eastern Hemisphere, no per-country limitation for the Western Hemisphere.

1976: The Immigration and Nationality Act Amendments, also called the Western Hemisphere Bill, equalized the provisions of law regulating immigration from the two hemispheres. The House Committee on the Judiciary in its report on this legislation stated, "This constitutes an essential first step in a projected long-term reform of U.S. Immigration law." The 20,000-per-country limit was extended to the Western Hemisphere. The limitation on colonies was raised from 200 to 600.

1978: The separate quotas for the two hemispheres were replaced by a worldwide numerical limitation on immigration of 290,000 annually. On the basis of the "immediate relatives" clause, about 22,000 Chinese enter legally each year, and the rate is increasing. There are also special quotas in effect for Southeast Asian refugees, most of whom are of Chinese ancestry. In the last decade, the ethnic Chinese population of the United States has doubled. The 1980 census may show a million or more.

The China Man also went to Alaska to strike-it-rich in gold mining. At the top of the world, people wrote in their diaries for entertainment; they recorded the weather and described their health, their daily farming, hunting, and cooking, and the executions they witnessed. Many of them wrote about seeing an old Indian put to death in the middle of a public street: The tribe feasted and drank whiskey. Then while they drummed on walrus hide, the old father calmly brought out a walrus hide thong. A son or a brother came from behind him, noosed his throat, pushed a foot against his back, and broke his neck. There was also a stoning of an Indian woman in Juneau.

The strongest court of law was the miners' meetings, and the code of self-defense was the miners' law. Citizenship was cheaper in Alaska; the Citizenship Judge, who followed the prospectors, only asked for a pinch of gold dust. The white miners voted in 1885 that the chinamen be shipped out for fighting with the Indian miners. Posters and newspapers announced that on a certain day in July, chinamen were to report to the waterfront on Douglas Island. Diaries glowed with the weather: "It was a beautiful sight, and one of the few days when the channel was smooth the day it was done." (Beauty was different in those days, the foliage along the edges of Douglas Island was dead because of the sulphur from the gold mills. After the ore was pounded a hundred and twenty times by nine-hundred-pound pistons, the gold was broken free, and the sulphur was slagged onto the land and into the channel.) Demons came from miles around to see the Driving Out done. There were no fights. The whites stood on the shore with guns and tools; the Indians in their colors paddled fifty war canoes into the channel and rowed away "the entire Chinese population" of one hundred. In Juneau they were put on a schooner to Puget Sound, where they were released.

The area was rid of chinamen except for China Joe, who was a baker in Juneau. He had saved the miners in the Cassiar District from starvation and bad winters by giving bread away. He had opened his stores to everyone. "He was the most loved person in Alaska," a diarist wrote. When he died, Juneau held the largest funeral Alaska had ever seen.

As soon as they touched shore in Puget Sound, the China Men found ways to return and take back their mines, jobs, houses, and girl friends.

So the next year, there had to be another shipping out (unless it only happened once with two versions of the same event and the dates mixed up). This time the white miners went on strike against the Treadwell Mining Company, and ninety Chinese scabs took their jobs. Treadwell blackballed the strikers, who hired rustlers, claim jumpers, trap looters, to get rid of the chinamen. One of these rowdies or bummers wrote in his diary: "The citizens of Juneau did not approve of the mining company's employing them and appealed to us to aid them in getting rid of the orientals which we did in the month of July." The China Men asked Treadwell for guns to defend themselves, but the mining company refused to arm them. Some citizens wrote to the governor to send help: "They are commencing the dynamiting business against the Chinese." The governor himself came. But one day in July 1886, the demons walked the chinamen at gunpoint to the harbor, no Indians with war canoes this time. They were forced to board an old ship, and the ship was set adrift at sea. Some say there were two old schooners. There was no food or water, and the hundred

China Men were so crowded together, they could not lie down. After eight days at sea, they steered the ship to Wrangel, a hundred and fifty miles south of Douglas Island. A white man named Captain Carroll gave them water and food and berths on his ship, the *Ancon*. He offered to sail them home, and they said, Yes, they would take him up on that. "Take us home," said the sourdough China Men, "to Douglas Island."

The only China Man not set adrift was China Joe, who owned a laundry and a big garden. He had provided vegetables during the bad winters. As French Pete was probably the name of more than one man, as were Dutch John and Missouri Frank and Arkansas Jim and French Charley, Dago Joe, and Indian Joe – one of the Citizenship Judges himself was named French Pete – perhaps any China Man was China Joe.

THE MAKING OF MORE AMERICANS

To visit grandfathers, we walked over three sets of railroad tracks, then on sidewalks cracked by grass and tree roots, then a gray dirt path. The roadside weeds waved tall overhead, netting the sunlight and wildflowers. I wore important white shoes for walking to the grandfathers' house.

The black dirt in their yard set off my dazzling shoes – two chunks of white light that encased my feet. "Look. Look," said Say Goong, Fourth Grandfather, my railroad grandfather's youngest brother. "A field chicken." It was not a chicken at all but a toad with alert round eyes that looked out from under the white cabbage leaves. It hopped ahead of my shoes, dived into the leaves, and disappeared, reappeared, maybe another toad. It was a clod that had detached itself from the living earth; the earth had formed into a toad and hopped. "A field chicken," said Say Goong. He cupped his hands, walked quietly with wide steps and caught it. On his brown hand sat a toad with perfect haunches, eyelids, veins, and wrinkles – the details of it, the neatness and completeness of it swallowing and blinking. "A field chicken?" I repeated. "Field chicken," he said. "Sky chicken. Sky toad. Heavenly toad. Field toad." It was a pun and the words the same except for the low tone of *field* and the high tone of *heaven* or *sky*. He put the toad in my hands – it breathed, and its heart beat, every part of it alive – and I felt its dryness and warmth and hind feet as it sprang off. How odd that a toad could be both of the field and of the sky. It was very funny. Say Goong and I laughed. "Heavenly chicken," I called, chasing the toad. I carefully ran between the rows of vegetables,

385

where many toads, giants and miniatures, hopped everywhere. Which one was the toad in my hand? Then suddenly they were all gone. But they clucked. So it isn't that toads look or taste like chickens that they're called chickens; they cluck alike! Dragonflies held still in the air, suddenly darted. Butterflies in pairs flew far away from their partners, then together again. I stepped into a green hallway in the corn and sat in a teepee grown of vines over lattices; from ceilings and walls hung gourds, beans, tomatoes, grapes, and peas, winter melons like fat green prickly piglets, and bitter melons like green mice with tails. But the real marvel was the black dirt, which was clean and not dirty at all.

In one corner of the yard was a pile of horse manure taller than an adult human being. "Aiya! Aiya!" our parents, grand-fathers, and neighbors exclaimed, eyes open in wonder as they stood around the pile, neighbors and friends invited especially to view it. "Come here! Come look. Oh, just look at it!" – I could tell that the adults felt what I felt, that I did not feel it alone, but truly. This pile hummed, and it was the fuel for the ground, the toads, the vegetables, the house, the two grandfathers. The flies, which were green and turquoise-black and silvery blue, swirling into various lights, hummed too, like excess sparks. The grandfathers boxed the horse manure, presents for us and their good friends to take home. They also bagged it in burlap. It smelled good.

Say Goong took my hand and led me to a cavernous shed black from the sun in my eyes. He pointed into the dark, which dark seemed solid and alive, heavy, moving, breathing. There were waves of dark skin over a hot and massive some-thing that was snorting and stomping – the living night. In the day, here was where the night lived. Say Goong pointed up at a wide brown eye as high as the roof. I was ready to be terrified but for his delight. "Horse," he said. "Horse." He contained the thing in a word – *horse*, magical and earthly sound. A horse was a black creature so immense I could not see the outlines. Grasping Say Goong's finger, I dared to walk past the horse, and then he pointed again, "Horse." There was a partition, and on the other side of it – another horse. There were two such enormities in the world. Again and again I looked inside the stalls to solve the mystery of what a horse was. On the outside of the shed was horse shit, on the inside, the source of horse shit.

What I could see in its entirety because inanimate was the vegetable wagon, which was really a stagecoach. I climbed up a wheel and into the seat. I opened the compartments, drawers, and many screened doors. A scale hung in back, and in front were reins and two long prongs.

When I heard hooves clippity-clopping down our street, I ran to the upstairs window and saw two grandfathers and the two horses, which were contained between the prongs. They had blinders cupping their eyes. I had discovered the daily shape of horses. My mother opened the window, and she and I made up a song about grandfathers and horses; we sang it to them in the interplaying rhythm of hooves on the street:

> *Third Grandfather and Fourth Grandfather,*
> *Where are you going?*
> *Hooves clippity-clopping four by four,*
> *Where are you going?*

"We're going to the north side to sell lettuce," they said. Or, the horses facing another direction, "We're going to the feed store," or "We're going home." "We're going on our route of demonesses." The grandfathers could understand demon talk; they told us how the demonesses praised the tomatoes all the same size. "Allee sem," said the demonesses.

Sometimes under our very windows, the grandfathers fitted nosebags of oats over the horses' muzzles. The water for the horses had run into two buckets from a block of ice that sat melting in the middle of the wagon. The grandfathers sprinkled the vegetables with a watering can while the horses drank. Neighbors who had waited until late in the day for bargains circled the wagon. Through the screens they looked shrewdly at the red, yellow, and green vegetables. The god with the gourd had a gourd like the ones the grandfathers sold. At New Year's, tangerines hung by the branch from the roof, and in the fall, persimmons. In summer the grandfathers sold watermelons, which grew in China too, only there the meat was light pink and nobody we knew had ever tasted it. A railing along the top of the stagecoach kept the sacks of potatoes and yams from rolling off. Our family got what remained for free.

One time I went to the shed to have a look at the horses, and they were gone. "Where are the horses?" I asked. "They're gone," said both my parents with no surprise or emphasis. Not satisfied with the answer, I asked them again and again. Such vastness could not possibly have disappeared so completely. But they said, "They've been gone a long time." I walked inside each bare stall. "Where are the horses? Where are they?" No more horses. "What happened to them?" "They've been gone for a long time." No explanation. Did they trot away down the street without the stagecoach and the grandfathers? Time must have gone by, then, since I'd last come to visit them, though the visits seemed like the same time, no time at all, time just one time, but it must have been later, a last time. I looked inside the first stall, looked again in the other one but found no aliveness there, bright now and not dark with horses. I could see boards and into corners, no vestige of horses, no hay spilling over the troughs, not a single yellow straw sticking out of a crack, floor not covered with straw and horse shit, everything swept clean. Manure pile gone. I have looked for proof of horses, and found it in the family album, which has photographs of horses with blinders, though the men standing in front of the wagons are not the grandfathers but the uncles, the same ones who later had their pictures taken with cars and trucks.

The stagecoach was still there. I sat in the seat, shook the reins, and looked in the distance for Indians and bisons.

One day Sahm Goong, Third Grandfather, came to our house alone, and he said to my mother, "Say Goong is standing in the stable."

"No," said my mother. "He's dead."

"He's in the stable. I saw him. I left him there just now, standing by the wall near the door."

"What was he doing?"

"Just standing there. Not working."

"You know he's dead, don't you?"

"Yes. It must be his ghost standing there. He comes to visit me every day."

"What does he have to say?" she asked.

"Nothing. I talk to him, but he doesn't answer."

"You tell him to go home," said my mother. "Scold him. 'Go home!' Loud. Like that. 'Go home, Say Goong!'" They both called him that even though he was my fourth grandfather and not theirs.

Sahm Goong walked back home. He sat on a crate in the empty stable, the gray floorboards awash with afternoon sun. There in the shade beside the door stood his brother.

"How nice of you to visit me again," said Sahm Goong.

Say Goong did not reply. He was wearing his good clothes, his new bib overalls, a white shirt, a tie, his cardigan, and his cloth cap, which he had worn when working in the yard or driving the stagecoach. His fine white hair caught the light like a halo.

"Sit down," invited Sahm Goong, but his brother did not want to. He certainly could not be seen through, and he was not floating; he had his feet on the floor. The high work shoes were polished.

Third Grandfather stood up and walked over to Fourth Grandfather, the two of them the same size. They did not touch each other. "I am very well, you know," the live grandfather said. "My health is good. Yes, the rest of the family is fine too. Though there are a lot of girls. We're all well." Say Goong did not say a thing. Sahm Goong walked sideways and examined him in profile; he certainly looked as usual. Then Sahm Goong sat down again, looking a moment into the garden. When he looked back, his brother was still there, no shimmering, no wavering, just as solid and real as ever before. The two brothers stayed with each other until suppertime. Then Sahm Goong went in the house to cook and eat.

After dinner he took his flashlight and went again into the shed. He shone it into the place where the ghost had been. He was still there. He turned off the flashlight so as not to glare it in his face and sat in the dark with his brother. When he felt sleepy, he said, "Good night," and went back up to bed.

The next morning, he ate breakfast, then watered the yard, left the hose trickling. He went into the stable and did not see his brother, but the next time he checked, there he was again. Again he sat with him for a while. Then he got up and looked into the familiar old face. They were alike, two wispy old men, two wispy old brothers.

"Do you need to say something to me?" Sahm Goong asked.

The ghost did not answer.

"You don't have something to tell me then? No message?" Sahm Goong paced about. "What are you doing here?" he asked. "What do you want? You don't have something to tell me? No message? Why are you here?" He waited for a reply. "What do you want?"

But Say Goong's ghost said nothing.

"It's time to go home, then," said Sahm Goong. He said it louder. "Go home! It's time for you to go home now. What's the use of staying here any more? You don't belong here. There's nothing for you to do here. Go home. Go back to China. Go."

There did seem to be a flickering then. All was still, no sound of bird or toad, no aroused insect, only the humming that could have been the new refrigerator. "Go home," Sahm Goong said sternly. "Go back to China. Go now. To China." His voice was loud in the bare shed.

Say Goong disappeared, as if the vehement voice had filled the space he had been using. He had been startled away, reminded of something. He did not come back again. Later Sahm Goong couldn't say whether he had been looking directly at his brother at the moment of disappearance. He might have looked aside for a second, and when he looked again, Say Goong was gone. A slant of light still came in at the door.

Then Third Grandfather too disappeared, perhaps going back to China, perhaps dead here like his brother. When their descendants came across the country to visit us, we took them to the place where two of our four grandfathers had had their house, stable, and garden. My father pointed out where each thing had stood, "They had two horses, which lived in a stable here. Their house stood over there." The aunts and uncles exclaimed, "Their horses were here, then," and said it again in English to their children. "And their house over there." They took pictures with a delayed-shutter camera, everyone standing together where the house had been. The relatives kept saying, "This is the ancestral ground," their eyes filling with tears over a vacant lot in Stockton.

Third Grandfather had a grandson whom we called Sao Elder Brother to his face, but for a while behind his back, Mad Sao, which rhymes in our dialect. Sao firmly established his American citizenship by serving in the U.S.

Army in World War II, then sent for a wife from China. We were amazed at how lovely and kind she was even though picked sight unseen. The new couple, young and modern (*mo-dang*), bought a ranch house and car, wore fashionable clothes, spoke English, and seemed more American than us.

But Sao's mother sent him letters to come home to China. "I'm growing old," she said or the letter writer said. "If you don't come home now you'll never see me again. I remember you, my baby. Don't wait until you're old before coming back. I can't bear seeing you old like me." She did not know how American he had looked in his army uniform. "All you're doing is having fun, aren't you?" she asked. "You're spending all the money, aren't you? This is your own mother who rocked you to sleep and took care of you when you were sick. Do you remember your mother's face? We used to pretend our rocker was a boat like a peapod, and we were peas at sea. Remember? Remember? But now you send paper boats into my dreams. Sail back to me." But he was having his own American babies yearly, three girls and a boy. "Who will bury me if you don't come back?" his mother asked.

And if she wasn't nagging him to return, she was asking for money. When he sent photographs of the family with the car in the background, she scolded him: "What are you doing feeding these girls and not your mother? What is this car, and this radio? A new house. Why are you building a new house in America? You have a house here. Sell everything. Sell the girls, and mail the profits to Mother. Use the money for ship fare. Why are you spending money on photographs of girls? Send me the money you give the photographers so I can send you *my* picture, the face you've forgotten." She did not know that he owned his own camera. His family was one of the first to own a shower, a lawn, a carport, and a car for passengers rather than for hauling.

"You're doing everything backward," his mother wrote. "I'm starving to death. In the enclosed picture, you can see my bones poking through the skin. You must be turning into a demon to treat a mother so. I have suffered all my life; I need to rest now. I'll die happy if you come home. Why don't you do your duty? I order you to come back. It's all those daughters, isn't it? They've turned your head. Leave them. Come back alone. You don't need to save enough money to bring a litter of females. What a waste to bring girls all the way back here to sell anyway. You can find a second wife here too. A Gold Mountain Sojourner attracts ten thousand rich fat women. Sell those girls, apprentice the boy, and use the money for your passage." Of course, though Mad Sao favored his son, there was no question but that, being very American, he would raise and protect his daughters.

"Let me tell you about hunger," wrote his mother. "I am boiling weeds and roots. I am eating flowers and insects and pond scum. All my teeth have fallen out. An army drafted the ox, and soldiers took the pigs and chickens. There are strangers in the orchard eating the fruit in its bud. I tried to chase them away. 'We're hungry. We're hungry,' they kept explaining. The next people through here will gnaw the branches. The sly villagers are hoarding food, begging it, and hiding it. You can't trust the neighbors. They'd do anything. I haven't eaten meat for so long, I might as well have been a nun who's taken a vegetable vow. You'd think I'd be holy by now and see miracles. What I see are the hungry, who wander lost from home and village. They live by swindling and scheming. Two crazed villagers are stealing a Dragon King statue from each other. It goes back and forth and whoever's doorstep it lands on has to pay for a party. There's no goodness and wisdom in hunger. You're starving me. I see you for what you are — an unfaithful son. Oh, what blame you're incurring. All right, don't bring yourself to me. I don't need a son. But send money. Send food. Send food. I may have been exaggerating before, but don't punish me for playing the boy who cried wolf. This time there really is a wolf at the door." He shut his heart and paid his house mortgage. He did nothing for her, or he did plenty, and it was not enough.

"Now we're eating potato leaves," she wrote. "We pound rice hulls into paste and eat it. At least send money to bury me." (Sao felt the terror in *bury*, the dirt packing the nose, plugging the eyes and mouth.) "I've wasted my life waiting, and what do I get for my sacrifices? Food and a fat old age? No. I'm starving to death alone. I hold you responsible. How can you swallow when you know of me?" Some letters were long and some short. "The beggar children who came to the door on your sister's wedding day were the worst-looking beggars in many years," she wrote. "Give them food? Huh. I should have kidnapped them and sold them. Except that people don't buy children any more, not even boys. There's a baby on the rich family's doorstep every morning. Oh, it's so pathetic. The mother hides behind bushes to watch the rich lady bring the baby inside. There are people eating clay balls and chewing bark. The arbor we sat under is gone, eaten. No more fish in the rivers. Frogs, beetles, all eaten. I am so tired. I can't drive the refugees off our property. They eat the seeds out of the dirt. There'll not be harvest again."

Other relatives wrote letters about their hunger: "We'd be glad to catch a rat but they're gone too," a cousin wrote. "Slugs, worms, bugs, all gone. You think we're dirty and depraved? Anything tastes good fried, but we can't buy oil." "We're chewing glue from hems and shoes," wrote another cousin. "We steal food off graves if people are rich enough to leave some. But who tends the dead any more?" "Starving takes a long time." "No more dogs and cats. No more birds. No mice. No grasshoppers." "We've burned the outhouse for fuel. Didn't need it anyway. Nothing comes out because nothing goes in. What shall we do? Eat shit and drink piss? But there isn't any coming out." "I can't sleep for the hunger.

If we could sleep, we'd dream about food. I catch myself opening cupboards and jars even though I know they're empty. Staring into pots." "I searched under my own children's pillows for crumbs." "Soon I won't be able to concentrate on writing to you. My brain is changing. If only the senses would dull, I wouldn't feel so bad. But I am on the alert for food." "There are no children on some streets." "We know which weeds and berries and mushrooms and toads are poisonous from people eating them and dying." "Fathers leave in the middle of the night, taking no food with them." "The dead are luckier."

When the relatives read and discussed one another's hunger letters, they said, "Perhaps it's more merciful to let them die fast, starve fast rather than slow." "It's kinder either to send a great deal of money or none at all," they said. "Do you think people really go into euphoria when they die of hunger? Like saints fasting?"

"How can you leave me to face famine and war alone?" wrote Mad Sao's mother. "All I think about is you and food. You owe it to me to return. Advise me. Don't trick me. If you're never coming home, tell me. I can kill myself then. Easily stop looking for food and die." "The neighbors heard rumors about food inland to the north," she wrote next. "Others are following an army their sons joined. The villagers are moving. Tell me what to do. Some people are walking to the cities. Tin miners are coming through here, heading for the ocean. They spit black. They can't trade their tin or money for food. Rich people are throwing money into the crowds. I've buried the gold. I buried the money and jewels in the garden. We were almost robbed. The bandit used the old trick of sticking a pot like his head bulging against the curtain, and when I clubbed it, it clanged. At the alarm he fled. I had nothing to steal anyway." Hearing that money couldn't buy food relieved Mad Sao of feeling so guilty when he did not send money.

"Since everyone is traveling back and forth, I might as well stay put here," wrote his mother. "I'm frightened of these hungry eaters and killer soldiers and contagious lepers. It used to be the lepers and the deformed who hid; now the fat people hide."

"Shall I wait for you? Answer me. How would you like to come home and find an empty house? The door agape. You'll not find me waiting when you get here. It would serve you right. The weather has changed; the world is different. The young aren't feeding the old any more. The aunts aren't feeding me any more. They're keeping the food for their own children. Some slaves have run away. I'm chasing my slaves away. Free people are offering themselves as soldiers and slaves."

"I'm too old. I don't want to endure any more. Today I gave my last handful of rice to an old person so dried up, I couldn't tell whether it was man or woman. I'm ready to die." But she wrote again, "The fugitives are begging for burial ground and make a cemetery out of our farm. Let them bury their skinny bodies if they give me a little funeral food. They ask if Jesus demons have settled nearby; they leave the children with them. If you don't have stories that are equally heart-rending, you have nothing better to do with your money than send it to me. Otherwise, I don't want to hear about your mortgage payment or see photographs of your new car. What do you mean mortgage payment? Why are you buying land there when you have land here?"

"If only I could list foods on this paper and chew it up, swallow, and be full. But if I could do that, I could write your name, and you'd be here."

"I keep planning banquets and menus and guests to invite. I smell the food my mother cooked. The smell of puffed rice cookies rises from tombs. The aunts have left me here with the babies. The neighbors took their children with them. If they find food, they can decide then what to do with the children, either feed them or trade them for the food. Some children carry their parents, and some parents carry their children."

Mad Sao wished that his mother would hurry up and die, or that he had time and money enough to pay his mortgage, raise all his children, and also give his mother plenty.

Before a letter in a white envelope reached us saying that Sao Brother's mother had died, she appeared to him in America. She flew across the ocean and found her way to him. Just when he was about to fall asleep one night, he saw her and sat up with a start, definitely not dreaming. "You have turned me into a hungry ghost," she said. "You did this to me. You enjoyed yourself. You fed your wife and useless daughters, who are not even family, and you left me to starve. What you see before you is the inordinate hunger I had to suffer in my life." She opened her mouth wide, and he turned his face away not to see the depths within.

"Mother," he said. "Mother, how did you find your way across the ocean and here?"

"I am so cold. I followed the heat of your body like a light and fire. I was drawn to the well-fed."

"Here, take this, Mother," he cried, handing her his wallet from the nightstand.

"Too late," she said. "Too late."

With her chasing him he ran to the kitchen. He opened the refrigerator. He shoved food at her.

"Too late."

Curiously enough, other people did not see her. All they saw was Mad Sao talking to the air, making motions to the air, talking to no voice, listening to someone who moved about, someone very tall or floating near the ceiling. He yelled and argued, talked, sobbed. He lost weight from not eating; insomnia ringed his eyes. That's when people began to call him Mad Sao.

He knew how his grandfather had helped Fourth Grandfather by scolding him on his way. "Go home, Mother!" he was heard to scold, very firm, his face serious and his voice loud. "Go home! Go back to China. Go home to China where you belong." He went on with this scolding for days and nights, but it did not work. She never left him for a moment.

"I'm hungry," she cried. "I'm hungry." He threw money at her; he threw food at her. The money and food went through her. She wept continually, most disturbingly loud at night; though he pulled the covers over his ears and eyes, he heard her. "Why didn't you come home? Why didn't you send money?"

"I did send money."

"Not enough."

"It's against the law to send money," he told her – a weak excuse. "But even so, I sent it."

"I'm not a rich man," he said. "It isn't easy in this country either."

"Don't lie to me," she said. She pointed toward the kitchen, where the refrigerator and freezer were filled with food, and at the furniture, the radio, the TV. She pointed with her chin the way Chinese people point.

"Since you're here, Mother," he tried to bribe her, "you may have all the food I have. Take it. Take it."

She could see her surroundings exactly, but though she could see food, she could not eat it.

"It's too late," she mourned, and passed her hand through the footboard of his bed. He drew his feet up. He could not bear it if she should pass her hand through his feet. His wife beside him saw him gesturing and talking, sleepwalking and sleeptalking, and could not calm him.

"I died of starvation," his mother said. She was very thin, her eye sockets hollow like a Caucasian's. "I died of starvation while you ate."

398

He could not sleep because she kept talking to him. She did not fade with the dawn and the rooster's crowing. She kept a watch on him. She followed him to work. She kept repeating herself. "You didn't come home. You didn't send money."

She said, "I've got things to tell you that I didn't put in letters. I am going to tell them to you now. Did you know that when children starve, they grow coarse black hairs all over their bodies? And the heads and feet of starving women suddenly swell up. The skin of my little feet split open, and pus and blood burst out; I saw the muscles and veins underneath.

"One day there was meat for sale in the market. But after cooking and eating it, the villagers found out it was baby meat. The parents who had sold their children regretted it. 'We shouldn't have sold her,' they said. The rich people had bought the babies and resold them to butchers."

"Stop it, Mother," he said to the air. "I can't stand any more."

Night after night, she haunted him. Day after day. At last he drove to the bank. She sat in the back seat directly behind him. He took a lump of money out of his savings. Then he ran to a travel agency, his mother chasing him down the street, goading him. "Look, Mother," he was heard to say, sounding happier as he showed her the money and papers. "I'll take you home myself. You'll be able to rest. I'll go with you. Escort you. We're going home. I'm going home. I'm going home at last, just as you asked. I'll take you home. See? Isn't it a wonderful idea I have? Here's a ticket. See all the money I spent on a ticket, Mother? We're going home together." He had bought an oceanliner ticket for one, so it was evident that he knew she was a ghost. That he easily got his passport proves that he was indeed an American citizen and in good standing with the Immigration and Naturalization Service. It was strange that at a time when

399

Americans did not enter China, he easily got a visa also. He became much calmer. He did not suddenly scream any more or cry or throw food and money.

The family told him that there were no such things as ghosts, that he was wasting an enormous amount of savings, that it was dangerous to go to China, that the bandits would hold him hostage, that an army would draft him. The FBI would use our interest in China to prove our un-Americanness and deport all of us. The family scolded him for spending a fortune on a dead person. Why hadn't he mailed her the money when she was alive if he was going to spend it anyway? Why hadn't he gone to see her earlier? "Why don't you give the money to some wretch instead of wasting it on a vacation for yourself, eh?" He reminded them of a ghost story about a spirit that refused ghost money but had to have real money. They shook their heads. When my father saw that Mad Sao would not be swayed, he bought two Parker 51 fountain pens for fifty-five dollars, kept one for himself, and told Mad Sao to deliver the other to a most loved relative in China.

Mad Sao packed a small bag, all the time talking, "See, Mother? We're on our way home now. Both of us. Yes, I'm going home too. Finally going home. And I'm taking you home. We're together again, Mother." He hardly heard the live people around him.

All the way up the gangway, he was waving her on, "This way, Mother," leading her by the hand or elbow. "This way, Mother. This way." He gave her his bed and his deck chair. "Are you comfortable, Mother?" "Yes, Mother." He talked to no other passenger, and did not eat any of the ship's meals, for which he had already paid. He walked the decks day and night. "Yes, Mother. I'm sorry. I am sorry I did that. Yes, I did that, and I'm sorry."

He returned his mother to the village. He went directly to her grave, as if led by her. "Here you are, Mother," he said, and the villagers heard him say it. "You're home now. I've brought you home. I spent passage fare on you. It equals more than the food money I might have sent. Travel is very expensive. Rest, Mother. Eat." He heaped food on her grave. He piled presents beside it. He set real clothes and real shoes on fire. He burned mounds of paper replicas and paper money. He poured wine into the thirsty earth. He planted the blue shrub of longevity, where white carrier pigeons would nest. He bowed his forehead to the ground, knocking it hard in repentance. "You're home, Mother. I'm home too. I brought you home." He set off firecrackers near her grave, not neglecting one Chinese thing. "Rest now, heh, Mother. Be happy now." He sat by the grave and drank and ate for the first time since she had made her appearance. He stepped over the fires before extinguishing them. He boarded the very same ship sailing back. He had not spent any time sightseeing or visiting relatives and old friends except for dropping off the Parker 51. He hurried home to America, where he acted normal again, continuing his American life, and nothing like that ever happened to him again.

Another grandfather we had was Kau Goong, the ex-riverboat pirate, our grandmother's brother. When a neighbor boy called him Kau Goong too, I saw rush across the old man's face, pleasure at being the Great Uncle, a title with loft, but he said, "I'm not *your* kau goong," scornful of an American boy, a Ho Chi Kuei, who did not know the titles. Kau Goong was the longest-lived and biggest human being I had ever seen, and my mother said that Grandmother was the same size; in fact this was her younger brother. He had to duck under doorways. We tied rags around the pipes in the basement to cushion him when he hit his head; we let strips hang down to warn him. He carried trunks, stones, trees, the railroad ties. He was lucky, and won for us a TV set and a vacuum cleaner, which were raffled off at the Chinese

Community Fourth of July Annual Picnic. He also gave us Nabisco wafers, one entire box for each kid. This same Great Uncle had been a murderer in Cuba and a second-story man in New York, a city he climbed the way King Kong climbed the Empire State Building. That killing must have been done not in stealth but in hand-to-hand fight, no weapons but his enormous hands. A second-story man, we learned, clamps his mouth shut when jumping so he doesn't bite his tongue off upon landing. At the laundry Kau Goong worked without pay doing the heaviest work, which was pressing overalls and Levi's.

Another of his chores was to walk my youngest sister from kindergarten. Once when she came home alone, a wino knocked all afternoon on the doors and windows. She barricaded herself under the dining table with chairs tight all around. When we found her in there among the legs, she was still scared. After that Kau Goong met her at school and walked her to the laundry.

My brothers remember him as a generous old man; he took them to a smoking place where men with silver and wood pipes gave them presents and praised them. The only times he spoke to me were to scold and to give orders. "Bad girl," he said.

There was a day when he was shouting for me, probably to do some chore, clean house or wash dishes, rinse the rice, some routine work, which I suddenly did not want to do. I did not want to hear him order me to make a phone call or address an envelope; I would not fill out a form or take something to the laundry or whatever. I did not want to see him or hear him or be in his bossy presence. I dashed downstairs into the basement, where I locked myself into the storeroom, and sat on the stairs under the cellar door as in *The Wizard of Oz*. I liked hiding in the dark, which could be anywhere. The cellar door sloped overhead, a room within the storeroom within the basement. I listened to footsteps above the rafters. He would not come down to the basement, where he had to duck the pipes and walk stooped. I was safely tucked away among the bags of old clothes and shoes, the trunks and crates the grown-ups had brought with them from China, the seabags with the addresses in English and Chinese, the tools, the bags and bottles of seeds, the branches of seeds and leaves and pods hanging upside down, and the drying loofahs. Outside the cellar door, the pigeons purred, the chickens squawked, and a turkey and a dog, a rooster, a train made their noises. In the middle of the basement, the swing my father had hung from a beam bounced and squeaked when Kau Goong walked over it; at night ghosts played on that swing.

I thought over useless things like wishes, wands, hibernation. I talked to the people whom I knew were not really there. I became different, complete, an orphan; my partners were beautiful cowgirls, and also men, cowboys who could talk to me in conversations; I named this activity Talking Men.

But today, interrupting the conversations were the stomping and roaring overhead. "Children. Children. Where are you?" He sounded angry. But that was his usual voice. The basement ran the length of the house, and his footsteps went everywhere across the ceiling. He was stomping from room to room, opening and slamming doors, closet doors too. I stretched my legs out on the cement and put one elbow on the highest step, my back against one wall and toes against the other. I belonged here; everything was my size. The air smelled of anise from the drying stalks. Kau Goong was calling out our names one by one. I wondered where my brothers and sisters were; one of them ought to be answering by now. If one of them answered, Kau Goong would forget about me. But I heard no reply. Maybe they were hiding in other places – the ledge along the top of the neighbor's goose pen, which was roofless but tall enough for the lazy geese not to fly away, or under the grape leaves on top of the pigeon coop, or on top of wardrobes, behind the boxes. We had many special places. My brothers and sisters were good at chores too, but Kau Goong mostly called me because I was the oldest and took blames. A long time had passed, and he was still calling. He did not give up; he would not forget about it. We had to be there somewhere; the front door had been open, that was how he had got in, and so somebody had to be home.

The longer he looked, I realized, the less plausibly I'd be able to step out of the basement and say, acting natural, "Yes, Kau Goong, were you calling me?" I tried the appropriate facial expression, erased guile and worry from my face, casually said, "Here I am." But then he would say, "Where have you been?" And then what would I say? I couldn't say, "I was in the bathroom." He had checked every room. I couldn't say, "I was watering the yard," or "I was feeding the chickens and rabbits," because he had made the rounds of the yard too. I had seen his legs at the basement windows.

Then his footsteps came across the kitchen and down the basement stairs. He would know I was in the storeroom – I had latched the door from the inside. Trapped. How dumb. Stupid. If he found me while I was doing something of use like sweeping out the basement or restacking the lumber or roller skating on the concrete or drawing on the walls, then all would have been right, but to be found doing nothing, to be found hiding, I could not explain. He walked past the storeroom door. Through its screen, I saw him from the shoulders to the waist, the rolled-up sleeves over the long arms. He growled; he lumbered past. I darted out of the corner, unlatched the door, and hid again. Even if he opened the door and looked in, maybe I could count on his eyes not being used to the dark. He walked to the end of the basement. He shouted into the corners. He walked over to the pile of sawdust which we used to outline borders when we played Cities, walked around the Texas rice, the onion pile, the potato pile, and the woodpile of boards and railroad ties. The upright stakes were transfixing vampires. Over where there were treasures buried underneath the front stairs (I had buried some myself in cigar boxes), he roared my name several times. I should either stay hidden or come out. Miraculously, he passed the door again without looking inside. I didn't feel sorry for him calling through an empty house, and it was not as if my name were a tether to me, but I got up, opened the door, and said to his big back, "Hello, Kau Goong. Did I hear you calling me?" Then scooted around him and ran up the stairs. "Yes," he said. From the basement he would only be able to see my feet. "Oh, here and there," I mumbled in case he was saying, "Where were you?" "I was just on my way to finish my work," I said, sweeping something into the dustpan I'd grabbed. He did not scold me taking so long to answer. I must have fooled him.

When he was over ninety, and his forehead grown very high, his wife, Great Aunt, wrote to him: "Now we're surely in our old age. Why don't you come back, and let's spend a few years together before we die." But in China he would have to have a hole drilled in his head and warm soapy water slooshed through, brainwashed into a Communist. He would have to stand up night after night without sleep until his brain turned Communist. Great Aunt wrote, however, that the Communists had quit breaking up families; men no longer lived in separate houses from women. Some children had been taught to inform on their parents, but some were only pretending they'd do so. Now that families were reuniting, couldn't the two of them also meet again? "You only have a few years left anyway," she wrote, "so don't be afraid of plane crashes or ships sinking. Haven't you had your life of adventure? Now it's time to come home."

"What are you going to do?" asked my mother, who read him his letters.

"Who knows?" he roared and stomped out of the house to his room at the Benevolent Association, so he wouldn't have to discuss this going back to China.

"What do you think he should do?" MaMa asked. "If he goes back to China, he'll see his wife again. But he may have to suffer Communism and famines. And we'll never see him again." We children thought about Kau Goong finding the way street by street to an ocean, then over the Atlantic or the Pacific, then distinguishing the coast of Asia from Africa. Finding was a power not a one of us had, and we too had to go someday on that same quest, for which our mother had made us memorize the directions in syllables. "If he stays here," MaMa analyzed, "he'll grow old and never see his wife again, but he'll always have food to eat." There was no question of Great Aunt coming here, against the law to leave Communist China, also against the law to enter the United States. "She's so old too," MaMa said. "On the other hand, they saw each other when they were young and not again for the rest of their lifetimes; what difference does it make if they don't see each other a little longer? It would only be a sentimental indulgence." *If*, *old*, *but* – terrible words. Gapping, gaping spaces. Two old people with a planet between them, and the planet unfathomable with its hunger and wars and laws.

One day MaMa said, "He ought to go back," and I did not see how she came to this conclusion, what bridges of reasoning she took to arrive at it, why this conclusion was better than the other possibility. It must have been Father who had decided and she was doing the announcing. "You must go back, Kau Goong," she said. "Here you're all alone. What use are you here?" She asked him several times, "What have you decided?" But his growl didn't sound like a Yes or a No. He left the house without talking about the decision he had to make and did not visit again for a week or two.

Then she told us, "Kau Goong has decided he's not going back." *Never, forever* – two more terrible words.

"Why?" I asked. "How did he decide that? Why? How come?"

So Great Aunt, who was also more than ninety years old, saved seventy-five dollars and bribed a farmer, who hid her under the potatoes in his cart, and he smuggled her out of Communist China. "I could hear the border guard talking with the farmer," she wrote. "They even talked about people hiding in sacks – under potatoes. 'Eyes among the eyes,' they said. Then they laughed, and we went on. A donkey drew the cart. I'm now in Hong Kong. You don't have to worry about Communists any more. They're not of any consideration whatsoever. We can spend our old age in Hong Kong. I'll wait for you here." I wondered, if she had been hiding under corn would they have said, "Ears among the ears," whether Chinese also think corn comes in ears.

More weeks passed while the adults thought over this new development. He has to go now, I thought; he cannot leave her alone and old in a foreign country. But Great Uncle, who was standing by the window, the profile of his big head against the glass and peach trees, the long tendons of his neck stretching, his big Adam's apple bobbing, said, "I've decided to stay in California." He said, "California. This is my home. I belong here." He turned and, looking at us, roared, "We belong here."

My mother wrote Great Aunt about the decision. Not much later, Great Aunt wrote that she had bribed another farmer to smuggle her back into China. Another seventy-five dollars. She said she was not going to spend the rest of her life alone in a strange city. Her return was a clue that Red China couldn't have been as horrible as everyone made out.

Not many years after his decision, Great Uncle grew shorter and thinner, though he was still bigger than most people. He did not appear for dinner one day, and he was dead.

We and the old men sat in rows at the funeral. Some of the old men were: the storekeeper who had torn up his accounts and stopped keeping them when he saw he was not getting ahead, the delivery man who whistled on leaves, the hatchet man who sang opera, the artist uncle who said how paper and pencil are cheap and how inexpensive it is to be an artist, the piano player who lived in the basement and played without depressing the keys so as not to disturb the people upstairs, the Old Man of the North disguised as Uncle Camel Face, the uncle who lived with the Mexican lady, and Uncle Bing Sun Who Laughed Twice (which rhymes). They wore their brown or blue jackets and sweaters; some took off their tweed caps, and others kept them on. Only my father wore a matching suit. I thought about myself dying and about parents dying. We were the only children; the old men admired children.

MaMa sat for a moment, then left, hurried back with four dented buckets filled with sand. She stuck incense sticks any old how into the sand and put the buckets around the coffin. She lit the incense and sat down, having filled the room with smells and broken up the symmetry of the demon mortuary. I looked at the mortician demons, who stood in the back of the room, to see if they were going to upbraid her and remove the buckets. The coffin was brown and very long as if it were made with doors nailed together. He was that tall; he was inside. One old man, then another one, stood up, walked in front of the coffin, and made a speech. They seemed to speak in a higher language than when talking to children; I did not understand most of what they said. Perhaps on this serious occasion, they did not put things into many synonyms until they hit on one a kid could understand. I listened to find out more about Kau Goong's pillages, his plunders, and sackings, and for some details about how he had killed a man, but they did not mention his crimes though he was safe from deportation now. I should have yelled questions at him. I shouldn't have hidden from him. He was almost a hundred years old; Chinese live a long time – to do many things and to make their ages span the legal immigration dates. The old men and a politician told how Kau Goong had come to the Gold Mountain and stayed. He was a Gold Mountain Man. They said "Gold Mountain" a lot, "Gum Sahn" many times. "Long time Califoon," they said in English.

Mad Sao wept. I did not think that men had feelings; it was women who missed people, minded the distances, the time, and cared about whether or not they saw someone again. But Mad Sao was an unusual man.

After the speeches, the mourners got up to go, but when the demons saw everybody leaving, they started nabbing pall-bearers. We hadn't known we were to designate some. My parents asked the old men to carry the coffin, my father asking and my mother tugging them by the sleeves. They were doing us a favor saying Yes, not wanting to do it, reluctant to associate with death. The white demons handed them white gloves, which the men shoved their splintery hands into. There must have been a demon taboo against touching a coffin with one's bare hands. Father, Mad Sao, and four men not in our family each took a coffin handle and, fumbling and stumbling, jostled it between the chairs and out the door. It wasn't like the processions in the movies but like moving furniture, some pallbearers facing forward and some backward, bumping out the door and down the steps, then lifting the big coffin into the hearse.

The limousine unfolded inside; jump seats came up out of the floor and the walls. My mother walked around to the windows in back – we were like the children who ride in station wagons – and gave us strips of white paper the size of dollar bills. "Throw this money out the window," she said, but she was unceremonious; I thought it would be better to dole the "money" out, scatter it in intervals along the way, not just dump it. "Use it up," was all she said. We would not have to save any of it. Luxury. We divided the paper evenly amongst us. "Wait until the car starts so that it'll fly," we instructed one another.

When the car moved, we flung out a few white bills, budgeting them so that we would not run out before reaching the cemetery. For lack of adult explanations, we children made up what was happening. "It's for him to spend in heaven," we said. It may have also been for the waif ghosts lining the streets, or it was like a carrot on a stick to entice Kau Goong, who was lingering behind or hovering overhead, to the cemetery. The hearse, the vegetable trucks, the pickup trucks, and Mad Sao's automobile moved in procession through Stockton. We drove to the places where Kau Goong went when he was alive as if we were following him on his rounds, very slowly, as if gathering him in. His ghost was not to stay at the club where he smoked his water pipe or at the school, where he waited to pick us up. We drove to our house and paused there, engines running. Perhaps he'd come for his things – the trunk and wicker baskets that he had brought from China, his water gourd, his ceramic jug, the rags on the pipes, the TV set, the vacuum cleaner – that is, the invisible duplicates of these things, or perhaps he'd left some of his anima in them and was collecting that. "We're taking him on a last look," we explained to one another. "Or we're looking for him." We next drove to Chinatown, where we idled in front of the Benevolent Association. In the window of his room on the second floor, the gauze curtains were slightly parted and still. His room overlooked the square where the hoboes and winos slept under the palm trees. On one side of the square was the Chinese school, whose classrooms were also on the second floor; he had heard us at our lessons and seen us lean on the balconies. On the other side of the square was the Catholic church, where the hoboes and winos were lined up for lunch an hour ahead of time; a cop walked by with his dog, and the poor men stiffened to attention like an army. One of them drank water out of the gutter. Beneath Kau Goong's room was the store where the old men sat out on the sidewalk among the big tin cans full of tofu and bean sprouts and live snails and turtles; the bench between the parking meters was empty, the sitters at the funeral. Next to the store was the closed-up place that used to be our gambling house. Next to that was the herbalist's, and at the corner was the Filipino grocery store. At the other corner was the demon liquor store all lit up no matter what time of day or night; in the window, a black scotty and a white scotty, run by batteries behind the cardboard, wagged their tails and tongues. A loudspeaker mounted above the door played country music loud enough for everyone to hear. Once I was crossing the street and heard machine-gun fire full blast and a grenade and a long scream – "Aaaaaa!" – then the announcer saying, "Another G.I. shot down in battle," more shooting and the scream again, striking me stock-still in the intersection. We did not drive through the middle of Chinatown, which was the one block with the uncles' businesses on both sides of the street. The cars crossed Washington Street, and from the intersection we looked down Chinatown at the grocery stores, the butcher shops, the shoe store, the restaurants, the candy-and-tobacco store. Leaving Skid Row, we drove to the laundry, where we slowed a moment and then sped onto the highway. The wind twisted the white money, pulled it out of our hands, and carried it away. It went whipping and spinning over the alfalfa fields, and caught in the fruit trees and the tumbleweeds.

We stopped at the Chinese cemetery, which is not on a hillside in China but beside Interstate 5 on the flat San Joaquin Valley floor. The pallbearing uncles carried the coffin and lowered it into the grave. We may have been one man short, for a demon helped carry. The mortician demons threw their white gloves into the grave, and so the uncles did too. As she does wherever she goes, my mother brought food, which she arranged on the ground around the grave. It was like birthday food, the whole chicken, pork, beef, vegetables. She filled a shot glass with whiskey; my father poured it into the grave and bowed three times. She refilled the glass and did that too. Then, according to her directions, starting with my oldest brother, who was younger than I, and ending with the girls, each of us kids poured a glass of the amber and fumy whiskey into the blackening dirt and on the coffin, and bowed three times. Whenever we had to do this bowing at political meetings or assemblies at Chinese school, we kids giggled. Now I felt my body slop and shuffle, lean crooked on one foot like an informal American punk – there being something wrong with bowing, something embarrassing, awkward. Not looking at one another, we did some quick nods.

My mother burned Kau Goong's clothes and shoes in the black incinerator at the end of a row of graves. I looked inside the grate; I saw black shoes and red mouths, blood and eyes. She shut the lid before I finished looking. She gave us and the pallbearers red paper with money inside; it was to end the death and begin the luck again.

We went to the big expensive restaurant in the middle of Chinatown, where my parents ordered a moderate amount of food, not like the profusion at wedding banquets. I thought it typical of us to order stingily, but it was only lunch, and we had the grave food left over. As if there were no funeral a moment ago, the adults laughed, talked, ate.

When we got home, we did not burn a pile of leaves and newspapers at the curb. We were modern. We children had seen such piles and women stoking them. When we asked, "Is it so that the ghost won't follow you in? Is it so that you're no longer contagious?" the adults scolded, "It's nothing. Don't talk about it." We went directly indoors, a relief not to be jumping over fire like Indians or Africans or South Seas Islanders in front of the neighbors and passersby.

That was the only time our family went to the cemetery. Other families go every year and even twice a year to bring food, flowers, and paper to their relatives. They eat with or for the dead. "Superstitious backward peasants," my parents say. "We don't have that custom in our family," MaMa says proudly. "Nothing happens to you after you die. You just disappear. No afterlife. Right?" "Right," says BaBa. We treat Kau Goong and any other grandfathers who may be in that cemetery like any American dead.

I had a dream about Kau Goong one morning. MaMa asked, "What did he say?" I couldn't remember and was tempted to make up something extravagant. "Sometimes there's a message," she said. In another family, a grandfather came to one of them in a dream and said that the kids were to bury their parents correctly; after that they would be absolved of all duties to ancestors since they were now Americans.

We had an uncle, a second or third cousin maybe, who went back to China to be a Communist. We called him Uncle Bun, which might have been his name, but could also be a pun, Uncle Stupid. He was a blood relative and not just a villager. He was very talkative. In fact, he hardly ever stopped talking, and we kids watched the spit foam at the corners of his mouth. He came to the laundry and sat, or if it was very hot, he stood near the door to talk and talk. It was more like a lecture than a conversation. He repeated himself so often that some of what he said seeped into the ears. He talked about wheat germ. "You ought to eat wheat germ," he said, "because wheat germ is the most potent food in the world. Eat it and you'll stay young for a long time; you'll never get sick. You'll be beautiful and tall and strong, also intelligent. The reason for so much unhappiness and strife is that people have been eating wrong. Meat turns them into animals. Wheat germ, which we can digest easier, can help us evolve into better people. Wheat germ is full of vitamins (*why-huh-ming*), and it is very cheap. A, C, thiamine, riboflavin, niacin, calcium, carbohydrates, fats, iron (*eye-yun*)." He was a scientific and up-to-date man who used English scientific terms. In two weighty syllables, both equally accented, a spondee, he said "Wheat Germ." Wheat germ would fatten up my father and also fatten up all the skinny children. Unlike the rest of the men in the family, who were thin and had white hair, this uncle was round and bald with black hair above his ears and around the back of his head. He wore a pearl gray three-piece suit and a necktie with a gold tiepin, the gold chain of his pocket watch linking one vest pocket to the other, the last button of his vest open over his prosperous paunch. He opened his eyes wide to see everything through his round gold-framed eyeglasses.

"Wheat germ – you can put it into any food," he said. "Sprinkle it on the rice and strew it on all the accompaniments. Stir it into milk and juices. Drink it in soups and beverages; it melts right in. Mix it with ice cream and strawberries. Combine it with flour. Combine it with rice. Beat it into cakes and pancakes. Scatter it on fried eggs for a crunchy texture. You can eat it by itself. Eat it by the handful, cooked or raw. Add it to cold food or hot food, sauces and gravies. Rain it on vegetables. Coat fish, meat, and fowl with it. Use it as a binder in meatballs and fishcakes. It goes with anything." Wheat germ. I could not imagine this miracle food, whether it was sweet or salty, what size it was, what it was, what color, whether it tasted good. Was it a liquid or a solid? Was *germ* the same germ as in bacteria? "Wheat germ is golden brown," he said, "though the color blends with whatever you're cooking. A pinch of it changes regular food into a medicine." It sounded like a fairy-tale elixir, fairy food. "You cannot taste or detect its presence in other foods," he said. "Yet you can eat it by itself like cornflakes," which he also pronounced spondaically in his accent, *Coon Flex*. "Wheat germ is the heart of the wheat," he said, "the heart of bread and wheat, which is more nutritious in the first place than rice. It repairs broken parts and tissues."

"Hum," said my father and mother.

"We ought to buy some, don't you think?" I asked my parents, hating to ask them to spend more money, but we might be wasting away from the lack of a vital food.

"He's crazy," my mother said. "Anything that necessary has to have been invented long ago."

He brought us some sample wheat germ, which tasted like raw peas or raw oats.

Although he was about my father's age, Uncle Bun, like many of the old men, did not appear to have a job and was able to afford entire mornings, afternoons, days, and evenings sitting and chatting while we worked. Maybe his sons sent money from Chicago. My father did join him talking politics, a man's topic as gray as newspapers. They talked about Sun Yat Sen and Chiang Kai Shek and Mao Tse Tung, about their moves and countermoves, their strategies, the Red Army and the White Army, and the Japanese maneuvering here, marching there, meeting and retreating, circling, war for years. My father scoffed at Chiang and Mao, at their ineptness. Their inconsistencies made him laugh. Since Sun's death, nobody could unite China.

"The way Chiang solves poverty is to print paper money," my father said.

"We have to examine the causes of poverty," said Uncle Bun. "The world has never experimented to find out if it is rich enough and big enough to support all its people. It probably is. Look at all the rich people who own too much, and you can see there's extra food, land, and money. And certainly, there's always work enough. Only the distribution is wrong; we have to divide up the goods evenly." We kids divided every five-cent candy bar and all the chores. "Who really owns the land?" he asked. "The man who farms it with his sweat and piss or the man whose name is on the paper? And shouldn't the worker on the assembly line own his labor and the results of his labor?"

"The farmers should own the land," he answered himself. "The workers should own the factories – and the profits. The rich pigs turn profit into extra cars, ostrich-feather hats, and golf parks. When it ought to be distributed as food among the poor. We have the airplanes and ships and trains for the distribution. The true purpose of the diesel engine is to rush food to everyone on every continent and island. Every child has the right to food."

"And would the owners, landlords, and bosses voluntarily give away their holdings?" asked my father. "And the house-wives their slaves?"

"Yes!" shouted Uncle Bun. "Either we educate them, to see the right way, or we, the poor of the earth, will take what's ours by revolution. The takeover by the poor is inevitable. The poor become more and more numerous as the rich become fewer. Haven't you noticed how many poor people there are and how few rich? We will overcome them with our numbers. I get so angry that a boss can deny a worker his job. Why should another man own my muscles and brains and what I make with my hands and my time?" He told again about some fight he had had with the boss at one of his past jobs, his face red and his spit spraying. "How dare he treat me like that? I'm a man and he's a man. In a fair system, the worker would be the more valuable man, and the supervisor serve him and make his job easier."

My father had ideas too but merely an observation here and there that changed from day to day. Uncle Bun said the white demons were not the only oppressors, that upper-class Chinese made their money off lower-class ones; the immi-grants got twenty-five cents an hour if they were lucky. No day off. We children made exactly twenty-five cents an hour.

"You're in trouble at the cannery if the forelady is Chinese," my mother agreed. "She'll make trouble for you to impress the boss." (*Fo-laydee, chup-bo* – trouble – *bossu, day offu,* Chinese American words.)

"Actually these aren't dreams or plans," Uncle Bun said. "I'm making predictions about ineluctabilities. This Beautiful Nation, this Gold Mountain, this America will end as we know it. There will be one nation, and it will be a world nation. A united planet. Not just Russian Communism. Not just Chinese Communism. World Communism."

He said, "When we don't need to break our bodies earning our daily living any more, and we have time to think, we'll write poems, sing songs, develop religions, invent customs, build statues, plant gardens, and make a perfect world." He paused to contemplate the wonders.

"Isn't that great?" I said after he left.

"Don't get brainwashed," said my mother. "He's going to get in trouble for talking like that. He's going to get us in trouble; the barbarians think that Communists and Chinese are the same."

Even when the uncles were killed during the Revolution and the aunts tortured, Uncle Bun did not change his mind about Communism. "We have to weigh the death of a few against the lives of millions of poor workers and the coming generations," he said.

"A fermentation of dreams," said my father. Uncle Bun should not have said such Communist things against our dead relatives. His fingers followed the gold chain to the gold watch in his vest pocket; he looked at the time and left. BaBa snorted, "Foolish man. Silly man. Long winded." "Long winded," the same metaphor in Chinese and English. "Fermenting dreams," said Baba. "Dreams fermenting." I heard in his scorn and words how dreams ferment the way yeast and mold do, how dreams are like fungus.

Next time Uncle Bun came over, he said that Mao himself had had to leave his sick wife and child behind on the Long March, his dedication to Communism that strong. With spit flying, Uncle Bun talked about the glory of the Long March. The lame and weak sacrificed their bodies for use as ladders and fords so that others could leap mountains and rivers. Yes, some of his own family – our family – had given their lives too, though unwillingly. He talked about five-year plans. It frightened me that someone could keep something in mind for five years – keeping track for five years.

"Ah, sad, sad America, which does not respect the poor," he said. "The poor are important. And look, look, even if we distribute everything, and it's spread so thin that we're all poor – that's good. Consider the culture we poor have invented – vegetarianism and fasting, pencil sketches, pottery, singing without instruments, mending, saving and reusing things, quilting, patchwork, the poetry written on leaves, rocks, and walls, acrobatics, dancing, and kung fu, which doesn't require expensive sports equipment. Oh, let's value the poor, who in a way are all of us. Even with money, the rich can't buy good food. They eat white bread and poisoned food. What they ought to do is eat wheat germ."

Amazing! His two big ideas – wheat germ and Communism – connected.

His ideas had come together neater and neater as the months and years passed. "Not just China," he said, "and not just America, but the world. We will organize the entire world. End world hunger. And we will have world peace." What scope. What neatness. World peace. How amazingly his ideas connected up.

Then one day, he announced in a whisper, "The milk demon is poisoning me. The grocer demon is poisoning me. They have a plot against me. They put poison in my milk and eggs."

My mother said, "It's impossible to inject poison into eggs. Look how perfect the shells are."

But he said, "Science. Science can do anything."

When he connected his two big ideas, he touched wrong wires to each other, shot off sparks, and shorted out. He had become a paranoiac. "They're trying to poison me," he said, running into the laundry, his red face bursting above the collar and tie. "I've discovered their plot. They think they can get away with it but because of the sharp senses I've developed on wheat germ, I can detect poisons. I smelled the poison, and did not eat or drink it. I've discontinued milk delivery, and I'm going to buy groceries at a different store." He looked canny. "Why do you suppose they're after me?" he asked. "It must be because I've hit on the truth and discovered the plot against the poor. And so they want to get me." He entered rooms as if pursued, stepping in and out of doorways, checking behind him, peeping out of windows, and pressing his back to walls. He continually surveyed the street. "I've noticed a pattern," he said. "They put the poison into white food – eggs, bread, milk, vanilla ice cream, flour, sugar, white beans. They're thinking that the seeming purity of white food would fool me, and it would disguise the poison, but I know that they have developed an invisible dissolvable poison. I'm outsmarting them. I'll shop at a different store every day. I'll keep changing stores."

"He's gone crazy," my mother diagnosed. "He's getting crazier. When he comes to the house, and we're at the laundry, you kids don't let him in."

He became more and more agitated. "I saw the wholesale demon open a bottle of milk. Yes, I saw him lift the lid. He dropped in a pellet of poison. I could tell by the way he cupped his hand. Then he pressed the lid back on. Sleight of hand. Lately the tops of milk bottles have been looser. That's evidence. And today's evidence is that I saw the wholesale demon tampering with the vacuum seal. He placed the bottle in the exact spot where I had picked my last bottle. They're out to get me because –" and he held his breath on "because" – "I am a Communist." "FBI," he whispered. "Secret police. House Un-American Activities Committee. Coconut. Inside the husk. They've even gotten inside the coconut with their scientific know-how."

"His head is a coconut," said BaBa.

Another day Uncle Bun came in, said nothing, sat. His face was red and purple. "How much did you spend for the kids' bikes?" he asked. "Where did you get the extra money? Roller skates. Then bikes." He whirled on my father, poked his face and finger at him. "Where's my money?" he shouted.

"I don't know," said BaBa. "Did you lose your money?"

"Half the money is gone from my savings account," he shouted. He looked as if he were in a fit, his mouth foaming. Breathing, snorting, bursting, he yelled, "Where is it?" His round body expanded.

"You shouldn't be accusing me," said BaBa, and continued ironing. "Banks are very careful," he said. "No one can get your money without your signature and your passbook. Did you lose your passbook and your I.D.'s?"

"No, I didn't lose my passbook and my I.D.'s," said Uncle Bun, imitating hatefully. "You took them, and you withdrew my money. You disguised yourself as me. They see a chinaman and can't tell it's not me. You know a lot about hand-writing, you forger." Then he stopped explaining. "Give me my money," he shouted. He took his glasses off. Red shot out of his eyes. "Give me back my money." He had changed from the jolly roly-poly man; I had not seen him jolly for quite a while. My mother had stopped letting him take the baby for walks, but lately he had not asked to baby-sit her either. "Thief!" he yelled. As in other emergencies, we kids kept working steadily, acting normal so that the rest of the world would return to normal too. I wished that my father would say soft, cajoling words, even pay him some money, but that was part of the fear too, that my father does not give in. "You walked into the bank with my passbook, and you took half, thinking that I wouldn't notice. You thought I was going mad and had forgotten how to add and subtract. You're very good at pen and abacus. I see you. I know you. You did it. Give me back the money, or I'll call the cops. Then you'll be sorry."

He was a hard, perverse man. He might just do that, call the police and get us deported. A man crazy enough to be glad that his relatives had been killed by Communists was capable of treachery.

"Why don't you phone your son long distance in Chicago?" said BaBa. "Tell him what happened. Or why don't you go to Chicago and stay with him until you feel better?"

"I don't see how I'm going to have money for train fare with you siphoning it. How long have you been dipping in, huh? A little at a time or one lump sum? I'm going to the cops."

"Why don't you look at the dates in the passbook?" said my father.

"I'm going to the police station," said Uncle Bun and ran out.

"He may get violent," said my mother. "Don't let him in the house."

He returned to the laundry the next day for further accusations, his open passbook in his hand, pointed at figures, and shouted out numbers. "Proof!" he said. "Proof!" and slapped the little book with the back of his hand.

BaBa took the passbook and studied it. "Look. There are no entries in the withdrawal column."

"Of course not. You didn't do it with this passbook. You did it so that it wouldn't show on this passbook. You told them you had lost the passbook. You filled out a special form."

"I'll go to the bank with you," said BaBa. He was taking Uncle Bun very seriously, setting down his iron, offering to take a break from work for him.

"Just watch it," said Uncle Bun. "When they see the two of us together, they'll put you in jail. They'll know which is really me." Which was very crazy; they looked the opposite of each other. When they returned from the bank, Uncle Bun had stopped talking about missing money.

He did come to our house one day when neither of our parents were home. Unfortunately, the front door was wide open, so we couldn't hide and pretend we were out. It would be embarrassing to tell him why he couldn't come in. Being the oldest, I decided that we children would go outside and talk to him on the porch. It was pleasant out there under the grapevines. We stood between him and the red door and asked him questions to distract him. He usually walked right in. "What exactly is wheat germ?" we asked, but he seemed not as interested in wheat germ as before. "How's shopping at the new grocery store?" "Fine. Fine," he said. "May I have a drink of water?" he asked. "We'll get it," we said, some of us blocking his way while one ran inside, very rude, a guest having to ask for refreshments. He drank the entire glassful quickly. "You must finish all your water," he advised us. "When you have milk, finish all of it. Finish your food. Eat everything. Don't leave scraps. Scraps turn into garbage. Food one moment, garbage the next. Same with paper. Don't blotch it, and if you do, save it for scratch paper. Cross out the mistakes rather than crumple the paper. Make every page count." He did not go berserk, did not break into the house and throw himself against the sofa like a padded cell, did not act like a maniac at all. He sounded like other adults, advising this, advising that, advising eat.

At the laundry, where it would be dangerous to run amok among the hot machines, he announced: "*They* are not *only* hiding the poison in my food. I am on the verge of discovering the *real* plot. Have you noticed – oh, surely, you must have been alarmed by it – you must have seen how many garbage demons there are in this country?" "Yes, there are," said my mother. "Do you see," he asked, "how the white demons are very careful with garbage? And how much garbage there is?"

Now, our family knew a great deal about garbage and how much of it was not garbage at all. On our way home on garbage nights, we visited bins that belonged to the stores and found valuables – mannequin heads and hands, sheet music, hats, magazines, comics, English-language news-papers, a cardboard Eiffel Tower, the black and white scotties, books of rug samples, Christmas card samples, wallpaper, perfectly good boxes. To lower our garbage bill, we left a sack or two of our own garbage – marrowed bones, papers written on front and back, shoes that couldn't be repaired. At the grocery stores, we found carrots and lettuce for our rabbits, the outer leaves for the rabbits. Sometimes we split up to cover the route faster, meeting one another with loot at another corner. So we understood garbage better than most people.

"The white demons are very careful with garbage, aren't they?" said Uncle Bun. "The city pays men to sweep the gutters and pick up paper with a stick and nail. They attach wire baskets to the signal poles, and on other street corners they have tax-paid trash cans right next to the mailboxes. And every week, regularly, on a highly organized schedule, teams of garbage demons come to each house and collect garbage. Truckloads." All this we agreed to seeing, and it did not, after all, seem crazy. You could see what he was talking about for yourself. "Have you ever thought about what they're saving the garbage for?" he asked. "What are they doing with it? Why are they so diligent? Today I saw children put their candy wrappers in their lunchboxes. And the hoboes who pick up cigarette butts and put them in their pockets – do you assume they're going to smoke them later? There has got to be a purpose behind this storing up and bagging and chuting. Have you seen the buildings with chutes? Garbage from every floor plunges to the basement. The government pays armies of collectors to take it somewhere for a purpose."

"They take it to the dump," my mother said. "They leave it there in heaps, which they burn. They take wet garbage from restaurants and feed it to pigs. Or they use it for fertilizer. They re-pulp paper and make newspaper."

"Oh, you think so?" he asked. "Have you ever seen any of this paper-making? Have you ever followed the garbage truck when it leaves your house? Too early in the morning for you to bother, isn't it? Have you seen any of these restaurant pigs?" Then he left very mysteriously, abruptly.

A few days later he again came running into the laundry. He was highly excited and frightened, as if he were being chased. "I've discovered what they do with the garbage." He was sweating. "They're collecting it for me. They're going to feed it to me. They'll capture me and tie me down and shovel it into my mouth. They're going to make me eat it. All of it. It's all for me. You must see what a big plot it is. Everybody is manufacturing garbage constantly, some knowing the purpose and some just because everyone else is doing it. It all ties in with the poisoning, don't you see? The newspapers and radios are in on it too, telling them to buy, buy, and then they turn everything they buy into garbage as fast as they can. They're preparing and saving for the day when they'll shovel it into my mouth. They've been collecting for years, and I didn't see the plot till now. That day is coming soon. They'll make me eat it."

"Why should they do that to you?" asked my mother.

"Because of my talk about Communism," he said.

"The garbage is not for you," said my father. "The garbage isn't that important. You're not that important. Forget the garbage."

"You should go to a mind doctor," said my mother.

He got offended and left. "You'll be sorry when the day arrives, and you see it all come true. Feeding day."

His stomach got thinner. He refused most food; he ate only greens and browns, leaving not a scrap, not contributing to the garbage that "they" would feed him later. "Paper garbage too," he said. "Paper cups, paper plates, paper napkins, Kleenex, gum and gum wrappers."

At last he said, "I'm going back to China. I've outsmarted them. I know which day the feeding will be on, and I'll leave before then. It was not like this in China. Remember? In fact, they couldn't poison your milk and bread because we didn't drink milk; only babies drank milk. And we didn't eat much bread. We used everything thoroughly in China. Remember? There was hardly any garbage. We ate all the food. Remember how we could see with our own eyes that the hogs ate the peelings? If the human beings didn't eat rinds, the animals did, and the fish bones got plowed into the fields. Remember how paper gatherers collected paper that had writing on it and burned it in word furnaces? Remember we saved the bags and boxes? Why, this –" he picked up a cornflakes box – "we would have treasured a pretty box like this, such bright colors, such sturdy cardboard. We would have opened the flaps carefully and used it to store valuable and useful things in. We'd have taken good care of it, made it last, handed it down. I'm going back to New Society Village."

"But New Society Village isn't there any more," said MaMa. "It's been Communized. You'd have to sleep in a men's barracks and eat in a dining hall with hundreds of strangers. You'd have to eat whatever they cook. The Communists will take away your bank account."

"That's right," he said, and he blinked as if clearing his eyes. "That's the way the world should be."

From that decision on, he acted saner and saner, happier, and stopped talking about the garbage except to say, "I'm returning to China before feeding day." "Returning" is not to say that he necessarily had ever been there before.

He talked about how he was using only a part of his money for passage and giving the rest to the new China. If they were suspicious of his years in America and did not let him in, he would sneak in from Hong Kong.

The day he left, he spoke to my youngest sister, who was about three years old. He bent over so that she could hear and see him very well. "Don't forget me, will you?" he asked. "Remember I used to play with you. Remember I'm the man who sang songs to you and gave you dimes. What's my name?" She laughed that he would ask her such a silly, easy question. Of course, she knew his name. He coaxed her to say it several times for him. "You won't forget? Tell me you won't forget."

"I won't forget," she said. He seemed satisfied to leave, and we never saw him or heard from him again.

For a while I reminded my sister, "Do you remember Uncle Bun, the bald fat man who talked a lot? Do you remember him asking you not to forget him?"

"Oh, yes, the funny man. I remember."

I reminded her periodically. But one day, I noticed that I had not asked her for some time. "Do you remember the funny man who talked a lot, the one who smuggled himself into Red China?"

"Who?" she asked.

"Uncle Bun. Remember?"

"No," she said.

With no map sense, I took a trip by myself to San Francisco Chinatown and got lost in the Big City. Wandering in a place very different from our own brown and gray Chinatown, I suddenly heard my own real aunt calling my name. She was my youngest aunt, my modern aunt just come from Hong Kong. We screamed at each other the way our villagers do, hugged, held hands. "Have you had your rice yet?" we shouted. "I have. I have had my rice." "Me too. I've eaten too," letting the whole strange street know we had eaten, and me becoming part of the street, abruptly not a tourist, the street mine to shout in, never mind if my accent be different. She had been talking with a couple of women, to whom I said, "Hello, Aunt. Hello, Aunt," mumbling because there are different kinds of aunts depending on whether they're older or younger than one's mother. They'd tease you for being too distant, for addressing them as Lady or Mademoiselle, affectations, and also for being familiar.

"Who is this?" the women asked, one of them pointing at me with her chin, the other with her rolled up newspaper. This talking about me in the third person, this pointing at me – I shoved the resentment down my throat. They do not mean disdain – or they *do* mean disdain, but it's their proper way of treating young people. Mustn't dislike them for it.

"This is my own actual niece come to visit me," my aunt said, as if I had planned to run into her all along. The women were to understand that I was not just somebody she called a niece out of politeness, but a blood niece. "Come see my new apartment," she said to me, turned around, and entered the doorway near which we were standing.

I followed her up the stairs, flight after flight, and along a hallway like a tunnel. But her apartment need not be dismal, I thought; these doors could open into surprisingly large, bright, airy apartments with shag carpets. "Our apartment is very small," she warned, her voice leading the way. "Not like a regular house. Not like your mother's big house." So she noticed space; I had thought perhaps people from Hong Kong didn't need room, that Chinese people preferred small spaces. Some early mornings if we went down into our basement, we found two straight-backed chairs facing one another, blankets and shawls still cupped in shapes of the women who had sat there. The cord of the electric heater rose to a ceiling socket. Coffee cups and footstools sat on the floor. Our mother and this aunt had stayed up all night talking again. I might have known from the good times they could have in the basement that it would be the smallest apartment I had seen in my life. The door didn't open up all the way because of a table, which had stuff stored on top and underneath. The half of the table away from the wall was cleared for eating and studying.

"Coffee? Tea?" Auntie asked.

"Coffee," I said. "Black."

"How can you drink it like that? How about some meat? Fish?"

"MaMa has started drinking it black," I said, giving her the news. "MaMa has switched to black at her age."

Big and medium-sized blonde dolls sat and stood on tops of stacks of things. Their pink gauze dresses fluffed against the cellophane windows of their cardboard boxes. They were expensive dolls with little socks and gloves, purses and hats. I felt very relieved that my cousin, who was about ten or twelve years old, did not have to share one doll, the naked kind that one had to make clothes out of scraps for; she had two bride dolls. My relatives were not bad off, not as poor as we used to be. They had luxuries.

Auntie went into the kitchen, which did not have room for another person. I snooped about at the desk in one corner of the living room; looked at the desk calendar and the statuettes of the guardians of Happiness, Money, and Long Life, read the appointments pinned among the cut-outs of flowers on the wall. It was this aunt who had given my mother a nice set of the guardians mounted on wood and red velvet. There were some Christian pamphlets on a shelf over the desk; I couldn't remember whether this was the aunt who had converted to Christianity and was sending my parents tracts and Bibles or whether it was another aunt in Hong Kong who was sending to both of them. Or maybe she'd been accosted by a missionary working Chinatown. ("Are you a Christian?" my mother asks periodically. "No, of course not." "That's good. Don't be a Christian. What *do* you believe in?" "No religion. Nothing." "Why don't you take the Chinese religion, then?" And a few minutes later, "Yes, you do that," she'd say. "Sure, Mom. Okay.") Next to the telephone were notebooks, pads, very sharp pencils, a pencil sharpener, another luxury. They had shaving lotion and hand lotion, toiletries on the shelf too.

"The bathroom is over there," she shouted as if it were a huge house. I went into the bathroom, which was the closet next to the kitchen, to spy some more. They had built shelves with stores of sale toilet paper and soap, which was in fancy shapes prettily boxed. They aren't so poor, I thought. They are above subsistence; we have been worse off.

I stood by the kitchen door and watched my aunt cut cake. A corner of the floor was stacked with shiny gallon cans without labels. "My husband baked these cakes," she said. *Hus-u-bun*, she called him, a clever solution; some wives get so embarrassed about what to call their husbands, their names and *husband* such intimate words (like *rooster* − or *cock*), that they call him So-and-so's Father. My uncle worked at a famous bakery whose name is stamped on pink boxes that people carry about Chinatown.

"Cake?" asked my aunt. "Pie? Chuck-who-luck? Le-mun?"

"I just ate," I said, which was true, but took a plate anyway. The biggest difference between my aunt and my mother was that my mother would have forced me to eat it. I sat on the sofa, facing the front door. There was another door near the desk; it must have been to the next apartment.

Auntie got herself some chocolate cake and lemon pie and sat next to me. I enjoyed looking at this aunt, who was how my mother would have been if she were the youngest instead of the oldest, the city woman rather than the peasant. She was wearing a white blouse with sharp lapels; I also liked the straight gray skirt and intelligent glasses.

"I saw those hoppies they tell about in the newspaper," she said. "Some of them talked to me. 'Spare change?' That's what they say. 'Spare change?' I memorized it." She held out her hand to show their ways. "'Spare change?' What does 'spare change' mean?" "They're asking if you have extra money." "Oh-h, I see," she said, laughing. "'Spare change?' How witty." She was silly compared to my mother. She giggled and talked about inconsequentials. "Condo," she would say. "Cottage cheese. Football? Foosball?"

But here I was alone with her, and no adults to distract her; maybe I could ask her things, two equal adults, talk the way Americans talk. Talk grown-up. "Is it hard to endure?" I asked like an old Chinese lady, but because I was not brave enough to hear the answer, quickly said on top of it, "Where did you go? Were you grocery shopping? Going for a walk? Visiting neighbors?"

"I was coming from the beauty parlor, getting my hair done," she said, and I wished that I had noticed to compliment her on how nice she looked, but her hair looked the way she always wore it, in stiff black curls. "Otherwise, it wouldn't be this black," she said. "It's really white, you know." She went to beauty parlors. Another luxury, I enumerated. Leisure.

"Are you working?" I asked because it was odd that she was having her hair done in the middle of a workday. "Is it your day offu?"

"No. I'm not working any more."

"What happened to your hotel job? Didn't you have a hotel job? As a maid?" I said *maid* in English, not knowing the Chinese word except for *slave*. If she didn't know the word, she wouldn't hear it anyway. Languages are like that.

"I've been fired," she said.

"Oh, no. But why?"

"I've been very sick. High blood pressure," she said. "And I got dizzy working. I had to clean sixteen rooms in eight hours. I was too sick to work that fast." Something else I liked about this aunt was her use of exact numbers. "Ten thousand rooms per second," my mother would have said. "Uncountable. Infinite." Half an hour per unit, including bathrooms. "People leave the rooms very messy," she said, "and I kept coughing from the ashes in the ashtrays. I was efficient until I fell sick. Once I was out for six weeks, but when I came back, the head housekeeper said I was doing a good job, and he kept me on." She worked at a famous hotel, not a flop house in Chinatown. She'd given us miniature cakes of soap whenever she came to visit. "The head housekeeper said I was an excellent worker." My mother was the same way, caring tremendously how her employer praised her, never so hurt as when a boss reprimanded her, never so proud as when a forelady said she was picking cleanly and fast. "He said I speak English very well," Auntie said. She was proud of that compliment.

"What do you do all day long now that you aren't cleaning hotel rooms?"

"The days go by very slowly. You know, in these difficult times in the Big City mothers can't leave their children alone. The kidnappers are getting two thousand dollars per child. And whoever reports a missing child the FBI turns over to Immigration. So I posted ads, and one in the newspaper too, that I wanted to mind children, but I haven't gotten any customers. When the mothers see the apartment, they say No." Of course. No place to run, no yard, no trees, no toys except to look at the dollies. Being poor in Stockton was better than this Big City poverty; we had trees and sloughs and vegetable gardens and animals. Also there were jobs in the fields. "I could mind four or five children," she said. "I'd make as much money as cleaning the hotel. They don't want me to watch their children because I can't speak English."

"But you do," I said. "You know lots of English." When I could not think of the Chinese for something, she always knew the English word.

She was flattered. "No, I don't," she said. "Now, *you* speak Chinese well," but I was speaking well because I was talking to her; there are people who dry up language.

"You speak like your mother. She used to sound like a city person, but American people speak peasant accents, village accents, so she talks that way now."

"Do my mother and father speak alike?"

"Why, yes," she said, but maybe she couldn't hear the difference; being a city person she lumped the village accents together.

"My own son doesn't talk to me," she said. "What's *nutrition*?"

"It has to do with food and what people ought to eat to keep healthy."

"You mean like cooking? He's going to college to learn how to cook?"

"Well, no. It's planning menus for big companies, like schools and hospitals and the Army. They study food to see how it works. It's the science of food," but I did not feel I was giving an adequate explanation, the only word for *science* I knew was a synonym or derivative of *magic*, something like *alchemy*. "He could work in public health, and that's a field that has lots of jobs right now. He could work for cafeterias and college dormitories, restaurant chains, mass production food plants that make frozen TV dinners, canned foods, cake mixes."

"And *engineering*?" she asked.

"Building things, designing them, like designing bridges and mines and electrical things. Do you know what kind of engineering he's studying?"

"No, they shout at me and tell me I'm too stupid to understand. They hardly come home, and when I ask them what they're doing, they say I'm dumb. Oh, my sons have turned out very bad, and after all I've suffered for them."

I did not want to hear how she suffered, and then I did. I did have a duty to hear it and remember it. She started by telling me how my mother had suffered. "Oh, the suffering," she said. "Think of it. Both of your mother's babies died. How painful it must be to watch your babies die after they can walk and talk and have personalities. Aiya! How hard to endure."

"What did they die of?"

"Firecrackers. The village women exploded firecrackers to scare germs and bad spirits away, but instead they scared away the babies. They filled the air with smoke so the babies couldn't breathe. And then a few years later, it happened again; when you were a baby, you suddenly stopped breathing, and she pounded on the floor for the downstairs neighbor to help. The fire trucks and the police came, and they revived you. She wrote to me about that."

"Probably all babies, having recently been nothing, have a tenuous hold on life," I observed. MaMa would have sat on the floor and held the babies to her or laid them on blankets in the middle of the house. I remembered the floor, the linoleum patterns and smells of it. Under the linoleum I had hidden milk bottle caps, flattening into lovely disks.

In the falling afternoon, I looked out the windows at the neighbors' windows. For a short while light had pushed through the curtains making little suns and a haze. We faced west and caught the last pale sun. The fog rolled between the buildings, and the foghorns were sounding already. My aunt made no move to switch on the lights. Her eyes were very bright. It aggravated me how easily tears came to women her age, not hardened at all by the years. "I suffered terribly too," she said. I would never be able to talk with them; I have no stories of equal pain.

Now she was telling her part of the story: When she was born, the blind fortuneteller said that she would be alternately very rich and very poor many times but end up rich. Sure enough, they were poor until her father went to the Gold Mountain, whence he traveled three times; each time he got richer and twice brought back wives. He hired teachers for his daughters, who learned to read and write. Between his trips they were poor. He died when she was ten. She was poor from then until she married a rich man. When Communism transformed the villagers, they chased her family out of their house. She hid with her two boys in the pig house. It was winter, and all they had on were cotton clothes. The boys knew better than to cry, learned instantly. The next morning, she found her husband. He said that the Communists had assigned them a place to live – the leper house. "That's where you belong," said the Communists. Lepers, the "growing yin" people, who have too much cold wind in them, died in there. The rest of the family had disappeared; his mother had run away alone with the gold and jade. They never saw her again. The Communists kept an eye on them in the leper house, waited for them to make a false move. One day her husband caught a pair of doves and hid them to feed the family. "And do you know how the Communists killed him?"

"I think my mother said they stoned him in the tree where the birds were."

"They pressed him between millstones," she said.

Of course. In stories, stones fall crash bang crash bang like pile drivers. It was the sound of harvest and executions. After battle, no matter what farmhouse or courtyard a villain or hero used, when it was time for executions, he always had a device handy – the millstones.

"Aiya," I said. "That's horrible. How hard to endure."

Then she escaped to Hong Kong. She gave her wedding ring to get on the ship, her earrings for food, her necklace to get off the ship. She and the two boys slept on the sidewalks; they ate the rice they begged though the Communists threw sand into it, saying "Have some salt." The oldest boy, Big Baby she called him, and her second son, Little Baby, got angry at her when they were hungry or too hot or too cold. "What did you do today?" she asked them after separating to beg on different streets. "What do you care?" they said. "What do you know?"

She noticed a man who was selling shoes alone in a stall. She bade him "Good morning" daily and thus made his acquaintance. He let her sit in the customer's chair under the awning in rain and in the noon sun. Whenever he shared his lunch with her, she hid some for the boys. One day she said – she said it for me with a giggle – "Sir, why doesn't your lady come help you work these long hours?" (Hong Kong people are more refined than us and don't say *old lady* for *wife* or *old rooster* for *husband*.)

"I don't have a lady," he said.

"I'll help you then," she said, and did so. Soon they got married, the first self-matched marriage in the family. They built the stall up into a store, then added a wholesale outlet, then a factory, and she was rich again. They had a boy and a girl of their own, much younger than the other two.

But she did not forget the accurate blind fortuneteller: a downfall imminent. The people who lived in crates on the hillsides and the boat people who had never touched land would soon rise up and kill the rich people and the British. There are rich people who don't see poor people, but she never stopped seeing them. She took varying routes from home to store so the beggars wouldn't recognize her and mark her. "The Revolution is coming," she kept saying, and her husband agreed, "Yes, it's going to happen," but went on building his business. Each downfall had been worse than the last – the Japanese, then World War II, then the Revolution. "The Hong Kong Revolution will be fought with nuclear bombs," she predicted. Her husband called her a superstitious peasant.

At last she said, "My name is at the top of the Refugee List. Let's leave for the United States." But her husband did not want to go; the business was doing very well. He told her that if she went, she would have to go alone. She took the two older boys and left him with the daughter and son. "Badger him to bring you to the Gold Mountain," she instructed these two youngest, and left.

"Father," they said with their little arms out supplicating, the boy especially naughty, "take us to the Gold Mountain. We want to see Ah Ma. Why won't you take us? Do you want us to get killed by Communists? Ah Ba, take us to America and buy us some American toys. You're a selfish father not to take us traveling. All right then. When we're old enough, we're leaving you. We'll go find her. You're cheap, that's why you won't take us."

My mother showed her the street corners where she was to wait for the farm buses to take her to the tomatoes and grapes. Yes, life in America was meaner, but no signs of revolution; the beggars in the street were young and fat "hoppies," who begged for fun. She hoped that this Gold Mountain poverty counted for the next fall in her fortunes. Her husband wrote that he was definitely not about to leave his homeland and his family. And didn't she miss having servants and friends talking her own language? She suggested that he not sell the shoe store but export the shoes to the United States, send them to her here. She had already gotten her American relatives to promise to take cases of sample shoes from store to store. She said a war in Indochina was going to spread to other Asian countries, and the Pentagon would bomb China. She outwrote him. He said, "All right.

436

I'm coming to the United States, but only to have a look at it and to bring you back."

He brought the two younger children with him. What luxury, I thought. World travel. No more deciding once and for all on a country sight unseen. He took one look at the Los Angeles International Airport, and said, "Let's go back." But she said to give the Gold Mountain a chance. Be a tourist. Take a vacation. For a couple of months he complained how there were no jobs, then how hard he had to work, and how he had to obey a boss. Both of them complained about doing hard work for only a fraction of the money they were making in Hong Kong.

I remember they rented a house with peeling and flaking paint; they did not plaster the cracks, did not hang curtains. They slept on the floor until my sister brought them mattresses. They used their suitcases instead of dressers. Chinese people are like that, we sisters and brothers told one another – no frills, cheap. My sister bought them sheets, then a bedspread. The two older boys, whom we refused to call Big BiBi and Little BiBi, did not talk to us but looked away if we caught their eyes, answered direct questions Yes or No, and never asked us questions in return. Like old uncles, they talked to our parents in Chinese. They were F.O.B.'s all right. Fresh Off the Boat.

The youngest boy was more sociable. He opened our refrigerator door and stood there and ate; he knocked over furniture and sassed his mother in two languages. He asked us questions, and his hair spiked up all over his head as if every hair were listening. "Why do you look like that?" "How do they do instant replay so fast?" "How much money do you make? Yeah, what's your salary?" But when we asked his name, he suddenly stood still. He and his sister looked at one another and down at their shoes. The girl, who was older, pointed to her brother and muttered something, and he turned red. "What?" I asked. She said it again. It was his

Chinese name, and we could hardly hear it. "Her name is Lucille," he said. And *Lucille* was easy for him to say and easy to hear. He was proud to be able to give an American name though it wasn't his. So, they'd already learned to be shamed by a Chinese name.

When I Fu, Aunt's Husband, said, "I'm going back. You do as you please, but I'm going back," Auntie went with him. They took the two younger children. Our older cousins decided that they would stay in the United States; they were never going back; they would finish school, apply for citizenship, risk getting drafted – it was worth it. How foreign they were. Another generation of heartless boys leaving their family. Only my mother and aunt showed regret at leaving each other.

My mother nagged her nephews if they took any time off from work and study whatsoever. "My own children study all the time," she scolded, to which the F.O.B.'s replied, "They must not be very bright if they have to study that hard." She told us that retort, stirring up suspicions, establishing a pecking order, which must have been the way in China. They lived down in our basement with a bare light bulb. They were not to put their belongings in our closets or drawers, nor to ride our bikes or watch our TV or listen to the radios. MaMa said, "They're not my children." When they came home from school or from the grocery store, where they worked for twenty-five cents an hour, they were to go to the cellar.

Meanwhile in Hong Kong, Auntie was enjoying another one of her high fortunes. But one day I Fu stood up from a customer's feet and told a clerk to finish up. A surge of chemicals or light had rushed through him. He went back to his office and unlocked his desk. He walked to the bank. The walk he took was magical: Inanimate objects glowed, but, oh, the animate – the trees and flowers and bugs and dogs were spraying colors. Human beings flared haloes around their heads and the rest of their bodies. Bands of light connected couples. He explained later how he understood the stopping quality of red light and the go of green. The city was not making a general roar or hum. His ears separated out the sounds of various motors, the gas pipes and water mains under the city, each bicycle wheel, the way the rubber peeled off the asphalt. It was a good thing it had been a sunny seaport day and not San Francisco; a foghorn would have melted him with sorrow. He passed a bookstore. Jets of colored lights jumped along the books' spines; he wanted to stop and see whether *Red Chamber Dream* and Communist books were red, the Clear River poems blue and green, Confucius's writings a white light, and the *I Ching* yellow or saffron, but he had to hurry on. The seats, handlegrips, and pedals of the pedicabs and bicycles pulsed like fire. The newspapers were aflame in reds and oranges. He passed a drugstore and saw the little drawers leaking squares of light.

At the bank, he filled out a withdrawal slip with the very figure that was the last balance in his account. He said later those digits had had a numerological significance. He took the money in cash – and money had its own brilliance. It was so much money, the bank let him keep the canvas bag to carry it in. The teller and manager asked if he were certain he didn't want a check or money order, and he said Yes. He liked the feeling of the Yes escaping warm out of his body. He also liked voices warming his ears. He would have to remember to go to the theater more often. He carried the money through the streets. He was certain that thieves would not snatch it; he was choreographing the movements of people and the weather. Time and fate were his invention and under the control of his will. He walked into a part of Hong Kong where he had never gone before, but he knew where to go. Fences made out of air guided his way. He entered the correct building and in the elevator knew which floor to choose. He walked through a particular door into a particular room. There were several men he had never seen before, but he knew just which one to approach and what to say. He gave this man all the money he had in the world. He walked out. Free of money. Free of burden. Purpose fulfilled. He flew home. "I can control the weather," he said earnestly. "You can too." His wife and the employees kept asking if he were all right. They planted in him the possibility of his not being all right.

"You look sick," his wife said.

"Stop saying that," he said, and he crashed down to normal. "I've been robbed," he said. "I've been robbed. I was drugged by the bandits that prey on Gold Mountain Sojourners. They slipped a drug into my lunch. And their post-hypnotic suggestion was for me to take all the money out of the bank. I gave it all to them. We're ruined. Why didn't you stop me?"

"What are you talking about?" my aunt asked. "That's impossible. A drug, you say? Hypnosis? How could I have stopped you? Is there such a drug? You gave all our money away? All of it? It wasn't gambling?"

"It was like sleepwalking," he said. "I could see everything; the world was the same, but the story behind it was different. I thought strangely. I thought it was a friend I gave the money to, that he was doing me a favor taking it." According to the passbook, which he found in his pocket, the account had been closed out. "Our life savings."

Husband and wife dashed outside, trying to trace where he had walked. They ran about asking if anyone had seen him come this way. "Did you see me go by a little while ago?" "The bookstore," he said. "I remember it. And that drugstore." The unknown neighborhood had disappeared as if the bandits had set it up, then taken the buildings away. They ran to the bank, which was closed. They went to the police station, though they knew that the police were themselves crooks.

440

They and a policeman were at the doors when the bank opened in the morning. The teller who had waited on I Fu confirmed that he had been at that window the day before, and he had withdrawn all his money. "Was there anyone with him?" his wife asked. "Did you see anyone behind him? Could there have been someone behind him with a gun?" The tellers had not seen anyone. I Fu told the bank manager that he had been drugged or hypnotized to take out all his money and give it away. The bank manager could do nothing about that. "We don't insure against that," he said. Hong Kong was full of criminals, tricksters, shysters, cheaters, con artists, plotters. People made their living by eating other people, by catching pigs. At lunch, a customer who followed him to the back room might have waved a hand over I Fu's food, and the drug had poured down a sleeve or slipped out of a button or a hinged ring. "Maybe so," said the policeman. Pig-catching was a game among the southern people. The shoe clerks and his relatives were probably in on it too, and the police too.

"We shouldn't have left the United States," Auntie complained. "American police and American people are honest."

When I Fu made change for the last customer of the day, when the bell dinged in the cash register, the spell came over him again. He scooped up the bills and put them in a shoe box. "Where are you going?" cried Auntie, alarmed at his pinpointy, jumpy eyes. "Where are you going? Stop it. You're doing it again. You told me to stop you. It's come over you again. Snap out of it. Put the money back. Give it to me. Wake up." She clapped her hands and shook him, but he pushed her aside "with superhuman strength," she said. "Hold him," she called to the customers and employees. "He's under a spell. Don't let him go. He's got all the petty cash we have left in the world."

"Leave me alone," he said. "It's my money." He broke from their grasp and ran through the streets. The after-work crowds moved aside and closed behind him.

"Stop him. Stop him," Auntie and the employees called, but the people did not want to grab the wild man. Auntie hunted for him, but he had entered a side street into another world. She went back to the store, terrified at what the thieves were capable of.

I Fu returned, walking slowly; he looked fatigued, having been run about like a puppet. "Let's sell the shoe business," he said, giving in at last, "and go back to the United States." "Return," he said. "Return to the United States."

"Be warned not to travel to China," Auntie told me. "Chinese are crooks. Travelers disappear and are never heard of again."

My aunt and uncle sold their businesses before someone could trick them into signing them away. With that money, they went for the second time to the Gold Mountain, where they arrived no better off than other immigrants. They would never go back; they said good-bye properly, good-bye forever.

"He got the job at the bakery, and I got the one at the hotel," said Auntie. "But I've been sick and can't work any more."

"You look well."

"I get dizzy when I work. By the time I carry my vacuum cleaner and linens up the stairs, I'm so dizzy I have to lie down on the landing. High blood pressure. I'll not fly in an airplane again."

"Do you keep seeing a doctor?"

"Yes."

"The doctor gave you some pills?"

"Yes, but I'm not taking them. It's not the blood pressure that makes me dizzy; it's the pills. I've discovered a cure. The Chinatown women, who all have high blood pressure, say that fresh, unprocessed, pure honey is good for hypertension, and I've been drinking it by the quart. I'm going to get your mother started on the pure honey cure too. I feel so much better on the honey than the pills. Too many side effects with the pills."

"Is that honey in the cans in the kitchen?"

"Yes, I like to stock up when a fresh supply comes into Chinatown. It comes from a special farm with special bees."

"I think you ought to keep taking the pills," I said. "How does the honey have that effect?"

"I'm not sure. Maybe it smooths out the blood so it takes less pressure to move through the veins."

There was no use talking her out of it. I would have to persuade my mother to continue taking the pills along with the honey.

"I'm glad you've decided to quit your job," I said. "You're lucky to be able to stay home and be a housewife."

"But I need a job badly, very badly. My husubun insists on one thing," she said. "He makes six hundred dollars a month. Exactly three hundred goes to China. He's a rescuer. Out of our three hundred dollars, we have to pay rent, food, clothes, everything. So you see why I have to get a job. He's been saying that I don't know how to save money, that I spend too much. He's so stingy; ever since I lost my job, he's been doing the grocery shopping himself. I had to refuse to cook until I got control of the grocery money again. I went on strike." She laughed. "Sometimes when the two of us are carrying the groceries home, he puts his bag down on the sidewalk and walks away swinging his arms free. I have to hurry home with my bag and run back for his before somebody takes it. Men from Kwangtung are arrogant like that. Independent."

"I'll cook if you stay for dinner," she added.

"I have to go," I said.

"Well, I know there isn't much room to play," she said, as if I were a child, or perhaps she meant "stroll" or "tour."

"No, it's not that. I have some tasks that I have to do. Was your apartment in Hong Kong bigger than this one?"

"No. No. About this size." Oh, such relief that the Chinese life they keep regretting leaving is no better than this.

"Do you want to move outside Tang People's Street?" I asked.

"No. No. Here my husubun can walk to and from work. He can wake up five minutes before the bakery opens and get there on time. And I can talk to the neighbors. The children walk across the street to Chinese school." I hoped that she was drawing the conclusion that she and her family were well off, that they were living in this room by choice, in a way.

"Stay for dinner," she urged. "There won't be good food, but stay."

"I can't," I said. "I have work to do."

"Then let me phone my husubun to bring home a cake for you."

"No, thank you. You don't need to do that. I just ate some cake."

"You can give it to someone, your brothers and sisters." She picked up the phone (another luxury, I counted) and called the bakery. "Bring a cake for my niece," she said. "The best kind – lemun kuk." "The bakery is just around the corner," she said to me. "He'll get off work in five minutes and be here in another minute or two."

It would only be polite to stay and say hello to my uncle. Also I wanted to take a good look at him after what I had heard about him. I did feel nervous that he would walk in angry at me for causing him to have to carry a lemon cake through the streets. A request right before closing time. What if he had to whip together a lemon cake on his own time or humble himself to ask the boss for a remainder cake, or, worse yet, if he had to take it out of his pay? My mother would want me to protest a gift, argue and tussle, my aunt and I trying to give the cake away, running back and forth, her yelling, "All right, then, I take it back. No cake for you," tucking it into clothes, hiding it in bags, throwing it in and out of windows, pushing the windows up and down, pulling the box back and forth until I gave up and took it. Being rude because young and American, taking advantage of that, I planned to say "Thank you" and take the cake.

I Fu arrived at the front door at exactly 5:05, as I could see by the alarm clock on the desk. Watching the knob turn, I thought, What if he were filled with years of gall, furious from kneeling at people's feet and carrying groceries? He would be mad at me for making my aunt sit all afternoon, no dinner started. But he seemed ordinary, handing over the cake box, a man not particularly burdened by money, smiling, not wide-eyed on drugs, the *Gold Mountain Times* under his arm. I stood up, old enough to have manners without being told. "How do you do, I Fu?" I said, shaking his hand. He did not look like a tough businessman who had built and lost a shoe empire or one who could marry a flirtatious beggarwoman from off the street or dash through Hong Kong giving away bags of money. He asked me what I was doing in the Big City. He sat down, asked if I wanted to eat anything. Then he couldn't resist any longer, rolled the rubber band off his newspaper, shook it open, and began to read, exactly as my father would have done. He looked just like my father behind the newspaper, the very same newspaper, skinny legs and hands sticking out.

"Why don't you come visit my parents at Christmas time?" I invited my aunt, figuring out a way to leave.

Just then the door opened again, and my girl cousin came home. She glanced at me, startled, and headed straight for the locked door, which I had thought led to the next apartment. She bent and unlocked it with one of the keys on the chain around her neck. I could see inside; it was the children's room, larger than the rest of the apartment, girl's stuff in one half, boy's stuff in the other.

"Lucille," scolded my aunt. "Say hello to Big Sister."

"Hello," she said, her whole body leaning to get into her own room.

"Lucille is returning from Chinese school," said Auntie.

The only times I had ever gotten Lucille to sit down with me was when playing games; she methodically set out to win everything on the board, only talking to clarify a rule.

"I was trying to explain to Big Sister what your brothers are studying at college," said Auntie.

"Nutrition and engineering," said my cousin.

"I see," I said, wishing my aunt would let her go. I Fu could have said something from behind the newspaper, like "I'm a baker and didn't have to study nutrition," but he didn't.

"Where's your youngest son?" I asked my aunt, and while she answered, Lucille went quickly inside her room and locked it.

"In the streets I guess," Auntie said. "Sometimes he doesn't come home until all the stores and restaurants are closed." He was only about ten years old.

"What does he do out there all night?"

"I don't know. Explores."

"Aren't you afraid of kidnappers and gangs getting him?"

"Yes, of course, but there's nothing we can do about him."

I asked her, "Will you walk me a short distance and point out which way I ought to go?" I said good-bye to my uncle, who looked up and said, "Leaving so soon?" My cousin did not come out of her room. Auntie and I walked for a block and a half until I recognized where I was, though the night and the street lights were coming on. We stood on a corner and shouted good-byes, me carrying a box of food with a red string, so Chinese, shouting and carrying food, shouting good-bye.

Once MaMa telephoned her brother after not having seen him for fifty years. This was the Singapore uncle who had spent his first fortune throwing a party for friends in Hong Kong. ("Americans get steadily richer building up their savings; Chinese save for years, then spend it all and go into debt for a party.") She told me to be ready to get up at 5 a.m. to do the dialing. They had written letters agreeing on this day, January 2, when it would be a cheap time and 8 p.m. in Singapore. "Oh, the size of the world," she exclaimed. "Look at that time difference. That's not three hours but fifteen hours apart. How far away."

I heard the alarms go off all over the house at 4:30 a.m. and leapt out of bed for nervousness. Wrapped in my blanket, I dialed the operator. After hearing my uncle's phone ring once, I handed the receiver to my mother. She heard a ring and handed it back to me. "Here, you talk to him." "No," I yelped, "I've never met him. He's your brother. You talk to him." Besides, I didn't want to scare him. My parents' friends hang up when we forget to answer with a Chinese accent.

The index finger of my mother's hand that held the phone tapped involuntarily against her cheek; it was the only part of her that shook. "Happy New Year, Wah," she yelled in her loudest voice, no titles, just his name, her baby brother, named after the Chinese Republic. "Is this Wah? Are you well? You're all well, aren't you? Everyone well. Yes, we're all fine too. Yes, very good. Everyone is good. Do you celebrate this New Year's day? Ours is very festive. All my children come back, eating at everybody's houses every day. We go from one of my children's house to another's eating. No, I can't come visit you. Five years ago I could have visited you. But I'm old now. Yes, I'm old now too. Are you old? Do you work hard? Did you just now come home from work? How hard do you work? I still work. Yes. Yes. Thirty employees, huh? That's good. Yes, my children are all working. Everyone working. Happy New Year. Yes, you have a good year too. Good year, good business, good health. Your son has

447

his own corporation? Why don't you come visit me? No, I don't fly. Yes, we're all well. Doing well. Fine. Good jobs. It's five a.m. here. What time is it there? It's January second now. What day is it there? You're home from work? Let me talk to your wife." Then she talked to his first wife, repeating just about everything. My father said, "Nine minutes," and she said, "That's enough. Be well. Good-bye," and hung up.

"Well," she said, "nothing significant said." She tried repeating the conversation to us. "He employs thirty people. He says that he wishes his children were smart. They're horses and oxen, he said. His son is in the construction business too, but has a different company. He says it's eight p.m., January second there in Singapore." I noticed she had not asked him how his second wife was, nor how the children of that family were. "Fifty years since we've talked, and we didn't say anything important," she said.

"That's the nature of phone calls," my father said. "You just hear each other's voices. That's enough."

"You can call again next year, you know," I said. "You can call again any time."

For eight months in 1975, residents on the edge of Green Swamp, Florida, had been reporting to the police that they had seen a Wild Man. When they stepped toward him, he made strange noises as in a foreign language and ran back into the saw grass. At first, authorities said the Wild Man was a mass hallucination. Man-eating animals lived in the swamp, and a human being could hardly find a place to rest without sinking. Perhaps it was some kind of a bear the children had seen.

In October, a game officer saw a man crouched over a small fire, but as he approached, the figure ran away. It couldn't have been a bear because the Wild Man dragged a burlap bag after him. Also, the fire was obviously man-made.

The fish-and-game wardens and the sheriff's deputies entered the swamp with dogs but did not search for long; no one could live in the swamp. The mosquitoes alone would drive him out.

The Wild Man made forays out of the swamp. Farmers encountered him taking fruit and corn from the turkeys. He broke into a house trailer, but the occupant came back, and the Wild Man escaped out a window. The occupant said that a bad smell came off the Wild Man. Usually, the only evidence of him were his abandoned campsites. At one he left the remains of a four-foot-long alligator, of which he had eaten the feet and tail.

In May a posse made an air and land search; the plane signaled down to the hunters on the ground, who circled the Wild Man. A fish-and-game warden "brought him down with a tackle," according to the news. The Wild Man fought, but they took him to jail. He looked Chinese, so they found a Chinese in town to come translate.

The Wild Man talked a lot to the translator. He told him his name. He said he was thirty-nine years old, the father of seven children, who were in Taiwan. To support them, he had shipped out on a Liberian freighter. He had gotten very homesick and asked everyone if he could leave the ship and go home. But the officers would not let him off. They sent messages to China to find out about him. When the ship landed, they took him to the airport and tried to put him on an airplane to some foreign place. Then, he said, the white demons took him to Tampa Hospital, which is for insane people, but he escaped, just walked out and went into the swamp.

The interpreter asked how he lived in the swamp. He said he ate snakes, turtles, armadillos, and alligators. The captors could tell how he lived when they opened up his bag, which was not burlap but a pair of pants with the legs knotted. Inside, he had carried a pot, a piece of sharpened tin, and a small club, which he had made by sticking a railroad spike into a section of aluminum tubing.

The sheriff found the Liberian freighter that the Wild Man had been on. The ship's officers said that they had not tried to stop him from going home. His shipmates had decided that there was something wrong with his mind. They had bought him a plane ticket and arranged his passport to send him back to China. They had driven him to the airport, but there he began screaming and weeping and would not get on the plane. So they had found him a doctor, who sent him to Tampa Hospital.

Now the doctors at the jail gave him medicine for the mosquito bites, which covered his entire body, and medicine for his stomach-ache. He was getting better, but after he'd been in jail for three days, the U.S. Border Patrol told him they were sending him back. He became hysterical. That night, he fastened his belt to the bars, wrapped it around his neck, and hung himself.

In the newspaper picture he did not look very wild, being led by the posse out of the swamp. He did not look dirty, either. He wore a checkered shirt unbuttoned at the neck, where his white undershirt showed; his shirt was tucked into his pants; his hair was short. He was surrounded by men in cowboy hats. His fingers stretching open, his wrists pulling apart to the extent of the handcuffs, he lifted his head, his eyes screwed shut, and cried out.

There was a Wild Man in our slough too, only he was a black man. He wore a shirt and no pants, and some mornings when we walked to school, we saw him asleep under the bridge. The police came and took him away. The newspaper said he was crazy; it said the police had been on the lookout for him for a long time, but we had seen him every day.

We had a book from China about a sailor named Lo Bun Sun, who as a child had a calling to go to sea. His father, a man from a foreign country, ordered him and his two brothers to settle down working in the family business. But Lo Bun Sun did not enjoy the business nor did he learn a trade or study law. He signed on a ship. "Heaven will not bless you," his father said.

A storm came upon his ship, which sprang a leak. He escaped in a lifeboat, and from there watched the ship sink. Other sailors told him that this unfortunate first voyage was a warning that he give up the sea, but he signed on another ship, which was besieged by pirates. After escaping from them, he bought land in Brazil and planted sugarcane. But one day he became tempted to go to sea again, this time on a slave-trading ship. The ocean reared black waves that knocked the sailors off the decks. Masts snapped, and the ship broke against the reef of an unknown shore. The deck splintered under Lo Bun Sun, and he dropped into the water. Waves big as buildings fell on him whenever he surfaced, and drove him under.

Then he had a sense of coming back from a distance. His dream was that he had been flying but clutching something in his hand; he had tried to open his fingers to drop it, but the burden had pulled him down to this beach. The storm had thrown the ship here also, its stern in the air and its head in the sea. No shipmates had landed with him, not even their bodies.

He put his forehead against the ground and thanked the heavenly beings for protecting him. After resting some more, he swam to the wreckage. With pieces of topmast and spars, he fashioned a raft, on which he loaded sacks of grain – rice, barley, and wheat. In the bread room, he filled his pockets with biscuits. Eating as he worked, he helped himself to ink, paper, and pens, barrels of flour and bolts of cloth, clothes of men and officers, tools – an adze, hatchets, axes, a saw; he took tobacco and rum, guns, pistols, muskets, and shot.

And happily a dog and two cats, glad to see him, came out of hiding. The dog swam; Lo Bun Sun carried one cat in his arms, and the other jumped from the wreck onto the raft. Also for delight, the illustrator had drawn rats climbing down ropes; the rats had wonderfully long tails and whiskers.

The first night, Lo Bun Sun covered himself with a piece of sail and slept in a tree.

He set up a work schedule, rescuing things against the next obliterating wave. Every day he worked during the daylight hours just as if he had a job, stopping only to eat at set mealtimes. He ate the beef jerky and drank water from the ship's barrels; he ate lemons and pickles also. According to the drawings, the clay water jugs and wine jugs, the water gourds, and vinegar jugs leaned together in rows and stacks padded with straw; one or two jugs had broken into graceful shards.

MaMa repeated exactly what things Lo Bun Sun took from the ship (this was one of the more boring tales she read – no magicians, no beautiful ladies, no knights, or warrior poets): rice, barley, wheat flour, clothes, bolts of cloth, ink, pens, and paper, biscuits, jerked beef, water, fruit and vegetables, guns, pistols, muskets, bullets, adze, hatchet, ax, saw, tobacco, rum, a dog, two cats.

He also found a chest of gold coins, and although he had not seen a place to spend money, lugged it onto the raft.

One morning, he awoke and the ship was gone. No manmade hulk served as a marker against all that sea. He might have been born on the island.

He walked around the island and saw no signs of another human being. He decided on places to build two houses. One was a dry cave ("such as the cave I lived in when the Japanese bombed China"). He bolstered the roof and sides with planks and planted a wall of stakes, which sprouted and grew around the entrance. The other house was in the woods on an opposite part of the island; if enemies found it, they would be satisfied, diverted. He called his dwellings castles.

A rescue ship would probably come any moment now. Food grew plentifully on the island, and Lo Bun Sun had taken abundant stores from the shipwreck, yet he did not loaf and tan himself on the beach; neither did he nap or play. Lo Bun Sun worked. He was never idle, never lazy. He farmed the island. There is drudgery in his name: *Lo* is "toil," what one does even when unsupervised; he works faithfully, not cheating. *Lo* means means "naked," man "the naked animal," and *lo* also sounds like the word for "mule," a toiling animal, a toiling sexless animal. *Bun* is the uncle who went to China to work on a commune. And *sun* is like "body" and also "son" in English and "grandson" in Chinese. *Sun* as in "new." Lo Bun Sun was a mule and toiling man, naked and toiling body, alone, son and grandson, himself all the generations. There is still another meaning of *lo*, the *lo* in "lohan"; like "arhat," like "bodhisattva." There were eighteen lohans, two of them Chinese and sixteen Hindu, personal disciples of the Buddha who enjoyed an easy life like the life on the island of lotus eaters.

Lo Bun Sun marked the days with notches on a board, but on the first busy days when he was hurrying to unload the wreck, he had not yet started this system and might have been thrown off a day.

After physical labor, he wrote in his diary, with which he kept his spirits up. He would leave a record. He ruled a page down the middle and listed the advantages and disadvantages of his island life. The two columns were entitled "Evil" and

"Good." One of the Evils was the desolation; that he had not drowned was the balancing Good. Other Goods were food and water and the tropical weather that made up for his dearth of clothes. An Evil was that he had no one to talk to. His Good list outstripped the Evil list; Good may always preponderate in this method of reckoning.

Another way he wrote was: "I really ought to stop complaining because I could be writing that . . ." He began fictions about raving death, starvation, and mutilation, but stopped to continue chronicling his chores, which were endless. He built a table for writing and eating. He preserved eggs in vinegar and some in wine. He spread wild grapes to dry for raisins. He built barricades. He opened a turtle and admired its thirty gold eggs in the shell bowl. (*Lo* also connotes the mystic markings on the tortoise shell.)

When he felt poorly, he drank liquor in which he had soaked tobacco, a mixture also good for rubbing bruises. He grew beans and made tofu and bean sauce. He shot and snared goats; he penned the kids in corrals for domestication.

From the start, he worried about using up his ink and paper, so he decided he would record only "the most remarkable events of my life." He wrote how he planted rice in dry ground, and it did not grow. Then he planted the seeds in boxes, where the shoots remained from twenty-five to fifty days. Next to a stream, he dug pools and built clay walls into dams and sluices to make paddies of water and soil two to four inches deep, which he stirred, *lo* connoting "dike" and "libation," and he transplanted the young plants by hand. One day he counted thirty panicles of rice, and he wrote that down. "Miracle. Miracle." He reaped the heavy tops, handshocked and dried them. Then he carefully ground the brown hulls with rocks. The husks blew away like insect wings. The rice straw was thatch for his roof, slippers, an umbrella, a raincoat; he wove a winnow for next harvest. He searched the ground at the feet of the cut shafts and picked the grains that had fallen; this he used for seed. (My father came to listen to this part of the story, and he told it again, retelling the gleaning several times.) Birds also picked the seed grain, but he scared them away by shooting three birds, which his dog retrieved, and hanging them in the field. From planting to harvest was one year.

Lo Bun Sun shaped pots out of clay and baked them in the sun, which was not hot enough. He built an oven of rocks sealed with clay. When he saw how well it fired, he began decorating the pots. He dipped them in a mixture of mud and beach sand, which melted into a glaze. He wove nets around the outsides of wet pots; the grass burned off, leaving decorations. Sometimes he wove baskets around the cooled pots; he tied the straw into handles.

He made bread without yeast. There was a picture of him with a hand on his stomach; he was sniffing the loaves from which savory steam arose in wavy lines. The same oven baked bread as well as pottery because of vents that regulated the temperature.

He built a boat and rowed around the island. The waves took him farther and farther out. He had to fight his way back, desiring his island. "There's no miserable condition of mankind that heaven can't make worse," he wrote.

He knocked a young parrot out of a tree, and after some years taught it to say his name so that he would hear a voice other than his own, a voice calling him by name. "Poor Lo Bun Sun," it said. "Poor, poor Lo Bun Sun. Where are you? Where have you been? How come you here? Poor Lo Bun Sun, and how did I come here?"

If there were migratory geese on the island, he could have bound a letter to the leg of a goose.

More years passed, and he used up the brushes, inks, and paper. How to replace the Four Valuable Things? When the rice stalks dried to a pale yellow, he crisscrossed them in a woven mat. The squares were the right size for a word each.

He also soaked rice straw, pounded it, and pressed the mash into sheets. And there was a tree whose bark peeled off in soft layers; he called it a paper bark tree. He sewed its pages into notebooks. If he had not found these things, he could have written on stones. He could have written on leaves. For brushes he used goat hairs.

Making good ink took years of experimentation. He hunted for berries dark enough; he crushed leaves, opened reeds, bled trees, but the sap ran clear or amber and sticky or milky. (Plants with milky sap are poisonous to eat.) He tried swamp mud. He caught squid offshore to see if the black in them was ink. But no dirt or flower or blood flowed correctly and lasted. He wrote with oil and dipped the paper in berry stain. What he ate, he fed to parrot, dog, cats, goats, and fields, and he also wrote with it. At last, he discovered the juice of the sandalwood, whose bark and flowers he crushed to produce red. And he found woad, whose leaves look like arrows and writing brushes, and he wrote in indigo. He used red and purple; he was king of his own island.

Still more years went by, and now he was dressed entirely in straw and skins, straw coat, goatskin vest and pants, straw shoes. His pants were open at the knees for movement. He carried a straw umbrella in the sun and a skin umbrella in the rain; the hair was on the outside of the umbrella so the water ran off. Hair grew long on his face and head. A picture showed him trimming his hair with the scissors he treasured, looking at his mirror face and talking to himself. The sea continued empty and the nights black.

One day while patrolling the beach, where the crabs rolled seaweed bubbles across the sand, Lo Bun Sun saw something that sent a burning fear up his spine – a human footprint. He ran to one of his fortifications. He chattered, "It can't be. It can't be." After starving for human company for twelve years, he did not shout, "Where are you? Who are you? Hey, where are you? Come on out. Welcome. Welcome.

I'm here. I'm over here." Instead, he became scared and henceforth timid on his island. His eyelid began to twitch. He took up the musket, which he always kept loaded anyway, and never again walked abroad without it. He stuck loaded pistols and rifles into gunports in his walls. For days he shivered in his cave, peeked through cracks in every direction, jumped at noises of winds and animals. He had another look at the print. Perhaps he had construed a human foot rather than paw or hoof or claw because of his loneliness. In need of human company, he had imagined the five toes and a heel. But, no, there it was — unmistakably the imprint of a naked human foot. The drawing showed Lo Bun Sun kneeling propped against his musket and regarding a footprint, inky like a baby's on a birth certificate. "It must be my own," he said aloud, but the footprint was bigger than his foot. He clapped his hand over his mouth like a Japanese; he did not know how loud or soft was normal any more. He returned to puzzle over the footprint until the wind and rain wore it away. From then on in case some accident disabled him, he planted two or three years' supply of grain.

For more than a decade, he thought about the footprint and sometimes thought he had dreamed it. But one dawn he saw a light on the beach and crept up hidden behind rocks and trees to see who was there. Around a campfire in the warm climate, nine black demons danced and ate. Then they rowed off, leaving the beach strewn with human bones, heads, hands, and feet.

Lo Bun Sun fortified his hiding places. He planted vegetables in small separate patches and split his goats into small herds. He tied the muskets on tripping lines so that he could pull seven triggers in two minutes. He established burrows, coverts, and camouflages everywhere, and planted twenty thousand trees in all. The cannibals might come when he was doing his chores or sleeping. He comforted himself by recalling a hero, Kao Chung, who overcame the cooking-and-eating sea monster, and then ate its food on the beach. Several more times in later years, the black demons held their ghastly feasts, and Lo Bun Sun found the remains. Once he also found a wrecked galleon and the body of a drowned sailor.

Thirteen and a half years after the footprint and twenty-five and a half years after his arrival, five canoes landed. From his watchtower in a tree, Lo Bun Sun looked through his spyglass at the black figures against the yellow sand. In the ink drawings, they were silhouettes and far away, so we could not study facial expressions. They slaughtered one prisoner and dressed the meat in front of the others. Suddenly a prisoner broke loose, his ropes falling from him. Two or three savages gave chase – all running directly toward Lo Bun Sun's hiding place. The savages swam a creek, where one pursuer was left behind because he could not swim. Standing between the pursued and pursuers, Lo Bun Sun shot the oncoming cannibals. One of the wounded men returned to the others, who quickly paddled off. The poor man who might have been eaten fell to his knees. He lifted Lo Bun Sun's foot and set it on his head. This was the first human being Lo Bun Sun had touched and who had touched him in over a quarter of a century. One of the cannibals had only been wounded, and when Lo Bun Sun pointed to him, the rescued savage cut his head off. "I name you Sing Kay Ng," said Lo Bun Sun, "because I saved your life on a Friday." "Sing Kay Ng," he pointed to the savage. "You name Sing Kay Ng. My name Teacher."

Sing Kay Ng buried the dead men, then took his first lesson in the Teacher's language. Lo Bun Sun pointed at everything – "*Goat. Jar. Fence. Man.*" Sing Kay Ng pointed to the graves and gestured: "Let's dig them up and eat them." Lo Bun Sun acted as if he were vomiting. He let Sing Kay Ng know that he would kill him if he offered him any human meat or showed his cannibal tastes in any way again.

Sing Kay Ng understood the calendar, the arc his arm made from horizon to horizon, sunrise to sunset to sunrise, one mark. They walked on the island measuring off a distance, which Lo Bun Sun said was one li. "One hundred and twenty li away," said Sing Kay Ng. "I come from land one hundred and twenty li in that direction." The people fought, and the winners brought the losers here for eating. In his country, it was the custom to worship The Old Man Who Had Made Everything. "All things do say 'O' to him," he said. He said that he had a father.

Lo Bun Sun gave his servant and pupil a notebook and a brush with a gold cap and many brushes in bamboo tubes so that he too could record his thoughts and life. Every day the Naked Toiling Mule and Friday sat like two scholars at their desks, reading, studying, writing, recording plantings, harvests, bird migrations, the seasons, the weather, and how many goats had kids.

Lo Bun Sun armed Sing Kay Ng for hunting. Also they would be in league should the cannibals return. "'A real hero will take on a village,'" Lo Bun Sun taught.

Three years later, twenty-one savages and three prisoners, two of whom looked like Lo Bun Sun and one like Sing Kay Ng, came sailing to the island in a fleet of canoes. The companions fired from their ambuscade, killing seventeen cannibals and wounding one, three escaping by boat. When the boat was out of sight, the victors came out and untied the prisoners. Suddenly Sing Kay Ng was jumping up and down and shouting in his own language, "O joy! O glad!" He was embracing the man who looked like himself, and when he untied him, they held each other and wept. It was his father. The father praised Sing Kay Ng for waiting all these years on this island to save him. What a good son he had raised.

One of the other prisoners was a sea captain who had lost his ship in a mutiny. "I have loyal men on the mainland," he said. "If I can just reach them, I'll come back here and take you home." Arming themselves from Lo Bun Sun's store, the captain and Sing Kay Ng's father took the wounded cannibal as a hostage and left in a canoe.

Another ship came to the island, and Lo Bun Sun was in such a rush, he left on it. He took with him one of his parrots, his goatskin cap, an umbrella, his money, and his man, Sing Kay Ng, and returned to his native land.

"But that isn't the end of the story," said my mother. At about sixty years of age Lo Bun Sun found a wife and had two sons and a daughter. When his wife died, he went to sea again. He and Sing Kay Ng had many adventures in barbarous lands; they fought wolves, bears, and bandits. Once, surrounded by a wolfpack, they remembered that the fiercest beasts are terrified by the voice of man; at their shouting, the wolves retreated.

A nostalgia for his island came over Lo Bun Sun, and he sailed back there without telling Sing Kay Ng their destination. Sing Kay Ng recognized it on sight, clapped his hands, and cried, "O yes, O there, O yes, O there," pointing to the site of one of their houses and dancing like mad. The island was now inhabited by mutineers and savages, who had formed a society. They felt no need for rescue, nor did their children have any curiosity about their ancestral countries.

And Sing Kay Ng found his father again; he had seen him from a distance so far at sea that Lo Bun Sun could descry no human shape even through his perspective glass. Sing Kay Ng embraced his father, kissed him, stroked his face, hugged him again, picked him up and set him down under a tree, lay down by him, then stood and looked at him for a quarter of an hour at a time, stroked his old feet and kissed them, and got up again and stared at him. He walked along the beach leading his father by the hand as if he were a lady. He went back and forth to the ship, fetched him a lump of sugar, a drink, a cookie. He danced about him, and he talked and talked, telling him of his travels.

The island was warring with another island, and the ship became caught in the war. A thousand canoes attacked the ship. Lo Bun Sun ordered Sing Kay Ng to go on deck and talk to the attackers in their own language and translate. Three hundred arrows flew at him, and Sing Kay Ng was killed. He was buried at sea with an eleven-gun salute. After more adventures, Lo Bun Sun returned to the land where he was born; he retired at the age of seventy-two.

THE AMERICAN FATHER

In 1903 my father was born in San Francisco, where my grandmother had come disguised as a man. Or, Chinese women once magical, she gave birth at a distance, she in China, my grandfather and father in San Francisco. She was good at sending. Or the men of those days had the power to have babies. If my grandparents did no such wonders, my father nevertheless turned up in San Francisco an American citizen.

He was also married at a distance. My mother and a few farm women went out into the chicken yard, and said words over a rooster, a fierce rooster, red of comb and feathers; then she went back inside, married, a wife. She laughs telling this wedding story; he doesn't say one way or the other.

When I asked MaMa why she speaks different from BaBa, she says their parents lived across the river from one another. Maybe his village was America, the river an ocean, his accent American.

My father's magic was also different from my mother's. He pulled the two ends of a chalk stub or a cigarette butt, and between his fingers a new stick of chalk or a fresh cigarette grew long and white. Coins appeared around his knuckles, and number cards turned into face cards. He did not have a patter but was a silent magician. I would learn these tricks when I became a grown-up and never need for cigarettes, money, face cards, or chalk.

He also had the power of going places where nobody else went, and making places belong to him. I could smell his presence. He owned special places the way he owned special things like his copper ashtray from the 1939 World's Fair and his Parker 51. When I explored his closet and desk, I thought, This is a father place; a father belongs here.

One of his places was the dirt cellar. That was under the house where owls bounced against the screens. Rats as big as cats sunned in the garden, fat dust balls among the greens. The rats ran up on the table where the rice or the grapes or the beans were drying and ate with their hands, then took extra in their teeth and leapt off the table like a circus, one rat after another. My mother swung her broom at them, the straw swooping through the air in yellow arcs. That was the house where the bunny lived in a hole in the kitchen. My mother had carried it home from the fields in her apron. Whenever it was hopping noiselessly on the linoleum, and I was there to see it, I felt the honor and blessing of it.

When I asked why the cellar door was kept locked, MaMa said there was a "well" down there. "I don't want you children to fall in the well," she said. Bottomless.

I ran around a corner one day and found the cellar door open. BaBa's white-shirted back moved in the dark. I had been following him, spying on him. I went into the cellar and hid behind some boxes. He lifted the lid that covered the bottomless well. Before he could stop me, I burst out of hiding and saw it – a hole full of shining, bulging, black water, alive, alive, like an eye, deep and alive. BaBa shouted, "Get away." "Let me look. Let me look," I said. "Be careful," he said as I stood on the brink of a well, the end and edge of the ground, the opening to the inside of the world. "What's it called?" I asked to hear him say it. "A well." I wanted to hear him say it again, to tell me again, "Well." My mother had poured rust water from old nails into my ears to improve them.

"What's a well?"

"Water comes out of it," BaBa said. "People draw water out of wells."

"Do they drink it? Where does the water come from?"

"It comes from the earth. I don't think we should drink it without boiling it for at least twenty minutes. Germs."

Poison water.

The well was like a wobble of black jello. I saw silver stars in it. It sparked. It was the black sparkling eye of the planet. The well must lead to the other side of the world. If I fall in, I will come out in China. After a long, long fall, I would appear feet first out of the ground, out of another well, and the Chinese would laugh to see me do that. The way to arrive in China less obtrusively was to dive in head first. The trick would be not to get scared during the long time in the middle of the world. The journey would be worse than the mines.

My father pulled the wooden cover, which was the round lid of a barrel, back over the well. I stepped on the boards, stood in the middle of them, and thought about the bottomless black well beneath my feet, my very feet. What if the cover skidded aside? My father finished with what he was doing; we walked out of the cellar, and he locked the door behind us.

Another father place was the attic of our next house. Once I had seen his foot break through the ceiling. He was in the attic, and suddenly his foot broke through the plaster overhead.

I watched for the day when he left a ladder under the open trap door. I climbed the ladder through the kitchen ceiling. The attic air was hot, too thick, smelling like pigeons, their hot feathers. Rafters and floor beams extended in parallels to a faraway wall, where slats of light slanted from shutters. I did not know we owned such an extravagance of empty space. I raised myself up on my forearms like a prairie dog, then balanced sure-footed on the beams, careful not to step between them and fall through. I climbed down before he returned.

The best of the father places I did not have to win by cunning; he showed me it himself. I had been young enough to hold his hand, which felt splintery with calluses "caused by physical labor," according to MaMa. As we walked, he pointed out sights; he named the plants, told time on the clocks, explained a neon sign in the shape of an owl, which shut one eye in daylight. "It will wink at night," he said. He read signs, and I learned the recurring words: *Company*, *Association*, *Hui*, *Tong*. He greeted the old men with a finger to the hat. At the candy-and-tobacco store, BaBa bought Lucky Strikes and beef jerky, and the old men gave me plum wafers. The tobacconist gave me a cigar box and a candy box. The secret place was not on the busiest Chinatown street but the street across from the park. A pedestrian would look into the barrels and cans in front of the store next door, then walk on to the herbalist's with the school supplies and saucers of herbs in the window, examine the dead flies and larvae, and overlook the secret place completely. (The herbs inside the hundred drawers did not have flies.) BaBa stepped between the grocery store and the herb shop into the kind of sheltered doorway where skid-row men pee and sleep and leave liquor bottles. The place seemed out of business; no one would rent it because it was not eyecatching. It might have been a family association office. On the window were dull gold Chinese words and the number the same as our house number. And delightful, delightful, a big old orange cat sat dozing in the window; it had pushed the shut venetian blinds aside, and its fur was flat against the glass. An iron grillwork with many hinges protected the glass. I tapped on it to see whether the cat was asleep or dead; it blinked.

BaBa found the keys on his chain and unlocked the grating, then the door. Inside was an immense room like a bank or a post office. Suddenly no city street, no noise, no people, no sun. Here was horizontal and vertical order, counters and tables in cool gray twilight. It was safe in here. The cat ran across the cement floor. The place smelled like cat piss or eucalyptus berries. Brass and porcelain spittoons squatted in corners. Another cat, a gray one, walked into the open, and I tried following it, but it ran off. I walked under the tables, which had thick legs.

BaBa filled a bucket with sawdust and water. He and I scattered handfuls of the mixture on the floors, and the place smelled like a carnival. With our pushbrooms leaving wet streaks, we swept the sawdust together, which turned gray as it picked up the dirt. BaBa threw his cigarette butts in it. The cat shit got picked up too. He scooped everything into the dustpan he had made out of an oil can.

We put away our brooms, and I followed him to the wall where sheaves of paper hung by their corners, diamond shaped. "Pigeon lottery," he called them. "Pigeon lottery tickets." Yes, in the wind of the paddle fan the soft thick sheaves ruffled like feathers and wings. He gave me some used sheets. Gamblers had circled green and blue words in pink ink. They had bet on those words. You had to be a poet to win, finding lucky ways words go together. My father showed me the winning words from last night's games: "white jade that grows in water," "red jade that grows in earth," or – not so many words in Chinese – "white water-jade," "redearthjade," "firedragon," "waterdragon." He gave me pen and ink, and I linked words of my own: "rivercloud," "riverfire," the many combinations with *horse*, *cloud*, and *bird*. The lines and loops connecting the words, which were in squares, a word to a square, made designs too. So this was where my father worked and what he did for a living, keeping track of the gamblers' schemes of words.

We were getting the gambling house ready. Tonight the gamblers would come here from the towns and the fields; they would sail from San Francisco all the way up the river through the Delta to Stockton, which had more gambling than any city on the coast. It would be a party tonight. The gamblers would eat free food and drink free whiskey, and if times were bad, only tea. They'd laugh and exclaim over the poems they made, which were plain and very beautiful: "Shiny water, bright moon." They'd cheer when they won. BaBa let me crank the drum that spun words. It had a little door on top to reach in for the winning words and looked like the cradle that the Forty-niner ancestors had used to sift for gold, and like the drum for the lottery at the Stockton Chinese Community Fourth of July Picnic.

He also let me play with the hole puncher, which was a heavy instrument with a wrought-iron handle that took some strength to raise. I played gambler punching words to win – "cloudswallow," "riverswallow," "river forking," "swallow forking." I also punched perfect round holes in the corners so that I could hang the papers like diamonds and like pigeons. I collected round and crescent confetti in my cigar box.

While I worked on the floor under the tables, BaBa sat behind a counter on his tall stool. With black elastic armbands around his shirtsleeves and an eyeshade on his forehead, he clicked the abacus fast and steadily, stopping to write the numbers down in ledgers. He melted red wax in candle flame and made seals. He checked the pigeon papers, and set out fresh stacks of them. Then we twirled the dials of the safe, wound the grandfather clock, which had a long brass pendulum, meowed at the cats, and locked up. We bought crackly pork on the way home.

According to MaMa, the gambling house belonged to the most powerful Chinese American in Stockton. He paid my father to manage it and to pretend to be the owner. BaBa took the blame for the real owner. When the cop on the beat walked in, BaBa gave him a plate of food, a carton of cigarettes, and a bottle of whiskey. Once a month, the police raided with a paddy wagon, and it was also part of my father's job to be arrested. He never got a record, however, because he thought up a new name for himself every time. Sometimes it came to him while the city sped past the barred windows; sometimes just when the white demon at the desk asked him for it, a name came to him, a new name befitting the situation. They never found out his real names or that he had an American name at all. "I got away with aliases," he said, "because the white demons can't tell one Chinese name from another or one face from another." He had the power of naming. He had a hundred dollars ready in an envelope with which he bribed the demon in charge. It may have been a fine, not a bribe, but BaBa saw him pocket the hundred dollars. After that, the police let him walk out the door. He either walked home or back to the empty gambling house to straighten out the books.

Two of the first white people we children met were customers at the gambling house, one small and skinny man, one fat and jolly. They lived in a little house on the edge of the slough across the street from our house. Their arms were covered with orange and yellow hair. The round one's name was Johnson, but what everyone called him was Water Shining, and his partner was White Cloud. They had once won big on those words. Also *Johnson* resembles *Water Shining*, which also has *o*, *s*, and *n* sounds. Like two old China Men, they lived together lonely with no families. They sat in front of stores; they sat on their porch. They fenced a part of the slough for their vegetable patch, which had a wooden sign declaring the names of the vegetables and who they belonged to. They also had a wooden sign over their front door: TRANQUILITY, a wish or blessing or the name of their house. They gave us nickels and quarters; they made dimes come out of noses, ears, and elbows and waved coins in and out between their knuckles. They were white men, but they lived like China Men.

When we came home from school and a wino or hobo was trying the doors and windows, Water Shining came out of his little house. "There's a wino breaking into our house," we told him. It did occur to me that he might be offended at our calling his fellow white man a wino. "It's not just a poor man taking a drink from the hose or picking some fruit and going on his way," I explained.

"What? What? Where? Let's take a look-see," he said, and walked with us to our house, saving our house without a fight.

The old men disappeared one by one before I noticed their going. White Cloud told the gamblers that Water Shining was killed in a farming accident, run over by a tractor. His body had been churned and plowed. White Cloud lived alone until the railroad tracks were leveled, the slough drained, the blackbirds flown, and his house torn down.

My father found a name for me too at the gambling house. "He named you," said MaMa, "after a blonde gambler who always won. He gave you her lucky American name." My blonde namesake must have talked with a cigarette out of the side of her mouth and left red lip prints. She wore a low-cut red or green gambling dress, or she dressed cowgirl in white boots with baton-twirler tassels and spurs; a stetson hung at her back. When she threw down her aces, the leather fringe danced along her arm. And there was applause and buying of presents when she won. "Your father likes blondes," MaMa said. "Look how beautiful," they both exclaimed when a blonde walked by.

But my mother keeps saying those were dismal years. "He worked twelve hours a day, no holidays," she said. "Even on New Year's, no day off. He couldn't come home until two in the morning. He stood on his feet gambling twelve hours straight."

"I saw a tall stool," I said.

"He only got to sit when there were no customers," she said. "He got paid almost nothing. He was a slave; I was a slave." She is angry recalling those days.

After my father's partners stole his New York laundry, the owner of the gambling house, a fellow ex-villager, paid my parents' fares to Stockton, where the brick buildings reminded them of New York. The way my mother repaid him – only the money is repayable – was to be a servant to his, the owner's, family. She ironed for twelve people and bathed ten children. Bitterly, she kept their house. When my father came home from work at two in the morning, she told him how badly the owner's family had treated her, but he told her to stop exaggerating. "He's a generous man," he said.

The owner also had a black servant, whose name was Harry. The rumor was that Harry was a half-man/half-woman, a half-and-half. Two servants could not keep that house clean, where children drew on the wallpaper and dug holes in the plaster. I listened to Harry sing "Sioux City Sue." "Lay down my rag with a hoo hoo hoo," he sang. He squeezed his rag out in the bucket and led the children singing the chorus. Though my father was also as foolishly happy over his job, my mother was not deceived.

When my mother was pregnant, the owner's wife bought her a dozen baby chicks, not a gift; my mother would owe her the money. MaMa would be allowed to raise the chicks in the owner's yard if she also tended his chickens. When the baby was born, she would have chicken to give for birth announcements. Upon his coming home from work one night, the owner's wife lied to him, "The aunt forgot to feed her chickens. Will you do it?" Grumbling about my lazy mother, the owner went out in the rain and slipped in the mud, which was mixed with chicken shit. He hurt his legs and lay there yelling that my mother had almost killed him. "And she makes our whole yard stink with chicken shit," he accused. When the baby was born, the owner's wife picked out the scrawny old roosters and said they were my mother's twelve.

Ironing for the children, who changed clothes several times a day, MaMa had been standing for hours while pregnant when the veins in her legs rippled and burst. After that she had to wear support stockings and to wrap her legs in bandages.

The owner gave BaBa a hundred-and-twenty-dollar bonus when the baby was born. His wife found out and scolded him for "giving charity."

"You deserve that money," MaMa said to BaBa. "He takes all your time. You're never home. The babies could die, and you wouldn't know it."

When their free time coincided, my parents sat with us on apple and orange crates at the tiny table, our knees touching under it. We ate rice and salted fish, which is what peasants in China eat. Everything was nice except what MaMa was saying, "We've turned into slaves. We're the slaves of these villagers who were nothing when they were in China. I've turned into the servant of a woman who can't read. Maybe we should go back to China. I'm tired of being Wah Q," that is, a Sojourner from Wah.

My father said, "No." Angry. He did not like her female intrigues about the chickens and the ironing and the half-man/half-woman.

They saved his pay and the bonuses, and decided to buy a house, the very house they were renting. This was the two-story house around the corner from the owner's house, convenient for my mother to walk to her servant job and my father to the gambling house. We could rent out the bottom floor and make a profit. BaBa had five thousand dollars. Would the owner, who spoke English, negotiate the cash sale? Days and weeks passed, and when he asked the owner what was happening, the owner said, "I decided to buy it myself. I'll let you rent from me. It'll save you money, especially since you're saving to go back to China. You're going back to China anyway." But BaBa had indeed decided to buy a house on the Gold Mountain. And this was before Pearl Harbor and before the Chinese Revolution.

He found another house farther away, not as new or big. He again asked the owner to buy it for him. You would think we could trust him, our fellow villager with the same surname, almost a relative, but the owner bought up this house too – the one with the well in the cellar – and became our landlord again.

My parents secretly looked for another house. They told everyone, "We're saving our money to go back to China when the war is over." But what they really did was to buy the house across from the railroad tracks. It was exactly like the owner's house, the same size, the same floor plan and gingerbread. BaBa paid six thousand dollars cash for it, not a check but dollar bills, and he signed the papers himself. It was the biggest but most run-down of the houses; it had been a boarding house for old China Men. Rose bushes with thorns grew around it, wooden lace hung broken from the porch eaves, the top step was missing like a moat. The rooms echoed. This was the house with the attic and basement. The owner's wife accused her husband of giving us the money, but she was lying. We made our escape from them. "You don't have to be afraid of the owner any more," MaMa keeps telling us.

Sometimes we waited up until BaBa came home from work. In addition to a table and crates, we had for furniture an ironing board and an army cot, which MaMa unfolded next to the gas stove in the wintertime. While she ironed our clothes, she sang and talked-story, and I sat on the cot holding one or two of the babies. When BaBa came home, he and MaMa got into the cot and pretended they were refugees under a blanket tent. He brought out his hardbound brown book with the gray and white photographs of white men standing before a flag, sitting in rows of chairs, shaking hands in the street, hand-signaling from car windows. A teacher with a suit stood at a blackboard and pointed out things with a stick. There were no children or women or animals in this book. "Before you came to New York," he told my mother, "I went to school to study English. The classroom looked like this, and every student came from another country." He read words to my mother and told her what they meant. He also wrote them on the blackboard, it and the daruma, the doll which always rights itself when knocked down, the only toys we owned at that time. The little *h*'s looked like chairs, the *e*'s like lidded eyes, but those words were not *chair* and *eye*. "'Do you speak English?'" He read and translated. "'Yes, I am learning to speak English better.' 'I speak English a little.'" "'How are you?' 'I am fine, and you?'" My mother forgot what she learned from one reading to the next. The words had no crags, windows, or hooks to grasp. No pictures. The same *a*, *b*, *c*'s for everything. She couldn't make out ducks, cats, and mice in American cartoons either.

During World War II, a gang of police demons charged into the gambling house with drawn guns. They handcuffed the gamblers and assigned them to paddy wagons and patrol cars, which lined the street. The wagons were so full, people had to stand with their hands up on the ceiling to keep their balance. My father was not jailed or deported, but neither he nor the owner worked in gambling again. They went straight. Stockton became a clean town. From the outside the gambling house looks the same closed down as when it flourished.

My father brought his abacus, the hole punch, and extra tickets home, but those were the last presents for a while. A dismal time began for him.

He became a disheartened man. He was always home. He sat in his chair and stared, or he sat on the floor and stared. He stopped showing the boys the few kung fu moves he knew. He suddenly turned angry and quiet. For a few days he walked up and down on the sidewalk in front of businesses and did not bring himself to enter. He walked right past them in his beautiful clothes and acted very busy, as if having an important other place to go for a job interview. "You're nothing but a gambler," MaMa scolded. "You're spoiled and won't go looking for a job." "The only thing you're trained for is writing poems," she said. "I know you," she said. (I hated her sentences that started with "I know you.") "You poet. You scholar. You gambler. What use is any of that?" "It's a wife's job to scold her husband into working," she explained to us.

My father sat. "You're so scared," MaMa accused. "You're shy. You're lazy." "Do something. You never do anything." "You let your so-called friends steal your laundry. You let your brothers and the Communists take your land. You have no head for business." She nagged him and pampered him. MaMa and we kids scraped his back with a porcelain spoon. We did not know whether it was the spoon or the porcelain or the massage that was supposed to be efficacious. "Quit being so shy," she advised. "Take a walk through Chinatown and see if any of the uncles has heard of a job. Just ask. You don't even need to apply. Go find out the gossip." "He's shy," she explained him to us, but she was not one to understand shyness, being entirely bold herself. "Why are you so shy? People invite you and go out of their way for you, and you act like a snob or a king. It's only human to reciprocate." "You act like a piece of liver. Who do you think you are? A piece of liver?" She did not understand how some of us run down and stop. Some of us use up all our life force getting out of bed in the morning, and it's a wonder we can get to a chair and sit in it. "You piece of liver. You poet. You scholar. What's the use of a poet and a scholar on the Gold Mountain? You're so skinny. You're not supposed to be so skinny in this country. You have to be tough. You lost the New York laundry. You lost the house with the upstairs. You lost the house with the back porch." She summarized, "No loyal friends or brothers. Savings draining away like time. Can't speak English. Now you've lost the gambling job and the land in China."

Somebody – a Chinese, it had to be a Chinese – dug up our loquat tree, which BaBa had planted in front of the house. He or she had come in the middle of the night and left a big hole. MaMa blamed BaBa for that too, that he didn't go track down the tree and bring it back. In fact, a new loquat tree had appeared in the yard of a house around the corner. He ignored her, stopped shaving, and sat in his T-shirt from morning to night.

He seemed to have lost his feelings. His own mother wrote him asking for money, and he asked for proof that she was still alive before he would send it. He did not say, "I miss her." Maybe she was dead, and the Communists maintained a bureau of grandmother letter writers in order to get our money. That we kids no longer received the sweet taste of invisible candy was no proof that she had stopped sending it; we had outgrown it. For proof, the aunts sent a new photo-graph of Ah Po. She looked like the same woman, all right, like the pictures we already had but aged. She was ninety-nine years old. She was lying on her side on a lounge chair, alone, her head pillowed on her arm, the other arm along her side, no green tints at her earlobes, fingers, and wrists. She still had little feet and a curved-down mouth. "Maybe she's dead and propped up," we kids conjectured.

BaBa sat drinking whiskey. He no longer bought new clothes. Nor did he go to the dentist and come back telling us the compliments on his perfect teeth, how the dentist said that only one person in a thousand had teeth with no fillings. He no longer advised us that to have perfect teeth, it's good to clamp them together, especially when having a bowel movement.

MaMa assured us that what he was looking forward to was when each child came home with gold. Then he or she (the pronoun is neutral in the spoken language) was to ask the father, "BaBa, what kind of a suit do you want? A silk gown? Or a suit from the West? An Eastern suit or a Western suit? What kind of a Western suit do you want?" She suggested that we ask him right now. Go-out-on-the-road. Make our fortunes. Buy a Western suit for Father.

I went to his closet and studied his suits. He owned gray suits, dark blue ones, and a light pinstripe, expensive, successful suits to wear on the best occasions. Power suits. Money suits. Two-hundred-dollars-apiece New York suits. Businessmen-in-the-movies suits. Boss suits. Suits from before we were born. At the foot of the closet arranged in order, order his habit, were his leather shoes blocked on shoe trees. How could I make money like that? I looked in stores at suits and at the prices. I could never learn to sew this evenly, each suit perfect and similar to the next.

MaMa worked in the fields and the canneries. She showed us how to use her new tools, the pitters and curved knives. We tried on her cap pinned with union buttons and her rubber gloves that smelled like rubber tomatoes. She emptied her buckets, thermoses, shopping bags, lunch pail, apron, and scarf; she brought home every kind of vegetable and fruit grown in San Joaquin County. She said she was tired after work but kept moving, busy, banged doors, drawers, pots and cleaver, turned faucets off and on with *kachunks* in the pipes. Her cleaver banged on the chopping block for an hour straight as she minced pork and steak into patties. Her energy slammed BaBa back into his chair. She took care of everything; he did not have a reason to get up. He stared at his toes and fingers. "You've lost your sense of emergency," she said; she kept up her sense of emergency every moment.

He dozed and woke with a jerk or a scream. MaMa medicated him with a pill that came in a purple cube lined with red silk quilting, which cushioned a tiny black jar; inside the jar was a black dot made out of ground pearls, ox horn, and ox blood. She dropped this pill in a bantam broth that had steamed all day in a little porcelain crock on metal legs. He drank this soup, also a thick beef broth with gold coins in the bottom, beef teas, squab soup, and still he sat. He sat on. It seemed to me that he was getting skinnier.

"You're getting skinny again," MaMa kept saying. "Eat. Eat. You're less than a hundred pounds."

I cut a Charles Atlas coupon out of a comic book. I read all the small print. Charles Atlas promised to send some free information. "Ninety-seven-pound weakling," the cartoon man called himself. "I'll gamble a stamp," he said. Charles Atlas did not say anything about building fat, which was what my father needed. He already had muscles. But he was ninety-seven pounds like the weakling, maybe ninety pounds. Also he kicked over chairs like in the middle panel. I filled in the coupon and forged his signature. I did not dare ask him how old he was, so I guessed maybe he was half as old as his weight: age forty-five, weight ninety. If Charles Atlas saw that he was even skinnier than the weakling, maybe he would hurry up answering. I took the envelope and stamp from BaBa's desk.

Charles Atlas sent pamphlets with more coupons. From the hints of information, I gathered that my father needed lessons, which cost money. The lessons had to be done vigorously, not just read. There seemed to be no preliminary lesson on how to get up.

The one event of the day that made him get up out of his easy chair was the newspaper. He looked forward to it. He opened the front door and looked for it hours before the mailman was due. *The Gold Mountain News* (or *The Chinese Times*, according to the English logo) came from San Francisco in a paper sleeve on which his name and address were neatly typed. He put on his gold-rimmed glasses and readied his smoking equipment: the 1939 World's Fair ashtray, Lucky Strikes, matches, coffee. He killed several hours reading the paper, scrupulously reading everything, the date on each page, the page numbers, the want ads. Events went on; the world kept moving. The hands on the clocks kept moving. This sitting ought to have felt as good as sitting in his chair on a day off. He was not sick. He checked his limbs, the crooks of his arms. Everything was normal, quite comfortable, his easy chair fitting under him, the room temperature right.

MaMa said a man can be like a rat and bite through wood, bite through glass and rock. "What's wrong?" she asked.

"I'm tired," he said, and she gave him the cure for tiredness, which is to hit the inside joints of elbows and knees until red and black dots — the tiredness — appear on the skin.

He screamed in his sleep. "Night sweats," MaMa diagnosed. "Fear sweats." What he dreamed must have been ax murders. The family man kills his entire family. He throws slain bodies in heaps out the front door. He leaves no family member alive; he or she would suffer too much being the last one. About to swing the ax, screaming in horror of killing, he is also the last little child who runs into the night and hides behind a fence. Someone chops at the bushes beside him. He covers his ears and shuts his mouth tight, but the scream comes out.

I invented a plan to test my theory that males feel no pain; males don't feel. At school, I stood under the trees where the girls played house and watched a strip of cement near the gate. There were two places where boys and girls mixed; one was the kindergarten playground, where we didn't go any more, and the other was this bit of sidewalk. I had a list of boys to kick: the boy who burned spiders, the boy who had grabbed me by my coat lapels like in a gangster movie, the boy who told dirty pregnancy jokes. I would get them one at a time with my heavy shoes, on which I had nailed toe taps and horseshoe taps. I saw my boy, a friendly one for a start. I ran fast, crunching gravel. He was kneeling; I grabbed him by the arm and kicked him sprawling into the circle of marbles. I ran through the girls' playground and playroom to our lavatory, where I looked out the window. Sure enough, he was not crying. "See?" I told the girls. "Boys have no feelings. It's some kind of immunity." It was the same with Chinese boys, black boys, white boys, and Mexican and Filipino boys. Girls and women of all races cried and had feelings. We had to toughen up. We had to be as tough as boys, tougher because we only pretended not to feel pain.

One of my girl friends had a brother who cried, but he had been raised as a girl. Their mother was a German American and their father a Chinese American. This family didn't belong to our Benevolent Association nor did they go to our parties. The youngest boy wore girls' dresses with ruffles and bows, and brown-blondish ringlets grew long to his waist. When this thin, pale boy was about seven, he had to go to school; it was already two years past the time when most people started school. "Come and see something strange," his sister said on Labor Day. I stood in their yard and watched their mother cut off his hair. The hair lay like tails around his feet. Mother cried, and son cried. He was so delicate, he had feelings in his hair; it hurt him to have his hair cut. I did not pick on him.

There was a war between the boys and the girls; we sisters and brothers were evenly matched three against three. The sister next to me, who was like my twin, pushed our oldest brother off the porch railing. He landed on his face and broke two front teeth on the sidewalk. They fought with knives, the cleaver and a boning knife; they circled the dining room table and sliced one another's arms. I did try to stop that fight – they were cutting bloody slits, an earnest fight to the death. The telephone rang. Thinking it was MaMa, I shouted, "Help. Help. We're having a knife fight. They'll kill each other." "Well, do try to stop them." It was the owner's wife; she'd gossip to everybody that our parents had lost control of us, such bad parents who couldn't get respectable jobs, mother gone all day, and kids turned into killers. "That was Big Aunt on the phone," I said, "and she's going to tell the whole town about us," and they quit after a while. Our youngest sister snuck up on our middle brother, who was digging in the ground. She was about to drop a boulder on his head when somebody shouted, "Look out." She only hit his shoulder. I told my girl friends at school that I had a stepfather and three wicked stepbrothers. Among my stepfather's many aliases was the name of my real father, who was gone.

The white girls at school said, "I got a spanking." I said we never got spanked. "My parents don't believe in it," I said, which was true. They didn't know about spanking, which is orderly. My mother swung wooden hangers, the thick kind, and brooms. We got trapped behind a door or under a bed and got hit anywhere (except the head). When the other kids said, "They kissed me good night," I also felt left out; not that I cared about kissing but to be normal.

We children became so wild that we broke BaBa loose from his chair. We goaded him, irked him – *gikked* him – and the gravity suddenly let him go. He chased my sister, who locked herself in a bedroom. "Come out," he shouted. But, of course, she wouldn't, he having a coat hanger in hand and angry. I watched him kick the door; the round mirror fell off the wall and crashed. The door broke open, and he beat her. Only, my sister remembers that it was she who watched my father's shoe against the door and the mirror outside fall, and I who was beaten. But I know I saw the mirror in crazy pieces; I was standing by the table with the blue linoleum top, which was outside the door. I saw his brown shoe against the door and his knee flex and the other brothers and sisters watching from the outside of the door, and heard MaMa saying, "Seven years' bad luck." My sister claims that same memory. Neither of us has the recollection of curling up inside that room, whether behind the pounding door or under the bed or in the closet.

A white girl friend, whose jobless and drunk father picked up a sofa and dropped it on her, said, "My mother saw him pushing *me* down the stairs, and *she* was watching from the landing. And I remember him pushing *her*, and *I* was at the landing. Both of us remember looking up and seeing the other rolling down the stairs.'"

He did not return to sitting. He shaved, put on some good clothes, and went out. He found a friend who had opened a new laundry on El Dorado Street. He went inside and chatted, asked if he could help out. The friend said he had changed his mind about owning the laundry, which he had named New Port Laundry. My father bought it and had a Grand Opening. We were proud and quiet as he wrote in gold and black on big red ribbons. The Chinese community brought flowers, mirrors, and pictures of flowers and one of Guan Goong. BaBa's liveliness returned. It came from nowhere, like my new idea that males have feelings. I had no proof for this idea but took my brothers' word for it.

BaBa made a new special place. There was a trap door on the floor inside the laundry, and BaBa looked like a trap-door spider when he pulled it over his head or lifted it, emerging. The basement light shone through the door's cracks. Stored on the steps, which were also shelves, were some rolled-up flags that belonged to a previous owner; gold eagles gleamed on the pole tips.

We children waited until we were left in charge of the laundry. Then some of us kept a lookout while the rest, hanging on to the edge of the hole, stepped down between the supplies. The stairs were steep against the backs of our legs.

The floor under the building was gray soil, a fine powder. Nothing had ever grown in it; it was sunless, rainless city soil. Beyond the light from one bulb the blackness began, the inside of the earth, the insides of the city. We had our flash-lights ready. We chose a tunnel and walked side by side into the dark. There are breezes inside the earth. They blow cool and dry. Blackness absorbed our lights. The people who lived and worked in the four stories above us didn't know how incomplete civilization is, the street only a crust. Down here under the sidewalks and the streets and the cars, the builders had left mounds of loose dirt, piles of dumped cement, rough patches of concrete tamping down and holding back some of the dirt. The posts were unpainted and not square on their pilings. We followed the tunnels to places that had no man-made materials, wild areas, then turned around and headed for the lighted section under the laundry. We never found the ends of some tunnels. We did not find elevators or ramps or the undersides of the buckling metal doors one sees on sidewalks. "Now we know the secret of cities," we told one another. On the shelves built against the dirt walls, BaBa had stacked boxes of notebooks and laundry tickets, rubber stamps, pencils, new brushes, blue bands for the shirts, rolls of wrapping paper, cones of new string, bottles of ink, bottles of distilled water in case of air raids. Here was where we would hide when war came and we went underground for gorilla warfare. We stepped carefully; he had set copper and wood rat traps. I opened boxes until it was time to come up and give someone else a chance to explore.

So my father at last owned his house and his business in America. He bought chicks and squabs, built a chicken run, a pigeon coop, and a turkey pen; he dug a duck pond, set the baby bathtub inside for the lining, and won ducklings and goldfish and turtles at carnivals and county fairs. He bought rabbits and bantams and did not refuse dogs, puppies, cats, and kittens. He told a funny story about a friend of his who kept his sweater on while visiting another friend on a hot day; when the visitor was walking out the gate, the host said, "Well, Uncle, and what are those chicken feet wiggling out of your sweater?" One morning we found a stack of new coloring books and follow-the-dot books on the floor next to our beds. "BaBa left them," we said. He buried wine bottles upside down in the garden; their bottoms made a path of sea-color circles. He gave me a picture from the newspaper of redwoods in Yosemite, and said, "This is beautiful." He talked about a Los Angeles Massacre, but I wished that he had not, and pretended he had not. He told an ancient story about two feuding poets: one killed the other's plant by watering it with hot water. He sang "The Song of the Man of the Green Hill," the end of which goes like this: "The disheveled poet beheads the great whale. He shoots an arrow and hits a suspended flea. He sees well through rhinoceros-horn lenses." This was a song by Kao Chi, who had been executed for his politics; he is famous for poems to his wife and daughter written upon leaving for the capital; he owned a small piece of land where he grew enough to eat without working too hard so he could write poems. BaBa's luffa and grapevines climbed up ropes to the roof of the house. He planted many kinds of gourds, peas, beans, melons, and cabbages – and perennials – tangerines, oranges, grapefruit, almonds, pomegranates, apples, black figs, and white figs – and from seed pits, another loquat, peaches, apricots, plums of many varieties – trees that take years to fruit.

In the epic elegy *Li Sao*, or *Lament on Encountering Sorrow* (also translated *Sorrow After Departure* and *Sorrow in Estrangement*), Ch'ü Yüan, who is Kwut Ngin in our dialect, China's earliest known poet, a Homer, told how he wandered in exile. He lived during the Warring States period when China was twelve states.

("All Chinese know this story," says my father; if you are an authentic Chinese, you know the language and the stories without being taught, born talking them.)

Ch'ü Yüan, who was born on a Tiger day, was a minister in the Chou Kingdom. He advised the king not to go to war against Ch'in, but the king listened to the warmongers and fought a losing war. Because he had expressed an unpopular opinion, Ch'ü Yüan, also called Ch'ü P'ing, meaning "Peace," was banished. He had to leave the Center; he roamed in the outer world for the rest of his life, twenty years. He mourned that he had once been a prince, and now he was nothing. And the people were so blind, they thought he was a wrongdoer instead of the only righteous man left in the world. His love for his country was not returned. He sang poems wherever he went, haggard and poor, always homesick, roving from place to place on foot like an old beggar. Paintings show him floating above the tips of trees and horned houses, over other people's heads, his gown blowing with the clouds at his feet.

He braided a gown out of cress leaves and lilies, and traveled south into the barbarous lands. He met the Goddess of the Hsiang River and the Lady of the Hsiang River, the

wonderful women on either side of the water, who decorated him with clinking jade stones, winterthorn, orchids,
angel herbs, and selineas. Flying horses, swift green dragons,
and phoenixes with gold plumes pulled his chariot, which
was a winged dragonboat made of jade and ivory and
entwined with ivy leaves. He rowed with cedar oars and flew
orchids for flags; orchids were woven in the rigging, and the
boat was harnessed to the whirlwind. He left the land of gray
plane trees. He drank dew from lotus leaf and magnolia cups.
His food was aster petals. Which may all be a way of saying
that he had nothing but the outdoors, the mist, the rivers,
stones, lightning (his gold whip), and his imagination and
dreams. He reached heaven's gate and climbed the roof of
the world.

He had many adventures. He followed the phoenix to the
uttermost parts of the earth, crossed and recrossed the sky.
No home anywhere. He saw the entire world, but not his
homeland. He crossed the quicksand; he crossed the burning
river red as blood. The Emperor of the West helped him, and
the Great Emperor of the East listened to his odes of sacrifice. His steeds drank at the lake where the sun bathes. He
brushed the sun with a golden bough. The Lady of the
Clouds took him to nine continents and four seas. The
Princess of the West, however, declined to meet him, and
the falcon refused to act as go-between; the capricious
turtledove offered to go, but sent the phoenix, who failed
him. Some say he cast his jasper pendant on the earth, where
it blossomed; some say he cast his jade pendant into the
Hsiang River. He sang to the goddess who dries her hair in
the rising sun. He gave spiced rice to the wizard who makes
circles with green feathers, shoots the dog star with a shaft,
casts rainbows, and pours cassia wine from the North
Star. He traveled on the nine waters and among the islands
with the God of the Yellow River, who rides on a white tortoise beneath the water. He visited the Dragon Halls, purple

and pearly red palaces with walls that glittered like fish scales.

When winter came, he journeyed in thunder and rain. The monkeys and hyenas moaned at night, and he cried that he could not find his king and home. "Time runs like water and takes my youth," he wrote. He told the God of Law how he had been wronged and exiled; the king had gone hunting and the queen had been stolen by a false friend. His king did not aid the suffering people. "I am the phoenix dispossessed," said Ch'ü Yüan. In all these travels, he could not find one uncorrupted human being. He was once rich and handsome with moth-wing eyebrows; now he had no reputation and was misunderstood by Southern Savages. "I am the naked roaming saint whose head was shaved like a slave's." The distance between him and home grew farther each day. "My old wife has gone to a strange district; wind and snow separate us." "Birds fly back to last year's nest; foxes face the hill to die, but I cannot go home." "No go-between anywhere." He was an orphan who traveled everywhere because one place was denied him.

He wrote a poem made of one hundred and seventy questions with no answers. "Soothsayers who use tortoise shell and yarrow," he asked, "what is the order of creation?" "Who built the sky?" "Where does it end?" "What supports the sky?" "Shall I be one of the common herd or a skylark?" "Why do I try to bank up the waters in the dark sea when I am not a great whale?" "Can I convince people one by one about what is right?" The soothsayer said, "I cannot help you." The Witch of the Future, to whom he gave mistletoe, asked him, "Why do you want just that one country?"

From his dragonboat, he looked down at his home and realized that escape and return were equally impossible.

At last he walked along the Tsanglang River while reciting poems. He met a fisherman and told his story again. He had seen the entire corrupt world, and "the crowd is dirty," but he had never given up the ideal of good government. "The crowd is drunk; I alone am sober, I alone am clean, so I am banished. The world has gone bad. Even the reliable orchid has changed."

"Why should you be aloof?" asked the fisherman. "When the water's clear, I wash my tassels, but when it's too muddy for silk, I can still wash my feet."

Upon hearing these words, Ch'ü Yüan decided that he would use the river too. He sang all his poems and his elegy, his requiem. He danced at the edge of the river to make his last moments happier. He threw himself into the water and drowned. "There is no wisdom in the world," says the commentary to the *Li Sao*. "Its people are too corrupt to deserve a man like this."

After he drowned, the people realized his sincerity and their loss. Too late, they felt guilt for their waywardness. They tried to call him back. Poets stood by the river and told him how uncomfortable death was: "Return, O Soul," they sang, "from the empty places and the wrong things. Do not go where the titans live who are a thousand cubits tall, and ten suns eat stone, bronze, and gold. Don't wander among the Blackteeth. Don't go where the demons sacrifice men's flesh and grind their bones. Return, O Soul, from the land where cobras move like grass, and foxes rule for a thousand miles. Don't sink into the thousand-mile quicksand or the pool that thunders. Don't go where red ants grow big as elephants and black wasps big as gourds. No crops grow in the dead lands, and human beings eat thorns and weeds. Return from the land of icebergs like mouths. Don't go to the heaven where tigers guard nine gates, serpents have nine heads, and the giant with the nine heads tears up nine thousand forests. Stay away from the devil with the tiger's forehead and three eyes. Stay away from the eater of human beings."

Then they enticed him with the pleasures of earth: "Return to earth. Return to earth where you have your own room with no surprises, your home warm in winter and cool in summer. Return to the porch with the balustrade and enter again the doors with the red squares. Return, O Soul, to the earth's great halls, domes, towers, and terraces. Remember the flowers and the birds, wild ducks, black cranes, wild geese." They chanted food poems and long, long lists of food: "Pepper with honey, steak, bitter melon soup, lamb, turtle, sugarcane juice." They reminded him of his clothes, the red belts, the silks. "Remember candles and early wheat, salt vinegar, ginger, and water." They sang about girls as mouthwatering as salt plums and lemons. "Come back and listen to the singing girls, who have made new songs. Play the urn and drum. Do the wind dance. Play the drums for war songs. Walk in the fields and sing the rustic songs from sea countries. Look again at the actresses playing warriors. Play chess. Hunt the rhino. Return, O Soul. Return."

The people threw rice into the river for his ghost to eat. They did this every year on the anniversary of his death, and they raced dragonboats up and down the river in memory of his travels or in search of him. Ch'ü Yüan was such a smart man that one day he managed to send his ghost out of the river and say, "Oh, you foolish people. The fish are eating the rice, and I'm going hungry. Wrap it in leaves for me." For a change they listened to him. And so on the fifth day of the fifth month, we eat rice and barley cooked in sausage and pork and salted eggs and beans, and a yellow gelatin, shaped by ti leaves. Not just Chinese but the people in Korea, Japan, Vietnam, Malaysia, and America remember Ch'ü Yüan the incorruptible.

THE BROTHER IN VIETNAM

My mother holding my hand, I went through a curtain into a dark, out of which came explosions and screams, voices shouting things I did not understand. In a rectangle of light – which grew and shrank according to how close or far away I thought it – men with scared eyes peered over the top of a big hole they were in. Helmets weighed down their skulls. Their cheekbones were black. The men ran, clutching guns, and fell, and crawled. The explosions rolled them screaming on the ground. I saw the undersides of their boots. Their faces and hands were not flesh-color. Everyone wore the same outfits. The color had gone out of the world. I stumbled tangle-legged into my mother's skirt and the curtain and screamed with the soldiers.

Suddenly they were all gone like a dream, and I was crying in the street. Years later I figured it had only been a movie, a war movie, an old sepia-tone. "Did you take me to an American movie when I was a baby?" I've asked. Usually my father took us to American movies, my mother to Chinese movies, where she could visit with friends during the boring parts, and children played and shouted without getting ejected. MaMa said, "You cried so much that the usher ghost threw me out of the theater." I worried about making her waste money on a ticket, and so she diverted me from the actual horror – I had seen a vision of war.

There has always been war, whether or not I knew about it. My tall parents even taller standing on ladders and covering the windows with black curtains, playing theater in the bright interstice, had been thinking about war. The curtains fell long and black, but the inside of the room shone. My father cut a picture out of a magazine and pinned it on the wall. The yellow light came from it. "You look like this," he said, or "This girl looks like you." She was shining because of her golden hair, a golden girl. It couldn't have been the blonde curls that made her look like me, so it must have been the round face with the fat cheeks. "Shirley Temple also looks like this girl." I had been diverted again, and for some years the importance of that day seemed the blonde girl when those were blackout curtains for World War II.

There is no word like *vision* for what one hears. I heard *earthquake* – it may have been during an earthquake – and listened to the world, which was a blue and green sphere with lines of meridians, spinning against a wood fence. It did not clatter against the fence but hummed. "The earth," I said, and did not say "quake" because of the mightiness of it, *earth* the same word as *world* in "World War II."

About the fourth and fifth things I remember – and each thing has to do with war – were my two youngest brothers being born. My sister and brother and I were alone; the adults were in a room across the hall. They had said, "Stay here," but did not shut us in. My sister and I were standing on the bed when we noticed that through a crack at the door-jamb coincidentally lined up with the crack of the door across the hall, we could see into that other room, which was filled with light. MaMa was squatting over a basin, and blood was pouring from her. So that was how babies were born. Our room turned white, and through the window flew a white Christmas card like a dove and landed on the floor. It had fluttered in the air. Forgetting about what we had seen through the cracks, my sister and I picked up the card. It was very beautiful with snow and sparkles. "There's no envelope," we said. "No stamp. No name. No mailman. How could it come through the window?" I checked the window; someone must have snuck up to the open window and thrown the card in. But screen and glass were shut tight against the winter. "You saw it too, didn't you?" my sister and I asked each other, our brother only about a year old and no help. "Yes, it flew through the glass near here." We pointed out the pane, one of the top ones. "How did this card come into the room?" we asked when an adult entered. "The baby's born," said the adult. That baby was my brother who was born on Christmas day. Later the adults said that they found him naked under a pine tree, but I knew what I had seen: blood and a flash of white flying, a flash of flying white.

In addition to his American name, this new brother was named Han Bridge like a bridge between Han and here. We're Han People from the Han Dynasty. Bridge is the name of my brothers' generation. The Chinese name of the brother who waited with us is Incorruptible Bridge or Pure Bridge.

Two years later when our youngest brother was born, I knew days and hours in advance that we were going to have another brother. My mother and the lady doctor locked themselves in a bedroom. I was in charge of my sister and two brothers and decided that we had to arrange to see this birth. Each of us carried a crate or a stool outside and lined it up on the porch under the window (where the card had flown in). We climbed up in a row and saw the doctor lift a white bundle like a snowdrop on a hook. A foot stuck out. The baby had been born. He was being weighed. We heard him cry. Joy swelled the world. We jumped up and down and sang a song the animals in fables sing when they are happy. " 'Jump like a squirrel. Bob like a bluejay. Tails in the air. Tails in the air.' " We added our own lines, "The baby's born. The baby's born." Our parents motioned for us to come inside.

This youngest brother was long, thin, and red with very black hair; the other brother had been pale. His fists were tight like fern curls. I pried the fingers open, careful not to break one; there was lint in there already. I put my finger in his hand so that it would feel as if he were holding my hand.

MaMa said that a tightfisted baby is lucky because his father saves money, and the baby will also save money. I was glad to see that he had that good useful trait to keep him safe. BaBa named him Bright Bridge, also translated Severe Bridge.

"Where did the baby come from?" I asked the doctor as I walked her to the door.

"I brought him in my black bag." Adults were always diverting us from the awful. They wanted to protect us, as I wanted to protect the baby, who a moment ago had been nothing and could easily slip back.

I made sure the windows were locked over the baby's crib, and patrolled those locks and latches. I watched the winos and hoboes. Once, we found one of my brothers sitting in the lap of a black man, who was sitting on the sidewalk. I saw burglars carry off the tuba from the Filipino Marching Band's basement. I watched shadows in the neighbors' windows strangling one another. Feet dangled from ceilings and trees. A big gray bomb slowly covered the skies between houses, but it was only a Navy blimp. Airplanes flew over, but their bomb hatches stayed shut. *Life* magazine showed black and white photographs of dead bodies, limbs, and heads in impossible positions, rib cages barely covered with skin, faces that one could not stop staring at. Piles of skeletons with teeth and eye sockets and hair. "Is this real?" "Yes, it's real." "What happened to these people?" "They were killed in the war."

The Chinese magazines had war cartoons. In the first panel an ugly man in the cockpit of an airplane laughed as he divebombed villagers and water buffaloes. "What is he, MaMa?" "He's an enemy person." So that was what the enemy looked like. He had an evil black pointed moustache, a skullcap, and goggles. She did not say enemy people were Japanese, so for a time, I thought they were from outer space. In the next panel an enemy bayoneted an old man, spurting his blood. A bayonet was a gun that shot knives. An enemy threw two naked babies into the air, and another enemy caught one on his bayonet. The second baby fell to the ground and smashed. A booted enemy stepped on its head. The mother had her arms raised toward the babies. Then the mother was in a cage, the father in another cage, a crowd of children in another, the mother's and father's and children's arms reaching toward one another through the bars. The cells were like cages for ducks and chickens at market. In one panel the huge mother was grimacing, her stomach bloated. She was drinking from a jug. MaMa explained that the Japanese were forcing her to drink water until she burst. They would bounce on her stomach and it would explode. They were torturing her children in front of her, and stopped whenever she drank. If she peed, she had to drink her own urine. The children's mutilation was so gruesome, the cartoonist did not show it.

The adults told us how the Japanese tortured the American soldiers they captured: They tied the prisoner to a stake, and while slicing and poking, they cut an opening in his side and knotted a rope to one of his large intestines. A Japanese, pretending to be friendly, loosened the rope that bound his hands and feet. The American ran, and the rope pulled his guts out in a stream behind him. The Japanese laughed, as they did at the bursting mother and the skewered baby.

While watching for lurkers come to kidnap the babies, I saw many first stars, and wasted them wishing for peace. I was careful to define *peace* so the tricky gods didn't make the earth peaceful by killing everything on it. War used up the magic rings, bracelets, wands, the fairies with dandelion skirts, the fish I let go. I wrote a spell, a one and zeroes all the way around the rims of the lamp shades on my parents' nightstands, turned on the lights, and said, "I wish MaMa and BaBa to live as many years as I have written around this lamp." Black ribbons, black wreaths, and pennants with stars hanging in windows and on doors meant the sons of those houses had been killed in war.

Each time we went to the Confucius Hall for meetings and Chinese movies, everybody together bowed three bows, and somebody on stage lit three sticks of incense, the first to wish happiness to the ruler, the second for World Peace, and the third, good harvest. Sun Yat Sen's and Chiang Kai Shek's pictures were on the stage next to the American and Chinese flags. (My father's small picture was among the other founders' in the foyer.) We sang the Chinese National Anthem, and heard hours of speeches about war and the obligations of us Wah People, then pledged money to help China.

At the parades, where tanks and rockets rolled by and soldiers and sailors marched, Chinese Americans carried a giant red Chinese flag that covered the street for people to throw money on. The dragon in those days came to our houses. We tied lettuce and new dollar bills from the porch eaves, and the dragon jumped for its food. All this money was used for rescuing war refugees.

The houses where the Japanese American families lived were shut down, and the gardens overgrown as if enchanted. We kids explored empty houses and called them haunted. We walked around the yards, climbed in doors and windows, wandered about the rooms, sat on the furniture. A boy fell through a floor. And once we saw a foot step out of a doorway. We ran from it and lost one of the girls, who sat on a curb bent over with a stomach-ache. The foot was in white socks and oxfords.

All the talk was about war and death. Even the story about the squirrel and the blue jay was about their burying a friend. Buried. Fa Mu Lan bled from sword wounds until her armor was soaked red. Ngok Fei's arms were tied behind his back, and the blood squeezed out from the wooden collar around his neck. Grandfather was bayoneted in the head for

patriotically withholding information from a Japanese soldier. My mother's family, which had four girls, had saved the
only boy, the youngest, Uncle Wah, who dodged the draft.
He had been fifteen years old, maybe only fourteen, Chinese
adding a year, when they gave him all their money and
helped him escape to Singapore.

"'The superior man minds his own business; fools con-
cern themselves with public matters,'" said the adults, talking
politics. "'Fan Kuei was a butcher before becoming a general.'" "'Warlords confiscate the land, and kidnap the farmer
to guard some obscure border.'" "'To go to war is to
mingle with the desert sands.'"

"Armies enter the village with draft lists, and there are
dots against our names," sang Tu Fu. "Boys come back with
their hair white." He wrote that giving birth to daughters is
better than sons. "We can still give her in marriage, keep her
as a neighbor, but a son is buried without ceremonies among
the hundred grasses." "Soldiers ravage and burn even the
print blocks." He sang a threnody for a woman sewing the
head back on her husband's dead body. "A wife of a soldier is
a wisteria clinging to an old tree." "A woman married to a
soldier is rabbit silk clinging to wild chrysanthemum and
hemp."

Soldiers wrote their poems on the paper money they'd
been paid and let the money fly away in the wind at
crossroads.

In his last five poems before he died in battle, Wang Tsan, a
poet with eidetic memory in Ts'ao Ts'ao's army, witnessed
the final days of the Han Dynasty. He saw a woman throw
her child into yellow weeds, which were studded with skulls.
While he wandered in the embers and ashes of once-tall
cities, he cupped his hands like blinders beside his eyes.

There was a farmer in Mei Chia village, who knew that
he would be drafted. Recruiters told the hungry farmer
about the food, clothes, and shoes the army would give him

free. He could send all the pay home to his mother. Whichever army reached the village first would force him to fight on its side or shoot him for an enemy, so he might as well volunteer. His mother told him that she did not want that money. But the farmer said he would have to get some sleep if he was to go to war in the morning. That night as he lay sleeping, his mother stabbed his eyes out with her two hairpicks.

Freedom from the draft was the reason for leaving China in the first place. The Gold Mountain does not make war, is not invaded, and has no draft. The government does not capture men and boys and send them to war.

My father was exactly the right age for the draft. So was Uncle Bun's son and Big Brother Sao. Everybody suggested ways to get out of war. Certain butchers were supposed to be efficient cutting off the trigger finger with one blow of the cleaver. "He's faster than a surgeon." There were diets to get thinner and diets to get fatter. So-and-so had gained ten pounds on the day of the physical by eating ten pounds of bananas. They discussed the advantages and dangers of staying awake for a week drinking coffee. They rehearsed flunking ear tests – not to turn around when a tester whispered behind them, for example.

"There was a poet who took a drug that paralyzed his vocal cords. I wonder what drug that was."

"Chlorine bleach and ammonia. The effect, unfortunately, is permanent."

"What you do to foil the X-ray machine is drink ink straight. Then the photograph comes out black."

"Is ink poisonous?"

"A brother in Los Angeles drank ink. He's gotten out of the draft, and he's still healthy. Wouldn't you rather die drinking ink than be blown up by a land mine?"

Borax, alum, rat poison. Run for twenty miles a day while smoking cigarettes.

I sniffed at the undiluted ink; it smelled metallic sweet. The men were brave and desperate to drink it. It made my teeth clench.

"Drink two quarts before the X-rays."

They experimented how to make more phlegm, how to ruin the stomach, how to control temperature and blood pressure by will power and breath.

"That inking the X-rays is not going to work," my father said. "It's only a superstition; it won't work." He was interested because he had been drafted.

BaBa did not sleep after he got drafted. I planned to be always awake too, alert, on guard. I would make time pass deliberately, like a slow train, but suddenly my mother and two of the children and I were on a train. Our father was not with us; we were traveling with the owner of the gambling house. He was the most powerful of the Stockton Chinese, an American citizen, an English speaker; he dealt with white people on our behalf. They knew him as a good citizen and Chinese community spokesman. The seat did not fit; I stood on it or in the aisle. Everything moved. We did not have to walk on top of the train, nor did we have to sneak aboard a boxcar. We were going where the tracks went, to Sacramento, Second City. "Look," said my mother. "Sheep. Look at the sheep." I was standing at the window, but did not see anything until she said "Sheep," and they appeared, white in the sun. I looked at her, and when I turned back, they were gone. The train whistled regularly ahead of us. At bends the engine and the caboose looked like other trains. We were on our way to rescue BaBa from the United States Army.

In Second City we took taxis and walked to places that were like train stations. We sat on benches waiting, or stood against MaMa on sidewalks and in hallways. We waited in lobbies decorated with posters of Army, Navy, and Marine demons. The baby didn't cry. Father's employer went away to talk to generals; then he also waited. BaBa was somewhere inside this city. Homeless and fatherless, I did not see how we were going to find the train tracks again. My mother said, "I'm going to go into the general's office and beg him not to take your father. I'll say, 'These children's lives depend on him.' Then all of you cry, 'BaBa. BaBa. Don't take our BaBa away from us.'" I would hang on to her coat, my sister to her hand, my brother be the babe in arms.

MaMa was wearing her black New York coat with the black fur collar; I wore my maroon coat with the brown fur collar, and my sister, her powder blue coat with the gray fur collar.

This waiting was like when villagers waited in the landlord's courtyard to pay taxes. The other reason for leaving China was the taxes paid with grain. There was a story about a widow who paid with the heads of her two children. The peasants cried Aiya when she poured their heads out of a rice bag. "Here are your taxes," she said as the heads rolled out at the feet of the landlord. Landlords and generals and governments "pare and peel the ignorant country people." Families had to sell the mother or a sister, leave her there at the landlord's.

At last, suddenly, BaBa came out of a door, laughing and talking. Time rippled again. He told MaMa what had happened to him: "We had to take all our clothes off, and file past the doctor demon. The white man in front of me was white and fat — rolls of fat. And there I was next to him — skinny with rows of ribs. The doctor flunked us both at once. Too fat and too skinny. He took one look at us, and said, 'Four F.' Mr. Too Fat and Mr. Too Thin. We pointed at each other and laughed." He told this miracle many times.

All of us together again, we found the train and went home. As soon as we got in the door, MaMa started fattening him up, but it never worked. She had been using her old doctoring skills poisoning him, and his weight had dropped permanently. "I poisoned him to keep him out of World

War II," she says. "Now all these years, I've been trying to plump him up with food and medicine, but he stays skinny. His metabolism is ruined. He eats a lot but doesn't gain weight."

The cousins who were not clever enough to avoid the war – in fact some foolhardy ones enlisted – sent pictures from Europe. They looked like the good soldiers in the movies. Uncle Bun's son, who had been the most enthusiastic about drinking ink and shooting off toes, had posed for a studio portrait of himself in a helmet with antennae. His hands in gauntlets held a machine with nozzles; the hose was draped around his neck. Big Brother Sao, an officer, wore a creased hat in some pictures and a brimmed hat in others; he is looking sideways into the camera to show off the bars on his collar. A Boston cousin was among a group of soldiers kneeling and standing in front of their tent. Their hair was inside hats and helmets, and they wore rumpled uniforms. My mother said they were army doctors. I kept asking which were men and which women, but she didn't know either. We guessed the pretty ones were women. The ones with beard stubbles and big knuckles were definitely men. The one that was our cousin had the chin strap of his helmet unbuckled, and it hung down jauntily and war-wearily. If he had not written which one he was, we would not have been able to pick him out; he did not look peculiarly Chinese. It must have been the uniform. Another cousin sent a picture of himself leaning against a palm tree; he looked like he was in a war musical.

One cousin was in the Fourteenth Service Squad, the Chinese American Air Force Battalion, the first American soldiers into China. What they found in Chungking was a city of primitive natives who did not understand Cantonese. The soldiers hired them as houseboys, carriers, and road builders. Two by two the Chinese carried bombs tied to a pole between them. They moved fifty-gallon drums of fuel.

The Chinese Americans drove their trucks on the new road while thousands of natives built it before them. Men, women, and children broke rocks into gravel so fast the drivers did not have to step on their brakes.

We had a family portrait taken to send to the faraway relatives. One brother was dressed in a kid army uniform with a leather strap across his chest and another brother in a baby navy uniform with white middy collar and white shorts, his sweet knees showing.

We went to a movie where the attendants gave each kid a free picture of an atomic bomb explosion. Smoke boiled in a yellow and orange cloud like a brain on a column. It was a souvenir to celebrate the bombing of Japan. Since I did not own much, I enjoyed the ownership of the V. J. picture. At the base of the explosion, where the people would have been, the specks didn't resolve into bodies. I hid the picture so the younger children could not see it, to protect them against the fear of such powerful evil, not to break the news to them too soon. Occasionally, I took it out to study. I hid it so well, I lost it. I drew billows and shafts of light, and almost heard the golden music of it, the gold trumpets with drums of it.

For a while after the soldiers in the family came home, they looked like their photographs; they wore the uniforms visiting. But then they put on their regular slacks and white shirts. Their hair grew out, and their wives trimmed it with home clippers. Their noses rounded out, the bridges receding, and their tight jaws softened. They did not walk from the shoulders like football players and boxers any more. They started speaking Chinese loud again. Big Brother Sao's eyes began looking at things far away again.

The one family of AJA's, Americans of Japanese Ancestry, on our block came out of relocation camp. They did not seem capable of killing 10 million Chinese civilians, but then these were Americans and not Japanese. We had not broken into their house; it had stood shut for years. They pruned the bushes back into neat balls; they preferred ornamentals over vegetables. They gave us their used comic books, and were the only adults who gave us toys instead of clothes for Christmas. We kids, who had peasant minds, suspected their generosity; they were bribing us not to lynch them. The friendlier they were, the more hideous the crimes and desires they must have been covering up. My parents gave them vegetables; we would want them to be nice to us when the time came for us Chinese to be the ones in camp. No matter how late we walked home from the laundry, as we passed their house, they switched on their porch light to light our way.

A comic book they gave us each month was *Blackhawk*, which is about a squadron of allied pilots. Chop Chop was the only Blackhawk who did not wear a blue-black pilot's uniform with yellow and black insignia. He wore slippers instead of boots, pajamas with his undershirt showing at the tails, white socks, an apron; he carried a cleaver and wore a pigtail, which Chinese stopped wearing in 1911. He had buck teeth and slanted lines for eyes, and his skin was a muddy orange. Fat and half as tall as the other Blackhawks, who were drawn like regular human beings, Chop Chop looked like a cartoon. It was unclear whether he was a boy or a little man. He did not pilot his own plane but rode behind the main Blackhawk, the American. "Very clever, these Chinese," Blackhawk kept saying; "I always said little Chop Chop is the smartest of the Blackhawks." And not being clever myself, I took these words as compliments. Tall dragon ladies with cigarette holders said, "I'd kill for a kiss from those lips," meaning Blackhawk's or André's. I thought I had to learn to like Chop Chop; it was certainly true that we used cleavers, and we admired fat people, and I for one was short. We decided the Japanese family must not have known what those comics meant, or they wouldn't have bought them.

The cousins who had gone to war didn't talk about what they had seen or done, just as the AJA's did not mention the camps. They must have been too ashamed. They might have talked among themselves, and shut up in front of an outsider like me, not a soldier, not an AJA. The stories unfit for children must have been worse than guts hanging out, legs and brains hurtling through the air, cities and countries bombed into insanity, my own cousins killing Germans and Italians. I wouldn't tell children such things either.

The next enemy was the Communists. Our parents agreed that we should not meet at a designated place should Stockton be bombed but be free to escape with our teachers if we were at school or to run with the neighbors. But we children privately planned to meet at the big tree, wait for each other there, come back to the tree years later if we got lost in the city altered by bombing. The scary thing about going to school was that I might come home to find a bomb crater, or the house would be empty. I would walk from room to room calling, and then the sun would go down. The AJA children must have come home from school and waited on the porch for their parents to open the door, but they had been taken to camp.

Grandmother and the aunts wrote letters on the deaths of every last uncle. If the uncles could have figured out what the Communists wanted of them, they would have complied, but Communism made no sense. It was something to do with new songs, new dances, and the breaking up of families. Maybe it had to do with no sex; the men were separated from the women. Children were put into motherless, fatherless camps for training; they were taught to report on their parents instead of guarding family secrets. The Communists were not simply after property; they wanted the people to say certain things. They had to sing ugly Communist songs. "Stoop and scoop, stoop and scoop," they sang, and genuflected, swooping their red scarves from air to ground. The aunts waved their kerchiefs vigorously; they memorized fast and sang loud, but still they had to kneel on ground glass, and their thumbs were broken. They did whatever they thought the Communists wanted, but the Communists were not satisfied. Communists were people who had gone crazy and perverted. They made order by rationing food, a cup of oil per family per week. They held court trials, which they thought were the same as entertainment and theater. The torturers asked riddles with no correct answers. The uncles had listened to the answers of the people ahead of them, but the Communists wanted peculiar responses; the same answer did not fit everyone. Communist schools taught from strange books. The uncles had been kept awake at night to study. "If Uncle doesn't get some sleep soon, he's going to die. He's working from four a.m. to eleven p.m., then has to study how to be a Communist in his spare time. If he doesn't memorize a page a day perfectly, he can't have his dinner." The Communists were monkeys trying to be human beings; they were pretending to explain and reason, putting on serious faces. They were saying nonsense, pretending they knew the classics when they were not teaching from real books. Communist schools, Communist books, Red art work, Red courts, theaters, customs were almost like real ones but off. The shrewd villagers were not fooled. The Japanese had tortured people for the fun of it; the Communists wanted something else: their monkey civilization. Neighbors informed against one another to prove they were true Communists. The number of people the Communists killed was 60 million.

After the uncles were killed, the aunts fled to Hong Kong, Canada, and the United States. That the Communists were holding their distant cousins as hostages did not deter them.

"I wish the Japanese had won," my mother said.

For the Korean War, we wore dog tags and had Preparedness Drill in the school basement. We had to fill out a form for what to engrave on the dog tags. I looked up "religion" in the *American-Chinese Dictionary* and asked my mother what religion we were. "Our religion is Chinese," she said. "But that's not a religion," I said. "Yes, it is," she said. "We believe in the Chinese religion." "Chinese is our race," I said. "Well, tell the teacher demon it's Kung Fu Tse, then," she said. The kids at school said, "Are you Catholic?" "No." "Then you're a Protestant." So our dog tags had O for religion and O for race because neither black nor white. Mine also had O for blood type. Some kids said O was for "Oriental," but I knew it was for "Other" because the Filipinos, the Gypsies, and the Hawaiian boy were O's. Zero was also the name of the Japanese fighter plane, so we had better watch our step. The teachers gave us anti-Communist comic books and Civil Defense pamphlets about atomic bomb attacks. We did a scientific experiment about chain reactions by arranging matches in triangles, the first match burning and lighting two, and those two igniting four, and so on until the whole world was on fire. The earth would quake and split in half.

"The War," I wrote in a composition, which the teacher corrected, "Which war?" There was more than one.

Before the letter writers stopped complaining about the Communists, the Vietnam war had begun. The government said that Viet Cong weapons came from China. We ought to bomb China into the Stone Age, the generals said. Soon the war would be Chinese Americans against Chinese. And my brothers old enough to be drafted.

One brother got married a few months before the draft exemption for married men was canceled. But one brother enlisted in the Navy and the other was commissioned as an officer in the Air Force.

I drove my youngest brother to the airport in the middle of the night. He didn't want the flowers I brought; he had already refused to carry the chickens and puddings that MaMa had cooked. He was in his uniform like the middy that he wore in his baby picture. He said not to wait for him to board or for the plane to take off. "Go on," he said. "Don't wait around." So I only got to see him check his luggage. As I drove past the terminal, I saw him sitting by himself on a cement bench under a light.

The brother tried to get into the Coast Guard, which he thought rescued surfers and sailboats and directed traffic around buoys. He drove to Santa Cruz and Monterey, and there were no openings; everybody else who did not want to go to war had had the same idea. Then the Coast Guard were sent to Vietnam to fight on the rivers there.

The Japanese and Chinese Americans warned one another what would happen if they got captured: the Vietnamese would flay Asian Americans alive. Unless you die of shock, you're still alive after being skinned. You had to die fighting. Imagine the eyes looking out of a skinless body. During World War II the United States had tactfully sent the 442nd Go-For-Broke AJA's to Europe, not Asia or the Pacific. But for this war, there was not that special consideration.

The rumor also went that the brother's draft board was channeling hippies and blacks into the infantry. And "Orientals" belonged over there in Asia fighting among their own kind. The only way that he would be able to get classified as a Conscientious Objector was to have a religion, and he did not have one. He did not want to end up a medic in this immoral war anyway.

While deciding what to do, as time ran out, the brother did his job, which was teaching high school. He had been teaching for months, but had not gotten over his surprise at how dumb the students were. Most of them had an I.Q. of 100, the average, which permitted them to read by sounding out each word. The human race was not smart.

During Current Events, he told his class some atrocities to convince them about the wrongness of war. The students looked at the pictures of napalmed children and said, "Sure, war is hell." Where had they learned that acceptance? He told them the worst torture he knew: the Vikings used to cleave a prisoner-of-war's back on either side of the spine, and pull the lungs out, which fluttered like wings when the man breathed. This torture was called the Burning Eagle. The brother felt that it was self-evident that we ought to do anything to stop war. But he was learning that upon hearing terrible things, there are people who are, instead, filled with a crazy patriotism.

"Who owns the electricity?" a boy with an 85 I.Q. and a third-grade reading level asked one day. The brother recognized a "teachable moment," as these happy seconds were called in college. He explained how water, electricity, gas, and oil originally belonged to nobody and everybody. Like the air. "But the corporations that control electricity sell it to the rest of us," he said. "Well, of course they do," said the student; "I'd sell the air if I had discovered it." "What if some people can't afford to buy it?" "Whoever discovered it deserves to be paid for it," said the stubborn boy. "It's Communist not to let him make all the money he can." Although the students could not read or follow logic, they blocked him with their anti-Communism, which seemed to come naturally to them, without effort or study. He had thought that it was self-evident that air, at least, belongs to all of us. The students' parents were on welfare, unemployment, and workmen's compensation, but they defended capitalism without knowing what it was called.

"Can you invent a plan where a person can always find a job, and with that job make a living?" the brother asked. "How do we go about making food instead of bombs?" "What steps can we take to stop the war in Vietnam?"

"You think like that because you're a Communist," the kids replied. "That's a Communist question." Any criticism he had of America they dismissed as his being gookish.

Students were dropping out, not in protest like college students but to volunteer for the Army, Navy, and Marines. He had a few months, a few weeks, days to educate them before they got killed or killed others in Vietnam. Or until he himself had to go. He had to make up words of advice on the spot. Supposedly men, the dropouts came back to the hallways to show off their sturdy uniforms and good shoes. They looked more substantial, taller, smoothed out, as if some kind of potential had been fulfilled. "Take care of yourself," he told them. To those who dropped out to work on assembly lines, he said, "Find out what you're making."

In the one class that wasn't remedial, strange things happened to the literature. After the lessons on how to fill out employment forms, checks, income tax forms, drivers' license and health insurance applications, after reading and discussing the motor vehicle code, he introduced *Romeo and Juliet* with a movie of it, models of the Globe, role-playing, and the sound track from *West Side Story*. But upon its reading, *Romeo and Juliet* became a horror story about children his students' age whispering, tiptoeing, making love, and driven mad in the dark. They killed and were killed in dark streets and dark rooms. They married in the dark. Plague infested the country, and drugs poisoned instead of cured. Children were buried alive among their ancestors' bones, with which Juliet feared she would dash in her brains. She was locked in a tomb with her dead husband, a young suicide, and her cousin festering green. The brother could not shift the emphasis; he felt he had spoiled the love story for a generation of students.

Between classes he found secret torn books hidden underneath shelves and stuffed behind other books. Somebody had jammed books behind the radiator and up the air vent, "Fuck you, basturds" scrawled on their pages. Books that he had bought for a classroom library were ripped in half along the bindings.

The students shamed by Remedial Reading covered their books with paper bags or oil cloth. The remedials had no brotherly feeling toward one another. "Dummy," they said. "Stupid." "Shut up, Stupid." There were hardly any girl remedials; when girls landed in those classes, they improved quickly and got out.

His students stole anything. They shot up bowling alleys, and beat up hippies and whores ("Hors Welcome" they painted on their cars). One boy collected German helmets, bayonets, knives ("with real bloodstains"), swastikas, atrocity and Hitler photos, flags, iron crosses, grenades. He had big hands but quit football practice for the brother's private reading lessons. When the poor boy stayed at third-grade, 3.0, reading level, he banged his head against the wall. His file said that he had had two older brothers who died when they reached third grade; one drowned and the other fell off a roof. One boy tied rocks around the necks of dogs and watched them struggle and drown. He bragged about killing two tied together. He also jumped dogs and slit their throats. One boy had three babies by three different girl friends, and persuaded all of them to keep the children; the brother gave him three Doctor Spock books. One student was a vampire boy, who wore a cape and would not go out into the sun. The others pulled him away from the shade along the walls, tore off his clothes, held him down, and trained magnifying glasses on his skin. Many students acted like animals: One, Benjie, lowered his heavy head snarling over his papers, peeped and spied over his left arm so nobody could cheat off his poor paper. He held his pencil straight up and down in a fist that stuck out of an unraveling sweater sleeve. His eyebrows jerked; growls came from inside his arms. Whenever his pencil broke, he walked all the way around the room to the sharpener, and wrote *fuck* and *chink* on the blackboards.

"Why does he think he's so smart?" Benjie asked, pointing with his middle finger at a yearbook picture of the student body president. "People who get *A*'s don't have fun. They're fairies. Fuckin' fairies. That guy's such a fairy, if I hit him, he'd fall over like anybody else. Is it true about that ten-year-old kid who's going to college?"

"Yes," said the brother, "but there are hardly any people like him. He's sort of a freak of nature."

"If I hit him, he'd fall over." He threw something, then retreated behind his arms, came out again. "You don't think I'm smart, do you? You think I'm dumb. Stu-pee-do."

"No, you're not so dumb. In three months you went from third-grade books to fourth-grade books. That's very fast. Three more months and you can read fifth-grade books. Two years' improvement in one year. At that rate in about two years you'll catch up to twelfth grade. You are the most improved person in the class."

"Most improved means I started out the dumbest. In a class of stupidos. But I'm in the twelfth grade right now. Eighteen years old. I ain't no dumb Mexican from Mexico. I been speaking English all my life. All my life." He put his head down inside the cave of his arms.

The next day he said, "Is it true about that three-year-old kid studying physics in Korea?"

"Yes."

Benjie hit himself hard on the face.

To give the students something they would read, the brother brought them a pile of comic books. "They're coming out with the first black superheroes," he said. "Too bad, though, they're starting to make Oriental villains again with yellow skin and long fingernails."

"That's supposed to be a chink?" Benjie asked, interested. "You're making a mistake this time. That doesn't look like no chink." He took the comic book and read it. "Don't feel bad. I just read it all the way through. That's not a chink. They draw him ugly to show how bad he is, that's all." Fu Manchu. The Mandarin. Yellow Claw. The brother was touched at Benjie's trying to protect his feelings.

The first of the brother's students to go to Vietnam was Alfredo Campos, who was twenty-one years old, the age at which the brother had graduated from college. Alfredo had emigrated alone from Mexico when he was nineteen. He was going to school to get a job away from the grape fields. He asked the brother to help him write letters to his eleven brothers and sisters, who practiced English for coming to the United States someday. But suddenly, in the middle of the semester, Alfredo dropped out and went to Vietnam. "I send honor to you, Teacher," he wrote from there. "I send congratulations to you, my Teacher, on Christmas day." His sister, who was eighteen, took his place in class. She brought slides he had sent from Vietnam.

The brother showed the pictures to the class: A puff of orange smoke was artillery fire. A row of tanks fired into what looked like a prairie. Guns mounted on wheels taller than men shot at a mountain. Rows of shit-colored helicopters blotched the sky. No dead bodies, though. Alfredo and his prisoner smiled side by side at the camera; they were both small, dark boys. Alfredo and a Vietnamese girl friend, who was dressed in a leopard mini-skirt, stood with their arms around each other's waist. Children cut his hair and shined his shoes; they did not seem to heed their broken arms and missing legs. He and his buddies, all Latins, toasted his former classmates with beer and made *V*'s with their fingers. Women rummaged through garbage cans marked PROPERTY OF USA. The sun made everybody's eyes squint.

The brother did not say anything. The students also did not say much. He showed the slides to all five of his classes, and therefore got to see them himself five times. He didn't find anything to say about them. It was just as well; it would be unfair to say anything, Alfredo being in the war, more fair to let the students draw their own conclusions seeing actual pictures of Vietnam taken by somebody they knew.

The third or fourth time around, the pictures seemed very happy, very attractive: Alfredo, grown, not lonely, almost married to a large and happy leopard-skinned wife. The sun shining orange in their cottage. Smoking an after-dinner cigarette while children played at his feet. Children laughing around his head, all their faces catching the light. Many friends, compadres. In winter Alfredo had jungles, not leaf-less trees in concrete. Even the prisoner was smiling. A lovely day. Sunshine and palm trees. The old woman held up half a potato and laughed.

The brother had to answer Alfredo's letters. "Dear Alfredo," he wrote, and could not think of the next thing to say. "I hope you are well," he wrote because that was the truth. He did hope he was well. "Take care of yourself," he wrote, but not "Take *good* care of yourself"; Alfredo might have to kill someone in order to do that. He did not write, "I showed your slides to the class"; he did not want to encourage him to take more dramatic shots. The brother kept writing the same letter: "I am fine. I hope you are too." He did not send any war or history books or peace pam-phlets; Alfredo might let down his guard at a crucial moment and not defend himself. He did not mention religion though he knew Alfredo had one; if he put doubt into him, maybe he would hesitate at the wrong moment and get shot. Nor did he ask if he had killed anybody yet.

The schools started atomic attack drills again. The teachers had to sign a paper to be Civil Defense deputies. The brother did not turn it in, as he had not submitted his loyalty oath. Nobody noticed. If the principal said a code sentence on the P.A. system, "The fire department will be inspecting Buildings C and D at two o'clock today," it meant that a bomb was really coming. The students were not to know so that they wouldn't panic. For drill, the brother was assigned to take his group to the weight room, where the P.E. Department stored the body-building equipment. He sat in the dark with the remedials and waited for the all-clear bell. The boys rolled the weights about, lifted them in the wrong postures, dropped them on the wood floor, punched one another. He would not like being trapped under rubble with them. He'd be the only rational, unselfish adult there, the only one with an idea of order, responsible for the safety of all of them, the only one who would question cannibalism. No, these would not be the people he would wish to die with. "Stop throwing the barbells," he ordered.

He could not escape induction. He did not have physical disabilities. He was not married. He was not in a job vital to defense. The Army would not assign him to some easy NATO duty like guarding a German border. They'd send a gook to fight the gook war. He had to do something, not leave his fate to the draft lottery, an all-or-nothing gamble. The chances had narrowed to two: go to Canada or enlist in the Navy. He decided against Canada though he had relatives in Vancouver Chinatown, Pender Street. He had no friends there. He had never met those relatives. He did not want to live the rest of his life a fugitive and an exile. The United States was the only country he had ever lived in. He would not be driven out.

So he enlisted in the Navy for four years. The Air Force was more apt to drop bombs. On the ocean, he would not have his heart broken at the sight of Vietnamese grandmothers and babies.

He arrived at his decision by reasoning like this: In a country that operates on a war economy, there isn't much difference between being in the Navy and being a civilian. When we ate a candy bar, drank grape juice, bought bread (ITT makes Wonder bread), wrapped food in plastic, made a phone call, put money in the bank, cleaned the oven, washed with soap, turned on the electricity, refrigerated food, cooked it, ran a computer, drove a car, rode an airplane, sprayed with insecticide, we were supporting the corporations that made tanks and bombers, napalm, defoliants, and bombs. For the carpet bombing. Everything was connected to everything else and to war. The Peace Movement published names of board members of weapons factories; they were the same people who were bankers and university trustees and government officials. Lines connected them in one interlocking system. The Pacifists' boycott lists included so many ordinary things, we couldn't live day-to-day American lives without adding to the war. Universities, funded with government grants, were inventing eerie new weapons: cobalt bombs, cluster bombs, scatter bombs, porpoise delivery systems, shrapnel that couldn't be X-rayed, fires that water did not put out, spider-web sensors that picked up body heat and relayed its presence to computers and from computers to satellites to bombers. Fragmentation bombs, "guavas," embedded pellets that sent out radio signals to be traced to hideouts. Seismologists were not just studying the natural quaking of the earth but the impact of bombs. Electronics companies in the United States and the Far East, headed by retired admirals and generals, were building missiles, firebombs, and nuclear weapons for warfare on land and under water. Bugs monitored conversations miles away. Engineers and psychologists were researching police systems for riot control in American cities. Computer companies were keeping track of everyone by cross-indexing our banking and social security numbers, drivers' licenses, airline tickets, birth certificates, jail records, and purchases. The metals and stones of the abundant continent were being changed into weapons, which were funneled to Vietnam.

The way to contribute less to the war was to go on welfare and eat out of garbage bins in back of grocery stores. Women were having babies at home to help them escape the draft in future wars or this war, which might not end by the time they grew to adolescence. There were drop-outs in a wagon train leaving California for Alaska, a Texas wagon train having already reached Canada. People were living in caves in Nevada and in the California north woods. A family from Hawai'i had had all their teeth replaced with metal ones; they went to live on a secret island forever. Families and friends bought boats and would live on the sea. The brother knew people leaving for the New Hebrides, Honduras, New Zealand. But he enlisted.

He resolved that in the Navy he would follow orders up to a point short of a direct kill. He would not shoot a human being; he would not press the last button that dropped the bomb. But he would ride the ship that brought he bombs, which his taxes had already paid for. If ordered to shoot at a human target, he would then go AWOL to Canada or Sweden. But up until then, he would be a Pacifist in the Navy rather than in jail, no more or less guilty than the ordinary stay-at-home citizen of the war economy.

When the new Secretary of Defense called the Chinese "the enemy of the world" and predicted all-out nuclear war before 1970, the brother stopped reading newspapers. There wasn't any news; it would be news if the war ended. The news didn't change; only the numbers kept going up.

When the brother handed in his resignation, the principal told him that he would get credit for being in the service; he would rise four years on the salary schedule just as if he'd been teaching all along. The school would have a job for him later, give him preference. "You don't have to do that," he said. He did not tell his students where he was going or that he was leaving. The last thing he tried to teach them was: "The military draft is not an American tradition. Protest against it is a longer tradition."

His mother said, "Bring a wife home. Look for a Chinese girl, but Japanese are okay too, Koreans okay. Just as long as she has a soft smile." His father stood at the door waving good-bye. "Good-bye," he said. "So long," like leaving for college.

Basic training wasn't bad; he had expected worse, like in *D.I.* with Jack Webb. He did not have to fight and die like Prewitt and Maggio. Nobody called him chink or gook or slope or Commie. The only personal racial harassment was when the Company Commander stopped in front of him and hollered, "Where you from?" and he had to shout out his hometown, Sir. "Louder. Where you from?" "Stockton, California, Sir." "Where is that?" "West Coast, Sir." "What country?" "U.S.A., Sir." Each time the Chief shouted at him, it wasn't about his shoe shine or his attitude but "Where you from?" "Stockton, California, U.S.A." The chief didn't ask anyone else about his hometown. It was a racial slur, all right, as though he were saying, "Remember you're not from Vietnam. Remember which side you're on. You're no gook from Vietnam." That's right, he wasn't. Fat men got the worst chewing out; the Company Commander called them girls – pussies, twats, sows, cunts, girls, ladies – and assigned them to run extra laps. His fellow man was like the remedials.

For the first five weeks, the recruits, or "boots," were not allowed to talk during meals. At the brother's first dinner conversation, a big man across from him spread a hand and said, "See this? You know what it's for?"

"What?"

"It's to make this." He made a fist and nodded at it.

"Nah," said the brother. "It's to put good food in your mouth, not this swill." They were eating the same chili sauce they cleaned the metal urinals with. Heads over their plates, which they encircled with one arm, the men stoked their mouths.

The brother lost his appetite. From the first day of boot camp when the recruits were marched to breakfast, he did not want the food. No food tasted any better or worse than any other. Peanut butter, french fries, chocolate did not taste good. He had lost the sensation of hunger. His stomach did not growl no matter how long he did without food. Not eating gave him some extra time, privacy; there were men who had nothing better to do than line up in front of the mess hall long before mealtime. He would use his insensitivity to advantage; he would not have to plan his life around food. He had not eaten for days when it occurred to him that his appetite was unreliable; he could not depend on it to keep alive. He would never get hungry. "I have to eat to keep myself alive," he said aloud at table; he would remember better by saying it to those around him. He would have to use his reason instead of his instinct to eat and stay healthy. Each day, regularly, he would eat three meals, enough of each kind of food whether he wanted it or not. "I've got to keep eating," he said. He would eat by reason rather than appetite. He calculated what foods a body needed and ate them. He would take care of himself until his appetite returned. "Eat vegetables," he grumbled. "Eat salad. Why do they feed us canned peas and carrots? Why can't they get fresh vegetables to San Diego?"

Whether anybody listened or not, he muttered from morning till night. "They get us up at five-thirty before our brains can start functioning," he said. "My brain feels like wet cement. I can't see. Here I'm getting up, and I didn't even go to sleep yet. I didn't even have any dreams. Sorry. No dreams to tell. When I get out of the Navy, I'm never going to make a bed again. They're turning us into housewives. Make beds. Fold clothes. Shine shoes. Sweep. Swab. The Navy is housework. And the Navy is gym class. Hell is staying in P.E. forever." He mumbled while marching, "Foot blisters. Bone bruises. Shin splints. Slave labor." He mumbled while swimming, "Abandon ship. Sharks at my underbelly. The ocean covered with black oil and the oil igniting. Ears clogged with chlorine." Actually he was making up the sharks; the reasons for the training were not given. "Can't shit in peace," he said, sitting in the head while twenty people stared awaiting their turn, no doors and walls around toilets. "I'm getting dumber," he said. "I can feel it, the I.Q.'s are leaking away. Everybody here is so dumb." "Yeah," people agreed, "they sure are." He was ordered to mutter numbers in the tear-gas training room, to feel the gas burn before running out. He talked even in his sleep. "Cut it out," said the men in the next bunks or "racks," but he didn't hear them because he'd stuffed erasers in his ears.

Recruit training wasn't the first time he had handled a gun. Each New Year's eve, his father took a heavy box out of its hiding place, lifted the lid, unwrapped the wads of cloth, and took out the black pistol. The brothers and sisters passed it around with barrel upturned. Their father oiled it and loaded it. They followed him outside, and at midnight he fired one shot into the air over the slough, a year ending and a year beginning at that bang. On the rifle range, shooting at bull's-eyes, the rifle became so hot that when the brother looked at his hand, a flap of skin was rolled back. It did not hurt.

Because he could type, he escaped some of the clean-up. He was not as bad off as the others. He was older and had had something going for him before the Navy. Office work was in addition to other duties; he lost time the Navy allotted for letter-writing or study. He made schedules, and wrote out permits, attendance, and duty rosters. No exciting orders to kill Vietnamese.

On the last day of boot camp, his group voted him Champion Complainer. There were men who admitted that they hadn't taken a shit the entire ten weeks. He did not think he was any more full of hate and a desire to kill than before. Nor did his appetite return. At restaurants and at home on leave, he had no appetite for his favorite foods. If only the war were as easy as recruit training, he could take it.

Then for a while he was shuffled from one base to another without there seeming to be a plan. At a sort of holding barracks for homosexuals, his orders were to keep them from "bed-hopping," though they didn't seem ill. He sat at his lookout's desk watching TV or writing letters or reading. He didn't catch anybody.

One area he avoided was the dependents' housing, which he stumbled upon one lunchtime. Navy wives in curlers and bedroom slippers sat on benches, two facing benches in front of each doorway. Arms folded, they yelled at their kids in the accents of many nations and regions, but even the black women looked colorless. These were women and children who were loved. "The attack plans are not going to work," a family man had confided during man-your-stations drill. "If an enemy ever attacks this place, nobody is going to man his station. Do you think I'm coming to this desk during an attack? I'll be with my wife and kid. And everybody else will be with his wife and kids." As a single man, the brother had not considered dependents.

Next he was assigned to a ship, an aircraft carrier. The beams and cables of the Golden Gate Bridge swung overhead. A few people up there waved and gave the peace sign. The Bay was gray like the pewter-color rocket launchers bolted to the decks. For a frantic second the brother wanted to turn the ship around. It was like a moving island of planes and jeeps and tanks. Maybe those khaki torpedoes and silver rockets were H-bombs. Or they were flares. He didn't know what an H-bomb looked like, perhaps a cassette or a crystal chip.

The officers announced that the ship was on its way to Subic Bay in the Philippines. Still not Vietnam, still not time to jump ship. Some men were disappointed that the Navy did not immediately send them to Vietnam. "We're gonna miss the war," they said. They should have joined the Army, they said, or the Marines. They were children themselves so would not recognize the Vietcong as children; they would think they were fighting short men.

The brother's favorite activity was to stand watch in the flight control tower. He volunteered for extra duty hanging over the sea, sighting dolphins and sea conditions. When the ocean went gold with what he thought were low-flying birds, he climbed down and saw flying fish for the first time. Another day, in the swaying air he sighted an airplane speck, which turned out to be an albatross come to follow the ship. The slop jockeys soaked the garbage with hot sauce; the brutes guffawed as the albatross ate it and its throat jerked. Still it followed near and far, black wings against the sky, against the sunrise.

A personnel officer had read the brother's records, and gave him the collateral duty of teaching English classes on board ship, Remedial Reading to grown men who were so ignorant they did not know where Indochina was or Sweden or the various states.

"What do you see when you read?" he asked. "Describe what you see." They were not seeing the stories or ideas.

"I see small, small words, and they get darker and darker." Poor boys; they must have joined the Navy to get away from school, and here they were in school again.

"I see words, and the ink runs together. Then it's dark."

"I see letters at first, but they turn into colors that jump around."

"Colors. Blue, I think. Or purple."

"The words look like they're melting in water. They float."

"I see a mist. Like fog."

"Dark like a tunnel."

"Like in an elevator."

"Dark. Claustro."

"Like a tight cave. And I can hardly breathe."

"Can't I stop reading now? I'm getting dizzy."

"I have a headache."

"My eyes are watering."

"I can't breathe."

"My eyes hurt."

"Dark. Claustro."

He taught writing by having them write home. They had a Navy textbook with sample letters. "'Dear Mom,'" the boys printed. "'How are you? I am fine. I hope you are fine too. We sure have a lot to eat here. They keep you busy in the Navy. The weather has been cool/warm. Lots of love. Yours truly, Your Name.'" Some of the students copied it out just like that. "'Your Name,'" they wrote.

They took so long copying, class ended before he could give them some spelling or literature. There were people who didn't know all the letters of the alphabet, or they knew them but out of order, yet they had passed intelligence tests to get in the Navy. "The government lowered the standards to get our bodies," he told them. He showed them where Canada and Sweden were on a globe.

"You speak English pretty good," his students complimented him. When white people said that, he had figured out what to answer, "Thank you, so do you," but he was at a loss again. He did not feel like using sarcasm on these boys, nor would they understand it.

What he wrote to his own parents because his Chinese vocabulary was small was, "How are you? I am fine. I hope you are fine too." But when he wrote in English for his sisters to translate, he again said, "How are you? I am fine." He didn't want to worry them.

As the ship moved toward Asia, he dreamed fiercely. The dreams came more and more quickly; the land sent them: An army enters a city to free it from an enemy. A soldier of the rescuing army, he walks through a castle into the dungeons. Going down the stairs, he sees at face level – bodies hanging, some upside down, some brown and dried up, black hair and arms swaying, feet turning this way, then that, bodies with black hair in their middles, corpses with sections missing and askew, but mercifully all dead, hanging by hooks and ropes. Laundry tubs drain beneath the bodies. The live women and children on the ironing tables, the last captured, are being dissected. It has to be a dream or a movie, he thinks, but he blinks his eyes, and the sights do not go away. He takes up his sword and hacks into the enemy, slicing them; they come apart in rings and rolls. He grits his teeth and goes into a frenzy, cutting whatever human meat comes within range. When he stops, he finds that he has cut up the victims too, who are his own relatives. The faces of the strung-up people are also those of his own family, Chinese faces, Chinese eyes, noses, and cheekbones. He woke terrified. The live bodies he had cut up had not screamed or wept because their mouths had been gagged and eyes blindfolded. Scared awake, he looked at the underside of the rack above him and at the sleeping man across the aisle; it was only the closeness in these berths that had made him dream like that.

He went to sleep again, and another dream recurred: Armies crawl like alligators under barbed wire. They have been ordered to charge a beach like at Normandy – only the beach is as wide as the Sahara Desert or the Gobi or Death Valley. In a panic of attack all those miles, they crawl and charge for years. It is an army of burrowing animals, moles, groundhogs, prairie dogs, ostriches. Frightened by shadows and sounds, they dig deeper. Nursing cubs and kids wriggle beneath bigger animals. Turkeys burrow under one another and die in a pile. Administering first aid, he cuts open their chests and sees gross internal damage. He tries unstacking the animals, weaning them. The alligators, left arm and leg, then right arm and leg, crawl toward battle. Occasionally, a wild stallion rears up and is shot.

He woke again, wondering why he should have such disorderly animal dreams when the ship was a machine. These dreams must have come from his years of poultry chores. When he slept again, he dreamed that he was a barkless dog tied to a table leg in a kitchen equipped with a sink, oven, and operating table. Families – mother, father, and one child – are in kitchens like this all over the world. A voice comes over the loudspeaker: "Children, take up your knives; women, forks; men, spoons." The fathers take the children's knives and stab them quickly. Then with their arms around one another, the wife picks up the fork, and the husband the spoon. The loudspeaker says for them to kill themselves by forking and scooping. "Spoon, knife, or fork?" the loudspeaker asks the barkless dog, who knows that if he took the sharpest instrument, he would deprive someone else of a quick death. He chooses the spoon, but is not willing to gouge himself to death. Because he is a dog and not watched as closely as human beings, he runs out of the kitchen-surgery, but outside, the shooting war has begun. He runs in and out the door, unable to decide whether it is better to commit suicide or to kill.

His bunk neighbors told the brother he talked Chinese and yelled in his sleep, complaining even more in sleep than awake. Mornings in another life, his family had told their dreams while eating breakfast. He found some shipmates who listened, though he would have otherwise muttered to himself.

The people he had met in basic training or another base seemed old friends meeting again, homeboys. Bill, a hippie Pacifist, followed him around asking about Zen, macrobiotic diet, yang and yin, brush painting. Bill was often swabbing decks or peeling potatoes because his hair was too long or completely shaved off, or he saluted crooked, or he wouldn't stand at attention during "Anchors Aweigh." He questioned the cooks and officers about the chili, whether there was hamburger in it, whether the fish had been fried in lard or vegetable oil. "Use peanut oil," he suggested. He picked out the bacon bits from his salad in case they were really bacon instead of soy. Ordinarily the brother wouldn't have liked a person who had a thing for the Orient, a sinophile, but Bill badgered him. "Tell me about Buddhism," he said. "Do you know kung fu? Tai Chi? I want to be a Buddhist Pacifist. When the ship returns to San Francisco, I'm joining the flower children. When we get to Asia, I'm going to find my guru or stand on a street corner and let my guru find me. Come on, say a few words in Chinese. Go ahead." Bill spoke Chinese in a scholarly or citified or northern dialect. He was very annoying, but he liked listening to dreams and complaints. There would be no real friends in the Navy anyway; these people didn't stick together – they were stuck with one another, assigned to one another.

The brother also spent time with a chubby tenor who had dropped out of a seminary and did not become a priest. Louder than the country-and-western records the other men played, he sang Italian opera and Mozart, which filled the bunkroom, the showers, the corridors and flew out across the water to the albatross. The young sailors shunned him in case he was homosexual and contagious. He rummaged the ship for bits of history and showed the brother the bolt marks in their berthing compartment, where ten years ago the Navy had kept a small cell for jailing one sailor as a warning. The tenor found a pair of foils, and he and Bill or the brother fenced across the decks pretending to be Errol Flynn and Basil Rathbone, leaping off hatches and swinging from guy wires like riggings.

Instead of carrying out his lists of projects, his reading lists, guitar lessons, correspondence, the brother, like the other sailors, wasted time sitting around, bullshitting, complaining, going to the nightly movies. In the sudden lights after a movie, the audience looked especially depressing.

At Subic Bay the Commander ordered two hundred sailors to go to a dance with one hundred girls in an outlying town. The mayor, a woman, had invited them, but not enough sailors volunteered. The brother danced with some of the one hundred, "all schoolteachers," according to the mayor's speech. The food was plentiful, and he watched a cockfight in the middle of the dance floor. One of the one hundred schoolteachers promised that in case the brother went to Vietnam, she would write dates on his letters and periodically mail them to his parents.

The next port was Korea, the magic place, where the good ginseng comes from. The civilian workers read the brother's name tag and asked if he were Korean. They had that same last name. "Chinese," he said, "American. Chinese American." "Chinese American," the Koreans repeated. "Lucky, huh? Lucky." He bought ginseng, "man's heart," the root of life, the root in the shape of a human being, and sent it to his mother. She kept writing for him to buy more, red and yellow ginseng and many different grades, also instants and concentrates.

On Thanksgiving, the sailors gave a party for local children, who ate very seriously. The children hid bananas and oranges inside their coats, into which they or their relatives had sewn enormous pockets. "We'll give you a doggy bag," the men, who sat in every other seat, said. "Go ahead. Eat." But the kids stored it away. "Have another apple. Have some more cupcakes," the brother said to the kids next to him. "Take the whole bowl." He handed one boy the potatoes. "Say some Korean," men said to the kids. "Cat got your tongue?" "They don't talk much, do they?" they said. "Aren't they cute? Cute little fellas."

Next the ship went to Taiwan, where he would be stationed. He watched the real China pass by, the old planet his family had left light years ago. Taiwan was not China, a decoy China, a facsimile. He would not find out if the air and flowers of China smelled sweeter than California and the sky filled with golden birds, whether promises would come true, time move slower, and life last long.

In Taiwan he was for the first time in a country of Chinese people. The childish dream was that he would find like minds, and furniture that always fit his body. Chinese Americans talk about how when they set foot on China, even just Hong Kong, their whole lives suddenly made sense; their youth had been a preparation for this visit, they say. They realize their Americanness, they say, and "You find out what a China Man you are." An ophthalmology student from the ship, an American of Japanese Ancestry, who was proud of his "double-lids," said that the eyes of ethnic Asians have a naturally faraway focus. "If we lived in Asia," he said, "where everything is arranged according to our eyesight, we wouldn't need glasses." Clarity was a matter of preference and culture. "Americans zone cities and make billboards for Caucasian eyes," he said. "Blackboards are set so many feet from the students' desks, traffic signals at such a size and distance, newspapers and books in a certain size type. If we AJA's with our epicanthic eyes and peculiar focus went back to Japan, we wouldn't need glasses any more." The brother had American 20–20 vision, but didn't notice things getting either blurrier or sharper in Taiwan. That eye doctor trainee was a crackpot.

The brother, Bill the Buddhist monk, the opera singer, and the ophthalmologist decided to live on the economy. They rented a prefab house next to rice paddies with water buffaloes; it had a fireplace though the climate was hot. The others looked for a houseboy to do the cleaning and cooking. "We ought to clean up after ourselves," the brother argued. "A man ought to wash his own dishes and wash the clothes he wears. Like Truman. Truman washed his own socks. Cleaning up after yourself is the followthrough."

His friends said he was blithering again. "We're pumping bucks into the economy," they said. "We're paying top dollar and putting food in bellies. If we don't hire him, somebody else will make him work for less." They hired an old man for houseboy.

The brother hoped Bill would not point him out to the old man, "He's Chinese too," unleashing a whole set of customs. The old man would scorn him for speaking the wrong kind of Chinese, scold and mock, turn him into a child, a bad Chinese who couldn't speak right. "Ho Chi Kuei," he'd scold. "Ho Chi Kuei." He'd call him names for who knows what. For being in the Navy, for living with a gang of white devils, for going out with girls, for drinking, for coming in late, for smoking dope, for the invasion and colonization of Asia. The old man leaned on his iron pressing their uniforms sharp "inside out," as the sailors requested. The brother had pressed them this same way when he worked at the laundry. If he were living alone, he would have gotten rid of the old man. So the old man wouldn't see his father's Chinese writing on envelopes, the brother made sure his mail came to his office at the base.

Once he came home in the middle of the workday and found the old man asleep on the sofa, and left so as not to wake him. Another day while wandering in a market, he saw him with his wife and three children. When the old man introduced everyone, the brother felt surprisingly honored, as if the old man were letting him have something special, personal. The brother resolved he would return after he got out of the Navy and say Hello to him. He'd look him up. He had a list of things to do after the Navy, after the war was over, the endless war not even officially begun yet, the beginning let alone the end not in sight: he would take a cruise ship from San Francisco to Asia; he would see the Philippines and Taiwan as a civilian.

The Chinese workers at the base were curious about him. "What are you?" they asked. "Chinese American," he said.

"Lucky. You're lucky," they said in English just like the Koreans.

Life was getting to be a routine when in the Chinese New Year season, which the Vietnamese and Americans were calling Tet, the brother was assigned to the U.S.S. *Midway* for an attack mission to the Gulf of Tonkin. There were nuclear weapons on board, sidewinders, matadors, six-hundred-mile-range rockets with atomic warheads. The men discussed cyanide in case of torture. "If I were in the jungle, I'd carry cyanide." "But bringing cyanide is like having Thorazine on hand when dropping acid. Expecting a bad trip causes a bad trip. You set yourself up." The hippies were doping themselves silly. A sister ship was supposed to accompany the *Midway*, but a kid had dropped a wrench into the engine. It wasn't sabotage, just an accident. Pilots ejected themselves inside of hangars, mechanics got sucked into the jets, flight deck crew sliced by guy wires. It did not require precision to deliver the massive tonnage.

The brother did not go AWOL to Sweden or Canada. He was, after all, only coming a few miles physically closer to Vietnam, and his job of flipping switches and connecting circuits and typing was the same as on land, the numbers and letters almost the same.

So here he was on an aircraft carrier from whose flight deck hour after hour corps of planes took off. He could not take naps, his bunk was directly beneath the rocket launchers. Even using binoculars, he did not see much of the shore. Hanoi was an hour away by plane. He did not see the bombs drop out of the planes, whether they fell like long white arrows, or whether they turned and turned, flashing in the sun. During loading, when they were locked into place, they looked like neatly rolled joints; they looked like long grains of rice; they looked like pupae and turds. He never heard cries under the bombing. They were not attacking the enemy with surprise bombings but routine bombings or "air operations" in twelve-hour shifts. When the sister ship got there, there would be bombings through the night, round-the-clock bombings. The pilots flew out there, unloaded their quota, and came back. It took intelligence and imagination to think that they were in Vietnam in the middle of the heaviest American bombing. A man he'd eaten lunch with did not show up for dinner, and that meant the man's plane had gone down. He had to imagine his death because he saw no blood, no body. The pilots either came back or they did not come back. There were no wounded. Sometimes a pilot would say that he had returned with a dead co-pilot in the cockpit. The sailors did not mourn the pilots, an arrogant, strutting class who volunteered for the bombings. Nobody was drafted to drop bombs. "Extra dessert tonight," the sailors said. "He asked for it," they said. "Hot shot." "Gung ho." When the pilots returned alive, it was no different from a practice run. No celebrations and no mournings, just business, a job. An officer was assigned to sort the dead man's personal effects; he censored those things too embarrassing to send to the family, such as photographs of Asian women.

The brother did touch foot on Vietnam by visiting a base near Saigon. He did not explore the city. He met some infantrymen who told him that when they were ordered to patrol the jungle they made a lot of noise, clanged equipment, talked loud. The enemy did the same, everybody warning one another off. Once in a while, to keep some hawk officer happy, they fired rounds into the trees.

The brother was formally asked by his Commanding Officer to train as a pilot. He had the test scores, the potential, but he said No.

The pilots often invited their shipmates for the bombings. "Want to come along?" "Come on. Take a ride. Come along for the ride." The brother said No, "No, not me," many times. Then one day he said, "Sure. Why not? When? Sure, I'll come along for the ride." He put on a parachute and walked with the pilot and co-pilot across the flight deck on to the plane. He felt overheated, his head crammed into the helmet and his body pulled backward by the parachute. He had to duck through the door. Stuffed into his low seat, which was tilted toward the ceiling, he found with effort the seat belts and buckled himself in. The door slid shut. It was not too late to ask out. The plane was still lined up behind others waiting for takeoff. He could say he'd changed his mind and cause only a minor inconvenience. He wouldn't be embarrassed. The engine revved. He wasn't, after all, committing a worse act by riding on the plane than riding on the ship. The plane accelerated on its short runway, left the deck, and climbed over the water, the horizon slanting, dipping, and rising. Then there was the steadiness one feels riding in any plane, train, or car. The instruments, needles, dials, and lights made no alarming flashes or jumps. He put on a headset and heard familiar numbers and letters. He stood up against the gravity and looked out of the windshield, which was narrow like a pair of wraparound glasses. All that he witnessed was heavy jungle and, in the open skies, other planes that seemed to appear and disappear quickly, shiny planes and their decals and formations. The bombs must have gone off behind them. Some air turbulence might have been a bomb ejected. He heard no explosion. There did seem to be some turns and banks like a ride in any small plane. The plane turned in the direction from which they seemed to have come – he could tell by the sun now on the other side – and they were descending and landing. The plane caught in the wires, not needing the net. The door opened, and he climbed out. "Smooth run," said the pilot. "Yeah, smooth," said the co-pilot. The brother felt no different from before, but he made a decision never to go again.

He got promoted and transferred back to Taipei. His Commanding Officer dealt out personnel papers:

"Communications Specialist. Q Clearance," he heard. "You've been run through a security check –" (The brother's breath caught – his family deported.) "– and cleared. Congratulations. Secret Security."

"Thank you. Thank you. I got something out of the Navy," the brother blurted. "I'm getting something good out of the Vietnam war."

The government was certifying that the family was really American, not precariously American but super-American, extraordinarily secure – Q Clearance Americans. The Navy or the FBI had checked his mother and father and not deported them. Maybe that grandfather's Citizenship Judge was real and legal after all. So Uncle Bun's defection to Communism didn't matter, nor Father's gambling, nor Great Uncle's river piracy, second-story work, and murder. And the government had forgiven whoever it was who had almost gotten caught stowing away, or he had covered his tracks so well that they overlooked him, missed him, impervious to investigation. The Communist grandmother, aunts, and cousins, potential hostages, were not hurting his trustworthiness as an American. Maybe Uncle Bun was dead, never got to China; maybe he wasn't even really an uncle. His grandfather's and father's papers had indeed burned in the earthquake, and it was all right that his mother was an alien. The government had not found him un-American with divided loyalties and treasonous inclinations. Though he was conveniently close to China, the U. S. government, which could make up new laws, change the law on him, did not dump him there. While his services were needed for the undeclared American-Vietnam war, the family was safe. And the family had friends and neighbors who protected them during investigation.

His Commanding Officer said that the brother's record as a communications expert with language aptitude qualified him for the Monterey Language School. Wouldn't he like to study Chinese? Or Vietnamese? "You studied French," he said. "You speak Chinese too, don't you?" A vision of Monterey leapt up like a mermaid out of the sea and lured him. He wanted that Pacific coast, that sunshine and fog, the red tile roofs in the dark trees, the fiery and white bougainvillea, the walks on the streets leading to the ocean – and school again, to be a student a luxury. "Let me think about it," he said.

A letter came from his older brother, who had gotten a commission in the Air Force. He had just been given Top Secret Security Clearance. Maybe he was the one who had prompted the security check, too ambitious to remain a private. The NAC had processed both of them at once. So they had not only been checked but double-checked, and cleared, doubly cleared.

The brother found some language books in the library. If he learned Chinese better, or if he let on how much he already knew, the Navy would assign him to be a spy or an interrogator. There was only one use the military had for Chinese language – war, the same use it had for raw materials and science. He would be assigned to gouge Viet Cong eyes, cattle-prod their genitals. He would have to hang prisoners from helicopters, drop the dumb-looking ones, and tell the smart remaining ones to talk or else. It wouldn't be Chinese poetry he'd be memorizing but the Pentagon's *Vietnam Phrase Book*:

> Welcome, Sir. Glad to meet you. How many
> are with you? Show me on your fingers.
> Are you afraid of the enemy? Us?
> Do you place faith in America? Will the
> people fight for their freedom? We are here
> to help them in the struggle on the side of
> (1) the free world (2) the United States
> (3) the Allies (4) freedom (5) God.

> Would they (1) support (2) join (3) fight on
> the side of (4) work for (5) sacrifice their
> lives for U.S. troops?
> Your nickname will be —. My nickname is —.
> Do you believe in (1) U.S. victory (2) anni-
> hilation of Bolshevism?
> Open the door or we will force it.
> Is he your father? Village leader?
> Are you afraid? Why?
> If we cannot trust a man, (1) wink
> your right eye (2) place your left hand on
> your stomach (3) move your hand to the
> right, unnoticed, until we note your signal.

The Vietnamese call their parents Ba and Ma; *phuoc* means
"happiness," "contentment," "bliss," the same as Chinese; *lan*
is "orchid," the same as his mother's name; Vietnamese puns
are like Chinese puns, *lettuce*, *life*; they probably also bring
heads of lettuce home on holidays. *Study*, *university*, *love* – the
important words the same in Chinese and Vietnamese.
Talking Chinese and Vietnamese and also French, he'd be a
persuasive interrogator-torturer. He would fork the
Vietnamese – force a mother to choose between her baby
with a gun at its belly and her husband hiding behind the
thatch, to which she silently points with her chin.

"No," he told his Commanding Officer. He had been
given a choice, and he said No. "No, thank you." He would
not be like the scientists making plasma bombs and
supersonic brain scramblers for want of a better use of their
abilities.

On days off and after work, he and friends went to
museums, bars, the aborigine village, looked for girl friends,
wandered about the Taiwanese countryside, shopped for
stereo equipment. Passing many Chinese faces made him feel
vaguely rude for not greeting every last one the way he'd

been taught to do back home. As happened every time he went out, he heard somebody shout, probably at him, but he did not understand the words. Once in the middle of the night, someone came out of an alley and jumped him from behind. An arm hooked around his neck. He broke loose and ran, got away. Later his throat remembered the choke-hold of that arm. It had probably been a mugger, not someone after him personally. Off duty, he wore a white shirt, baggy pants, and civilian shoes to blend with the crowds. Yet he had not "returned." Of course, the Center was elsewhere. This island was not the Center, its people emigrants, rejects, and misfits. He'd be more at home if he walked straight away from this Taipei street to a military base. Sailors and soldiers didn't blend into American towns either.

He had two weeks' R and R and went on a vacation to Tokyo and Hong Kong. His parents had given him the names of relatives to visit. He liked Tokyo, where the Japanese were too busy to stare at strangers. They walked fast, had places to go, business to do. He bought Peace brand cigarettes for their packaging. Then, not able to delay any more, he went to Hong Kong, where he heard Cantonese almost like back home. Storekeepers and waiters told him that they had hard lives. "You're lucky," they said. He took a train tour, which included a trip to the border of the New Territories. He saw a valley and distant hills covered with wild vegetation. "There is the People's Republic of China," said the guide. If he had not said that, the brother would not have known. A solitary guard stood here and there, also local policemen in British uniforms. The brother saw no man-made crossings, tracks, bridges, or fences, or anything to hinder or facilitate a crossing. No red wall, no curtain. He walked on the overpass above the railroad tracks for a better look at Red China. Just as Hong Kong had a Communist wharf among other wharves, Communist shops among other shops, he saw no Red distinction.

He boarded another train back to the city to look for the street where his relatives lived. Shopping, he tried to remember what to bring on the occasion of meeting after many years. Oranges, black bean cake, a roast duck might have been appropriate for a harvest blessing or a month-old baby, and his relatives would make fun of him and call him Ho Chi Kuei and *jook tsing*. But he would bring gifts upon entering a nightmare. His aunts and cousins would be poor, and live in a cave or shack. He would find a cardboard and tin shack full of people. Out of a gray rag pile, thin hands would grope and beg, and mouths stretch wide open. "They will change my life," he worried. Their faces would resemble brothers' and sisters' and parents' and his own. He would need to rescue them. He would not be able to leave them. Or he would leave at great cost, pain, and guilt. He would end up like his parents, pledging his salary forever. The relatives would have no manners, no polite ways that would make his visit easy. But a cardboard box on a hillside was not the worst shelter; worse would be if he were a Vietnamese returning from Paris to his hootch or his hole underground.

Queen's Road led him away from the hills. He would rather have rich relatives, the kind who didn't notice beggars, the kind who said, "Why, the hill people and sampan people are lazy. They choose to live like that. Yes, they prefer it." They'd take him out to dinner and wouldn't let him pay. They'd say, "I've never met a poor Chinese. We Chinese are raised with discipline. We make it." He'd tell them his parents were well, and leave. He'd have no trouble leaving them. He came to apartment buildings or housing projects with balconies of laundry. As many little girls as little boys were out on the sidewalks.

But as he looked, the numbers on the doors skipped the one in his hand. There was a number higher and one lower. He was not shirking; he walked back. It was not there, no such number, his number missing. He went in the alleys and looked in the crates. He entered the buildings with addresses that were approximate. No one had heard of his relatives' names. Trying combinations of the numbers, he searched on parallel streets, searched an afternoon, and did not find the house or hovel or tenement where they lived. He left the perishable food in front of any door. The next morning he tried again. Finally he left the rest of the gifts by another door. Perhaps they did live in one of the shacks upon the hill and had put a fake address for their relatives not to worry.

The brother decided that after his time in the Navy and after the war, he'd try again, and also ride into China and look for the ones there.

It was just as well he hadn't found them. The ophthalmologist had gone to Japan and found his village and his relatives, who were very hospitable and gave him the main bed and meat. But on the last day, before dawn, he heard the door slide open. Through his eyelashes, faking sleep, he watched his uncle tiptoe across the room and leave a piece of paper on his chest. (The brother pictured it on his breast, but he must have meant the chest of drawers.) It was a day-to-day running account of all he had eaten, down to the numbers of helpings of rice, a list of the laundry his aunt had washed and ironed, the number of times the little girl cousin had polished his shoes, each cup of tea, an itemized list of all the presents and loans, the bathrobe and slippers, the number of baths in the hot-tub, the number of days and nights in his room, totaled neatly in yen and dollars. He had paid it, of course.

When the brother took a cargo plane on standby home – CONUS, the Continental United States – there were no other passengers; it was a plane especially to take him home. At night in lonely parts of airports, he saw electric conveyors move coffins draped with flags on and off planes. A soldier stood guard in front of stacks of them.

Mustered out at Treasure Island, he rode a Greyhound to Stockton. He walked the few blocks to his parents' house, in front of which many cars were parked. A party was just ending. Some of the guests were leaving. "He's back," they said, typically talking about him in the third person.

"Well, so you've come back," said his father, "you've come back." "You're back home," said his mother.

The chicken still sat whole on the table. Pieces of the roast pork from a whole pig, noodles, and lettuce remained. This was a very important, religious party, a thanksgiving that he had come back home, more than personal, not a party only for him, and that was why they hadn't had to wait for him to have it. He ate the rock sugar on red paper his mother handed him; he ate the leftover pork. She hacked the white chicken for him. No, his appetite hadn't come back yet; he'd have to do more duty-eating.

Three years after his return, the United States withdrew from Vietnam. For a time longer than that, the things people did seemed to have no value; nobody else saw this. But his appetite did gradually increase. He had survived the Vietnam war. He had not gotten killed, and he had not killed anyone.

The Hundred-Year-Old Man

There is a man who would be one hundred and seventeen years old now. He had a one-hundred-and-sixth birthday party in the Palolo Chinese Home in Hawai'i in 1969. He wore a wool cap. He told the guests he came to Hawai'i in 1885 on the S.S. *Coptic*. He brought with him pigs in cages, and chives and onions growing in cans. He had divided his ration of fresh water with the pigs, the chives, and the onions.

He worked in the sugarcane fields for four dollars a month, and his first job had been to clear the brush for planting. He lived in a grass house, but later moved into a dormitory, where he slept in a bunk covered with grass mats. He sent one half of his pay to his family in China. Here's how he spent the rest: He bought kerosene and wood; he paid off some of his debts, his passage to Hawai'i, and the twelve-dollar fee for processing his papers; he spent six dollars to join his Benevolent Association, which gave him room and board when he took his monthly trip to Honolulu on pay day. He rode to town in a horse cart for thirty cents; it carried five passengers. When he could not afford the thirty cents, he walked.

He rested by smoking opium, which the plantation foreman sold. A half-hour's worth of high was called a dragon seed and cost fifty cents. When Hawai'i outlawed opium, he switched to cigars.

He saw King Kalakaua and Prince Kuhio. In 1893 he did not go to town because of the American revolution against Queen Lili'u-okalani, who was "big and friendly," he said. "I was for the Americans," he added.

Since 1885 he has left the island twice, once to go to Maui and once to Kaua'i.

On this one-hundred-and-sixth birthday, the United States was still fighting in Vietnam, and people asked him how to stop the war. "Let everybody out of the army," he said.

"In one hundred and six years, what has given you the most joy?" the reporters asked.

He thought it over. He said, "What I like best is to work in a cane field when the young green plants are just growing up."

"In the end," said Tu Fu, "I will carry a hoe."

At a party, I met a Filipino scholar, who asked, "Do you know the Chinese came to the Philippines to look for the Gold Mountain?"

"No," I said. "I know hardly anything about the Philippines."

"They came in a ship in March of 1603," he said. "Three great mandarins landed at the Bay of Manila. The Filipinos were amazed to see them riding in ivory and gold chairs. They were higher class than the thirty thousand Chinese who were already living in Luzon. They had with them a Chinese in chains, who was to show them where to look for a gold needle in a mountain."

It was past midnight, or it was his accent, but I could not hear if he was saying that looking for the Gold Mountain was like looking for a needle in a haystack. "No. No," he said. "A gold needle." To sew the sails, was it? A compass needle, was it? "The mandarins asked for more ships, which they would fill with gold, some to give to the Filipino king, some to take back to the Queen of Spain, and some for the Emperor of China."

A group of Chinese Americans were gathering around the Filipino scholar. "Oh, yes," said a young man, "a Chinese monk went to Mexico looking for that mountain too, and either he came there with Cortez, or it was before that."

"And the Filipino king," continued the Filipino, "who had met conquistadores and knew about seven cities of gold and a fountain of youth, sent them to the town of Cabit."

"And they went to Weaverville, California," said another. "And in Weaverville, Cantonese laborers built a replica of their village in China."

"No, no," said someone else. "The way I heard it was that some cowboys saw mandarins floating over California in a hot-air balloon, which had come all the way from China."

"Now, these Chinese who were looking for the gold needle," I reminded the Filipino man, "what happened after they got to Cabit?"

"They sailed up a river farther and farther inland." And they built roads and railroads and cities on their way to this mountain. They filled swamps. They had children. "And on a certain mountain they sifted rocks and dirt looking for a gold needle. They asked the man in chains where the gold was, and he said that all they saw was gold."

Because I didn't hear everything, I asked him to repeat the story, and what he seemed to say again was "They found a gold needle in a mountain. They filled a basket with dirt to take with them back to China."

"Do you mean the Filipinos tricked them?" I asked. "What were they doing in Spain?"

"I'll write it down in a letter, and mail it to you," he said, and went on to something else.

Good. Now I could watch the young men who listen.

ABOUT THE INTRODUCER

MARY GORDON is the author of several novels, including *Pearl*, *Final Payment*, *Men and Angels*, and *The Company of Women*, and a memoir, *The Shadow Man*. She lives in New York City, and teaches at Barnard College.

CHINUA ACHEBE
The African Trilogy
Things Fall Apart

AESCHYLUS
The Oresteia

ISABEL ALLENDE
The House of the Spirits

THE ARABIAN NIGHTS
(in 2 vols, tr. Husain Haddawy)

MARGARET ATWOOD
The Handmaid's Tale

JOHN JAMES AUDUBON
The Audubon Reader

AUGUSTINE
The Confessions

JANE AUSTEN
Emma
Mansfield Park
Northanger Abbey
Persuasion
Pride and Prejudice
Sanditon and Other Stories
Sense and Sensibility

HONORÉ DE BALZAC
Cousin Bette
Eugénie Grandet
Old Goriot

GIORGIO BASSANI
The Garden of the Finzi-Continis

SIMONE DE BEAUVOIR
The Second Sex

SAMUEL BECKETT
Molloy, Malone Dies,
The Unnamable
(US only)

SAUL BELLOW
The Adventures of Augie March

HECTOR BERLIOZ
The Memoirs of Hector Berlioz

THE BIBLE
(King James Version)
The Old Testament
The New Testament

WILLIAM BLAKE
Poems and Prophecies

GIOVANNI BOCCACCIO
Decameron

JORGE LUIS BORGES
Ficciones

JAMES BOSWELL
The Life of Samuel Johnson
The Journal of a Tour to
the Hebrides

RAY BRADBURY
The Stories of Ray Bradbury

JEAN ANTHELME
BRILLAT-SAVARIN
The Physiology of Taste

CHARLOTTE BRONTË
Jane Eyre
Villette
Shirley and The Professor

EMILY BRONTË
Wuthering Heights

MIKHAIL BULGAKOV
The Master and Margarita

SAMUEL BUTLER
The Way of all Flesh

JAMES M. CAIN
The Postman Always Rings Twice
Double Indemnity
Mildred Pierce
Selected Stories
(in 1 vol. US only)

ITALO CALVINO
If on a winter's night a traveler

ALBERT CAMUS
The Outsider (UK)
The Stranger (US)
The Plague, The Fall,
Exile and the Kingdom,
and Selected Essays
(in 1 vol.)

GIACOMO CASANOVA
History of My Life

WILLA CATHER
Death Comes for the
Archbishop (US only)
My Ántonia

BENVENUTO CELLINI
The Autobiography of
Benvenuto Cellini